PHILOSOPHY
THE PATH TO WISDOM
Third Edition

D1411950

Joseph R. Mixie

Contents

Part IV. The Philosophy of Knowledge

Part V. Ethics

Part VI. Contemporary Ethical Issues: Abortion

Part VII. Political Philosophy

Part I
What is Philosophy?

Part I

What is Philosophy?

> *"The unexamined life is not worth living."*
> - **Socrates**
>
> *"A man who is good for anything ought not to calculate the chance of living or dying; he ought only to consider whether in doing anything he is doing right or wrong – acting the part of a good man or of a bad."*
> - **Socrates**
>
> *"Are you not ashamed of heaping up the greatest amount of money and honor and reputation, and caring so little about wisdom and truth and the greatest improvement of the soul, which you never regard or heed at all?"*
> - **Socrates**
>
> *"Wherefore, O judges, be of good cheer about death, and know of a certainty, that no evil can happen to a good man, either in life or after death."*
> - **Socrates**

Introduction

WHAT IS PHILOSOPHY?

The English word "philosophy" is derived from the two Greek words *philos*, which means love, and *sophia*, which means wisdom. Therefore, philosophy means the "love of wisdom." Wisdom is usually differentiated from knowledge in that whereas knowledge focuses upon facts, wisdom focuses upon how those facts are used. Wisdom is primarily interested in how people live their lives, not how much factual information they possess. This idea is reflected in the great statement of Socrates, "The unexamined life is not worth living." Socrates was concerned about how people live their lives. What are their goals, desires, purpose in life? These are questions we will be considering.

As we begin this course in the study of philosophy, I want to encourage each of you to take the time to seriously consider why you are here. Not here in this class, because I know it is a required course, but here on earth. What is the meaning of your life? What do you want to accomplish in your life? When you look back at your life at the age of 80, what do you want to have accomplished? Now is the time to think about that. Don't let life just happen to you.

It is generally assumed that the term philosophy was first coined by the ancient philosopher Pythagoras (572-497 B.C.). For the ancient Greeks, human beings could pursue wisdom and grow wiser, but they could never become completely wise. In this original sense, a philosopher was one who continually pursued wisdom, or "loved wisdom."

In this sense, philosophy is an activity and process as much as it is a body of knowledge. A lover of wisdom is someone who loves the pursuit of wisdom. It is someone who constantly tries to live a life of wisdom by making right choices and good decisions.

Although we can communicate factual knowledge and discoveries to others, we cannot pass on the accumulated wisdom and experience of others, except in a very limited way. Each person must experience life for themselves and develop their own wisdom. They can certainly learn from others, but no one can give their experiences and wisdom to others.

QUESTIONS

What distinguishes philosophy from the other academic disciplines are the questions it attempts to answer. In the beginning, all inquiries for knowledge were considered part of philosophy. There was no distinct separation between the different areas of study. Philosophy encompassed mathematics, physics, psychology, etc. This fact is still reflected in the modern university where the highest degree granted in all the academic disciplines is the Ph.D. – the doctor of philosophy.

As each of these disciplines began to develop experimental techniques and procedures which led to a distinct body of knowledge, they gradually broke off from the discipline of philosophy and became specific areas of inquiry in their own right.

The discipline of philosophy was left with those questions that experimental inquiry and the scientific method could not answer. Questions such as: Does God exist? How should we live? What is the basis for our knowledge?

A common criticism of philosophy is that it never settles anything. There never seems to be a concrete, generally agreed upon answer to the questions philosophy deals with. In fact, we are still dealing with the same questions that Plato and Aristotle dealt with 2,500 years ago. While this is true, it is not the discipline of philosophy that is at fault, but the very nature of the questions themselves that defy the same kind of certainty that science provides.

THE ESSENCE OF PHILOSOPHY

The essence of philosophy is critical inquiry. Philosophy seeks to analyze everything. It seeks to determine the basic principles of things. In this regard, there can be a philosophy of anything. A philosophy of automotive mechanics would explain the basic principles of automotive mechanics, its purpose and goals. A philosophy of education would explain the basic principles of education, its purpose and goals.

The distinguishing characteristic of philosophy is the argument. An argument is simply an explanation of reasoning. It explains why someone thinks and believes a certain way about a certain subject. Philosophers clarify terms and concepts. They analyze and test propositions. They investigate beliefs and methods. Whereas scientific experiments take place in laboratories and have procedures which attempt to record and verify objective empirical results, the laboratory of the philosopher is the mind where ideas, thoughts and imagination provide the experiments.

AREAS OF PHILOSOPHY

Although many academic disciplines have broken off from philosophy, here is a list of some of the major areas of philosophical study today.

Metaphysics deals with the study of ultimate reality. Specific areas metaphysics deals with are the mind-body problem, personal identity, and free will and determinism.

Epistemology deals with the study of knowledge. Specific areas epistemology deals with are the justification of knowledge and beliefs, the process of acquiring knowledge, and the possibility of absolute knowledge and truth.

Logic deals with the study of correct thinking and reasoning. Specific areas logic deals with are deductive, inductive and abductive arguments, truth tables, and fallacies.

Ethics deals with the study of correct behavior. As technology has advanced, new areas of study have developed which include: biomedical ethics, business ethics, environmental ethics, and legal ethics.

The Philosophy of religion deals with the study of world religions and proofs for the existence of God. The proofs for the existence of God include the cosmological, teleological, and ontological arguments. The problem of evil is also part of the study of the philosophy of religion.

Political Philosophy deals with the study of politics and government. Included in this study are the justification of governments, political and natural rights, and the analysis of different types of political systems.

Aesthetics deals with the study of beauty and art. This includes the study of different types of art and an analysis of the basic principles of art, and the definition of beauty.

There are many other areas within the study of philosophy such as the philosophy of language, the philosophy of history, the philosophy of psychology, the philosophy of mathematics, etc. As mentioned earlier, there can be a philosophy of anything.

As we begin this course on the study of philosophy, I again want to encourage all of you to use this time as an opportunity to ask the questions that you never get an opportunity to ask in all your other courses. Ask what you think are the most important questions of your life. And listen to the answers given by those who have lived before you.

The Apology

PLATO

Plato (427-347 B.C.) is one of the most important philosophers who ever lived. He lived in the great Greek democratic city-state of Athens. He was Socrates' disciple and the founder of the first school of philosophy, the Academy in Athens. He was also Aristotle's teacher. Among his important works are the *Republic*, the *Apology*, *Phaedo*, and *Timaeus*. It was Alfred North Whitehead who calls the whole history of Western philosophy "a series of footnotes to Plato."

Socrates (470-399 B.C.) is considered the father of moral philosophy. He lived in Athens under Pericles and enjoyed the freedoms of a democratic society. Much of his life was spent in the marketplace of Athens questioning and discussing philosophical issues with the citizens of Athens. Although Socrates saw himself as the gadfly of Athens, intending to help his fellow citizens examine their lives, many of the citizens saw him as a nuisance and eventually brought him to trial.

Written in dialogue form, the *Apology* recounts the trial of Socrates as told by his star student Plato. Although three Athenians, Meletus, Anytus, and Lycon, have brought charges against Socrates that he has corrupted the youth and doesn't believe in the Greek gods, the real cause of the trial is undoubtedly that Socrates has created many enemies in high places. In his pursuit of truth, he has embarrassed many of the leading citizens, politicians, artisans, poets, and orators of Athens. By employing the Socratic Method, he has publicly exposed their pretense to knowledge.

Vocabulary

Apology:	defense
Dithyrambic:	any extravagantly emotional speach or writing
Calumnies:	false statements, slanderous
Vindication:	to be cleared from criticism, blame, guilt
Inveterate:	habitual; chronic
Drachma:	ancient Greek silver coin worth about a soldier's daily wage. Today worth about 44 cents.
Impudent:	to feel shame; shamelessly bold or disrespectful
Wantonness:	undisciplined; unmanageable; senseless; unjustified; reckless
Facetious:	joking at an inappropriate time
Demigod:	the offspring of a human being and a god or goddess
Gadfly:	a person who annoys others or rouses them from complacency
Caricature:	a likeness or imitation that is distorted
Impious:	lacking respect

Concepts:

Socratic Wisdom:

Socratic Method:

Socrates' two conceptions of death:

The unexamined life is not worth living:

Questions:

1. What are the first set of charges leveled against Socrates? How does he respond to these charges?

2. What was the message of the Oracle of Delphi to Chaerephon about Socrates?

3. What was Socrates' response to this message? What method does he use to disprove the oracle?

4. Discuss Socrates' interaction with the politicians, poets, and artisans.

5. What are the second set of charges brought against Socrates?

6. According to Socrates, what should be a person's primary concern when deciding upon a course of action?

7. Why did Socrates refuse to live in Athens under the condition of his not being allowed to pursue the truth?

8. Why was Socrates considered the gadfly of Athens?

9. What was the outcome of the first vote?

10. According to the Athenian justice system, who proposed a penalty during the trial? What were the penalties?

11. According to Socrates why is the unexamined life not worth living?

12. What was the outcome of the second vote? Why do you think it was more decisive than the first vote?

13. What does Socrates means when he says that no evil can happen to a good man?

THE APOLOGY

HOW YOU, O ATHENIANS, have been affected by my accusers, I cannot tell; but I know that they almost made me forget who I was — so persuasively did they speak; and yet they have hardly uttered a word of truth. But of the many falsehoods told by them, there was one which quite amazed me;—I mean when they said that you should be upon your guard and not allow yourselves to be deceived by the force of my eloquence. To say this, when they were certain to be detected as soon as I opened my lips and proved myself to be anything but a great speaker, did indeed appear to me most shameless — unless by the force of eloquence they mean the force of truth; for if such is their meaning, I admit that I am eloquent. But in how different a way from theirs! Well, as I was saying, they have scarcely spoken the truth at all; but from me you shall hear the whole truth: not, however, delivered after their manner in a set oration duly ornamented with words and phrases. No, by heaven! but I shall use the words and arguments which occur to me at the moment; for I am confident in the justice of my cause: at my time of life I ought not to be appearing before you, O men of Athens, in the character of a juvenile orator — let no one expect it of me. And I must beg of you to grant me a favor: — If I defend myself in my accustomed manner, and you hear me using the words which I have been in the habit of using in the [market], at the tables of the money-changers, or anywhere else, I would ask you not to be surprised, and not to interrupt me on this account. For I am more than seventy years of age and, appearing now for the first time in a court of law, I am quite a stranger to the language of the place; and therefore I would have you regard me as if I were really a stranger whom you would excuse if he spoke in his native tongue, and after the fashion of his country: — Am I making an unfair request of you? Never mind the manner, which may or may not be good; but think only of the truth of my words, and give heed to that: let the speaker speak truly and the judge decide justly....

Well, then, I must make my defense, and endeavor to clear away in a short time, a slander which has lasted a long time. May I succeed, if to succeed be for my good and yours, or likely to avail me in my cause! The task is not an easy one; I quite understand the nature of it. And so, leaving the event with God, in obedience to the law I will now make my defense.

I will begin at the beginning, and ask what is the accusation which has given rise to the slander of me, and in fact has encouraged Meletus to prefer this charge against me. Well, what do the slanderers say? They shall be my prosecutors, and I will sum up their words in an affidavit: "Socrates is an evil-doer, and a curious person, who searches into things under the earth and in heaven, and he makes the worse appear the better cause; and he teaches the aforesaid doctrines to others." Such is the nature of the accusation: it is just what you have yourselves seen in the comedy of Aristophanes, who has introduced a man whom he calls Socrates, going about and saying that he walks in air, and talking a deal of nonsense concerning matters of which I do not pretend to know either much or little — not that I mean to speak disparagingly of anyone who is a student of natural philosophy. I should be very sorry if Meletus could bring so grave a charge against me. But the simple truth is, O Athenians, that I have nothing to do with physical speculations. Very many of those here present are witnesses to the truth of this, and to them I appeal. Speak then, you who have heard me, and tell your neighbors whether any of you have ever known me to hold forth in few words or in many upon such matters.... You hear their answer. And from what they say of this part of the charge you will be able to judge of the truth of the rest.

As little foundation is there for the report that I am a teacher, and take money; this accusation has no more truth in it than the other. Although, if a man were really able to instruct mankind, to receive money for giving instruction would, in my opinion, be an honor to him. There is Gorgias of Leontium, and Prodicus of Ceos, and Hippias of Elis, who go the round of the cities, and are able to persuade the young men to leave their own citizens by whom they might be taught for nothing, and come to them whom they not only pay, but are thankful if they may be allowed to pay them....

I dare say, Athenians, that someone among you will reply, "Yes, Socrates, but what is the origin of these accusations which are brought against you? There must have been something strange which you have been doing? All these rumors and the talk about you would never have arisen if you had been like other men: tell us, then, what is the cause of them, for we should be sorry to judge hastily of you." Now I regard this as a fair challenge, and I will endeavor to explain to you the reason why I am called "wise" and have such an evil fame. Please to attend then. And although some of you may think that I am joking, I declare that I will tell you the entire truth. Men of Athens, this reputation of mine has come of a certain sort of wisdom which I possess. If you ask me what kind of wisdom, I reply, wisdom such as may perhaps be attained by man, for to that extent I am inclined to believe that I am wise; whereas the persons of whom I was speaking have a superhuman wisdom, which I may fail to describe, because I have it not myself; and he who says that I have, speaks falsely, and is taking away my character. And here, O men of Athens, I must beg you not to interrupt me, even if I seem to say something extravagant. For the word which I will speak is not mine. I will refer you to a witness who is worthy of credit; that witness shall be the God of Delphi — he will tell you about my wisdom, if I have any, and of what sort it is. You must have known Chaerephon; he was early a friend of mine, and also a friend of yours, for he shared in the recent exile of the people, and returned with you. Well, Chaerephon, as you know, was very impetuous in all his doings, and he went to Delphi and boldly asked the oracle to tell him whether — as I was saying, I must beg you not to interrupt — he asked the oracle to tell him whether anyone was wiser than I was, and the Pythian prophetess answered that there was no man wiser. Chaerephon is dead himself; but his brother, who is in court, will confirm the truth of what I am saying.

Why do I mention this? Because I am going to explain to you why I have such an evil name. When I heard the answer, I said to myself, What can the god mean? And what is the interpretation of his riddle? For I know that I have no wisdom, small or great. What then can he mean when he says that I am the wisest of men? And yet he is a god, and cannot lie; that would be against his nature. After long consideration, I thought of a method of trying the question. I reflected that if I could only find a man wiser than myself, then I might go to the god with a refutation in my hand. I should say to him, 'Here is a man who is wiser than I am; but you said that I was the wisest.' Accordingly, I went to one who had the reputation of wisdom, and observed him — his name I need not mention; he was a politician whom I selected for examination — and the result was as follows: When I began to talk with him, I could not help thinking that he was not really wise, although he was thought wise by many, and still wiser by himself; and thereupon I tried to explain to him that he thought himself wise, but was not really wise; and the consequence was that he hated me, and his enmity was shared by several who were present and heard me. So I left him, saying to myself, as I went away: Well, although I do not suppose that either of us knows anything really beautiful and good, I am better off than he is — for he knows nothing, and thinks that he knows; I neither know nor think that I know. In this latter particular, then, I seem to have slightly the advantage of him. Then I went to another who had still higher pretensions to wisdom, and my conclusion was exactly the same. Whereupon I made another enemy of him, and of many others besides him.

Then I went to one man after another, being not unconscious of the enmity which I provoked, and I lamented and feared this: But necessity was laid upon me, — the word of God, I thought, ought to be considered first. And I said to myself, Go I must to all who appear to know, and find out the meaning of the oracle. And I swear to you, Athenians, by the dog I swear! — For I must tell you the truth — the result of my mission was just this: I found that the men most in repute were all but the most foolish; and that others less esteemed were really wiser and better. I will tell you the tale of my wanderings and of the 'Herculean' labors, as I may call them, which I endured only to find at last the oracle irrefutable. After the politicians, I went to the poets; tragic, dithyrambic, and all sorts. And there, I said to myself, you will be instantly detected; now you will find out that you are more ignorant than they are. Accordingly, I took them some of the most elaborate passages in their own writings, and asked what was the meaning of them — thinking that they would teach me something. Will you believe me? I am almost ashamed to confess the truth, but I must say that there is hardly a person present who would not have talked better about their poetry than they did themselves. Then I knew that not by wisdom do poets write poetry, but by a sort of genius and inspiration; they are like diviners or soothsayers who also say many fine things, but do not understand the meaning of them. The poets appeared to me to be much in the same case; and I further observed that upon the strength of their poetry they believed themselves to be the wisest of men in other things in which they were not wise. So I departed, conceiving myself to be superior to them for the same reason that I was superior to the politicians.

At last I went to the artisans, for I was conscious that I knew nothing at all, as I may say, and I was sure that they knew many fine things; and here I was not mistaken, for they did know many things of which I was ignorant, and in this they certainly were wiser than I was. But I observed that even the good artisans fell into the same error as the poets; —

because they were good workmen they thought that they also knew all sorts of high matters, and this defect in them overshadowed their wisdom; and therefore I asked myself on behalf of the oracle, whether I would like to be as I was, neither having their knowledge nor their ignorance, or like them in both; and I made answer to myself and to the oracle that I was better off as I was.

This inquisition has led to my having many enemies of the worst and most dangerous kind, and has given occasion also to many calumnies. And I am called wise, for my hearers always imagine that I myself possess the wisdom which I find wanting in others: but the truth is, O men of Athens, that God only is wise; and by his answer he intends to show that the wisdom of men is worth little or nothing; he is not speaking of Socrates, he is only using my name by way of illustration, as if he said, He, O men, is the wisest, who, like Socrates, knows that his wisdom is in truth worth nothing. And so I go about the world, obedient to the god, and search and make enquiry into the wisdom of anyone, whether citizen or stranger, who appears to be wise; and if he is not wise, then in vindication of the oracle I show him that he is not wise, and my occupation quite absorbs me, and I have no time to give either to any public matter of interest or to any concern of my own, but I am in utter poverty by reason of my devotion to the god.

There is another thing: — young men of the richer classes, who have not much to do, come about me of their own accord; they like to hear the pretenders examined, and they often imitate me, and proceed to examine others; there are plenty of persons, as they quickly discover, who think that they know something, but really know little or nothing; and then those who are examined by them instead of being angry with themselves are angry with me: This confounded Socrates, they say; this villainous misleader of youth! — And then if somebody asks them, why, what evil does he practice or teach? they do not know, and cannot tell; but in order that they may not appear to be at a loss, they repeat the ready-made charges which are used against all philosophers about teaching things up in the clouds and under the earth, and having no gods, and making the worse appear the better cause, for they do not like to confess that their pretence of knowledge has been detected — which is the truth; and as they are numerous and ambitious and energetic, and are drawn up in battle array and have persuasive tongues, they have filled your ears with their loud and inveterate calumnies. And this is the reason why my three accusers, Meletus and Anytus and Lycon, have set upon me; Meletus, who has a quarrel with me on behalf of the poets; Anytus, on behalf of the craftsmen and politicians; Lycon, on behalf of the rhetoricians; and as I said at the beginning, I cannot expect to get rid of such a mass of calumny all in a moment. And this, O men of Athens, is the truth and the whole truth; I have concealed nothing, I have dissembled nothing. And yet, I know that my plainness of speech makes them hate me, and what is their hatred but a proof that I am speaking the truth? - Hence has arisen the prejudice against me; and this is the reason of it, as you will find out either in this or in any future enquiry.

I have said enough in my defense against the first class of my accusers. I turn to the second class. They are headed by Meletus, that good man and true lover of his country, as he calls himself.... He says that I am doer of evil, and corrupt the youth; but I say, O men of Athens, that Meletus is a doer of evil, in that he pretends to be in earnest when he is only in jest, and is so eager to bring men to trial from a pretended zeal and interest about matters in which he really never had the smallest interest. And the truth of this I will endeavor to prove to you.

Come hither, Meletus, and let me ask a question of you. You think a great deal about the improvement of youth?

Yes, I do.

Tell the judges, then, who is their improver; for you must know, as you have taken the pains to discover their corrupter, and are citing and accusing me before them. Speak, then, and tell the judges who their improver is. — Observe, Meletus, that you are silent, and have nothing to say. But is not this rather disgraceful, and a very considerable proof of what I was saying, that you have no interest in the matter? Speak up, friend, and tell us who their improver is.

The laws.

But that, my good sir, is not my meaning. I want to know who the person is, who, in the first place, knows the laws.

The judges, Socrates, who are present in court.

What, do you mean to say, Meletus, that they are able to instruct and improve youth?

Certainly they are.

What, all of them, or some only and not others?

All of them.

By the goddess here, that is good news! There are plenty of improvers, then. And what do you say of the audience, — do they improve them?

Yes, they do.

And the senators?

Yes, the senators improve them.

But perhaps the members of the assembly corrupt them? — Or do they too improve them?

They improve them.

Then every Athenian improves and elevates them; all with the exception of myself; and I alone am their corrupter? Is that what you affirm?

That is what I stoutly affirm.

I am very unfortunate if you are right. But suppose I ask you a question: How about horses? Does one man do them harm and all the world good? Is not the exact opposite the truth? One man is able to do them good, or at least not many; — the trainer of horses, that is to say, does them good, and others who have to do with them rather injure them? Is not that true, Meletus, of horses, or of any other animals? Most assuredly it is; whether you and Anytus say yes or no. Happy indeed would be the condition of youth if they had one corrupter only, and all the rest of the world were their improvers. But you, Meletus, have sufficiently shown that you never had a thought about the young: your carelessness is seen in your not caring about the very things which you bring against me.

And now, Meletus, I will ask you another question — by Zeus I will: Which is better, to live among bad citizens, or among good ones? Answer, friend, I say; the question is one which may be easily answered. Do not the good do their neighbors good, and the bad do them evil?

Certainly.

And is there anyone who would rather be injured than benefited by those who live with him? Answer, my good friend, the law requires you to answer — does anyone like to be injured?

Certainly not.

And when you accuse me of corrupting and deteriorating the youth, do you allege that I corrupt them intentionally or unintentionally?

Intentionally, I say.

But you have just admitted that the good do their neighbors good, and evil do them evil. Now, is that a truth which your superior wisdom has recognized thus early in life, and am I, at my age, in such darkness and ignorance as not to know that if a man with whom I have to live is corrupted by me, I am very likely to be harmed by him; and yet I corrupt him, and intentionally, too — so you say, although neither I nor any other human being is ever likely to be convinced by you. But either I do not corrupt them, or I corrupt them unintentionally; and on either view of the case you lie. If my offence is unintentional, the law has no cognizance of

18

unintentional offenses: you ought to have taken me privately, and warned and admonished me; for if I had been better advised, I should have left off doing what I only did unintentionally — no doubt I should; but you would have nothing to say to me and refused to teach me. And now you bring me up in this court, which is a place not of instruction, but of punishment.

It will be very clear to you, Athenians, as I was saying, that Meletus has no care at all, great or small, about the matter. But still I should like to know, Meletus, in what I am affirmed to corrupt the young. I suppose you mean, as I infer from your indictment, that I teach them not to acknowledge the gods which the state acknowledges, but some other new divinities or spiritual agencies in their stead. These are the lessons by which I corrupt the youth, as you say.

Yes, that I say emphatically.

Then, by the gods, Meletus, of whom we are speaking, tell me and the court, in somewhat plainer terms, what you mean! For I do not as yet understand whether you affirm that I teach other men to acknowledge some gods, and therefore that I do believe in gods, and am not an entire atheist — this you do not lay to my charge, — but only you say that they are not the same gods which the city recog-

nizes — the charge is that they are different gods. Or, do you mean that I am an atheist simply, and a teacher of atheism?

I mean the latter — that you are a complete atheist.

What an extraordinary statement! Why do you think so, Meletus? Do you mean that I do not believe in the godhead of the sun or moon, like other men?

I assure you, Judges, that he does not: for he says that the sun is stone, and the moon earth.

Friend Meletus, you think that you are accusing Anaxagoras: and you have but a bad opinion of the judges, if you fancy them illiterate to such a degree as not to know that these doctrines are found in the books of Anaxagoras the Clazomenian, which are full of them. And so, forsooth, the youth are said to be taught them by Socrates, when there are not infrequently exhibitions of them at the theatre (price of admission - one drachma at the most); and they might pay their money, and laugh at Socrates if he pretends to father these extraordinary views. And so, Meletus, you really think that I do not believe in any god?

I swear by Zeus that you believe absolutely in none at all.

Nobody will believe you, Meletus, and I am pretty sure that you do not believe yourself. I cannot help thinking, men of Athens, that Meletus is reckless and impudent, and that he has written this indictment in a spirit of mere wantonness and youthful bravado. Has he not compounded a riddle, thinking to try me? He said to himself: — I shall see whether the wise Socrates will discover my facetious contradiction, or whether I shall be able to deceive him and the rest of them. For he certainly does appear to me to contradict himself in the indictment as much as if he said that Socrates is guilty of not believing in the gods, and yet of believing in them — but this is not like a person who is in earnest.

I should like you, O men of Athens, to join me in examining what I conceive to be his inconsistency; and do you, Meletus, answer. And I must remind the audience of my request that they would not make a disturbance if I speak in my accustomed manner.

Did ever man, Meletus, believe in the existence of human things, and not of human beings?... I wish, men of Athens, that he would answer, and not be always trying to get up an interruption. Did ever any man believe in horsemanship, and not in horses? Or in flute-playing, and not in flute-players? No, my friend; I will answer to you and to the court, as you refuse to answer for yourself. There is no man who ever did. But now please to answer the next question: Can a man believe in spiritual and divine agencies, and not in spirits or demigods?

Certainly they can.

But this is what I call the facetious riddle invented by you: the demigods or spirits are gods, and you say first that I do not believe in gods, and then again that I do believe in gods; that is, if I believe in demigods. For if the demigods are the illegitimate sons of gods, whether by the nymphs or by any other mothers, of whom they are said to be the sons — what human being will ever believe that there are no gods if they are the sons of gods? You might as well affirm the existence of mules, and deny that of horses and asses. Such nonsense, Meletus, could only have been intended by you to make trial of me. You have put this into the indictment because you had nothing real of which to accuse me. But no one who has a particle of understanding will ever be convinced by you that the same men can believe in divine and superhuman things, and yet not believe that there are gods and demigods and heroes.

I have said enough in answer to the charge of Meletus: any elaborate defense is unnecessary; but I know only too well how many are the enmities which I have incurred, and this is what will be my destruction if I am destroyed; — not

Meletus, nor yet Anytus, but the envy and detraction of the world, which has been the death of many good men, and will probably be the death of many more; there is no danger of my being the last of them.

Some one will say: And are you not ashamed, Socrates, of a course of life which is likely to bring you to an untimely end? To him I may fairly answer: There you are mistaken: a man who is good for anything ought not to calculate the chance of living or dying; he ought only to consider whether in doing anything he is doing right or wrong — acting the part of a good man or of a bad....

Strange, indeed, would be my conduct, O men of Athens, if I who, when I was ordered by the generals whom you chose to command me at Potidaea and Amphipolis and Delium, remained where they placed me, like any other man, facing death — if now, when, as I conceive and imagine, God orders me to fulfill the philosopher's mission of searching into myself and other men, I were to desert my post through fear of death, or any other fear; that would indeed be strange, and I might justly be arraigned in court for denying the existence of the gods, if I disobeyed the oracle because I was afraid of death, fancying that I was wise when I was not wise. For the fear of death is indeed the pretence of wisdom, and not real wisdom, being a pretence of knowing the unknown; and no one knows whether death, which men in their fear apprehend to be the greatest evil, may not be the greatest good. Is not this ignorance of a disgraceful sort, the ignorance which is the conceit that man knows what he does not know? And in this respect only I believe myself to differ from men in general, and may perhaps claim to be wiser than they are: — that whereas I know but little of the world below, I do not suppose that I know: but I do know that injustice and disobedience to a better, whether God or man, is evil and dishonorable, and I will never fear or avoid a possible good rather than a certain evil. And therefore if you let me go now, and are not convinced by Anytus, who said that since I had been prosecuted I must be put to death.... If you say to me, Socrates, this time we will not mind Anytus, and you shall be let off, but upon one condition, that you are not to enquire and speculate in this way any more, and that if you are caught doing so again you shall die; — if this was the condition on which you let me go, I should reply: Men of Athens, I honor and love you; but I shall obey God rather than you, and while I have life and strength I shall never cease from the practice and teaching of philosophy, exhorting anyone whom I meet and saying to him after my manner: You, my friend, — a citizen of the great and mighty and wise city of Athens, — are you not ashamed of heaping up the greatest amount of money and honor and reputation, and caring so little about wisdom and truth and the greatest improvement of the soul, which you never regard or heed at all? And if the person with whom I am arguing, says: Yes, but I do care; then I do not leave him or let him go at once; but I proceed to interrogate and examine and cross-examine him, and if I think that he has no virtue in him, but only says that he has, I reproach him with undervaluing the greater, and overvaluing the less. And I shall repeat the same words to every one whom I meet, young and old, citizen and alien, but especially to the citizens, inasmuch as they are my brethren. For know that this is the command of god; and I believe that no greater good has ever happened in the state than my service to the God. For I do nothing but go about persuading you all, old and young alike, not to take thought for your persons or your properties, but first and chiefly to care about the greatest improvement of the soul. I tell you that virtue is not given by money, but that from virtue comes money and every other good of man, public as well as private. This is my teaching, and if this is the doc-trine which corrupts the youth, I am a mischievous person. But if anyone says that this is not my teaching, he is speaking an untruth. Wherefore, O men of Athens, I say to you, do as Anytus bids or not as Anytus bids, and either acquit me or not; but whichever you do, understand that I shall never alter my ways, not even if I have to die many times....

And now, Athenians, I am not going to argue for my own sake, as you may think, but for yours, that you may not sin against the gods by condemning me, who am his gift to you. For if you kill me you will not easily find a successor to me, who, if I may use such a ludicrous figure of speech, am a sort of gadfly, given to the state by the gods; and the state is a great and noble steed who is tardy in his motions owing to his very size, and requires to be stirred into life. I am that gadfly which God has attached to the state, and all day long and in all places am always fastening upon you, arousing and persuading and reproaching you. You will not easily find another like me, and therefore I would advise you to spare me...

Perhaps it may seem strange to you that, though I go about giving this advice privately and meddling in others' affairs, yet I do not venture to come forward in the assembly and advise the state. You have often heard me speak of my reason for this, and in many places: it is that I have a certain divine sign, which is what Meletus has caricatured in his indictment. I have had it from childhood. It is a kind of voice which, whenever I hear it, always turns me back from something which I was going to do, but never urges me to act. It is this which forbids me to take part in politics. And I think it does well to forbid me. For, Athenians, it is quite certain that, if I had attempted to take part in politics, I should have perished at once and long ago without doing any good either to you or to myself. And do not be indignant with me for telling the truth. There is no man who will preserve his life for long, either in Athens or elsewhere, if he firmly opposes the multitude, and tries to prevent the commission of much injustice and illegality in the state. He who would really fight for justice must do so as a private citizen, not as an office-holder, if he is to preserve his life even for a short time.

I will prove to you that this is so by very strong evidence, not by mere words, but by what you value highly, actions. Listen then to what has happened to me, that you may know that there is no man who could make me consent to do wrong from the fear of death, but that I would perish at once rather than give way. What I am going to tell you may be a commonplace in the law court; nevertheless it is true. The only office that I ever held in the state, Athenians, was that of Senator. When you wished to try the ten generals who did not rescue their men after the battle of Arginusae, as a group, which was illegal, as you all came to think afterwards, the tribe Antiochis, to which I belong, held the presidency. On that occasion I alone, of all the presidents, opposed your illegal action and gave my vote against you. The speakers were ready to suspend me and arrest me; and you were clamoring against me, and crying out to me to submit. But I thought that I ought to face the danger, with law and justice on my side, rather than join with you in your unjust proposal, from fear of imprisonment or death. That was when the state was democratic. When the oligarchy came in, the Thirty sent for me, with four others, to the council-chamber, and ordered us to bring Leon the Salaminian from Salamis, that they might put him to death. They were in the habit of frequently giving similar orders, to many others, wishing to implicate as many as possible in their crimes. But, then, I again proved, not by mere words, but by my actions, that, if I may speak bluntly, I do not care a straw for death; but that I do care very much indeed about not doing anything unjust or impious. That government with all its powers did not terrify me into doing anything unjust; but when we left the council-chamber, the other four went over to Salamis and brought Leon across to Athens; and I went home. And if the rule of the Thirty had not been destroyed soon afterwards, I should very likely have been put to death for what I did then. Many of you will be my witnesses in this matter.

Now do you think that I could have remained alive all these years if I had taken part in public affairs, and had always maintained the cause of justice like an honest man, and had held it a paramount duty, as it is, to do so? Certainly not, Athenians, nor could any other man. But throughout my whole life, both in private and in public, whenever I have had to take part in public affairs, you will find I have always been the same and have never yielded unjustly to anyone; no, not to those whom my enemies falsely assert to have been my pupils. But I was never anyone's teacher. I have never withheld myself from anyone, young or old, who was anxious to hear me discuss while I was making my investigation; neither do I discuss for payment, nor refuse to discuss without payment. I am ready to ask questions of rich and poor alike, and if any man wishes not answer me, and then listen to what I have to say, he may....

I believe in the gods as not one of my accusers believes in them: and to you and to God I commit my cause to be decided as is best for you and for me.[The vote is taken and he is found guilty by 281 votes to 220.]

There are many reasons why I am not grieved, O men of Athens, at the vote of condemnation. I expected it, and am only surprised that the votes are so nearly equal; for I had thought that the majority against me would have been far larger. But now, had thirty votes gone over to the other side, I should have been acquitted. And I may say, I think, that I have escaped Meletus. I may say more; for without the assistance of Anytus and Lycon, anyone may see that he would not have had a fifth part of the votes, as the law requires, in which case he would have incurred a fine of a thousand drachmae.

And so he proposes death as the penalty. And what shall I propose on my part, O men of Athens? Clearly that which is my due. And what is my due? What return shall be made to the man who has never had the wit to be idle during his whole life; but has been careless of what the many care for — wealth, and family interests, and military offices, and speaking in the assembly, and magistracies, and plots, and parties. Reflecting that I was really too honest a man to be a politician and live, I did not go where I could do no good to you or to myself; but where I could do the greatest good privately to every one of you, thither I went, and sought to persuade every man among you that he must look to himself, and seek virtue and wisdom before he looks to his private interests, and look to the state before he looks to the interests of the state; and that this should be the order which he observes in all his actions. What shall be done to such a one? Doubtless some good thing, O men of Athens, if he has his reward; and the good should be of a kind suitable to him. What would be a reward suitable to a poor man who is your benefactor, and who desires leisure that he may instruct you? There can be no reward so fitting as maintenance in the Prytaneum, O men of Athens, a reward which he deserves far more than the citizen who has won the prize at Olympia in the horse or chariot race, whether the chariots were drawn by two horses or by many. For I am in want, and he has enough; and he only gives you the appearance of happiness, and I give you the reality. And if I am to estimate the penalty fairly, I should say that maintenance in the Prytaneum is the just return.

Perhaps you think that I am braving you in what I am saying now, as in what I said before about the tears and prayers. But this is not so. I speak rather because I am convinced that I never intentionally wronged anyone, although I cannot convince you — the time has been too short; if there were a law at Athens, as there is in other cities, that a capital cause should not be decided in one day, than I believe that I should have convinced you. But I cannot in a moment refute great slanders; and, as I am convinced that I never wronged another, I will assuredly not wrong myself. I will not say of myself that I deserve any evil, or propose any penalty. Why should I? Because I am afraid of the penalty of death which Meletus proposes? When I do not know whether death is a good or an evil, why should I propose a penalty which would certainly be an evil? Shall I say imprisonment? And why should I live in prison, and be the slave of the magistrates of the year — of the Eleven? Or shall the penalty be a fine, and imprisonment until the fine is paid? There is the same objection. I should have to lie in prison, for money I have none, and cannot pay. And if I say exile (and this may possibly be the penalty which you will affix), I must indeed be blinded by the love of life, if I am so irrational as to expect that when you, who are my own citizens, cannot endure my discourses and words, and have found them so grievous and odious that you will have no more of them, others are likely to endure me. No indeed, men of Athens, that is not very likely. And what a life should I lead, at my age, wandering from city to city, ever changing my place of exile, and always being driven out! For I am quite sure that wherever I go, there, as here, the young men will flock to me; and if I drive them away, their elders will drive me out at their request; and if I let them come, their fathers and friends will drive me out for their sakes.

Some one will say: Yes, Socrates, but cannot you hold your tongue, and then you may go into a foreign city, and no one will interfere with you? Now I have great difficulty in making you understand my answer to this. For if I tell you that to do as you say would be a disobedience to the God, and therefore that I cannot hold my tongue, you will not believe that I am serious; and if I say again that daily to discourse about virtue, and of those other things about which you hear me examining myself and others, is the greatest good of man, and that the unexamined life is not worth living, you are still less likely to believe me. Yet I say what is true, although a thing of which it is hard for me to persuade you. Also, I have never been accustomed to think that I deserve to suffer any harm. Had I money I might have estimated the offense at what I was able to pay, and not have been much the worse.

But I have none, and therefore I must ask you to proportion the fine to my means. Well, perhaps I could afford a mina, and therefore I propose that penalty: Plato, Crito, Critobulus, and Apollodorus, my friends here, bid me say thirty minae, and they will be the sureties. Let thirty minae be the penalty; for which sum they will be ample security to you.

[2nd vote: the jury decides for the death penalty by a vote of 360 to 141.]

Not much time will be gained, O Athenians, in return for the evil name which you will get from the detractors of the city, who will say that you killed Socrates, a wise man; for they will call me wise, even although I am not wise, when they want to reproach you. If you had waited a little while, your desire would have been fulfilled in the course of nature. For I am far advanced in years, as you may perceive, and not far from death.... The difficulty, my friends, is not to avoid death, but to avoid unrighteousness; for that runs faster than death. I am old and move slowly, and the slower runner has overtaken me, and my accusers are keen and quick, and the faster runner, who is unrighteousness, has overtaken them. And now I depart hence condemned by you to suffer the penalty of death, — they too go their ways condemned by the truth to suffer the penalty of villainy and wrong; and

I must abide by my award — let them abide by theirs. I suppose that these things may be regarded as fated, — and I think that they are well....

Friends, who would have acquitted me, I would like also to talk with you about the thing which has come to pass, while the magistrates are busy, and before I go to the place at which I must die. Stay then a little, for we may as well talk with one another while there is time. You are my friends, and I should like to show you the meaning of this event which has happened to me. O my judges — for you I may truly call judges — I should like to tell you of a wonderful circumstance. Hitherto the divine faculty of which the internal oracle is the source has constantly been in the habit of opposing me even about trifles, if I was going to make a slip or error in any matter; and now as you see there has come upon me that which may be thought, and is generally believed to be, the last and worst evil. But the oracle made no sign of opposition, either when I was leaving my house in the morning, or when I was on my way to the court, or while I was speaking, at anything which I was going to say; and yet I have often been stopped in the middle of a speech, but now in nothing I either said or did touching the mater in hand has the oracle opposed me. What do I take to be the explanation of this silence? I will tell you. It is intimation that what has happened to me is a good, and that those of us who think that death is an evil are in error. For the customary sign would surely have opposed me had I been going to evil and not to good.

Let us reflect in another way, and we shall see that there is great reason to hope that death is a good; for one of two things - either death is a state of nothingness and utter unconsciousness, or, as men say, there is a change and migration of the soul from this world to another. Now if you suppose that there is no consciousness, but a sleep like the sleep of him who is undisturbed even by dreams, death will be an unspeakable gain. For if a person were to select the night in which his sleep was undisturbed even by dreams, and were to compare with this the other days and nights of his life, and then were to tell us how many days and nights he had passed in the course of his life better and more pleasantly than this one, I think that any man, I will not say a private man, but even the great king will not find many such days or nights, when compared with the others. Now if death be of such a nature, I say that to die is gain; for eternity is then only a single night. But if death is the journey to another place, and there, as men say, all the dead abide, what good, O my friends and judges, can be greater than this? If indeed when the pilgrim arrives in the world below, he is delivered from the professors of justice in this world, and finds the true judges who are said to give judgment there, Minos and Rhadamanthus and Aeacus and Triptolemus, and other sons of God who were righteous in their own life, that pilgrimage will be worth making. What would not a man give if he might converse with Orpheus and Musaeus and Hesiod and Homer? Nay, if this be true, let me die again and again. I myself, too, shall have a wonderful interest in there meeting and conversing with Palamedes, and Ajax the son of Telamon, and any other ancient hero who has suffered death through an unjust judgment; and there will be no small pleasure, as I think in comparing my own sufferings with theirs. Above all, I shall then be able to continue my search into true and false knowledge; as in this world, so also in the next; and I shall find out who is wise, and who pretends to be wise, and is not. What would not a man give, O judges, to be able to examine the leader of the great Trojan expedition; or Odysseus or Sisyphus, or numberless others, men and women too! What infinite delight would there be in conversing with them and asking them questions! In another world they do not put a man to death for asking questions: assuredly not. For besides being happier than we are, they will be immortal, if what is said is true.

Wherefore, O judges, be of good cheer about death, and know of a certainty, that no evil can happen to a good man, either in life or after death. He and his are not neglected by the gods; nor has my own approaching end happened by mere chance. But I see clearly that the time had arrived when it was better for me to die and be released from trouble; wherefore the oracle gave no sign. For which reason, also, I am not angry with my condemners, or with my accusers; they have done me no harm, although they did not mean to do me any good; and for this I may gently blame them.

Still I have a favor to ask of them. When my sons are grown up, I would ask you, O my friends, to punish them; and I would have you trouble them, as I have troubled you, if they seem to care about riches, or anything, more than about virtue; or if they pretend to be something when they are really nothing, — then reprove them, as I have reproved you, for not caring about that for which they ought to care, and thinking that they are something when they are really nothing. And if you do this, both I and my sons will have received justice at your hands.

28

The hour of departure has arrived, and we go our ways — I to die, and you to live. Which is better god only knows.

From *Dialogues of Plato,* trans. Benjamin Jowett, Oxford, 1896.

Crito

PLATO

Written in dialogue form, Crito recounts the final days of Socrates' life. Socrates' friend, Crito, has secured Socrates' escape from prison and certain death, yet Socrates refuses to comply. He argues that for him to escape from the Athenian prison after due process of law has condemned him to death would be paramount to aiding the destruction of the Law of Athens and the city itself.

Vocabulary

Comely:	good looking
Confiscations:	that which is taken away, usually against one's will
Hobgoblin:	imaginary terrors
Enumerate:	number
Deteriorated:	destroyed
Retaliate:	to be revengeful
Truant:	one who avoids work, school, or required activities without permission
Interrogate:	to question
Revile:	to denounce with abusive language
Acquiesced:	to agree with; to comply with
Sentiments:	feelings

Covenants: promises or agreements
Subverter: one who overthrows
Metamorphosed: changed
Repining: fearful

Concepts

Justice:

Injustice:

Civil Disobedience:

Implied Contract:

Questions:

1. *According to Socrates, should we care about the opinion of the many? Explain.*
2. *Why does Socrates refuse to escape from prison?*
3. *Does Socrates believe it is acceptable to return evil for evil? Explain.*
4. *How would Socrates' Disobedience to the Laws of the State contribute to the States destruction?*
5. *What is the implied contract that each citizen of the state enters into with the State?*

PERSONS OF THE DIALOGUE: SOCRATES, CRITO.

SCENE: The Prison of Socrates

[Socrates] WHY have you come at this hour, Crito? It must be quite early.

[Crito] Yes, certainly.

[Soc.] What is the exact time?

[Cr.] The dawn is breaking.

[Soc.] I wonder why the keeper of the prison would let you in.

[Cr.] He knows me because I often come, Socrates; moreover, I have done him a kindness.

[Soc.] And have you only just come?

[Cr.] No, I came some time ago.

[Soc.] Then why did you sit and say nothing, instead of awakening me at once?

[Cr.] Why, indeed, Socrates, I myself would rather not have all this sleeplessness and sorrow. But I have been wondering at your peaceful slumbers, and that was the reason why I did not awaken you, because I wanted you to be out of pain. I have always thought you happy in the calmness of your temperament; but never did I see the easy, cheerful way in which you bear this calamity.

[Soc.] Why, Crito, when a man has reached my age he ought not to be repining at the prospect of death.

[Cr.] And yet other old men find themselves in similar misfortunes, and age does not prevent them from repining.

[Soc.] That may be. But you have not told me why you come at this early hour.

[Cr.] I come to bring you a message which is sad and painful; not, as I believe, to yourself, but to all of us who are your friends, and saddest of all to me.

[Soc.] What! I suppose that the ship has come from Delos, on the arrival of which I am to die.

[Cr.] No, the ship has not actually arrived, but she will probably be here to-day, as persons who have come from Sunium tell me that they have left her there; and therefore to-morrow, Socrates, will be the last day of your life.

[Soc.] Very well, Crito; if such is the will of God, I am willing; but my belief is that there will be a delay of a day.

[Cr.] Why do you say this?

[Soc.] I will tell you. I am to die on the day after the arrival of the ship.

[Cr.] Yes; that is what the authorities say.

[Soc.] But I do not think that the ship will be here until to-morrow; this I gather from a vision which I had last night, or rather only just now, when you fortunately allowed me to sleep.

[Cr.] And what was the nature of the vision?

[Soc.] There came to me the likeness

of a woman, fair and comely, clothed in white raiment, who called to me and said: O Socrates-

The third day hence, to Phthia shall thou go.

[Cr.] What a singular dream, Socrates!

[Soc.] There can be no doubt about the meaning, Crito, I think.

[Cr.] Yes: the meaning is only too clear. But, O! my beloved Socrates, let me entreat you once more to take my advice and escape. For if you die I shall not only lose a friend who can never be replaced, but there is another evil: people who do not know you and me will believe that I might have saved you if I had been willing to give money, but that I did not care. Now, can there be a worse disgrace than this- that I should be thought to value money more than the life of a friend? For the many will not be persuaded that I wanted you to escape, and that you refused.

[Soc.] But why, my dear Crito, should we care about the opinion of the many? Good men, and they are the only persons who are worth considering, will think of these things truly as they happened.

[Cr.] But do you see, Socrates, that the opinion of the many must be regarded, as is evident in your own case, because they can do the very greatest evil to anyone who has lost their good opinion?

[Soc.] I only wish, Crito, that they could; for then they could also do the greatest good, and that would be well. But the truth is, that they can do neither good nor evil; they cannot make a man wise or make him foolish; and whatever they do is the result of chance.

[Cr.] Well, I will not dispute about that; but please to tell me, Socrates, whether you are not acting out of regard to me and your other friends: are you not afraid that if you escape hence we may get into trouble with the informers for having stolen you away, and lose either the whole or a great part of our property; or that even a worse evil may happen to us? Now, if this is your fear, be at ease; for in order to save you, we ought surely to run this or even a greater risk; be persuaded, then, and do as I say.

[Soc.] Yes, Crito, that is one fear which you mention, but by no means the only one.

[Cr.] Fear not. There are persons who at no great cost are willing to save you and bring you out of prison; and as for the informers, you may observe that they are far from being exorbitant in their demands; a little money will satisfy them. My means, which, as I am sure, are ample, are at your service, and if you have a scruple about spending all mine, here are strangers who will give you the use of theirs; and one of them, Simmias the Theban, has brought a sum of money for this very purpose; and Cebes and many others are willing to spend their money, too. I say, therefore, do not on that account hesitate about making your escape, and do not say, as you did in the court, that you will have a difficulty in knowing what to do with yourself if you escape. For men will love you in other places to which you may go, and not in Athens only; there are friends of mine in Thessaly, if you like to go to them, who will value and protect you, and no Thessalian will give you any trouble. Nor can I think that you are justified, Socrates, in betraying your own life when you might be saved; this is playing into the hands of your enemies and destroyers; and moreover I should say that you were betraying your children; for you might bring them up and educate them; instead of which you go away and leave them, and they will have to take their chance; and if they do not meet with the usual fate of orphans, there will be small thanks to you. No man should bring children into the world who is unwilling to persevere to the end in their nurture and education. But you are choosing the easier part, as I think, not the better and manlier, which

would rather have become one who professes virtue in all his actions, like yourself. And, indeed, I am ashamed not only of you, but of us who are your friends, when I reflect that this entire business of yours will be attributed to our want of courage. The trial need never have come on, or might have been brought to another issue; and the end of all, which is the crowning absurdity, will seem to have been permitted by us, through cowardice and baseness, who might have saved you, as you might have saved yourself, if we had been good for anything (for there was no difficulty in escaping); and we did not see how disgraceful, Socrates, and also miserable all this will be to us as well as to you. Make your mind up then, or rather have your mind already made up, for the time of deliberation is over, and there is only one thing to be done, which must be done, if at all, this very night, and which any delay will render all but impossible; I beseech you therefore, Socrates, to be persuaded by me, and to do as I say.

[Soc.] Dear Crito, your zeal is invaluable, if a right one; but if wrong, the greater the zeal the greater the evil; and therefore we ought to consider whether these things shall be done or not. For I am, and always have been, one of those natures who must be guided by reason, whatever the reason may be which upon reflection appears to me to be the best; and now that this fortune has come upon me, I cannot put away the reasons which I have before given: the principles which I have hitherto honored and revered I still honor, and unless we can find other and better principles on the instant, I am certain not to agree with you; no, not even if the power of the multitude could inflict many more imprisonments, confiscations, deaths, frightening us like children with hobgoblin terrors. But what will be the fairest way of considering the question? Shall I return to your old argument about the opinions of men, some of which are to be regarded, and others, as we were saying, are not to be regarded? Now were we right in maintaining this before I was condemned? And has the argument which was once good now proved to be talk for the sake of talking; in fact an amusement only, and altogether vanity? That is what I want to consider with your help, Crito: whether, under my present circumstances, the argument appears to be in any way different or not; and is to be allowed by me or disallowed. That argument, which, as I believe, is maintained by many who assume to be authorities, was to the effect, as I was saying, that the opinions of some men are to be regarded, and of other men not to be regarded. Now you, Crito, are a disinterested person who is not going to

die to-morrow- at least, there is no human probability of this, and you are therefore not liable to be deceived by the circumstances in which you are placed. Tell me, then, whether I am right in saying that some opinions, and the opinions of some men only, are to be valued, and other opinions, and the opinions of other men, are not to be valued. I ask you whether I was right in maintaining this?

[Cr.] Certainly.

[Soc.] The good are to be regarded, and not the bad?

[Cr.] Yes.

[Soc.] And the opinions of the wise are good, and the opinions of the unwise are evil?

[Cr.] Certainly.

[Soc.] And what was said about another matter? Was the disciple in gymnastics supposed to attend to the praise and blame and opinion of every man, or of one man only- his physician or trainer, whoever that was?

[Cr.] Of one man only.

[Soc.] And he ought to fear the censure and welcome the praise of that one only, and not of the many?

[Cr.] That is clear.

[Soc.] And he ought to live and train, and eat and drink in the way which seems good to his single master who has understanding, rather than according to the opinion of all other men put together?

[Cr.] True.

[Soc.] And if he disobeys and disregards the opinion and approval of the one, and regards the opinion of the many who have no understanding, will he not suffer evil?

[Cr.] Certainly he will.

[Soc.] And what will the evil be, whither tending and what afflicting, in the disobedient person?

[Cr.] Clearly, affecting the body; that is what is destroyed by the evil.

[Soc.] Very good; and is not this true, Crito, of other things which we need not separately enumerate? In the matter of just and unjust, fair and foul, good and evil, which are the subjects of our present consultation, ought we to follow the opinion of the many and to fear them; or the opinion of the one man who has understanding, and whom we ought to fear and reverence more than all the rest of the world: and whom deserting we shall destroy and injure that principle in us which may be assumed to be improved by justice and deteriorated by injustice; is there not such a principle?

[Cr.] Certainly there is, Socrates.

[Soc.] Take a parallel instance; if, acting under the advice of men who have no understanding, we destroy that which is improved by health and deteriorated by disease- when that has been destroyed, I say, would life be worth having? And that is- the body?

[Cr.] Yes.

[Soc.] Could we live, having an evil and corrupted body?

[Cr.] Certainly not.

[Soc.] And will life be worth having, if that higher part of man be depraved, which is improved by justice and deteriorated by injustice? Do we suppose that principle, whatever it may be in man, which has to do with justice and injustice, to be inferior to the body?

[Cr.] Certainly not.

[Soc.] More honored, then?

[Cr.] Far more honored.

[Soc.] Then, my friend, we must not regard what the many say of us: but what he, the one man who has understanding of just and unjust, will say, and what the truth will say. And therefore you begin in error when you suggest that we should regard the opinion of the many about just and unjust, good and evil, honorable and dishonorable. Well, someone will say, "But the many can kill us."

[Cr.] Yes, Socrates; that will clearly be the answer.

[Soc.] That is true; but still I find with surprise that the old argument is, as I conceive, unshaken as ever. And I should like to know whether I may say the same of another proposition- that not life, but a good life, is to be chiefly valued?

[Cr.] Yes, that also remains.

[Soc.] And a good life is equivalent to a just and honorable one- that holds also?

[Cr.] Yes, that holds.

[Soc.] From these premises I proceed to argue the question whether I ought or ought not to try to escape without the consent of the Athenians: and if I am clearly right in escaping, then I will make the attempt; but if not, I will abstain. The other considerations which you mention, of money and loss of character, and the duty of educating children, are, I fear, only the doctrines of the multitude, who would be as ready to call people to life, if they were able, as they are to put them to death- and with as little reason. But now, since the argument has thus far prevailed, the only question which remains to be considered is, whether we shall do rightly either in escaping or in suffering others to aid in our escape and paying them in money and thanks, or whether we shall not do rightly; and if the latter, then death or any other calamity which may ensue on my remaining here must not be allowed to enter into the calculation.

[Cr.] I think that you are right, Socrates; how then shall we proceed?

[Soc.] Let us consider the matter together, and do you either refute me if you can, and I will be convinced; or else cease, my dear friend, from repeating to me that I ought to escape against the wishes of the Athenians: for I am extremely desirous to be persuaded by you, but not against my own better judgment. And now please to consider my first position, and do your best to answer me.

[Cr.] I will do my best.

[Soc.] Are we to say that we are never intentionally to do wrong, or that in one way we ought and in another way we ought not to do wrong, or is doing wrong always evil and dishonorable, as I was just now saying, and as has been already acknowledged by us? Are all our former admissions which were made within a few days to be thrown away? And have we, at our age, been earnestly discoursing with one another all our life long only to discover that we are no better than children? Or are we to rest assured, in spite of the opinion of the many, and in spite of consequences whether better or worse, of the truth of what was then said, that injustice is always an evil and dishonor to him who acts unjustly? Shall we affirm that?

[Cr.] Yes.

[Soc.] Then we must do no wrong?

[Cr.] Certainly not.

[Soc.] Nor when injured injure in

return, as the many imagine; for we must injure no one at all?

[Cr.] Clearly not.

[Soc.] Again, Crito, may we do evil?

[Cr.] Surely not, Socrates.

[Soc.] And what of doing evil in return for evil, which is the morality of the many-is that just or not?

[Cr.] Not just.

[Soc.] For doing evil to another is the same as injuring him?

[Cr.] Very true.

[Soc.] Then we ought not to retaliate or render evil for evil to anyone, whatever evil we may have suffered from him. But I would have you consider, Crito, whether you really mean what you are saying. For this opinion has never been held, and never will be held, by any considerable number of persons; and those who are agreed and those who are not agreed upon this point have no common ground, and can only despise one another, when they see how widely they differ. Tell me, then, whether you agree with and assent to my first principle, that neither injury nor retaliation nor warding off evil by evil is ever right. And shall that be the premise of our agreement? Or do you decline and dissent from this? For this has been of old and is still my opinion; but, if you are of another opinion, let me hear what you have to say. If, however, you remain of the same mind as formerly, I will proceed to the next step.

[Cr.] You may proceed, for I have not changed my mind.

[Soc.] Then I will proceed to the next step, which may be put in the form of a question: Ought a man to do what he admits to be right, or ought he to betray the right?

[Cr.] He ought to do what he thinks right.

[Soc.] But if this is true, what is the application? In leaving the prison against the will of the Athenians, do I wrong any? Or rather do I not wrong those whom I ought least to wrong? Do I not desert the principles which were acknowledged by us to be just? What do you say?

[Cr.] I cannot tell, Socrates, for I do not know.

[Soc.] Then consider the matter in this way: Imagine that I am about to play truant (you may call the proceeding by any name which you like), and the laws and the government come and interrogate me: "Tell us, Socrates," they say; "what are you about? Are you going by an act of yours to overturn us- the laws and the whole State, as far as in you lies? Do you imagine that a State can subsist and not be overthrown, in which the decisions of law have no power, but are set aside and overthrown by individuals?" What will be our answer, Crito, to these and the like words? Anyone, and especially a clever rhetorician, will have a good deal to urge about the evil of setting aside the law which requires a sentence to be carried out; and we might reply, "Yes; but the State has injured us and given an unjust sentence." Suppose I say that?

[Cr.] Very good, Socrates.

[Soc.] "And was that our agreement with you?" the law would say, "or were you to abide by the sentence of the State?" And if I were to express astonishment at their saying this, the law would probably add: "Answer, Socrates, instead of opening your eyes: you are in the habit of asking and answering questions. Tell us what complaint you have to make against us which justifies you in attempting to destroy us and the State? In the first place did we not bring you into existence? Your father married your mother by our aid and begat you. Say whether you have any objection to urge against those of us who regulate marriage?" None, I should reply. "Or against those of us who regulate the system of nurture and education of children in which you were trained? Were not the laws, who have the charge of this, right in commanding your father to train you in music and gymnastic?" Right, I should reply. "Well, then, since you were brought into the world and nurtured and educated by us, can you deny in the first place that you are our child and slave, as your fathers were before you? And if this is true you are not on equal terms with us; nor can you think that you have a right to do to us what we are doing to you. Would you have any right to strike or revile or do any other evil to a father or to your master, if you had one, when you have been struck or reviled by him, or received some other evil at his hands?- you would not say this? And because we think right to destroy you, do you think that you have any right to destroy us in return, and your country as far as in you lies? And will you, O professor of true virtue, say that you are justified in this? Has a philosopher like you failed to discover that our country is more to be valued and higher and holier far more than mother or father or any ancestor, and more to be regarded in the eyes of the gods and of men of understanding? Also to be soothed, and gently and reverently entreated when angry, even more than a father, and if not persuaded, obeyed? And when we are punished by her, whether with imprisonment or stripes, the punishment is to be endured in silence; and if she leads us to wounds or death in battle, thither we follow as is right; neither may anyone yield or retreat or leave his rank, but whether in battle or in a court of law, or in any other place, he must do what his city and his country order him; or he must change their view of what is just: and if he may do no violence to his father or mother, much less may he do violence to his country." What answer shall we make to this, Crito? Do the laws speak truly, or do they not?

[Cr.] I think that they do.

[Soc.] Then the laws will say: "Consider, Socrates, if this is true, that in your present attempt you are going to do us wrong. For, after having brought you into the world, and nurtured and educated you, and given you and every other citizen a share in every good that we had to give, we further proclaim and give the right to every Athenian, that if he does not like us when he has come of age and has seen the ways of the city, and made our acquaintance, he may go where he pleases and take his goods with him; and none of us laws will forbid him or interfere with him. Any of you who does not like us and the city, and who wants to go to a colony or to any other city, may go where he likes, and take his goods with him. But he who has experience of the manner in which we order justice and administer the State, and still remains, has entered into an implied contract that he will do as we command him. And he who disobeys us is, as we maintain, thrice wrong: first, because in disobeying us he is disobeying his parents; secondly, because we are the authors of his education; thirdly, because he has made an agreement with us that he will duly obey our commands; and he neither obeys them nor convinces us that our commands are wrong; and we do not rudely impose them, but give him the alternative of obeying or convincing us; that is what we offer and he does neither. These are the sort of accusations to which, as we were saying, you, Socrates, will be exposed if you accomplish your intentions; you, above all other Athenians." Suppose I ask, why is this? They will justly retort upon me that I, above all other men, have acknowledged the agreement. "There is clear proof," they will say, "Socrates, that we and the city were not displeasing to you. Of all Athenians you have been the most constant resident in the city, which, as you never leave, you may be supposed to love. For you never went out of the city either to see the games, except once when you went to the Isthmus, or to any other place unless when you were on military service; nor did you travel as other men do. Nor had you any curiosity to know other States or their laws: your affections did not go beyond us and our State; we were your especial favorites, and you acquiesced in our government of you; and this is the

State in which you begat your children, which is a proof of your satisfaction. Moreover, you might, if you had liked, have fixed the penalty at banishment in the course of the trial. The State which refuses to let you go now would have let you go then. But you pretended that you preferred death to exile, and that you were not grieved at death. And now you have forgotten these fine sentiments, and pay no respect to us, the laws, of whom you are the destroyer; and are doing what only a miserable slave would do, running away and turning your back upon the compacts and agreements which you made as a citizen. And first of all answer this very question: Are we right in saying that you agreed to be governed according to us in deed, and not in word only? Is that true or not?" How shall we answer that, Crito? Must we not agree?

[Cr.] There is no help, Socrates.

[Soc.] Then will they not say: "You, Socrates, are breaking the covenants and agreements which you made with us at your leisure, not in any haste or under any compulsion or deception, but having had seventy years to think of them, during which time you were at liberty to leave the city, if we were not to your mind, or if our covenants appeared to you to be unfair. You had your choice, and might have gone either to Lacedaemon or Crete, both of which you often praise for their good government, or to some other Hellenic or foreign State. Whereas you, above all other Athenians, seemed to be so fond of the State, or, in other words, of us her laws (for who would like a State that has no laws?), that you never stirred out of her: the halt, the blind, the maimed, were not more stationary in her than you were. And now you run away and forsake your agreements. Not so, Socrates, if you will take our advice; do not make yourself ridiculous by escaping out of the city.

"For just consider, if you transgress and err in this sort of way, what good will you do, either to yourself or to your friends? That your friends will be driven into exile and deprived of citizenship, or will lose their property, is tolerably certain; and you yourself, if you fly to one of the neighboring cities, as, for example, Thebes or Megara, both of which are well-governed cities, will come to them as an enemy, Socrates, and their government will be against you, and all patriotic citizens will cast an evil eye upon you as a subverter of the laws, and you will confirm in the minds of the judges the justice of their own condemnation of you. For he who is a corrupter of the laws is more than likely to be a corrupter of the young and foolish portion of mankind. Will you then flee from well-ordered cities and virtuous men? And is existence worth having on these terms? Or will you go to them without shame, and talk to them, Socrates? And what will you say to them? What you say here about virtue and justice and institutions and laws being the best things among men? Would that be decent of you? Surely not, but if you go away from well-governed States to Crito's friends in Thessaly, where there is great disorder and license, they will be charmed to hear the tale of your escape from prison, set off with ludicrous particulars of the manner in which you were wrapped in a goatskin or some other disguise, and metamorphosed as the fashion of runaways is- that is very likely; but will there be no one to remind you that in your old age you violated the most sacred laws from a miserable desire of a little more life? Perhaps not, if you keep them in a good temper; but if they are out of temper you will hear many degrading things; you will live, but how?- as the flatterer of all men, and the servant of all men; and doing what?- eating and drinking in Thessaly, having gone abroad in order that you may get a dinner. And where will be your fine sentiments about justice and virtue then? Say that you wish to live for the sake of your children, that you may bring them up and educate them- will you take them into Thessaly and deprive them

of Athenian citizenship? Is that the benefit which you would confer upon them? Or are you under the impression that they will be better cared for and educated here if you are still alive, although absent from them; for that your friends will take care of them? Do you fancy that if you are an inhabitant of Thessaly they will take care of them, and if you are an inhabitant of the other world they will not take care of them? Nay; but if they who call themselves friends are truly friends, they surely will.

"Listen, then, Socrates, to us who have brought you up. Think not of life and children first, and of justice afterwards, but of justice first, that you may be justified before the princes of the world below. For neither will you nor any that belong to you be happier or holier or juster in this life, or happier in another, if you do as Crito bids. Now you depart in innocence, a sufferer and not a doer of evil; a victim, not of the laws, but of men. But if you go forth, returning evil for evil, and injury for injury, breaking the covenants and agreements which you have made with us, and wronging those whom you ought least to wrong, that is to say, yourself, your friends, your country, and us, we shall be angry with you while you live, and our brethren, the laws in the world below, will receive you as an enemy; for they will know that you have done your best to destroy us. Listen, then, to us and not to Crito."

This is the voice which I seem to hear murmuring in my ears, like the sound of the flute in the ears of the mystic; that voice, I say, is humming in my ears, and prevents me from hearing any other. And I know that anything more which you will say will be in vain. Yet speak, if you have anything to say.

[Cr.] I have nothing to say, Socrates.

[Soc.] Then let me follow the intimations of the will of God.

From *Dialogues of Plato*, trans. Benjamin Jowett, Oxford, 1896.

Logic

Logic is the study of right or correct thinking. It focuses upon the analysis and construction of arguments. An argument is the reasons given for one's opinion. One's opinion should be supported by statements, sometimes called propositions or premises. The study of logic insures that these statements provide an acceptable inference to the conclusions.

> Premise #1 (Reason #1)
> Premise #2 (Reason #2)
> Conclusion

DEDUCTIVE ARGUMENTS

A deductive argument is one where the conclusion necessarily follows from the premises. It is an argument from a general principle to a specific example. Deductive arguments are said to yield *necessity*. A deductive argument is *valid* when following the correct form. Consider the following example:

Example #1:

> (1) All men are mortal.
> (2) Socrates is a man.
> (3) Therefore, Socrates is mortal.

The conclusion (3) necessarily follows from the premises (1 and 2). If all men have the characteristic of mortality and if Socrates is included in the group of men, then he must have the characteristic that the entire group has, namely mortality. The general principle of all men being mortal is applied to the specific example of Socrates. It is very important that the first premise state a general principle. General principles are indicated by a universal qualifier such as "all," "any," "every," "none," and "no."

Upon closer analysis, we find that the conclusion follows necessarily from the premises because it follows this particular form:

Example #2:

> All A's = B.
> C = A
> Therefore, C = B

Again, if all A's are B, and if C is an A, then C must also be a B.

It is interesting to note that this form will produce a logically necessary conclusion even if the premises are not true. Consider the following example:

Example #3:

> (1) All men have brown hair.
> (2) Joe is a man.
> (3) Therefore, Joe has brown hair.

This conclusion (3) follows necessarily from the premises (1 and 2) even though the premises (1 and 2) are not in fact true. It follows necessarily because of the form. This is a valid deductive argument. You see that it is possible to have a valid deductive argument that is, in fact, not true, as example #3 demonstrates.

When the premises are true, we say that the deductive argument is *sound*. Example #1 is such an example. It is true, in fact, that all men are mortal and that Socrates is a man. Therefore, Socrates must be mortal.

There are four other deductive argument forms the are important to know. They are called *modus ponens*, *modus tollens*, *disjunctive syllogism*, and *reducto ad absurdum*.

Modus Ponens (MP)

Modus Ponens means affirming the antecedent. In an "if, then" statement the first term is called the antecedent and the second term is called the consequent. For example:

Example #4:

> If A (antecedent), then B (consequent).

The *Modus Ponens* form indicates that if we affirm the antecedent, or if the antecedent is true, then we can affirm the consequent, or the consequent will be true. Consider the following examples:

Example #5:

> If P, then Q.
> We have P
> Therefore, we can affirm Q

Example #6:

> If Mary is a mother (P), then she must be a woman (Q).
> Mary is a mother (P).
> Therefore, she must be a woman (Q).

Because the previous argument is also naturally true, it provides us an opportunity to see what happens if we affirm the consequent, which is an *invalid* form. Consider the following example:

Example #7:

> If Mary is a mother (P), then she must be a woman (Q).
> Mary is a woman (Q).
> Therefore, she must be a mother (P).

We know from experience that this conclusion is not true because not all women are mothers. Therefore, in the form that was used, affirming the consequent has yielded a false conclusion and is therefore *invalid*.

Modus Tollens (MT)

Modus Tollens means denying the consequent. The *Modus Tollens* form indicates that if we deny the consequent, or the consequent is not true, then we must also deny the antecedent, or the antecedent is not true. Consider the following examples:

Example #8:

> If P, then Q.
> We do not have Q.
> Therefore, we do not have P.

Example #9:

If Mary is a mother (P), then she must be a woman (Q).
Mary is not a woman (-Q)
Therefore, she cannot be a mother (-P)

Because the previous argument is also naturally true, it provides us an opportunity to see what happens if we affirm the consequent, which is an *invalid* form. Consider the following example:

Example: #10:

If Mary is a mother (P), then she is a woman (Q).
Mary is not a mother (-P).
Therefore, she cannot be a woman (-Q)

Again, we know from experience that this conclusion is not true because not all women are mothers. Therefore, in the form that was used, affirming the consequent has yielded a false conclusion and is therefore *invalid.*

Disjunctive Syllogism (DS)

Disjunctive syllogism means deny the disjunct. In an "either / or" statement, each term is called a disjunct. Consider the following examples:

Example #11:

Either P or Q.		Either P or Q.
Not P.	or	Not Q.
Therefore Q.		Therefore P.

Example #12:

I have either $5 (P) or $10 in my pocket (Q).
I don't have $5 (-P).
Therefore, I must have $10 (Q).

Reductio ad Absurdem (RAA)

Reductio ad Absurdem means reduce to an absurdity. In logic an absurdity is a contradiction. Therefore, a *reduction* argument reduces an opponent's argument to a contradiction, which renders it illogical and, therefore, incorrect. Consider the following example:

Example #13:

You have said there is no absolute truth (-A).

But if there is no absolute truth, then no one ever makes a statement that is absolutely true (If -A, then –B).

But if no one ever makes a statement that is absolutely true, then the statement that there is no absolute truth cannot be absolutely true (If -B, then – C).

But you have purported to state a statement that is absolutely true (A), namely that there is no absolute truth.

Therefore, you have said there is no absolute truth (-A) and there is at least one absolute truth (A).

Therefore, your statement that there is no absolute truth is not true because it leads to a logical contradiction (Both A and –A).

The statement "there is no absolute truth," claims to be an absolute truth by asserting that there is absolutely no truth that is absolute. From the *reducto ad absurdem* argument, we can clearly see that this is an inherently false assertion. In other words, there is absolute truth.

INDUCTIVE ARGUMENTS

An inductive argument is one where the conclusion follows *probably* from the premises. It is an argument from specific examples to a general principle. Inductive arguments are said to yield *probability*. Consider the following example:

Example: #14:

Island A has palm trees.
Island B has palm trees.
Island C has palm trees.
Therefore, all islands have palm trees.

The conclusion (4) does not necessarily follow the premises (1, 2, and 3). It might be true, given the information in the premises, but it does not *necessarily* have to be true. We speak of *strong* and *weak* inductive arguments based upon the amount of evidence presented in the premises. The more evidence presented in the premises, the stronger the argument.

Given the nature of deductive and inductive arguments, *sound* deductive arguments are always to be preferred. But there are times when a deductive argument simply cannot be used. For example, when General Motors wants to demonstrate the safety of its cars, it can only test a small percentage of the total cars it manufactures because the testing process destroys the cars. It may test only 1% of the total number of cars it has manufactured during the year. But it infers the same safety standards of that 1% to the entire number manufactured. If General Motors wanted to develop a deductive argument for the safety of its cars it would have to test all its cars, which would mean the destruction of all the cars it manufactured. Obviously, it cannot do that. Therefore, an inductive argument is acceptable.

ABDUCTIVE ARGUMENTS

First formulated by the American philosopher Charles S. Peirce (1839-1914), abductive reasoning is better known as "inference to the best explanation." Like inductive arguments, abductive reasoning yields *probability*. Abductive reasoning is used in evaluating competing explanations or hypotheses.

There are four criteria philosophers use to determine the best explanation of observed phenomena. They are:

Do any of the competing explanations conflict with established background knowledge?
Is there more evidence supporting one explanation than the others?
Is there more evidence against one than the others?
Which explanation is simpler?

For example, suppose scientists are trying to determine the origin of the great statues on Easter Island. Further, suppose that there are only two competing hypotheses. Hypothesis #1 (H1) says that the statues are the product of aliens from another planet. Hypothesis #2 (H2) says that the statues are the product of ancient human beings who were very ingenious in their artistic and construction techniques. How are the scientists to determine the best explanation? They can apply abductive reasoning to find the inference to the best explanation.

Consider the first criterion; does H1 or H2 conflict with established background knowledge? The answer is yes! H1 conflicts with the established background knowledge that aliens do not exist. Therefore, according to this criterion, H2 is the better explanation.

Consider the second criterion; is there more supporting evidence for H1 or H2? The answer is yes! There is empirical evidence that ancient human beings designed and constructed extraordinary objects, such as the Pyramids in Egypt and The Mayan Temples in South America. There is no empirical evidence that aliens even exist, let alone have designed and built anything on earth. Therefore, according to this criterion, H2 is the better explanation.

Consider the third criterion; is there more evidence against H1 or H2? There is more evidence against H1 because there is no empirical evidence that aliens ever existed on earth. Therefore, there is no evidence that aliens ever designed and built anything on earth. There is evidence however that ancient people existed, designed and built objects on earth. Therefore, according to this criterion, H2 is the better explanation.

Consider the fourth criterion; which is the simpler explanation, H1 or H2? Here they both seem to be equal. Neither seems to be more complex. So let's say they tie on this criterion.

Considering all the criteria, H2 provides the best explanation for the statues on Easter Island.

FALLACIES

There are a number of common fallacies of reasoning that you need to be familiar with. A fallacy is an argument that sounds logical but upon closer inspection is found to be unsound.

Ad Hominem Argument (Arguing Against the Man):
This fallacy attacks the person instead of the issue. For example, when two candidates are debating and one candidate attacks the other candidate's morality instead of the issues.

Arguing in a Circle (Begging the Question):
This fallacy occurs when you assume to be true that which you are trying to prove. For example, you believe in God because the Bible tells you so and you believe in the

Bible because it's the Word of God. You have assumed the existence of God as the foundation for the Bible and appealed to the Bible to prove God's existence.

False Dilemma (Only Two Choices):

This fallacy occurs when only two choices are offered, when in fact there are several. For example, if a young woman gets pregnant and a counselor tells her that her only choices are an abortion or bringing up the child herself. These are not the only two choices because she could have the baby and then give it up for adoption.

Slippery Slope Fallacy (The Edge of the Wedge Argument):

This fallacy occurs when it is assumed that if one thing is allowed to happen, another very undesirable thing will inevitable follow. For example, during the Vietnam War it was argued that if Vietnam fell to the communists, all of Southeast Asia would follow. Vietnam did eventually fall to the communists, but all of Southeast Asia did not become communists.

Straw Man Argument:

This fallacy occurs when an opponent's position is restated as an inferior position and then this inferior version is argued against. This is an intentional distortion of an opponent's position. For example, a candidate might argue for a reduction in taxes, which most people would like. His opponent restates this position as attacking social programs designed to help the poor because these programs are supported by taxes. Because it is difficult to argue against reducing taxes, this position is intentionally distorted, and then the distorted position is argued against.

Argument from Ignorance:

Arguments of this form assume that since something has not been proven false, it is, therefore, true. Conversely, such an argument may assume that since something has not been proven true, it is, therefore, false. (This is a special case of a false dilemma since it assumes that all propositions must either be known to be true or known to be false.) As Davis writes, "Lack of proof is not proof."

Equivocation:

The same word is used with two different meanings. For example: A plane is a carpenter's tool, and the Boeing 747 is a plane. Therefore, the Boeing 747 is a carpenter's tool.

Part I: What is Philosophy? Review

Below is the review for *Part I: What is Philosophy?* Included in this review are the terms and concepts you should be familiar with to prepare for the exam. I have also included an example of the multiple choice questions that you will have to answer. It will give you an idea of the type of questions to expect.

We will be reviewing each of these terms and concepts and the multiple choice questions in class prior to the exam.

I. Terms and Concepts:

Metaphysics
Epistemology
Logic
Ethics
Aesthetics
Be familiar with Plato's *Apology*
Apology
Socratic Wisdom
Socratic Method
Socrates' Two Conceptions of Death
The Unexamined Life is not Worth Living
Be familiar with Plato's *Crito*

Justice

Injustice

Civil Disobedience

Implied Contract

Returning evil for evil

Deduction

Induction

Modus Ponens

Modus Tollens

Disjunctive Syllogism

Reducto as Absurdem

Abduction

Ad Hominem Argument

Arguing in a Circle

False Dilemma

Slippery Slope Fallacy

Straw Man Argument

Equivocation

Your exam will have several multiple choice questions. You will be asked to find the BEST answer to each of these questions. Here is an example of the questions you will be asked.

II. Multiple Choice Examples:

Which best describes Plato's *Apology*?

A. Written in dialogue form, this work by Plato describes the trial of Socrates who was accused of corrupting the youth of Athens. Socrates successfully defends himself and lives happily ever after.

B. Written in dialogue form, this work by Plato describes the trial of Socrates who was accused of corrupting the youth of Athens. In this work, we get a discussion of the most important issues of human life, such as how we should live our lives, what we should consider important, and what death might be like.

C. Written in dialogue form, this work by Plato describes the trial of Socrates who was accused of corrupting the youth of Athens. In this work, we get a discussion of the most important issues of human life, such as how we should live our lives, what we should consider important, and what death might be like. In the end, Socrates is condemned to death.

D. Written in dialogue form, this work by Plato describes the trial of Socrates who was accused of corrupting the youth of Athens. In this work, we get a discussion of the most important issues of human life, such as how we should live our lives, what we should consider important, and what death might be like. In the end, Socrates is sentenced to work as the maintenance man of Yankee Stadium.

Which best describes Plato's *Crito*?

A. The scene takes place in the prison where Socrates is being held for his execution. Crito, one of Socrates' friends, has come to persuade Socrates to escape as Crito and his friends have secured Socrates' escape. Socrates agrees and escapes to Thebes where he lives happily pursuing truth, justice, and the "examined" life.

B. The scene takes place in the prison where Socrates is being held for his execution. Crito, one of Socrates' friends, has come to persuade Socrates to escape as Crito and his friends have secured Socrates' escape. Socrates refuses because he believes that to escape would be agreeing with the opinion of the many.

C. Written in dialogue form, Crito recounts the final days of Socrates' life. Socrates' friend, Crito, has secured Socrates' escape from prison and certain death, yet Socrates refuses to comply. He argues that for him to escape from the Athenian prison after due process of law has condemned him to death would be paramount to aiding the destruction of the Law of Athens and the city itself.

D. Written in dialogue form, Crito recounts the final days of Socrates' life. Socrates' friend, Crito, has secured Socrates' escape from prison and certain death, yet Socrates refuses to comply. He argues that for him to escape from the Athenian prison after due process of law has condemned him to death would not be aiding the destruction of the Law of Athens and the city itself.

Part II
The Philosophy of Religion

Part II

The Philosophy of Religion

> "Therefore, it is necessary to stop at some first mover which is moved by nothing else. And this is what we all understand God to be."
>
> **- *Thomas Aquinas***
>
> *"The words, therefore, necessary existence, have no meaning; or, which is the same thing, none that is consistent."*
>
> **- *David Hume***
>
> *"Every indication of contrivance, every manifestation of design, which existed in the watch, exists in the works of nature, with the difference, on the side of nature, of being greater and more, and that in a degree which exceeds all computation."*
>
> **- *William Paley***
>
> *"But wherever you depart, in the least, from the similarity of the cases, you diminish proportionably the evidence; and may at last bring it to a very weak analogy, which is confessedly liable to error and uncertainty."*
>
> **- *David Hume***

"And, indeed, we believe that you are a being than which nothing greater can be conceived. Or is there no such nature, since the fool has said in his heart, there is no God?"

- *Anselm*

"For I do not yet say, no, I even deny or doubt that this being is greater than any real object."

- *Gaunilo*

"Hence it comes that, if there are as many risks on one side as on the other, the course is to play even, and then the certainty of the stake is equal to the uncertainty of the gain, so far is it from the fact that there is an infinite distance between them."

- *Blaise Pascal*

Introduction

THE PHILOSOPHY OF RELIGION

Arguments for the existence of God are divided into two main groups: *a priori* and *a posteriori*. An *a priori* argument begins with premises that can be known to be truly independent of experience of the world. The argument rests purely upon logical considerations based upon reflection and understanding of the meaning of concepts employed by the argument. The classical statement of an *a priori* argument for the existence of God is the ontological argument, which was first developed by St. Anselm, Abbot of Bec and later Archbishop of Canterbury, in his work entitled *Proslogium.*

An *a posteriori* argument depends upon premises that are known to be true by means of experience in the world. In this regard, *a posteriori* arguments are said to begin with statements of fact that are readily accepted, such as the world exists, events have causes, etc. The two major *a posteriori* arguments for the existence of God are the Cosmological Argument and the Teleological Argument.

Pascal offers an entirely different approach to belief in God. He argues that belief in God is simply a better bet, with higher rewards, than unbelief in God.

Many have criticized these classical proofs for the existence of God, most notably David Hume. One of Hume's criticisms is based upon his claim that there can be no certainty in matters of fact because the truth we arrive at in matters of fact is based upon induction, which can yield only probability.

Do you believe that God exists? If you do believe that God exists what is your proof? These questions have plagued humankind since philosophy first began. In this section, we will examine the leading answers and their criticisms. Who do you think has the stronger arguments?

The Five Ways

THOMAS AQUINAS (1225-1274)

Aquinas was an Italian theologian and philosopher who spent his life in the Dominican Order, teaching and writing. His writings set forth in a systematic form a complete theory of God, humanity, and the universe. He is generally regarded as the greatest scholastic thinker. Aquinas combined the revelation and interpretation of holy scripture with the secular metaphysical doctrines of Aristotle and the post-Aristotelian Greek and Roman philosophers.

Aquinas' philosophical synthesis of philosophy and theology became the accepted teaching of the Roman Catholic Church. It is known today as Thomism. It continues to exercise a profound intellectual influence both on Church doctrine and the philosophical works of Catholic and non-Catholic thinkers. Aquinas' two major works are *Summa Contra Gentiles* and *Summa Theologica* from which the following excerpt is taken.

Aquinas' famous "Five Ways" of proving the existence of God is the best known of his works. The first way argues that the fact of change or motion provides proof for the existence of an unmoved mover that originates change or motion. The second way argues from the fact that some things are caused to infer the existence of a first cause. The third way argues from the fact that some things are contingent to the existence of that which exists necessarily. The fourth way argues from the fact that there are degrees of excellence to infer the existence of a perfect being. The fifth way argues from the alleged fact that because natural objects behave purposefully, this infers the existence of an intelligence that directs the activities of natural objects.

Vocabulary

Potentiality:	that which is possible; possibility
Actuality:	that which exists in reality; that which is
Efficient cause:	the immediate cause of something
Contingent:	that which does not have to exist
Necessary:	that which must exist

Concepts

Change or motion:

Infinite regression:

First cause:

Necessary existence:

Perfect being:

Natural harmony:

Potentiality:

Actuality:

Efficient Cause:

Contingent:

Necessary:

Questions:

1. *Explain in your own words Aquinas' five ways.*
2. *What are the main ideas in each of his arguments?*
3. *What are some criticisms of Aquinas' arguments?*
4. *How do you think Aquinas would respond to those criticisms?*

THE FIRST WAY:
THE ARGUMENT FROM CHANGE

The first and clearest way is taken from the idea of motion. (1) Now it is certain, and our senses corroborate it, that some things in this world are in motion. (2) But everything which is in motion is moved by something else. (3) For nothing is in motion except in so far as it is in potentiality in relation to that towards which it is in motion. (4) Now a thing causes movement in so far as it is in actuality. For to cause movement is nothing else than to bring something from potentiality to actuality; but a thing cannot be brought from potentiality to actuality except by something which exists in actuality, as, for example, that which is hot in actuality, like fire, makes wood, which is only hot in potentiality, to be hot in actuality, and thereby causes movement in it and alters it. (5) But it is not possible that the same thing should be at the same time in actuality and potentiality in relation to the same thing, but only in relation to different things; for what is hot in actuality cannot at the same time be hot in potentiality, though it is at the same time cold in potentiality. (6) It is impossible, therefore, that in relation to the same thing and in the same way anything should both cause movement and be caused, or that it should cause itself to move. (7) Everything, therefore, that is in motion must be moved by something else. If, therefore, the thing which causes it to move be in motion, this too must be moved by something else, and so on. (8) But we cannot proceed to infinity in this way, because in that cause there would be no first mover, and in consequence, neither would there be any other mover; for secondary movers do not cause movement except they be moved by a first mover, as, for example, a stick cannot cause movement unless it is moved by the hand. Therefore, it is necessary to stop at some first mover which is moved by nothing else. And this is what we all understand God to be.

THE SECOND WAY:
THE ARGUMENT FROM CAUSATION

The Second Way is taken from the idea of the efficient cause. (1) We find that there is among material things a regular order of efficient causes. (2) But we do not find, nor indeed is it possible, that anything is the efficient cause of itself, for in that case it would be prior to itself, which is impossible. (3) Now it is not possible to proceed to infinity in efficient causes. (4) For if we arrange in order all efficient causes, the first is the cause of the intermediate, and the intermediate the cause of the last, whether the intermediate be many or only one. (5) But if we remove a cause the effect is removed; therefore, if there is no first among efficient causes, neither will there be a last or an intermediate. (6) But if we proceed to infinity in efficient causes there will be no first efficient cause, and thus there will be no ultimate effect, nor any intermediate efficient causes, which is clearly false. Therefore, it is necessary to suppose the existence of some first efficient cause, and this men call God.

THE THIRD WAY: THE ARGUMENT FROM CONTINGENCY

The Third Way rests on the idea of the "contingent" and the "necessary" and is as follows: (1) We find that there are certain things in the Universe which are capable of existing and of not existing, for we find that some things are brought into existence and then destroyed, and consequently are capable of being or not being. (2) But it is impossible for all things which exist to be of this kind, because anything which is capable of not existing, at some time or other does not exist. (3) If, therefore, all things are capable of not existing, there was a time when nothing existed in the Universe. (4) But if this is true there would also be nothing in existence now; because anything that does not

exist cannot begin to exist except by the agency of something which has existence. If, therefore, there was once nothing which existed, it would have been impossible for anything to begin to exist, and so nothing would exist now. (5) This is clearly false. Therefore, all things are not contingent, and there must be something which is necessary in the Universe. (6) But everything which is necessary either has or has not the cause of its necessity from an outside source. Now it is not possible to proceed to infinity in necessary things which have a cause of their necessity, as has been proved in the case of efficient causes. Therefore it is necessary to suppose the existence of something which is necessary in itself, not having the cause of its necessity from any outside source, but which is the cause of necessity in others. And this "something" we call God.

THE FOURTH WAY: THE ARGUMENT FROM DEGREES OF EXCELLENCE

The Fourth Way is taken from the degrees which are found in things. (1) For among different things we find that one is more or less good or true or noble; and likewise in the case of other things of this kind. (2) But the words "more" and "less" are used of different things in proportion as they approximate in their different ways to something which has the particular quality in the highest degree — e.g., we call a thing hotter when it approximates more nearly to that which is hot in the highest degree. There is, therefore, something which is true in the highest degree, good in the highest degree and noble in the highest degree; (3) and consequently there must be also something which has being in the highest degree. For things which are true in the highest degree also have being in the highest degree. (4) But anything which has a certain quality of any kind in the highest degree is also the cause of all the things of that kind, as, for example, fire, which is hot in the highest degree, is the cause of all hot things (as is said in the book). (5) Therefore, there exists something which is the cause of being, and goodness, and of every perfection in all existing things; and this we call God.

THE FIFTH WAY: THE ARGUMENT FROM HARMONY

The Fifth Way is taken from the way in which nature is governed. (1) For we observe that certain things which lack knowledge, such as natural bodies, work for an End. This is obvious, because they always, or at any rate very frequently, operate in the same way so as to attain the best possible result. (2) Hence it is clear that they do not arrive at their goal by chance, but by purpose. (3) But those things which have no knowledge do not move towards a goal unless they are guided by someone or something which does possess knowledge and intelligence — e.g., an arrow by an archer. Therefore, there does exist something which possesses intelligence by which all natural things are directed to their goal; and this we call God.

From Thomas Aquinas, *Summa Theologica*, trans. Laurence Shapcote, 1911.

Critique of Cosmological Argument

DAVID HUME (1711-1776)

David Hume is one of the most important philosophers in the history of philosophy. Born in Edinburgh, Scotland, Hume attended Edinburgh University. He enjoyed great popularity during his lifetime. His six-volume *History of England* established his reputation as an historian and man of letters. Hume also made many enemies with his skeptical doubts about religion and his attacks on the metaphysical doctrines of his Continental and British predecessors.

One of his most influential works, *Dialogues Concerning Natural Religion* (1779), which our present reading is from, was published after his death. His friends, like Adam Smith, persuaded him that the work was too controversial and might permanently damage his reputation.

David Hume's *Dialogues Concerning Natural Religion* is one of the most celebrated contributions to philosophical theology in Western thought. In this dialogue, a cast of three characters each represents a common attitude about God. Demea is a metaphysical theist whose arguments stand or fall on certain *a priori* notions about evidence. Cleanthes is an anthropomorphic theist who argues from the fact of the world to the necessity of a divine source. Philo is clearly Hume as the skeptic. In the sections that follow, both Cleanthes and Philo attack the rationalism of Demea. Cleanthes argues that matters of fact cannot be demonstrated by the introduction of *a priori* assertions. Philo argues that while Demea has assumed that rationality necessarily entails a divine mind, an equally acceptable explanation could be the absolute natural character of the universe.

Vocabulary:

Adhere: stick to
Sublime: noble
Infallible: incapable of error
Ascertained: determined
Efficacy: power to produce effects or desired results
Annihilation: complete destruction

Concepts:

A posteriori:
Infinity:
Necessary existence:
Chance:
Contradiction:
Infinite Regression
Contingency:
Matters of Fact:

Questions:

1. *Explain Hume's argument regarding matters of fact.*
2. *Explain Hume's argument regarding contingency.*
3. *Explain Hume's argument regarding infinite regression.*
4. *Do you feel that Hume correctly expresses the Teleological Argument?*
5. *Do you agree with Hume? Why or why not?*

Dialogues Concerning Natural Religion

But if so many difficulties attend the argument *a posteriori*, said Demea, had we not better adhere to that simple and sublime argument *a priori*, which by offering to us infallible demonstration, cuts off at once all doubt and difficulty? By this argument, too, we may prove the infinity of the Divine attributes, which, I am afraid, can never be ascertained with certainty from any other topic. For how can an effect, which either is finite, or, for aught we know, may be so; how can such an effect, I say, prove an infinite cause? The unity, too, of Divine Nature, it is very difficult, if not absolutely impossible, to deduce merely from contemplating the works of nature; nor will the uniformity alone of the plan, even were it allowed, give us any assurance of the attribute.

You seem to reason, Demea, said Cleanthes, as if those advantages and conveniences in the abstract argument were full proofs of its solidity. But it is first proper, in my opinion, to determine what argument of nature you choose to insist on; and we shall afterwards, from itself, better than from its useful consequences, endeavor to determine what value we ought to put upon it.

The argument, replied Demea, which I would insist on, is the common one. Whatever exists must have a cause or reason of its existence; it being absolutely impossible for anything to produce itself, or be the cause of its own existence. In mounting up, therefore, from effects to causes, we must either go on in tracing an infinite regression, without any ultimate cause at all; or must at last have recourse to some ultimate cause, that is necessarily existent. Now, that the first supposition is absurd, may be thus proved. In the infinite chain or succession of causes and effects, each single effect is determined to exist by the power and efficacy of that cause which immediately preceded; but the whole external chain or succession, taken together, is not yet determined or caused by anything; and yet it is evident that it requires a cause or reason, as much as any particular object which begins to exist in time. The question is still reasonable, why this particular succession of causes existed from eternity, and not any other succession, or no succession at all. If there be no necessarily existent being, any supposition which can be formed is equally possible; nor is there any more absurdity in nothing's having existed from eternity, than there is in that succession of causes which constitutes the universe. What was it, then, which determined something to exist rather than nothing, and bestowed being on a particular possibility, exclusive of the rest? External causes, there are supposed to be none. Chance is a word without meaning. Was it nothing? But that can never produce anything. We must, therefore, have recourse to a necessarily existent being, who carries the reason of his existence in himself, and who cannot be supposed not to exist, without an expressed contradiction. There is, consequently, such a being; that is, there is a Deity.

I shall not leave it to Philo, said Cleanthes, though I know that starting objections is his chief delight, to point out the weakness of this metaphysical reasoning. It seems to me obviously ill-grounded and at the same time of so little consequence to the cause of true piety and religion, that I shall myself venture to show the fallacy of it.

I shall begin with observing, that there is an evident absurdity in pretending to demonstrate a matter of fact, or to prove it by any argument *a priori*. Nothing is demonstrable, unless the contrary implies a contradiction. Nothing, that is distinctly conceivable, implies a contradiction. Whatever we conceive as existent, we can also conceive as non-existent. There is no being, therefore, whose non-existence implies a contradiction. Consequently, there is no being, whose existence is demonstrable. I propose this argument as entirely decisive, and am willing to rest the whole controversy upon it.

It is pretended that the Deity is a necessarily existent being; and this necessity of his existence is attempted to be explained by asserting that, if we knew his whole essence or nature, we should perceive it to be as impossible for him not to exist as for twice two not to be four. But it is evident, that this can never happen, while our faculties remain the same as at present. It will still be possible for us, at any time, to conceive the non-existence of what we formerly conceived to exist; nor can the mind ever lie under a necessity of supposing any object to remain always in being; in the same manner as we lie under a necessity of always conceiving twice two to be four. The words, therefore, necessary existence, have no meaning; or, which is the same thing, none that is consistent.

But further; why may not the material universe be the necessarily existent being, according to this pretended explication of necessity? We dare not affirm that we know all the qualities of matter; and for aught we can determine, it may contain some qualities, which, were they known, would make its non-existence appear as great a contradiction as that twice two is five. I find only one argument employed to prove, that the material world is not the necessarily existent being; and this argument is derived from the contingency both of the matter and form of the world. "Any particle of matter," it is said, "may be conceived to be annihilated; and any form may be conceived to be altered. Such an annihilation or alteration, therefore, is not impossible." But it seems a great partiality not to perceive, that the same argument extends equally to the Deity, so far as we have any conception of him; and that the mind can at least imagine him to be non-existent, or his attributes to be altered. It must be some unknown, inconceivable qualities, which can make his non-existence appear impossible, or his attributes unalterable: And no reason can be assigned, why these qualities may not belong to matter. As they are altogether unknown and inconceivable, they can never be proved incompatible with it.

Add to this, that in tracing an eternal succession of objects, it seems absurd to inquire for a general cause or first author. How can anything that exists from eternity, have a cause, since that relation implies a priority in time, and a beginning of existence?

In such a chain, too, or succession of objects, each part is caused by that which preceded it, and causes that which succeeds it. Where then is the difficulty? But the whole, you say, wants a cause. I answer, that the uniting of these parts into a whole, like the uniting of several distinct countries into one kingdom, or several members into one body, is performed merely by an arbitrary act of the mind, and has no influence on the nature of things. Did I show you the particular causes of each individual in a collection of twenty particles of matter? I should think it very unreasonable, should you afterwards ask me, what was the cause of the whole twenty? This is sufficiently explained in explaining the cause of the parts.

Though the reasoning which you have urged, Cleanthes, may well excuse me, said Philo, from starting any further difficulties, yet I cannot forbear insisting still upon another topic. It is observed by arithmeticians that the products of 9, compose always either 9, or some lesser product of 9, if you add together all the characters of which any of the former products are composed. Thus, of 18, 27, 36, which are products of 9, you make 9 by adding 1 to 8, 2 to 7, 3 to 6.

To a superficial observer, so wonderful a regularity may be admired as the effect of chance or design. But a skillful algebraist immediately concludes it to be the work of necessity, and demonstrates, that it must forever result from the nature of these numbers. Is it not probable, I ask, that the whole economy of the universe is conducted by a like necessity, though no human algebra can furnish a key which solves the difficulty? And instead of admiring the order of natural beings, may it not happen, that, could we penetrate into the intimate nature of bodies, we should clearly see why it was absolutely impossible they could never admit of any other disposition? So dangerous is it to introduce this idea of necessity into the present question and so naturally does it afford an inference directly opposite to the religious hypothesis!

From David Hume, *Dialogues Concerning Natural Religion*, 1779.

The Cosmological Argument Revisited

Joe Mixie (1956-)

Joe Mixie teaches Philosophy at Sacred Heart University located in Fairfield, CT. He is the author of *The Existence of God* (2004), *The Atheist Trap* (1994), and several articles.

In this article Mixie argues that the most accepted cosmological model for the origin of the universe, the standard hot big bang theory, and the ontological status of the big bang singularity provide evidence that supports a necessary cause for the universe which we call God.

Vocabulary:

Scientific Empiricism:	method of science in which all knowledge must be proved by repeated experiments
Constituents:	parts of a whole
Entrophy:	disorder
Tensor:	set of coordinates that represents the change in a system
Ex nihilo:	from nothing
Ontological:	refers to the state of being of something
Wave Function:	mathematical representation of all the possible phase paths for a quantum event
Universal	

Wave Function:	mathematical representation of all the possible phase paths for all the particles in the universe at the time of creation
Phase Path:	the possible paths or trajectories of particles represented in a quantum wave function
Epistemological:	refers to our knowledge of things or events

Concepts:

Big Bang Theory:
Big Bang Singularity:
Universal Wave Function:

Questions:

1. What is the "Big Bang?"

2. What is the Big Bang Singularity and why it is important to this argument?

3. What does the ontological status of the Big Bang Singularity refer to?

4. What are the implications of the ontological status of the Big Bang Singularity for the cosmological argument?

5. Evaluate this revision of the cosmological argument.

Introduction

Consider the following form of the cosmological argument:

(A) The physical universe exists.

(B) All physical existents must have a cause.

(C) That which causes something to exist (provides the sufficient reason for its existence) must be either:

(C1) another contingent cause,

or

(C2) a non-contingent (necessary) cause.

(D) If the cause is contingent (C1), then this contingent cause must itself have a cause ad infinitum.

(E) Therefore, that which causes (provides the sufficient reason) the existence of the universe must be either:

(E1) an infinite series of contingent causes,

or

(E2) a necessary cause.

(F) By appeal to the principle of inference to the best explanation, an infinite series of contingent causes does not provide the best explanation for the existence of the universe.

(G) Therefore, the best explanation for the existence of the universe is a necessary cause.

(H) By appeal to empirical evidence, the necessary cause for the existence of the universe is a necessary non-physical being, i.e. God.

By appeal to scientific empiricism, premises (A) and (B) are self-evident. One could argue that it is, in fact, the very nature of the scientific endeavor of humankind to understand the causes of physical existents. Without knowledge of the cause of a phenomenon, one cannot possess complete understanding of the phenomenon in question. This applies to the origin of the universe as well as the individual constituents of the universe.

Premises (C), (D), and (E) reflect the possible alternatives available which claim to provide a sufficient reason for the existence of the universe. Consider premise (E1):

(E1) That which causes (provides the sufficient reason for) the existence of the universe must be an infinite series of contingent causes.

When applied to a proposition, contingency denotes that the opposite of the proposition under consideration is logically possible. The truth value of the statement is dependent upon future conditions which may or may not be realized. When applied to a being, the word "contingent" means that the being either may or may not exist at some time. In his book entitled *The Cosmological Argument*, Bruce Reichenbach says:

Contingency as applied to existence is not a statement about some certainty or uncertainty that we have with respect to knowing whether an object exists; it is not reporting an epistemological state of affairs. Rather, it is telling us something about the ontology of the existent or future existent; it is informing us about the being itself, namely, that there is no logical or real necessity that it exists now or in the future; its nonexistence is as conceivable as its existence (Reichenbach 1972, 7).

Another concept which is often used to elucidate "contingent" is that of "dependency." When a being is categorized as a contingent being, it is dependent upon another being for its existence. More specifically, it is dependent upon another being as the cause of its existence. The being that provides the cause must actually exist prior to and simultaneously with that which it is causing to exist.

Premise (E2) provides an alternative hypothesis for the cause of the existence of the universe.

By appeal to the principle of inference to the best explanation, premise (F) denies that an infinite series of contingent causes empirically provides the best explanation for the existence of the universe. The hypothesis of an infinite regression of contingent causes fails on this account because:

(a) it conflicts with the established background knowledge supporting the current cosmological models of the origin of the universe;

(b) there is more supporting evidence for the hypothesis that a necessary cause exists, when the current cosmological models of the origin of the universe are integrated with the known elements of a quantum theory of gravity;

(c) there is less evidence against the hypothesis that a necessary cause exists than there is against an infinite regression of contingent causes, as per the current models of the origin of the universe;

(d) the necessary cause hypothesis is simpler than the hypothesis of an infinite series of contingent causes.

The preliminary conclusion (G) states that, by appeal to the inference to the best explanation, a necessary cause is the best explanation for the existence of the universe. This follows from premises (E1), (E2) and (F) via application of the rule of logic known as disjunctive syllogism.

The final conclusion (H) will be justified based upon the ontological status of the big bang singularity. Anticipating Kant's argument for the reduction of the cosmological argument to the ontological argument, the justification for the conclusion (H) is provided by an argument based upon empirical evidence (current cosmological models), not an *a priori* conception of a necessary being derived through logical and conceptual analysis.

The Standard Hot Big Bang Cosmological Model

I shall argue that the standard hot big bang theory and the ontological status of the big bang singularity provide evidence that not only is a necessary cause the best explanation for the origin of the universe, but the stronger claim that this necessary cause must be a non-physical, intelligent being which exists independently of the physical universe.

In his article entitled "A Big Bang Argument For God's Nonexistence," Quentin Smith summarizes the relevant aspects of the big bang theory as consisting of:

(i) Einstein's field equations which say that the curvature of space-time is determined by the distribution of mass and energy in space-time.

This implies that if there is sufficient density of matter in the universe, space-time will converge and intersect at a point, in the past or the future.

(ii) Accepting the Friedmann solutions as applying to our universe.

The Friedmann solutions assume that the universe is perfectly isotropic and homogeneous thus offering two possible descriptions of the current state of the universe; expansion at a decreasing rate or contracting at an increasing rate.

(iii) Applying the Hawking-Penrose singularity theorems to the Friedmann solutions.

Stephen Hawking, in his work entitled "Theoretical Advances in General Relativity," says that the implication of the solutions for the Hawking-Penrose singularity theorems is that there is a curvature singularity that will intersect every world line, a beginning of time.

The upshot of this is that approximately 10-15 billion years ago, all the matter which now comprises the universe, was squeezed into one point which had zero spatial dimensions, a singularity. When the singularity exploded, in what we refer to as the big bang, space, time and the universe as we understand them began. Smith says,

> The instantaneously existing point is a singularity, which means that it is an endpoint of space-time; there is no earlier time than the instant of the singularity for it itself is the first instant of time (Smith 1992, 220).

Roger Penrose, in his book entitled *The Emperor's New Mind* says,

According to standard theory, this gas was just spewed out as a result of the explosion which created the universe: the big bang. However, it is important that we do not think of this as an ordinary explosion of the familiar kind, where material is ejected from one central point into a pre-existing space. Here, the space itself is created by the explosion, and there is, or was, no central point (Penrose 1989, 326).

The idea of a beginning of space, time and the universe as we know it is generally accepted by cosmologists today. Recall premise (F):

(F) By appeal to the principle of inference to the best explanation, an infinite series of contingent causes does not provide the best explanation for the existence of the universe.

It is by appeal to the wide spread acceptance of the big bang singularity, which is based upon empirical evidence, that I argue premise (F) is justified.

The Big Bang Singularity

By its nature, or lack thereof, the big bang singularity is very difficult to describe. In his article entitled "Breakdown of Predictability in Gravitational Collapse," Hawking describes a singularity as,

...a place where the classical concepts of space and time break down as do all the known laws of physics because they are all formulated on a classical space-time background. (Hawking 1976, 246).

Some have mistakenly understood the break down of the known laws of physics and our resulting inability to predict the future as implying that the big bang singularity was a state of maximum chaos, involving complete entropy and lawlessness. It is further argued that the hypotheses of divine creation is inconsistent with the lack of physical laws governing the big bang singularity.

Not only is the conclusion dubious that divine creation is inconsistent with the preceding description of the big bang singularity, it is questionable whether the description itself is accurate. First, it is not accepted that the big bang singularity was in a state of complete entropy or maximally chaotic. This conclusion stems from the mistaken notion that the initial singularity at the big bang exhibits temporal symmetry with singularities found in black holes. Understanding this difference provides an explanation for the second law of thermodynamics, which asserts that the entropy (disorder) of an isolated system increases with time. On purely logical grounds, it should be clear that the initial singularity could not be a state of maximum entropy. For in that case, how could one explain the second law of thermodynamics? It is logically impossible for the universe to begin in a state of maximum entropy and then increase in entropy (the second law of thermodynamics) over time. Roger Penrose provides the empirical explanation. He says,

> We expect to find, indeed, that the curvature close to a final singularity is completely dominated by the tensor WEYL (the tidal distortion or initial change in shape, of a freely falling particle). This tensor goes to infinity. This appears to be the generic situation with a space-time singularity. Such behavior is associated with a singularity of high entropy (Penrose 1989, 337).

The WEYL tensor is used to denote the distortion effect of gravity on physical bodies, or the non-uniformity in the gravitational field. In the case of a "generic" singularity (any singularity except the big bang singularity), the physical body experiences a distortion of elongation because the gravitation force on that part of the body which first enters the singularity is greater than on that part which enters after. It is this infinite distor-

tion which is associated with high entropy.

However, this is not the state of affairs at the big bang singularity. Penrose continues,

> The standard models of the big bang are provided by the highly symmetrical Friedmann-Robertson-Walker space-times that we considered earlier. Now the distorting tidal effect provided by the tensor WEYL is entirely absent. Instead there is a symmetrical inward acceleration acting on any spherical surface of test particles. This is the effect of the tensor RICCI, (initial change in volume) rather than WEYL. In any FRW-model, the tensor equation WEYL = 0 always holds. As we approach the initial singularity more and more closely we find that it is RICCI that becomes infinite, instead of WEYL, so it is RICCI that dominates near the initial singularity, rather than WEYL. This provides us with a singularity of low entropy (Penrose 1989, 337).

The RICCI tensor is used to denote the change in volume. We see that at the big bang singularity, the volume becomes infinite with zero amount of tidal distortion because there is no space present in which a distortion could be present. The space (volume) that the singularity occupies is infinite. Therefore, there could be no distortions. Interestingly, Penrose mentions that because of Einstein's famous $E = mc^2$ formula, we could also interpret the RICCI tensor as the equivalent of the energy present. This means that in the big bang singularity there was an infinite amount of energy. In this case, that would mean that there was absolutely no energy present, or creation *ex nihilo*.

The Ontological Status of The Big Bang Singularity

Debate has continued regarding the ontological status of the big bang singularity. I shall argue that the ontological status of the big bang singularity is that of the Universal Wave Function for the possible phase paths of the entire universe. A possible phase path for a universe corresponds to a particular set of values for all the position coordinates and momentum coordinates for every single constituent particle that would be actualized within that universe were that particular phase path to collapse and become actualized. Therefore, the Universal Wave Function would contain at least all the sets of values for the possible phase paths for the particles that currently exist in the universe. This leaves open the question of whether or not the Universal Wave Function must contain all the sets of values for all the particles that may have

been possible but not realized in our universe.

Recall that Erwin Schrodinger shared the Nobel Prize in physics in 1933 for his work in developing wave mechanics. Although Schrodinger wanted to interpret the displacement of the electron wave as being real in the sense that the "true" electron was spread out and the displacement measured how much of the electron was at each point in space, Niels Bohr provided what is now the accepted interpretation of the wave function. Bohr reasoned that because there was too much evidence for the particle-like properties of the electron to allow it to be spread out in a classical wave, the electron should be thought of as a localized object, with the displacement of Schrodinger's electron wave at a particular point relating mathematically to the probability that a measurement would show the electron to be localized at that point. Schrodinger's wave equation predicts the properties of a probability wave with which we can predict the probability where an electron will be at a certain point if we should make a measurement.

The Universal Wave Function cannot be determined through physical law because of the limitation imposed by the singularity. Yet, we must guard against allowing epistemological limitation to dictate ontological status. The evidence for the existence of the Universal Wave Function is based upon our understanding of the special purpose which the quantum mechanical wave function has in quantum mechanics, which is to generate probabilities concerning the possible outcomes of measurements. We understand that for every observation (measurement) taken on the quantum level, there was a prior wave function which generated the probabilities associated with that quantum event and which collapsed, even if it was not or could not actually be calculated. Our inability to calculate does not change the ontological situation. Quantum wave functions exist prior to quantum observations.

Although we can distinguish the Universal Wave Function from a quantum wave function, when considering wave functions qua wave functions, both satisfy the conditions for being wave functions and therefore can be considered the same type species of cause and effect relationship. They differ only in origin and complexity. All wave functions require an observation to collapse. Therefore, the cause and effect relationship is of the same type. Further, the casual relationship between observation and the collapse of the quantum wave function may provide a

means of interaction between mind and matter.

This is not an argument from analogy where the Universal Wave Function is held to be analogous to a quantum mechanical wave function that proceeds according to the Schrodinger equation. This is the stronger claim that the Universal Wave Function is of the same type as that of the quantum mechanical wave function differing only in origin and complexity.

Implications Of The Ontological Status Of The Big Bang Singularity For The Cosmological Argument

The collapse of a wave function is caused by a measurement or observation being made. As long as one describes reality according to the Schrodinger wave equation, the wave function proceeds deterministically. However, when a measurement is taken, the wave function collapses and this collapse is governed according to probabilistic law. According to the Copenhagen Interpretation of quantum mechanics, the collapse of the wave function represents an actualization according to the probabilities as prescribed by Schrodinger's equation. According to the Many Worlds Interpretation of quantum mechanics, the Schrodinger wave function generates an endless proliferating number of different branches of reality. What is important to our discussion is that both of these interpretations agree on one basic point, it is an observation or measurement that causes the wave function to change.

"Observation" implies "observer" and "measurement" implies "measurer.". The wave function collapses during a measurement, and it is the interaction of consciousness with the physical system that is responsible for the collapse. What caused the Universal Wave Function to collapse and actualize our universe out of the infinite possible universes? Clearly, the cause cannot be contained within our universe or part of it because our universe did not exist. Nor can this cause be physical, spatial-temporal, or unconscious because matter, space and time do not exist prior to the big bang singularity and unconscious observers cannot make observations nor do unconscious measurers make measurements. The implication is clear, the cause of the collapse of the Universal Wave Function was a non-physical, a-temporal, conscious observer (God). The cause of the collapse of the Universal Wave Function is also the cause of the universe.

An argument for the necessary cause of the universe being an intelligent cause can be made from the low entropy singularity model proposed by Roger Penrose and referred to as the "orderly singularity school." In this model, the initial singularity had a very regular structure, with just enough irregularity to give rise to the stars and galaxies. This model is the only one which adequately explains the second law of thermodynamics. I have argued by appeal to the inference to the best explanation, that any form of order is best explained by intelligent design. When one contemplates the possible ways that the universe might have started off, the probability of ours being actualized is greater than one in $10^{10^{123}}$. Penrose has described this number as,

Even if we were to write a "0" on each separate proton and on each separate neutron in the entire universe – and we could throw in all the other particles as well for good measure – we should fall short of writing down the figure needed (Penrose 1989, 344).

At what point does it become irrational to suppose that chance is still a viable alternate explanation?

The existence of a necessary observer is based upon the empirical evidence that for our universe or any other universe to exist, there must be a collapse of the Universal Wave Function that corresponds to the existing universe and any collapse necessitates an observer.

Because the cosmological argument is an *a posterior* argument for the existence of God, it is not within the scope of the cosmological argument to address the issue of God's necessary existence in the absence of the existence of any universe. To address the concept of God's necessary existence not based upon empirical evidence is within the realm of the *a priori* ontological argument.

References:

Hawking, Stephen. 1976. "Breakdown of Predictability in Gravitational Collapse." *Physical Review Letters*. Vol. 17. pp. 234-252.

Penrose, Roger. 1989. The *Emperor's New Mind*. Oxford. England: Oxford University Press.

Reichenbach, Bruce. 1972. "Cosmological Argument and the Causal Principle." *International Journal for Philosophy of Religion*. Vol. 6. pp. 185-190.

Smith, Quentin. 1992. "A Big Bang Cosmological Argument for God's Nonexistence." *Faith and Philosophy*. Vol. 9. No. 2 pp. 205-220.

From Joe Mixie, *The Existence of God*, 2004.

The **Teleological Argument**

WILLIAM PALEY (1743-1805)

William Paley was an English churchman whose writings in defense of Christianity were widely read in the eighteenth and nineteenth centuries. His most important work is *Natural Theology, or Evidences of the Existence and Attributes of the Deity Collected from the Appearances of Nature* (1801). In this work Paley argues for the intelligent design of the universe based upon its similarity to objects we know to be the product of intelligent design, such as a watch. The present reading is from Chapter 1 of this work.

Vocabulary:

Heath:	path
Pitched:	hit
Apprehend:	to think
Contrivance:	something made up
Presupposes:	takes for granted, presumes
Agency:	active force, power; that by which something is done
Subserviency:	subordinate to
Computation:	the act of computing, calculating
Ingenuity:	cleverness

Concepts:

Argument by analogy:

The problem of induction:

Difference in species:

Questions:

1. *What does Paley compare the universe to?*
2. *What are the similarities?*
3. *What are the differences?*
4. *Explain each of Paley's eight points in your own words.*

STATEMENT OF THE ARGUMENT

IN CROSSING A HEATH, suppose I pitched my foot against a stone, and were asked how the stone came to be there, I might possibly answer, that, for anything I knew to the contrary, it had lain there forever; nor would it, perhaps, be very easy to show the absurdity of this answer. But suppose I found a watch upon the ground, and it should be inquired how the watch happened to be in that place, I should hardly think of the answer which I had given — that, for anything I knew, the watch might have always been there. Yet why should not this answer serve for the watch as well as for the stone? Why is it not as admissible in the second case as in the first? For this reason, and for no other; when we come to inspect the watch, we perceive (what we could not discover in the stone) that its several parts are framed and put together for a purpose, e.g. that they are so formed and adjusted as to produce motion, and that motion so regulated as to point out the hour of the day; that, if the different parts had been differently shaped from what they are, of a different size from what they are, or placed after any other manner, or in any other order than that in which they are placed, either no motion at all would have been carried on in the machine, or none which would have answered the use that is now served by it. To reckon up a few of the plainest of these parts, and of their offices, all tending to one result: — We see a cylindrical box containing a coiled elastic spring, which, by its endeavor to relax itself, turns around the box. We next observe a flexible chain (artificially wrought for the sake of flexure) communicating the action of the spring from the box to the fuse. We then find a series of wheels, the teeth of which catch in, and apply to, each other, conducting the motion from the fuse to the balance, and from the balance to the pointer, and, at the same time, by the size and shape of those wheels, so regulating that motion as to terminate in causing an index, by an equable and measured progression, to pass over a given space in a given time. We take notice that the wheels are made of brass, in order to keep them from rust; the springs of steel, no other metal being so elastic; that over the face of the watch there is placed a glass, a material employed in no other part of the work, but in the room of which, if there had been any other than a transparent substance, the hour could not be seen without opening the case. This mechanism being observed (it requires indeed an examina-

tion of the instrument, and perhaps some previous knowledge of the subject, to perceive and understand it; but being once, as we have said, observed and understood), the inference, we think, is inevitable, that the watch must have had a maker; that there must have existed, at some time, and at some place or other, an artificer or artificers who formed it for the purpose which we find it actually to answer; who comprehended its construction, and designed its use.

I. Nor would it, I apprehend, weaken the conclusion, that we had never seen a watch made; that we had never known an artist capable of making one; that we were altogether incapable of executing such a piece of workmanship ourselves, or of understanding in what manner it was performed; all this being no more than what is true of some exquisite remains of ancient art, of some lost arts, and, to the generality of mankind, of the more curious productions of modern manufacture. Does one man in a million know how oval frames are turned? Ignorance of this kind exalts our opinion of the unseen and unknown artist's skill, if he be unseen and unknown, but raises no doubt in our minds of the existence and agency of such an artist, at some former time, and in some place or other. Nor can I perceive that it varies at all the inference, whether the question arises concerning a human agent, or concerning an agent of a different species, or an agent possessing, in some respect, a different nature.

II. Neither, secondly, would it invalidate our conclusion, that the watch sometimes went wrong, or that it seldom went exactly right. The purpose of the machinery, the design and the designer, might be evident, and, in the case supposed, would be evident, in whatever way we accounted for the irregularity of the movement, or whether we could account for it or not. It is not necessary that a machine be perfect, in order to show with what design it was made; still less necessary, where the only question is, whether it were made with any design at all.

III. Nor, thirdly, would it bring any uncertainty into the argument, if there were a few parts of the watch, concerning which we could not discover, or had not yet discovered, in what manner they conduced to the general effect; or even some parts, concerning which we could not ascertain whether they conduced to that effect in any manner whatever. For, as to the first branch of the case, if by the loss, or disorder, or decay of the parts in question, the movement of the watch were found, in fact, to be stopped, or disturbed, or retarded, no doubt would remain in our minds as to the utility or intention of these parts, although we should be unable to investigate the manner according to which, or the connection by which, the ultimate effect depended upon their action or assistance; and the more complex is the machine, the more likely is this obscurity to arise. Then, as to the second thing supposed, namely, that there were parts which might be spread without prejudice to the movement of the watch, and that we had proved this by experiment, these superfluous parts, even if we were completely assured that they were such, would not vacate the reasoning which we had instituted concerning other parts. The indication of contrivance remained, with respect to them, nearly as it was before.

IV. Nor, fourthly, would any man in his senses think the existence of the watch, with its various machinery, accounted for, by being told that it was one out of possible combinations of material forms; that whatever he had found in the place where he found the watch, must have contained some internal configuration or other; and that this configuration might be the structure now exhibited, of the works of a watch as well as a different structure.

V. Nor, fifthly, would it yield his inquiry more satisfaction, to be answered, that there existed in things a principle of order, which had disposed the parts of the watch into their present form and situation. He never knew a watch made by the principle of order; nor can he even form to himself an idea of what is meant by a principle of order, distinct from the intelligence of the watchmaker.

VI. Sixthly, he would be surprised to hear that the mechanism of the watch was no proof of contrivance, only a motive to induce the mind to think so.

VII. And not less surprised to be informed, that the watch in his hand was nothing more than the result of the laws of *metallic* nature. It is a perversion of language to assign any law as the efficient, operative cause of anything. A law presupposes an agent; for it is only the mode according to which an agent proceeds; it implies a power; for it is the order according to which that power acts. Without this agent, without this power, which are both distinct from itself, the *law* does nothing, is nothing. The expression, "the law of metallic nature," may sound strange and harsh to a philosophic ear; but it seems quite as justifiable as some others which are more familiar to him such as "the law of vegetable nature," "The law of animal nature," or, indeed, as "the law of nature" in general, when assigned as the cause of phenomena in exclusion of agency and power, or when it is substituted into the place of these.

VIII. Neither, lastly, would our observer be driven out of his conclusion, or from his confidence in its truth, by being told that he knew nothing at all about the matter. He knows enough for his argument: he knows the utility of the end: he knows the subserviency and adaptation of the means to the end. These points being known, his ignorance of other points, affect not the certainty of his reasoning. The consciousness of knowing little need not beget a distrust of that which he does know....

APPLICATION OF THE ARGUMENT

Every indication of contrivance, every manifestation of design, which existed in the watch, exists in the works of nature; with the difference, on the side of nature, of being greater and more, and that in a degree which exceeds all computation. I mean that the contrivances of nature surpass the contrivances of art, in the complexity, subtlety, and curiosity of the mechanism; and still more, if possible, do they go beyond them in number and variety; yet in a multitude of cases, are not less evidently mechanical, not less evidently contrivances, not less evidently accommodated to their end, or suited to their office, than are the most perfect productions of human ingenuity....

From William Paley, *Natural Theology, or
Evidences of the Existence and Attributes of the
Deity Collected from the Appearances of
Nature*, 1801.

Critique of the Teleological Argument

DAVID HUME (1711-1776)

Dialogues Concerning Natural Religion contains the classical critique of the teleo-logical argument. In this dialogue, Cleanthes represents the position of natural theology; Demea represents the orthodox believer; and Philo represents the skeptic. Hume identified himself with Philo's position.

Vocabulary:

Contemplate:	to think
Contrivance:	something thought up, devised
A posteriori:	after experience
Sophism:	a fallacious argument
Candor:	being fair and honest
Analogy:	comparison
Dissimilitude:	difference
Zealous:	passionate
Scruples:	having uneasiness about an action due to its morality or acceptability
Fancy:	imagination
Scandalized:	to have received slander,
Alteration:	change

Anthropomorphism: attributing human characteristics to that which is not human

Ethereal: not earthly, heavenly

The Aeneid: a book by Virgil about the founding of Rome

Concepts:

Analogical reasoning:

The problem of induction:

Agnostic:

Questions:

1. *How does Cleanthes argue for God's existence?*
2. *What are Demea's objections to Cleanthes' argument?*
3. *What are Philo's objections to Cleanthes' argument?*
4. *What are Philo's six objections to the argument from design?*
5. *What are Cleanthes' responses to Philo's objections?*

Dialogues Concerning Natural Religion

CLEANTHES: LOOK ROUND THE WORLD: Contemplate the whole and every part of it: You will find it to be nothing but one great machine, subdivided into an infinite number of lesser machines, which again admit of subdivisions to a degree beyond what human senses and faculties can trace and explain.

All these various machines, and even their most minute parts, are adjusted to each other with an accuracy which ravishes into admiration all men who have ever contemplated them. The curious adapting of means to ends, throughout all nature, resembles exactly, though it much exceeds, the productions of human contrivance; of human design, thought, wisdom, and intelligence. Since, therefore, the effects resemble each other, we are led to infer, by all the rules of analogy, that the causes also resemble, and that the Author of nature is somewhat similar to the mind of man, though possessed of much larger faculties, proportioned to the grandeur of the work which he has executed. By this argument *a posteriori*, and by this argument alone, do we prove at once the existence of a Deity and his similarity to human mind and intelligence.

Demea: I shall be so free, *Cleanthes*, said *Demea*, as to tell you that, from the beginning, I could not approve of your conclusion concerning the similarity of the Deity to men; still less can I approve of the mediums by which you endeavor to establish it. What! No demonstration of the Being of God! No abstract arguments! No proofs a priori! Are these, which have hitherto been so much insisted on by philosophers, all fallacy, all sophism? Can we reach no farther in this subject than experience and probability? I will say not that this is betraying the cause of a Deity; but surely, by this affected candor, you give advantages to atheists which they never could obtain by the mere dint of argument and reasoning.

Philo: What I chiefly scruple in this subject, said *Philo*, is not so much that all religious arguments are by *Cleanthes* reduced to experience, as that

they appear not to be even the most certain and irrefragable of that inferior kind. That a stone will fall, that fire will burn, that the earth has solidity, we have observed a thousand and a thousand times; and when any new instance of this nature is presented, we draw without hesitation the accustomed inference. The exact similarity of the cases gives us a perfect assurance of a similar event, and a stronger evidence is never desired nor sought after. But wherever you depart, in the least, from the similarity of the cases, you diminish proportionably the evidence; and may at last bring it to a very weak *analogy*, which is confessedly liable to error and uncertainty. After having experienced the circulation of the blood in human creatures, we make no doubt that it takes place in Titus and Maevius; but from its circulation in frogs and fishes it is only a presumption, though a strong one, from analogy that it takes place in men and other animals. The analogical reasoning is much weaker when we infer the circulation of the sap in vegetables from our experience that the blood circulates in animals; and those who hastily followed that imperfect analogy are found, by more accurate experiments, to have been mistaken.

If we see a house, *Cleanthes*, we conclude, with the greatest certainty, that it had an architect or builder because this is precisely that species of effect which we have experienced to proceed from that species of cause. But surely you will not affirm that the universe bears such a resemblance to a house that we can, with the same certainty, infer a similar cause, or that the analogy is here entire and perfect. The dissimilitude is so striking that the utmost you can here pretend to is a guess, a conjecture, a presumption concerning a similar cause; and how that pretension will be received in the world, I leave you to consider.

Cleanthes: It would surely be very ill received, replied *Cleanthes*; and I should be deservedly blamed and detested did I allow that the proofs of a Deity amounted to no more than a guess or conjecture. But is the whole adjustment of means to ends in a house and in the universe so slight a resemblance? The economy of final causes? The order, proportion, and arrangement of every part? Steps of a stair are plainly contrived that human legs may use them in mounting; and this inference is certain and infallible. Human legs are also contrived for walking and mounting; and this inference, I allow, is not altogether so certain because of the dissimilarity which you remark; but does it, therefore, deserve the name only of presumption or conjecture?

Demea: Good God! cried *Demea*,

interrupting him, where are we? Zealous defenders of religion allow that the proofs of a Deity fall short of perfect evidence! And you, *Philo*, on whose assistance I depended in proving the adorable mysteriousness of the Divine Nature, do you assent to all these extravagant opinions of *Cleanthes*? For what other name can I give them? Or, why spare my censure when such principles are advanced, supported by such an authority, before so young a man as *Pamphilus*?

Philo: You seem not to apprehend, replied *Philo*, that I argue with *Cleanthes* in his own way, and, by showing him the dangerous consequences of his tenets, hope at last to reduce him to our opinion. But what sticks most with you, I observe, is the representation which *Cleanthes* has made of the argument *a posteriori*; and, finding that that argument is likely to escape your hold and vanish into air, you think it so disguised that you can scarcely believe it to be set in its true light. Now, however much I may dissent, in other respects, from the dangerous principle of *Cleanthes*, I must allow that he has fairly represented that argument, and I shall endeavor so to state the matter to you that you will entertain no further scruples with regard to it.

Were a man to abstract from everything which he knows or has seen, he would be altogether incapable, merely from his own ideas, to determine what kind of scene the universe must be, or to give the preference to one state or situation of things above another. For as nothing which he clearly conceives could be esteemed impossible or implying a contradiction, every chimera of his fancy would be upon an equal footing; nor could he assign any just reason why he adheres to one idea or system, and rejects the others which are equally possible.

Again, after he opens his eyes and contemplates the world as it really is, it would be impossible for him at first to assign the cause of any one event, much less of the whole of things, or of the universe. He might set his fancy a rambling, and she might bring him in an infinite variety of reports and representations. These would all be possible; but, being all equally possible, he would never of himself give a satisfactory account for his preferring one of them to the rest. Experience alone can point out to him the true cause of any phenomenon.

Now, according to this method of reasoning, *Demea,* it follows (and is, indeed, tacitly allowed by *Cleanthes* himself) that order, arrangement, or the adjustment of final causes, is not of itself any proof of design, but only so far as it has been experienced to proceed from that principle. For aught we can know *a priori*, matter may contain the source or spring of order originally within itself, as well as mind does; and there is no more difficulty in conceiving that the several elements, from an internal unknown cause, may fall into the most exquisite arrangement, than to conceive that their ideas, in the great universal mind, from a like internal unknown cause, fall into that arrangement. The equal possibility of both these suppositions is allowed. But, by experience, we find, according to *Cleanthes*, that there is a difference between them. Throw several pieces of steel together, without shape or form; they will never arrange themselves so as to compose a watch. Stone and mortar and wood, without an architect, never erect a house. But the ideas in a human mind, we see, by an unknown, inexplicable economy, arrange themselves so as to form the plan of a watch or house. Experience, therefore, proves that there is an original principle of order in mind, not in matter. From similar effects we infer similar causes. The adjustment of means to ends is alike in the universe, as in a machine of human contrivance. The causes, therefore, must be resembling.

I was from the beginning scandalized, I must own, with this resemblance which is asserted between the Deity and human creatures, and must conceive it to imply such a degradation of the Supreme Being as no sound theist could endure. With your assistance, therefore, *Demea*, I shall endeavor to defend what you justly call the adorable mysteriousness of the Divine Nature, and shall refute this reasoning of *Cleanthes*, provided he allows that I have made a fair representation of it.

When *Cleanthes* had assented, *Philo*, after a short pause, proceeded in the following manner.

That all inferences, Cleanthes, concerning fact are founded on experience, and that all experimental reasonings are founded on the supposition that similar causes prove similar effects, and similar effects similar causes, I shall not at present much dispute with you. But observe, I entreat you, with what extreme caution all just reasoners proceed in the transferring of experiments to similar cases. Unless the cases be exactly similar, they repose no perfect confidence in applying their past observation to any particular phenomenon. Every alteration of circumstances occasions a doubt concerning the event; and it requires new experiments to prove certainly that the new circumstances are of no moment or importance. A change in bulk, situation, arrangement, age, disposition of the air, or surrounding bodies; any of these particulars may be attended with the most unexpected consequences. And unless the objects be quite familiar to us, it is the highest temerity to expect with assurance, after any of these changes, an event similar to that which before fell under our observation. The slow and deliberate steps of philosophers here, if anywhere, are distinguished from the precipitate march of the vulgar, who, hurried on by the smallest similitude, are incapable of all discernment or consideration.

But can you think, *Cleanthes*, that your usual phlegm and philosophy have been preserved in so wide a step as you have taken when you compared to the universe houses, ships, furniture, machines; and, from their similarity in some circumstances, inferred a similarity in their causes? Thought, design, intelligence, such as we discover in men and other animals, is no more than one of the springs and principles of the universe, as well as heat or cold, attraction or repulsion, and a hundred others which fall under daily observation. It is an active cause by which some particular parts of nature, we find, produce alterations on other parts. But can a conclusion, with any propriety, be transferred from parts to the whole? Does not the great disproportion bar all comparison and inference? From observing the growth of a hair, can we learn anything concerning the generation of a man? Would the manner of a leaf's blowing, even though perfectly known, afford us any instruction concerning the vegetation of a tree?

But allowing that we were to take the operations of one part of nature upon another for the foundation of our judgment concerning the origin of the whole (which never can be admitted), yet why select so minute, so weak, so bounded a principle as the reason and design of animals is found to be upon this planet? What peculiar privilege has this little agitation of the brain which we call "thought," that we must thus make it the model of the whole universe? Our partiality in our own favor does indeed present it on all occasions, but sound philosophy ought carefully to guard against so natural an illusion.

So far from admitting, continued Philo, that the operations of a part can afford us any just conclusion concerning the origin of the whole, I will not allow any one part to form a rule for another part if the latter be very remote from the former. Is there any reasonable ground to conclude that the inhabitants of other planets possess thought, intelligence, reason, or anything similar to these faculties in men? When nature has so extremely diversified her manner of operation in this small globe, can we imagine that she incessantly copies herself throughout so immense a universe? And if thought, as we may well suppose, be confined merely to this narrow corner, and has even there so limited a sphere of action, with what propriety can we assign it for the original cause of all things? The narrow views of a peasant, who makes his domestic economy the rule for the government of kingdoms, is in comparison a pardonable sophism.

But were we ever so much assured that a thought and reason resembling the human were to be found throughout the whole universe, and were its activity elsewhere vastly greater and more commanding than it appears in this globe; yet I cannot see why the operations of a world constituted, arranged, adjusted, can with any propriety be extended to a world which is in its embryo state, and is advancing towards that constitution and arrangement. By observation we know somewhat of the economy, action, and nourishment of a finished animal; but we must transfer with great caution that observation to the growth of a fetus in the womb, and still more to the formation of an animalcule in the loins of its male parent. Nature, we find, even from our limited experience, possesses an infinite number of springs and principles which incessantly discover themselves on every change of her position and situation. And what new and unknown principles would actuate her in so new and unknown a situation as that of the formation of a universe, we cannot, without the utmost temerity, pretend to determine.

A very small part of this great system, during a very short time, is very imperfectly discovered to us; and do we, thence pronounce decisively concerning the origin of the whole?

Admirable conclusion! Stone, wood, brick, iron, brass, have not, at this time, in this minute globe of earth, an order or arrangement without human art and contrivance; therefore, the universe could not originally attain its order and arrangement without something similar to human art. But is a part of nature a rule for another part very wide of the former? Is it a rule for the whole? Is a very small part a rule for the universe? Is nature in one situation a certain rule and in another situation vastly different from the former?

And can you blame me, *Cleanthes*, if I here imitate the prudent reserve of *Simonides*, who, according to the noted story, being asked by *Hiero, What God was*? desired a day to think of it, and then two days more; and after that manner continually prolonged the term, without ever bringing in his definition or description? Could you even blame me if I had answered, at first, *that I did not know*, and was sensible that this subject lay vastly beyond the reach of my faculties? You might cry out skeptic and raillier, as much as you pleased; but, having found in so many other subjects much more familiar the imperfections and even contradictions of human reason, I never should expect any success from its feeble conjectures in a subject so sublime and so remote from the sphere of our observation. When two *species* of objects have always been observed to be conjoined together, I can *infer*, by custom, the existence of one wherever I see the existence of the other; and this I call an argument from experience. But how this argument can have place where the objects, as in the present case, are single, individual, without parallel or specific resemblance, may be difficult to explain. And will any man tell me with a serious countenance that an orderly universe must arise from some thought and art like the human because we have experience of it? To ascertain this reasoning it were requisite that we had experience of the origin of worlds; and it is not sufficient, surely, that we have seen ships and cities arise from human art and contrivance...

Philo: But to show you still more inconveniences, continued *Philo*, in your anthropomorphism, please to take a new survey of your principles. *Like effects prove like causes.* This is the experimental argument; and this, you say too, is the sole theological argument. Now it is certain that the liker the effects which are seen and the liker the causes which are inferred, the stronger is the argument. Every departure on either side diminishes the probability and renders the experiment less conclusive. You cannot doubt of the principle; neither ought you to reject its consequences.

All the new discoveries in astronomy which prove the immense grandeur and magnificence of the works of nature are so many additional arguments for a Deity, according to the true system of theism; but, according to your hypothesis of experimental theism, they become so many objections, by removing the effect still farther from all resemblance to the effects of human art and contrivance. For if *Lucretius*, even following the old system of the world, could exclaim:

> Who is strong enough to rule the sum? Who to hold in hand and control the mighty bridle of the unfathomable deep? who to turn about all the heavens at one time, and warm the fruitful worlds with ethereal fires, or to be present in all places and at all times.

If Tully esteemed this reasoning so natural as to put it into the mouth of his Epicurean:

> What power of mental vision enabled your master Plato to descry the vast and elaborate architectural process which, as he makes out, the deity adopted in building the structure of the universe? What method of engineering was employed? What tools and levers and derricks? What agents carried out so vast an understanding? And how were air, fire, water, and earth enabled to obey and execute the will of the architect?

If this argument, I say, had any force in former ages, how much greater must it have at present when the bounds of nature are so infinitely enlarged and such a magnificent scene is opened to us? It is still more unreasonable to form our idea of so unlimited a cause from our experience of the narrow productions of human design and invention.

The discoveries by microscopes, as they open a new universe in miniature, are still objections, according to you; arguments, according to me. The farther we push our researches of this kind, we are still led to infer the universal cause of all to be vastly different from mankind, or from any object of human experience and observation.

And what say you to the discoveries in anatomy, chemistry, botany? ...

Cleanthes: These surely are no objects, replied Cleanthes; they only discover new instances of art and contrivance. It is still the image of mind reflected on us from innumerable objects.

Philo: Add a mind like the human, said Philo.

Cleanthes: I know of no other, replied *Cleanthes*.

Philo: And the liker, the better, insisted Philo.

Cleanthes: To be sure, said *Cleanthes*.

Philo: Now, *Cleanthes*, said *Philo*, with an air of alacrity and triumph, mark the consequences. *First,* by this method of reasoning you renounce all claim to infinity in any of the attributes of the Deity. For, as the cause ought only to be proportioned to the effect, and the effect, so far as it falls under our cognizance, is not infinite: What pretensions have we, upon your suppositions, to ascribe that attribute to the Divine Being? You will still insist that, by removing him so much from all similarity to human creatures, we give in to the most arbitrary hypothesis, and at the same time weaken all proofs of his existence.

Secondly, you have no reason, on your theory, for ascribing perfection to the Deity, even in his finite capacity; or for supposing him free from every error, mistake, or incoherence, in his undertakings. There are many inexplicable difficulties in the works of Nature which, if we allow a perfect author to be proved *a priori*, are easily solved, and become only seeming difficulties from the narrow capacity of man, who cannot trace infinite relations. But according to your method of reasoning, these difficulties become all real; and, perhaps, will be insisted on as new instances of likeness to human art and contrivance. At least, you must acknowledge, that it is impossible for us to tell, from our limited views, whether this system contains any great faults or deserves any considerable praise if compared to other possible and even real systems. Could a peasant, if the *Aeneid* were read to him, pronounce that poem to be absolutely faultless, or even assign to it its proper rank among the productions of human wit, he who had never seen any other production?

But were this world ever so perfect a production, it must still remain uncertain whether all the excellences of the work can justly be ascribed to the workman. If we survey a ship, what an exalted idea must we form of the ingenuity of the carpenter who framed so complicated, useful, and beautiful a machine? And what surprise must we feel when we find him a stupid mechanic who imitated others, and copied an art which, through a long succession of ages, after multiplied trials, mistakes, corrections, deliberations, and controversies, had been gradually improving? Many worlds might have been botched and bungled, throughout an eternity, ere this system was struck out; much labor lost; many fruitless trials made; and a slow but continued improvement carried on during infinite ages in the art of world-making. In such subjects, who can determine where the truth, nay, who can conjecture where the probability lies, amidst a great number of hypotheses which may be proposed, and a still greater which may be imagined?

And what shadow of an argument, continued Philo, can you produce from your hypothesis to prove the unity of the Deity? A great number of men join in building a house or ship, in rearing a city, in framing a commonwealth; why may not several deities combine in contributing and framing a world? This is only so much greater similarity to human affairs. By sharing the work among several, we may so much further limit the attributes of each, and get rid of that extensive power and knowledge which must be supposed in one deity, and which, according to you, can only serve to weaken the proof of his existence. And if such foolish, such vicious creatures as man can yet often

unite in framing and executing one plan, how much more those deities or demons, whom we may suppose several degrees more perfect?

To multiply causes without necessity is indeed contrary to true philosophy, but this principle applies not to the present case. Were one deity antecedently proved by your theory who were possessed of every attribute requisite to the production of the universe, it would be needless, I own (though not absurd), to suppose any other deity existent. But while it is still a question whether all these attributes are united in one subject or dispersed among several independent beings; by what phenomena in nature can we pretend to decide the controversy? Where we see a body raised in a scale, we are sure that there is in the opposite scale, however concealed from sight, some counterpoising weight equal to it; but it is still allowed to doubt whether that weight be an aggregate of several distinct bodies or one uniform united mass. And if the weight requisite very much exceeds anything which we have ever seen conjoined in any single body, the former supposition becomes still more probable and natural. An intelligent being of such vast power and capacity as is necessary to produce a universe, or, to speak in the language of ancient philosophy, so prodigious an animal, exceeds all analogy and even comprehension.

But further, *Cleanthes*, men are mortal, and renew their species by generation; and this is common to all living creatures. The two great sexes of male and female, says *Milton*, animate the world. Why must this circumstance, so universal, so essential, be excluded from those numerous and limited deities?

And why not become a perfect anthropomorphite? Why not assert the deity or deities to be corporeal, and to have eyes, a nose, mouth, ears, etc.? *Epicurus* maintained that no man had ever seen reason but in a human figure; therefore, the gods must have a human figure. And this argument, which is deservedly so much ridiculed by *Cicero*, becomes, according to you, solid and philosophical.

In a word, *Cleanthes*, a man who follows your hypothesis is able, perhaps, to assert or conjecture that the universe sometime arose from something like design: But beyond that position he cannot ascertain one single circumstance, and is left afterwards to fix every point of his theology by the utmost license of fancy and hypothesis. This world, for aught he knows, is very faulty and imperfect, compared to a superior standard; and was only the first rude essay of some infant deity who afterwards abandoned it, ashamed of his lame performance: It is the work only of some dependent, inferior deity, and is the object of derision to his superiors: It is the production of old age and dotage in some superannuated deity; and ever since his death has run on at adventures, from the first impulse and active force which it received from him.... You justly give signs of horror, *Demea*, at these strange suppositions; but these, and a thousand more of the same kind, are *Cleanthes'* suppositions, not mine. From the moment the attributes of the Deity are supposed finite, all these have place. And I cannot, for my part, think that so wild and unsettled a system of theology is, in any respect, preferable to none at all.

Cleanthes: These suppositions I absolutely disown, cried *Cleanthes*: They strike me, however, with no horror, especially when proposed in that rambling way in which they drop from you. On the contrary, they give me pleasure when I see that, by the utmost indulgence of your imagination, you never get rid of the hypothesis of design in the universe, but are obliged at every turn to have recourse to it. To this concession I adhere steadily; and this I regard as a sufficient foundation for religion.

From David Hume, *Dialogues Concerning Natural Religion*, 1779.

The Teleological Argument Revisited

Joe Mixie (1956 -)

Joe Mixie teaches Philosophy at Sacred Heart University located in Fairfield, CT. He is the author of *The Existence of God* (2004), *The Atheist Trap* (1994) and several articles.

Our current reading is an adaptation from Chapter 7 of *The Existence of God* where Mixie presents a formulation of the argument from design which fulfills the requirements of scientific empiricism according to the school of falsificationism.

Vocabulary:

Falsificationism:	method of scientific empiricism in which the minimal requirement for a theory to be considered as scientific is that it be at least possible for it to be proven incorrect
Scientific Empiricism:	method of science in which all knowledge must be proved by repeated experiments
Intersubjectivity:	the requirement of scientific statements to be verified by observable repeated experiments
Universal Statement:	in logic any statement that is universal in scope
Existential Statement:	in logic any statement that is particular in scope
Anthropic Principle:	refers to the self-evident fact that human beings can

only observe a universe orderly enough to maintain human life

Corroborating: supporting, providing evidence for

Concepts:

Scientific Falsificationism:

Intersubjectivity:

Scientific Criterion:

Instances of Natural Order:

Instances of Spatial Order:

Instances of Temporal Order:

Questions:

1. *How does Mixie's formulation of the Argument from Design fulfill the requirements of scientific empiricism?*
2. *Evaluate Mixie's examples of natural order.*
3. *Evaluate Mixie's examples of spatial order.*
4. *Evaluate Mixie's examples of temporal order.*
5. *Do you find this restatement of the Argument from Design convincing? Why or why not?*

Introduction

Many philosophers think that any argument for the existence of God is "mere metaphysical speculation." Many times these philosophers use the criteria of scientific empiricism as the standard for an "acceptable" scientific theory, regardless of the subject matter. While acknowledging Kuhn's work, *The Structure of Scientific Revolutions*, and the insights it gives us regarding how the nature of scientific theories and paradigms change, it is still appropriate to ask whether any argument for the existence of God can be formulated in such a way so as to fulfill the currently acceptable criteria of scientific empiricism. I shall explore the possibility of formulating the argument from design as an empirical scientific theory.

One major school of thought regarding the criteria of scientific empiricism is that of falsificationism. Karl Popper was one of the leading exponents of falsificationism, and presented and defended that position in his works entitled *Science: Conjectures and Refutation* and *The Logic of Scientific Discovery*. For the purposes of this paper, I will adopt Popper's criteria of falsification.

Revised Teleological Argument

I shall consider a form of the argument from design which infers the existence of God from our experience of instances of natural order. I shall discuss the notion of natural order in greater detail later in this paper. I shall not count as instances of natural order those patterns which appear randomly in nature from time to time.

Consider the following formulation of the argument from design in *modus ponens* argument form:

(1) If there are instances of natural order (NO), then there is intelligent design of these instances of natural order (D).
(2) There are instances of natural order (NO).
(3) Therefore, (by modus ponens) there is intelligent design of these instances of natural order (D).

The acceptance of the truth of the conclusion that there is intelligent design depends upon the strength of the evidence for the antecedent-consequent relation in premise (1) between natural order (NO) and the existence of a designer (D). The evidence for the truth of the antecedent, required for premise (2), is provided in the section entitled "Instances of Natural Order" and I shall argue in the section entitled "Inference to the Best Explanation" for the acceptance of the truth of the antecedent-consequent relation.

The Scientific Criterion

Recall Popper's method of empirical falsification. According to Popper, for a claim to qualify as empirical, a minimal requirement is that there be some evidence from experience which would indicate the claim to be false. Popper writes in *The Logic of Scientific Discovery*,

> But I shall admit a system as empirical or scientific only if it is capable of being tested by experience. These considerations suggest that not the verifiability but the falsifiability of a system is to be taken as a criteria of demarcation. In other words: I shall not require of a scientific system that it shall be capable of being singled out, once and for all, in a positive sense; but I shall require that its local form shall be such that it can be singled out, by means of empirical tests, in a negative sense: it must be possible for an empirical scientific system to be refuted by experience (Popper 1959, 40-41).

It is important to point out that Popper argued that what differentiated empirical science from pseudo-science was that the "objectivity" of scientific statements lay in the fact that they can be intersubjectively tested. Popper says,

Kant was perhaps the first to realize that the objectivity of scientific statements is closely connected with the construction of theories – with the use of hypotheses and universal statements. Only when certain events recur in accordance with rules or regularities, as in the case with repeatable experiments, can our observations be tested – in principle – by anyone. We do not take even our own observations quite seriously, or accept them as scientific observations, until we have repeated and tested them. Only by such repetitions can we convince ourselves that we are not dealing with a mere isolated "coincidence," but with events which, on account of their regularity and reproducibility, are in principle the inter-subjectively testable (Popper 1959, 45).

It is clear that Popper defines an empirical test as a repeatable experiment under controlled conditions. The procedure is deductive. Singular statements, known as predictions, are deduced from the general theory and are then tested. As Popper says,

> Next we seek a decision as regards these (and others) derived statements by comparing them with the results of practical applications and experiments. If this decision is positive, that is, if the singular conclusions turn out to be accepted, or verified, then the theory has, for the time being, passed its test: we have no reason to discard it. But if the decision is nega-

tive, or in other words, if the conclusions have been falsified, then their falsification also falsifies the theory from which they were logically deduced (Popper 1959, 33).

Popper argued that empirical strict universal statements are falsifiable and cannot be verified, and empirical strict existential statements are verifiable and are not falsifiable. Again Popper writes,

Strict or pure statements, whether universal or existential, are not limited to space and time. They do not refer to an individual, restricted, spatio-temporal region. This is the reason why strict existential statements are not falsifiable. We cannot search the whole world in order to establish that something does not exist, has never existed, and will never exist. It is for precisely the same reason that strict, universal statements are not verifiable. Again, we cannot search the whole world in order to make sure that nothing exists which the law forbids. Nevertheless, both kinds of strict statements, strictly existential and strictly universal, are in principle empirically decidable; each, however, in one way only: they are unilaterally decidable. Whenever it is found that something exists here or there, a strictly existential statement may be verified, or a universal one falsified (Popper 1959, 70).

Popper argued that the only

"acceptable" method for scientific empiricism to employ is that of *modus tollens* (denying the consequent) argument form. Popper says,

Consequently it is possible by means of purely deductive inferences (with the help of the modus tollens of classical logic) to argue from the truth of singular statements to the falsity of universal statements. Such an argument to the falsity of universal statements is the only strictly deductive kind of inference that proceeds, as it were, in the inductive direction; that is, from singular to universal statements (Popper 1963, 41).

In this way, Popper tried to avoid the problem of induction which occurs when scientists employ the *modus ponens* form and commit the fallacy of affirming the consequent.

Modern analysis of the problem of induction begins with Hume and his celebrated analysis of causation in his work entitled *Enquiry Concerning the Human Understanding* (Sec. 5, Part 1). The problem of induction is that it is impossible to derive a universal statement from any number of existential statements. That is, no amount of specifically confirming instances can verify a universal law. For example, P (universal law) cannot be experimentally verified by particular instances of Q (P holding). The fallacy is shown as follows:

(4) If P (universal law), then Q (Particular instance).

(5) Q (Particular instance of P holding).

(6) Therefore, P (universal law).

Thus, Popper says in *Conjectures and Refutations*, "Every genuine test of a theory is an attempt to falsify it, or to refute it" (Popper 1963, 63). In other words, only one instance of a weight not falling when dropped from a tower disconfirms the universal law of gravity, while no number of instances of a weight actually falling from a tower when dropped can confirm the universal law of gravity. Popper does allow for corroboration of universal laws based upon confirming instances.

The argument from design as stated fulfills Popper's falsification criterion. All experiences of natural order may be taken as falsification of the negative hypothesis that a designer does not exist. In this case, the *modus ponens* argument may be translated via the rule of replacement known as transposition into the *modus tollens* form:

(7) If there is not intelligent design (-D), then there are no instances of natural order (-NO).

(8) There are instances of natural order (NO).

(9) Therefore, (by modus tollens), there is intelligent design (D).

The experience we have of instances of natural order falsifies the non-existence of intelligent design.

Instances of Natural Order

The term "natural order" refers to instances in nature of repeating patterns. These repeating patterns exhibit uniformity, symmetry and predictability. It is precisely because these instances of natural order are predictable and repeating that the theist argues they fulfill Popper's criterion of inter-subjectivity and can be verified.

I would like to discuss three types of natural order which are evident in this world. The three types are spatial order, temporal order, and informational order.

Spatial Order

I shall refer to instances of spatial order as instances of co-presence and distinguish co-presence from co-incidence by repetition. Co-presence is characterized by the repeating arrangement of a certain structure. I shall discuss the instances of atomic co-presence and anatomical co-presence.

The simplest and most striking

example of co-present order is that of the atom. Every electron that revolves around its nucleus does not revolve at just any distance from the nucleus. These orbits or shells have specific energy levels and can only contain a certain number of electrons. When any atom has more electrons than a specific shell can hold, the additional electrons begin to fill up the next shell. The atomic orbits of all electrons for each of the specific elements are identically spatially ordered. The electronic structure of even the most complex atoms can be viewed as a succession of filled levels increasing in energy, with the outermost electrons primarily responsible for the chemical properties of the element. Niels Bohr won the Nobel Prize in 1922 for this discovery. One of the basic ideas of quantum theory and quantum mechanics is that as these electrons jump from one shell or orbit to the next they move in discrete jumps exhibiting only a certain specific amount of energy. While studying blackbody radiation in 1900, Max Planck discovered that energy is absorbed and emitted in specific amounts. He called these amounts "quanta." In other words, these jumps from different orbits are not gradual but discontinuous. There is no in-between position. The periodic table of elements is based upon this spatial order.

I distinguish the spatial order (co-presence) present in atomic structure from mere co-incidence by appeal to the universality of the structure. If this structure occurred only sparingly or at random, then there might be an argument for referring to these incidences as coincidences. But, this is not an acceptable explanation of the atomic structure because it is an identically repeated pattern for each specific element.

Another instance of natural spatial order is that of the anatomical structure of animals and plants. The philosophers of the eighteenth century almost exclusively discussed this instance of co-presence. William Paley, in his work entitled *Natural Theology,* discussed the details of the anatomical structure of the eyes and ears and marveled at the minute precision which yielded high efficiency of operation.

It is possible to formulate an argument from the instance of anatomical order which is immune to Darwin's criticisms. Evolution can only occur given special natural laws. These laws include the chemical laws which specify how, under certain conditions, organic molecules combine, and subsequently how these combine to make organisms. There are also biological laws of evolution which govern offspring and the transference of those characteristics which are advantageous for survival. Those organisms that survive will be so structured that they will be able to more easily adapt to the changing environment than competitors. These organisms will exhibit greater anatomical spatial order than their competitors. Under these circumstances, nature guarantees that these instances of spatial order cannot be co-incidental.

Temporal Order

The instances of natural temporal order in our world are even more obvious than those of spatial order. These instances of order refer to the simple patterns of non-conscious behavior of physical objects. The regularity of day and night, the changes of the seasons, the succession of growth in plants and animals are all examples of temporal order. Any example of a physical object acting in accordance with the laws of nature and the laws of physics, such as the laws of gravity and motion, provide experimentally testable evidence of temporal order. Richard Swinburne in his article entitled "The Argument from Design," says "Almost all regularities of succession are due to the normal operation of scientific laws" (Swinburne 1969, 200). One need only look up in the sky to see examples of the predictable, uniform, temporal paths

that the heavenly bodies follow. The fact that we are able to predict any natural occurrence is evidence of temporal order. The universe could have naturally been chaotic.

Kant's criticism that, the idea that temporal order is the result of human beings imposing their order on an otherwise chaotic world, can be countered by arguing that since human beings can discriminate between order and disorder, this discrimination must be in response to something independent of human beings. The argument from design holds that the temporal order in the world is independent of human being's recognition of it. As such, temporal order has been, is, and will continue to be regardless of any human being present to observe it. Temporal order is a basic feature of the structure of the universe.

There has been much discussion of the many interpretations and definitions of the anthropic principle. In 1974, Brandon Carter coined the phrase in his book entitled *Confrontation of Cosmological Theories with Observations* (Carter 1974). Essentially, the anthropic principle refers to the self-evident and trivial fact that human beings can observe only a universe orderly enough to maintain human life. It is not my point to argue the validity of this principle. I would only like to provide a response to the potential objections which might be raised by this principle. The mere fact that order is a necessary condition for human beings to observe the universe does not dismiss the existence of order as less extraordinary and less in need of explanation. True, there would need to be a certain amount of order for human beings to exist, but there could be chaos outside the earth, so long as the planet earth was unaffected by it. As Richard Swinburne says in his book entitled *The Existence of God*,

> There is a great deal more order in the world than is necessary for the existence of humans. So men could still be around to comment on the fact even if the world were a much less orderly place than it is … The Teleologist's starting point is not that we perceive order rather than disorder, but that order rather than disorder is there (Swinburne 1969, 136).

Informational Order

The final instance of natural order in our world that I would like to consider is that which I refer to as informational order or order exemplified as information. Donald M. MacKay in his article entitled "The Wider Scope of Information Theory" said,

Information theory, in the more general sense it has developed over the past forty years, is concerned with all processes in which the spatio-temporal form of one set of objects or events (at A) determines the form of another set (at B) without explicit regard for the energetics involved. These are situations in which we say that information flows from A to B. In the operational context, then, we can define information as that which determines form, in much the same way as force is defined in physics as that which produces acceleration (Machlup 1983, 486).

Both energy and information are operationally defined by what they do. Mackay differentiates the two as follows,

> Whereas the work done by energy is physical in character, the work done by information is logical work. In talking about information, there is always a suppressed reference to a third party, since, as in the physical theory of relativity, we have to relate our definitions to an observer, actual or potential, before they become operationally precise" (Machlup 1983, 486).

The relation between information and order is that the spatio-temporal sets must be ordered sets. The individual members of these sets are arranged in an ordered pattern which determine form. Whereas the formation of a snowflake, in which a simple, structural pattern is repeated, involves high order but little information, the DNA and protein formation involve both high order and great information.

One instance of natural informational order is genetic material. Carl Sagan in his book entitled *The Dragons of Eden* writes,

> But complexity can also be judged by the minimum information content in the organism's genetic material. A typical human chromosome has one very long DNA molecule wound into coils, so that the space it occupies is very much smaller than it would be if it were unraveled. This DNA molecule is composed of smaller building blocks, a little like the rungs and sides of a rope ladder. These blocks are called nucleotides and come in four varieties. The language of life, our hereditary information, is determined by the sequence of the four different sorts of nucleotides ... The genetic instruction of all the other taxa on Earth are written in the same language, with the same code book (Sagan 1977, 23).

It is an accepted idea that information is transmitted between genetic material. Most introductory textbooks in modern genetics devote entire chapters to the topic. A typical example of this is seen in *An Introduction To Modern Genetics* by Donald Patt and Gail Patt. Chapter 4 of this book is entitled, "Transmission of Genetic Information" (Patt 1975, 51-78) and is devoted entirely to the discussion of information transfer between genetic material.

All books on genetics also make use of linguistic terms. In the 12th volume of *Frontiers of Biology* which is entitled "The Biological Code," editors A. Neuberger and E.L. Tatum make this point explicitly when they say, "A sequence of nucleotides or amino acids in a nucleic acid or a protein is a *text* and the residues are *letters*. *Reading* is a general term for any process which uses the sequence information in one polymer to produce a defined sequence in another" (Neuberger 1979, 7).

How much information is contained in a single human chromosome if this information were written down in ordinary printed book form in a modern human language? Carl Sagan in his book *The Dragons of Eden* addresses this question. To summarize Sagan's explanation: A single human chromosome contains twenty billion bits of information. Assuming that human language has no more than 64 individual characters (letters, numbers, and punctuation marks), and that it would take no more than 6 bits (6 questions) to determine any specific character, twenty billion bits are about equivalent to three billion characters. If we assume that there are 6 letters in the average word and 300 words on the average page of a book, and 500 pages in the average book, the information content of a single human chromosome would be roughly equivalent to 4000 five hundred page books. (Sagan 1977, 25).

Corroboration

Let us recall the formulation of the argument from design in *modus ponens* argument form:

(1) If there are instances of natural order (NO), then there is intelligent design of these instances of natural order (D).
(2) There are instances of natural order (NO).
(3) Therefore, there is intelligent design of these instances of natural order (D).

We have seen that this argument, when restated in its *modus tollens* form, fulfills Popper's criterion of falsifiability and thus qualifies as a scientific theory. We now must shift our focus from falsifiability to corroboration. The question which we are now engaged in is that given that our theory in question has passed the test of falsifiability, to what degree, if any, can we accept it as representing the truth of the matter to which it offers explanation?

According to Popper, if a hypoth-esis has survived continual and serious attempts to falsify it, then the hypothesis can be provisionally accepted. In *The Logic of Scientific Discovery*, Popper says,

> It should be noticed that a positive decision can only temporarily support the theory, for subsequent negative decisions may always overthrow it. So long as a theory withstands detailed and severe tests and is not superceded by another theory in the course of scientific progress, we may say that it has "proved its mettle" or that it is "corroborated" (Popper, 1959, 33).

After having rejected the verificationist ideas of Carnap and others because of the problem of induction, it is clear why Popper stresses the provisional nature of accepting any scientific theory.

This having been said, Popper does offer some criteria by which we may speak of the degree of corroboration of a theory. It is not simply the number of corroborating instances which determines the degree of corroboration, although this is taken into consideration, but the severity of the tests and the degree of testability of the theory in question. The degree of testability is directly proportional to the degree of falsifiability. Popper says, "In appraising the degree of corroboration of a theory we take into account its degree of falsifiability. A theory can be better corroborated the better testable it is" (Popper 1959, 269).

Inference to the Best Explanation

The statement of the argument from design that we have been concerned with here is intended to show that belief in the existence of intelligent design is the most experimentally acceptable hypothesis which attempts to account for the instances of natural order in the world. At this point we need to investigate the logic of accepting theories.

Implicit in the spirit of the scientific method is the principle of sufficient reason. According to Gottfried Leibniz, the principle of sufficient reason holds for all truths, especially contingent truth, such as we have been concerned with here. Leibniz expressed this principle simply as, "There must be a sufficient reason for anything to exist, for any event to occur, for any truth to obtain." The argument from design relies upon this principle that there must be a sufficient reason which explains the instances of natural order in the world.

In the case of competing hypotheses, appeal to the principle of sufficient reason will not resolve the dilemma. We need to appeal to another principle of reasoning, the inference to the best explanation.

Although the formulation of the argument from design that we have been discussing is stated in deductive logical form, the truth of premise (1) is not derived through deduction. Premise (1) is not derived through induction either. We could never conclude that instances of natural order require intelligent design from analysis of any number of individual instances of natural order. This is not a problem because, as we have seen, if the truth of premise (1) were arrived at through induction, we would be faced with the problem of induction. So how is the truth of premise (1) arrived at? I submit that the truth of premise (1) is arrived at through the principle known as "inference to the best explanation."

We have established the fact that there are many instances of natural order in the world. These instances of natural order are confirmed not only in our daily experiences, but also in the strictly controlled environment of scientific experimentation. We must now address the question of competing hypotheses because, as we have seen, in *modus ponens* argument form, the conclusion of the argument will follow deductively if premise (2) is accepted.

Many times several different

hypotheses claim to be the best explanation to some accepted set of observations. Under these circumstances, we employ the method of the inference to the best explanation in order to determine which of the competing hypotheses is, in fact, the best explanation.

What makes one hypothesis a better explanation than another? There are four criteria which logicians and scientists have traditionally cited in their attempt to clarify what makes one explanation of observed phenomena better than others. These are:

(A) Do any of the competing hypotheses conflict with established background knowledge?
(B) Is there more evidence supporting one hypothesis than the others?
(C) Is there less evidence against one than the others?
(D) Which hypothesis is simpler?

There are two major competing hypotheses that are usually argued to be better explanations for the existence of natural order in the world than intelligent design. These two hypotheses are:

(10) If there are instances of natural order in the world, then these instances of natural order are the result of chance.
(11) If there are instances of natural order in the world, then these instances of nat-

ural order are the result of self-ordering matter.

I will now argue that the instances of natural order in the world are better explained by intelligent design than by either of these two competing hypotheses.

Chance

Regarding premise (10), there are several reasons which indicate the weakness in this explanation.

First, recall the definition of order as repeating patterns exhibiting uniformity, symmetry and predictability. Premise (1) stands in contradiction with this definition of natural order. The *Encyclopedia of Philosophy* distinguishes chance events from other events "on the basis of whether or not men can predict their occurrence" (vol. 1, 73). The notion of an absolutely random pattern that predictably repeats is self-contradictory.

Second, premise (10) conflicts with the established background knowledge of scientific laws based upon repeatable scientific experiments. Recall Popper's notion of inter-subjectivity. Chance explanations, by their very nature, could not possibly fulfill this requirement. There is no chance involved regarding Newton's law of motion (force = mass X acceleration).

Third, theories of chance lead to

theories of probability that, it is claimed, provide an explanation of chance. Recall that only universal statements fulfill Popper's criterion of falsifiability. Carl Hempel in his book entitled *Aspects of Scientific Explanation and Other Essays in the Philosophy of Science* writes,

> But the distinction between law-like statements of strictly universal form and those of probabilistic form pertains, not to the evidential support of the statements in question, but to the claims made by them: roughly speaking, the former attribute (truly or falsely) a certain characteristic to all members of a certain class; the latter, to a specific proportion of its members (Hempel 1948, 376-386).

Regarding natural spatial order, the explanation of chance or co-incidence fails on two accounts. First, as I mentioned earlier when discussing atomic structure, there are instances of natural spatial order that are all-pervasive. No doubt chance arrangements of physical objects do occur in nature, but when these arrangements continually recur, the explanation of chance fails because we are able to formulate laws and make predictions as to their recurrence. There is no doubt that by mere chance there could exist a lake such that there could be a row of trees around the lake that alternated in a pattern of maple, oak, and pine. Were we to come

across such a lake with such an arrangement of trees, one acceptable explanation could be that this arrangement occurred by mere chance. But if we continually observed similar lakes with a similar arrangement of trees around them, the explanation of chance would cease to be an acceptable explanation in light of other possible explanations, such as intelligent design. Therefore the explanation of chance in this instance conflicts with the established background knowledge of predictability.

Self-ordering matter

Regarding premise (11), there is a major reason which indicates the weakness of this explanation.

First, quantum physics has discovered that all elementary particles, atoms, and even molecules are identical. In his book entitled *The Emperor's New Mind*, Roger Penrose says,

> According to quantum mechanics, any two electrons must necessarily be completely identical, and the same holds for any two protons and for any two particles whatever, of any one particular kind. This is not merely to say that there is no way of telling the particles apart: the statement is considerably stronger than that. If an electron in a person's brain were to be exchanged with an electron in a brick, then the state of the system would be

exactly the same as it was before, not merely indistinguishable from it. The same holds for protons and for any other kind of particle, and for whole atoms, molecules, etc. (Penrose 1989, 25).

The significance of this is clear. If all elementary particles of atoms and molecules are identical in kind, how does premise (11) explain the fact that some of these elementary particles become orderful patterns, i.e. atoms and molecules, and some do not? Quantum physics does not recognize order and disorder as intrinsic properties of elementary particles. There is no recognized property in physics known as self-ordering matter. Clearly, these unconscious entities do not possess the capability within themselves of creating order. If they did, then they would all be orderful.

An objection might be raised regarding the previous discussion of spatial order in reference to atomic structure. It is true that atoms exhibit order, but there is no evidence that this order is due to some intrinsic property of the elementary constituents of the atoms. Furthermore, not all electrons orbit around nuclei. There are free floating elementary particles. Therefore, premise (11) conflicts with established background knowledge.

Intelligent Design

In contrast to premises (10) and (11), premise (1) of the argument from design does have supporting evidence which qualifies it as the best explanation. I shall now discuss this evidence.

The strongest evidence a theist could provide in favor of intelligent design being the best explanation for the instances of natural order is that there is, in fact, a class of order which we know is the result of intelligent design, namely human order. Natural order and human order are not different in kind, but only in origin. This is not an argument from analogy. The theist is not saying that human order and natural order are merely similar or resemble one another. The theist can make the stronger claim that natural order and human order are identical in kind, but only differ in origin.

There are many examples of spatial human order. Books arranged in a library, streets arranged in a city, and even traffic lights are instances of spatial human order. Examples of temporal human order are any regularly scheduled event, such as train, bus, or airline schedules. Music also is an example of temporal human order. Examples of informational human order are also numerous. Any human language or communication is an example. Street signs and books are examples of human informational order. The list goes on and on. All these instances of human order are the result of intelligent design. Therefore the inference to the explanation that instances of natural order are also the result of intelligent design at least has more corroborating evidence than the others we have discussed.

What is important to notice about all instances of human order is that they all involved reference to some purpose or goal. Up to this point in the discussion I have purposely not introduced any notion whatsoever regarding purpose or intention. Regarding instances of human order, the elimination of purpose or intention is impossible.

I agree that the introduction of specific motives and desires pertaining to the intelligent design of the universe does employ the argument from analogy, but not the general notion that some motivation, though we may never know specifically what it is, does play a part in the design of the universe. This does not violate the scientific nature of the explanation. Carl Hempel and Paul Oppenheim wrote in their work entitled "Studies in the Logic of Explanation."

"The determining motives and beliefs, therefore, have to be classified among the antecedent conditions of a motivational explanation, and there is no formal difference on this account between motivational and causal explanations" (Hempel 1948, 45).

In conclusion, I submit that intelligent design is the best explanation for the instances of natural order in the universe. According to the criteria of inference to the best explanation, intelligent design (A) does not conflict with established background knowledge; (B) has more evidence supporting it; (C) has no evidence against it; (D) is simpler than any competing explanation.

References:

Carter, Brandon. 1974. *Confrontation of Cosmological Theories with Observation.* New York, NY: McGraw-Hill Book Company.

Hempel, Carl. and Paul Oppenheim 1948. "Studies in the Logic of Explanation." *Philosophy of Science.* Vol. 15. pp. 135-175.

Machlup, F. and U. Mansfield. 1983. *The Study of Information.* New York, NY: Macmillian Publishing Co., Inc.

Neuberger, A. and E.L. Tatum. 1979. *Frontiers of Biology.* New York, NY: North-Holland Publishing Company.

Patt, Donald I. and Gail R. Patt. 1975. *An Introduction to Modern Genetics*. Reading, MA: Addison-Wesley Publishing Company.

Popper, Karl R. 1959. *The Logic of Scientific Discovery*. New York, NY: Basic Books

Popper, Karl R. 1963. *Conjectures and Refutations*. New York, NY: Basic Books.

Sagan, Carl. 1977. *The Dragons of Eden*. New York, NY: Random House.

Swinburne, Richard. 1969. "The Argument From Design." *Philosophy*. Vol. 43. pp. 199-212.

Adapted from Joe Mixie, *The Existence of God,* 2004.

The Ontological Argument

ANSELM (1033-1109)

Anselm was born in Italy. A Benedictine monk, he was Abbot of Bec and later Archbishop of Canterbury. He wrote several important works on theological subjects. His most important philosophical work is the *Proslogium*, in which he set forth a startling and radically new proof for the existence of God. The proof is known as the Ontological Argument.

The Ontological Argument attempts to prove the existence of God by starting with nothing more than the mere concept of the most perfect being. The argument is as follows:

1. God is the Greatest Possible Being.
2. The Greatest Possible Being exists in the mind alone.
3. It is greater to exist in reality than in the mind alone.
4. Therefore, if the Greatest Possible Being exists in the mind alone, then it is not the greatest possible being.
5. Therefore, the Greatest Possible Being must exist in reality.
6. Therefore, God exists in reality.

Vocabulary

Ontology: the study of being
Importunity: persistence in requesting or demanding

Concepts:

To exist in the understanding alone:

Greatest Possible Being:

Existence as a predicate:

Questions:

1. *What is your concept of the Greatest Possible Being?*
2. *Would existence be one of its characteristics?*
3. *In your own words, explain Anselm's argument.*
4. *Are you convinced by it? Why or why not?*
5. *What is Gaunilo's criticism of the argument?*

PROSLOGIUM

. . . I BEGAN TO ASK MYSELF whether there might be found a single argument which would require no other for its proof than itself alone; and alone would suffice to demonstrate that God truly exists, and that there is a supreme good requiring nothing else, which all other things require for their existence and well-being; and whatever we believe regarding the divine Being.

Although I often and earnestly directed my thought to this end, and at some times that which I sought seemed to be just within my reach, while again it wholly evaded my mental vision, at last in despair I was about to cease, as if from the search for a thing which could not be found. But when I wished to exclude this thought altogether, lest, by busying my mind to no purpose, it should keep me from other thoughts, in which I might be successful; then more and more, though I was unwilling and shunned it, it began to force itself upon me, with a kind of importunity. So, one day, when I was exceedingly wearied with resisting its importunity, in the very conflict of my thoughts, the proof of which I had despaired offered itself, so that I eagerly

124

embraced the thoughts which I was strenuously repelling. . . .

And so, Lord, do you, who does give understanding to faith, give me, so far as you know it to be profitable, to understand that you are as we believe; and that you are that which we believe. And, indeed, we believe that you are a being than which nothing greater can be conceived. Or is there no such nature, since the fool has said in his heart, there is no God? But, at any rate, this very fool, when he hears of this being of which I speak — a being than which nothing greater can be conceived — understands what he hears, and what he understands is in his understanding; although he does not understand it to exist.

For, it is one thing for an object to be in the understanding, and another to understand that the object exists. When a painter first conceives of what he will afterwards perform, he has it in his understanding, but he does not yet understand it to be, because he has not yet performed it. But after he has made the painting, he both has it in his understanding, and he understands that it exists, because he has made it.

Therefore, even the fool is convinced that something exists in the understanding, at least, than which nothing greater can be conceived. For, when he hears of this, he understands it. And whatever is understood, exists in the understand-

ing. And assuredly that, than which nothing greater can be conceived, cannot exist in the understanding alone. For, suppose it exists in the understanding alone: then it can be conceived to exist in reality; which is greater.

Therefore, if that, than which nothing greater can be conceived, exists in the understanding alone, this very being, than which nothing greater can be conceived, is not the greatest possible being. But obviously this is impossible. Hence, there is no doubt that there exists a being, than which nothing greater can be conceived, and it exists both in the understanding and in reality....

And it assuredly exists so truly, that it cannot be conceived not to exist. For, it is possible to conceive of a being which cannot be conceived not to exist, and this is greater than one which can be conceived not to exist. Therefore, if that, than which nothing greater can be conceived, can be conceived not to exist, it is not that, than which nothing greater can be conceived. But this is an irreconcilable contradiction. There is, then, so truly a being than which nothing greater can be conceived to exist, that it cannot even be conceived not to exist; and this Being you are, O Lord, our God.

So truly, therefore, you do exist, O Lord, my God, that you can not be conceived not to exist; and rightly. For if a mind could conceive of a being better than Thee, the creature would rise above the Creator; and this is most absurd. And, indeed, whatever else there is, except Thee alone, can be conceived not to exist. To Thee alone, therefore, it belongs to exist more truly than all other beings, and hence in a higher degree than all others. For, whatever else exists does not exist so truly, and hence in a less degree it belongs to it to exist. Why, then, has the fool said in his heart, there is no God, since it is so evident, to a rational mind, that You do exist in the highest degree of all? Why, except that he is dull and a fool? ...

In Behalf of the Fool

AN ANSWER TO THE ARGUMENT OF ANSELM BY GAUNILO

...if it should be said that a being which cannot be even conceived in terms of any fact, is in the understanding. I do not deny that this being is, accordingly, in my understanding. But since through this fact it can in no wise attain to real existence also, I do not yet concede to it that existence at all, until some certain proof of it shall be given.

For he who says that this Being exists, because otherwise the Being which is greater than all will not be greater than all, does not attend strictly to what he is saying. For I do not yet say, no, I even deny or doubt that this Being is greater than any real object. Nor do I concede to it any other existence than this (if it should be called existence) which it has when the mind, according to a word merely heard, tries to form the image of an object absolutely unknown to it.

How, then, is the veritable existence of that Being proved to me from the assumption, by hypothesis, that it is greater than all other beings? For I should still deny this, or doubt your demonstration of it, to this extent, that I should not admit that this being is in my understanding and concept even in the way in which many objects whose real existence is uncertain and doubtful, are in my understanding and concept. For it should be proved first that this being itself really exists somewhere; and then, from the fact that it is greater than all, we shall not hesitate to infer that it also subsists in itself.

For example: it is said that somewhere in the ocean is an island, which, because of the difficulty, or rather the impossibility, of discovering what does not exist, is called the lost island. And they say that this island has an inestimable wealth of all manner of riches and delicacies in greater abundance than is told of the Islands of the Blessed; and that having no owner or inhabitant, it is more excellent than all other countries, which are inhabited by mankind, in the abundance with which it is stored.

Now if someone should tell me that there is such an island, I should easily understand his words, in which there is no difficulty. But suppose that he went on to say, as if by a logical inference: "You can no longer doubt that this island which is more excellent than all lands exists somewhere, since you have no doubt that it is in your understanding. And since it is more excellent not to be in the understanding alone, but to exist both in the understanding and in reality, for this reason it must exist. For if it does not exist, any land which really exists will be more excellent than it; and so the island already understood by you to be more excellent will not be more excellent."

If a man should try to prove to me by such reasoning that this island truly exists, and that its existence should no longer be doubted, either I should believe that he was jesting, or I know not which I ought to regard as the greater fool: myself, supposing that I should allow this proof; or him, if he should suppose that he had established with any certainty the existence of this island. For he ought to show first that the hypothetical excellence of this island exists as a real and indubitable fact, and in no wise as any unreal object, or one whose existence is uncertain, in my understanding.

ANSELM'S REPLY

But you say, it is as if one should suppose an island in the ocean, which surpasses all lands in its fertility, and which, because of the difficulty, or rather the impossibility, of discovering what does not exist, is called a lost island; and should say that there can be no doubt that this island truly exists in reality, for this reason, that one who hears it described easily understands what he hears.

Now I promise confidently that if any man shall devise anything existing either in reality or in concept alone (except that than which a greater cannot be conceived) to which he can adapt the sequence of my reasoning, I will discover that thing, and will give him his lost island, not to be lost again.

But it now appears that this being than which a greater is inconceivable cannot be conceived not to be, because it exists on so assured a ground of truth; for otherwise it would not exist at all.

Hence, if anyone says that he conceives this being not to exist, I say that at the time when he conceives of this either he conceives of a being than which a greater is inconceivable, or he does not conceive at all. If he does not conceive, he does not conceive of the nonexistence of that of which he does not conceive. But if he does conceive, he certainly conceives of a being which cannot be even conceived not to exist. For if it could be conceived not to exist, it could be conceived to have a beginning and an end. But this is impossible.

He, then, who conceives of this Being conceives of a Being which cannot be even conceived not to exist; but he who conceives of this Being does not conceive that it does not exist; else he conceives what is inconceivable. The nonexistence, then, of that than which a greater cannot be conceived is inconceivable.

From the *Proslogium*, translated by Sindey Norton Deane, 1903.

God is a Good Bet

Blaise Pascal (1623-1662)

A French scientist, philosopher, and mathematician, Pascal founded probability theory and made several important contributions to science and mathematics including number theory and geometry. In 1653 he converted to Catholicism and turned his attention to religious matters.

In our present reading he argues that it is in your self-interest to believe that God exists because it is a good bet.

Vocabulary:

Annihilation:	complete destruction
Infinite:	without end
Disproportion:	lack of appropriate relationship between parts
Substantial:	having substance; strong, firm
Extension:	range; property of a body by which it occupies space; additional time
Incomprehensible:	not able to be understood
Extremity:	the outer most point; the greatest degree
Imprudent:	unwise
Transgressing:	breaking (as a law); to go beyond
Adatement:	deducting or making smaller
Acuteness:	sensitivity; sharpness

Concepts:

Infinity:

Finitude:

Wagering:

Questions:

1. *What is the relationship between our finitude and infinity?*
2. *What does Pascal say regarding our knowledge of the nature of God?*
3. *Does Pascal believe that God's existence can be proven?*
4. *Explain the wager that Pascal advocates.*
5. *Do you think belief in God is a good bet? Why or why not?*

THOUGHTS

Infinite – nothing. – Our soul is cast into a body, where it finds number, time, dimension. Thereupon it reasons, and calls this nature, necessity, and can believe nothing else.

Unity joined to infinity adds nothing to it, no more than one foot to an infinite measure. The finite is annihilated in the presence of the infinite, and becomes a pure nothing. So our spirit before God, so our justice before divine justice. There is not so great disproportion between our justice and that of God, as between unity and infinity.

The justice of God must be vast like His compassion. Now, justice to the outcast is less vast, and ought less to offend our feelings than mercy towards the elect.

We know that there is an infinite, and are ignorant of its nature. As we know it to be false that numbers are finite, it is therefore true that there is an infinity in number. But we do not know what it is. It is false that it is even, it is false that it is odd; for the addition of a unit can make no change in its nature. Yet it is a number, and every number is odd or even (this is certainly true of every finite number). So we may well know that there is a God without knowing what He is. Is there not one substantial truth, seeing there are so many things which are not truth itself?

We know then the existence and nature of the finite, because we also are finite and have extension. We know the existence of the infinite, and are ignorant of its nature, because it has extension like us, but not limits like us. But we know neither the existence nor the nature of God, because He has neither extension nor limits.

But by faith we know His existence; in glory we shall know His nature. Now, I have already shown that we may well know the existence of a thing, without knowing its nature.

Let us now speak according to natural lights.

If there is a God, He is infinitely incomprehensible, since, having neither parts nor limits, He has no affinity to us. We are then incapable of knowing either what He is or if He is. This being so, who will dare to undertake the decision of the question? Not we, who have no affinity to Him.

Who then will blame Christians for not being able to give a reason for their belief, since they profess a religion for which they cannot give a reason? They declare, in expounding it to the world, that it is a foolishness, *stultitiam*; and then you complain that they do not

prove it! If they proved it, they would not keep their words; it is in lacking proofs, that they are not lacking in sense. "Yes, but although this excuses those who offer it as such, and takes away from them the blame of putting it forward without reason, it does not excuse those who receive it." Let us then examine this point, and say, "God is, or He is not." But to which side shall we incline? Reason can decide nothing here. There is an infinite chaos which separates us. A game is being played at the extremity of this infinite distance where heads or tails will turn up. What will you wager? According to reason, you can do neither the one thing nor the other; according to reason, you can defend neither of the propositions.

Do not then reprove for error those who have made a choice; for you know nothing about it. "No, but I blame them for having made, not this choice, but a choice, for, again, both he who chooses heads and he who chooses tails are equally at fault. They both are in the wrong. The true course is not to wager at all."

Yes, but you must wager. It is not optional. You are embarked. Which will you choose then? Let us see. Since you must choose, let us see which interests you least. You have two things to lose, the true and the good; and two things to stake, your reason and your will, your knowledge and your happiness; and your nature has two things to shun, error and misery. Your reason is no more shocked in choosing one rather than the other, since you must of necessity choose. This is one point settled. But your happiness? Let us weigh the gain and the loss in wagering that God is. Let us estimate these two chances. If you gain, you gain all; if you lose, you lose nothing. Wager then without hesitation that He is. "That is very fine. Yes, I must wager; but I may perhaps wager too much." Let us see. Since there is an equal risk of gain and of loss, if you had only to gain two lives, instead of one, you might still wager. But if there were three lives to gain, you would have to play (since you are under the necessity of playing), and you would be imprudent, when you are forced to play, not to chance your life to gain three at a game where there is an equal risk of loss and gain. But there is an eternity of life and happiness. And this being so, if there were an infinity of chances, of which one only would be for you, you would still be right in wagering one to win two, and you would act stupidly, being obliged to play, by refusing to stake one life against three at a game in which you had an infinity of an infinitely happy life to gain. But there is here an infinity of an infinitely happy life to gain, a chance of gain against a finite number

of chances of loss, and what you stake is finite. It is all divided; whatever the infinite is and there is not an infinity of chances of loss against that of gain, there is no time to hesitate, you must give all. And thus, when one is forced to play, he must renounce reason to preserve his life, rather than risk it for infinite gain, as likely to happen as the loss of nothingness.

For it is no use to say it is uncertain if we will gain, and it is certain that we risk, and that the infinite distance between the certainty of what is staked and the uncertainty of what will be gained, equals the finite good which is certainly staked against the uncertain infinite. It is not so, as every player stakes a certainty to gain an uncertainty, and yet he stakes a finite certainty to gain a finite uncertainty, without transgressing against reason. There is not an infinite distance between the certainty staked and the uncertainty of the gain; that is untrue. In truth, there is an infinity between the certainty of gain and the certainty of loss. But the uncertainty of the gain is proportioned to the certainty of the stake according to the proportion of the chances of gain and loss. Hence it comes that, if there are as many risks on one side as on the other, the course is to play even; and then the certainty of the stake is equal to the uncertainty of the gain, so far is it from the fact that there is an infinite distance between them. And so our proportion is of infinite force, when there is the finite to stake in a game where there are equal risks of gain and loss, and the infinite to gain. This is demonstrable; and if men are capable of any truths, this is one.

"I confess it, I admit it. But still is there no means of seeing the faces of the cards?" Yes, Scripture and the rest, etc. Yes, but I have my hands tied and my mouth closed; I am forced to wager, and I am not free. I am not released, and am so made that I cannot believe. What then would you have me do?"

Endeavor then to convince yourself, not by increase of proofs of God, but by the abetment of your passions. You would like to attain faith, and do not know the way; you would like to cure yourself of unbelief, and ask the remedy for it. Learn of those who have been bound like you, and who now stake all their possessions. These are people who know the way which you would follow, and who are cured of an ill of which you would be cured. Follow the way by which they began; by acting as if they believe, taking the holy water, having masses said, etc. Even this will naturally make you believe, and deaden your acuteness. "But this is what I am afraid of." And why? What have you to lose?

But to show you that this leads you there, it is this which will lessen the passions, which are your stumbling-blocks.

Now what harm will befall you in taking this side? You will be faithful, honest, humble, grateful, generous, a sincere friend, truthful. Certainly you will not have those poisonous pleasures, glory and luxury; but will you not have others? I will tell you that you will thereby gain in this life, and that, at each step you take on this road, you will see so great certainty of gain, so much nothingness in what you risk, that you will at last recognize that you have wagered for something certain and infinite, for which you have given nothing.

"Ah! This discourse transports me, charms me, etc."

If this discourse pleases you and seems impressive, know that it is made by man who has knelt, both before and after it, in prayer to that Being, infinite and without parts, before whom he lays all he has, for you also to lay before Him all you have for your own good and for His glory, so that strength may be given to lowliness.

From Blaise Pascal, *Thoughts*, translated by W.F. Trotter, 1910.

II. The Philosophy of Religion Section Review

Below is the review sheet for Part II: The Philosophy of Religion. Included in this review are the terms and concepts you should be familiar with to prepare for the exam. I have also included an example of the multiple choice questions that you will have to answer. It will give you an idea of what type of questions to expect.

We will be reviewing each of these terms and concepts and the multiple choice question in class prior to the exam.

You should be familiar with the following terms and concepts:

A priori
A posteriori
The Cosmological Argument
Aquinas' 5 Ways
1st way: Change / Motion
Potentiality
Actuality
Linear motion
Non-linear motion
2nd Way: Causation
First cause
Efficient cause

Infinite Regression
3rd Way: Contingency
Dependent
Non-dependent
Necessary
Criticisms of Cosmological Argument
Infinite regression
Matters of fact
Contingency
World is eternal
Aristotle's Four Causes
Analytic truths
Synthetic truths
4th Way: Excellence
5th Way: Harmony
Teleological Argument
Argument from design
Natural order
Spatial order
Informational order
William Paley's Version
Didn't see it being made
Doesn't work right all the time
Don't know how all parts work
Criticisms of Telelogical Argument
Evolution
Irreducible complexity
Design inference
Small probability

Recognizable pattern / specification

Ontological Argument

God as Greatest Possible Being

Descartes' Proof

Criticisms

Existence is not predicate

Pascal's Wager

Mixie's Teleological Argument

Scientific Falsificationism:

Intersubjectivity

Instances of Natural Order

Mixie's Cosmological Argument

Big Bang Theory:

Big Bang Singularity:

Multiple Choice Example:

Which is the best explanation of Aquinas' first way?

A. The First Way deals with the argument from change / motion. Change is the actualization of potentiality. This is an *a posteriori* argument.

B. The First Way deals with the argument from change / motion. These concepts deal with the ideas of potentiality and actuality. This is an *a priori* argument.

C. The First Way deals with the argument from change / motion. This includes linear and non-linear motion. Any change or motion is potentiality being actualized. For potentiality to be actualized, it must be acted upon by something actual. From this Way, we learn that God is pure actuality. This is an *a posteriori* argument.

D. The First Way deals with the argument from change / motion. These concepts deal with the ideas of potentiality and actuality. Any potentiality must be acted upon by something actual for its potentiality to be realized. From this Way we learn that God has actuality. This is an *a priori* argument.

137

Part III
The Problem of Evil

Part III

The Problem of Evil

> *If the maker of the world can do all that he wills, he wills misery, and there is no escape from the conclusion.*
> ### - *John Stuart Mill*

> *For the Omnipotent God, whom even the heathen acknowledge as the Supreme Power over all, would not allow any evil in his works, unless in his omnipotence and goodness, as the Supreme Good, he is able to bring forth good out of evil. What, after all, is anything we call evil except the privation of good?*
> ### - *Augustine*

> *Man has received the knowledge of good and evil. It is good to obey God, and to believe in Him, and to keep His commandments, and this is the life of man; as not to obey God is evil, and this is his death.*
> ### - *Irenaeus*

> *The world is seen, instead, as a place of "soul-making" in which free beings, grappling with the tasks and challenges of their existence in a common environment may become "children of God" and "heirs of eternal life."*
> ### - *John Hick*

Introduction

THE PROBLEM OF EVIL

The existence of evil in the world has always presented a problem for the traditional theistic position. The difficulty arises because of the paradox of an omnipotent and omnibenevolent God allowing the existence of evil. Theists affirm these three propositions:

1. God is omnipotent.
2. God is omnibenevolent.
3. Evil exists.

But if God is perfectly good, then surely he does not desire that evil exists. And if God is all-powerful, then surely he has the power to prevent evil from existing. These two points lead to the following propositions that complete the classical argument against the traditional theistic position for God's existence based upon the existence of evil in the world:

4. If God (omnipotent and omnibenevolent) exists, there would be no evil in the world.
5. Yet there is evil in the world.
6. Therefore, one of the following conclusions must be true:
    a. God does not exist.
    b. God exists and is omnipotent, but not omnibenevolent.
    c. God exists and is omnibenevolent, but not omnipotent.

Before we continue, it might be helpful to define what we mean by evil. Traditionally, Western thought has distinguished between two types of evil: *moral and natural*. Moral evil is the evil that human beings do to one another for which they are morally responsible. This includes acts such as murder, rape, theft, etc. Natural evil is the evil that is the result of natural forces, such as hurricanes, tornados, earthquakes, etc. The attempt to justify the existence of God who is both omnipotent and omnibenevolent is called a theodicy. This term comes from two Greek words, *theos*, which means God and *dike*, which means justice. It is the attempt to reconcile the unlimited goodness of an all-powerful God with the reality of evil.

The religions of the world have offered basically three types of solutions to the problem of evil. (1) There is the monism of the Vedanta teachings of Hinduism. According to this religion, the phenomenal world, with all its evils, is *maya,* or illusion. A Westernized version of this position is found in Christian Science which affirms that "evil is but an illusion, and it has no real basis. Evil is a false belief" (Mary Baker Eddy, *Science and Health*, 1934, 480). (2) There is the dualism exemplified in ancient religions, such as Zoroastrianism, which holds that there are opposing forces of good and evil with equal strength. Taoism, with its concept of ying and yang is a form of dualistic religion. (3) The Christian religion presents an ethical dualism within an ultimate metaphysical monism, in which evil is real, but the result of the exercise of creaturely free will and moral respon-sibility. It is here that a theodicy is required because Christianity (like Judaism and Islam) is committed to a doctrine of God as absolute in goodness and power and the creator of the universe *ex nihilo.*

The Problem of Evil

John Stuart Mill (1806-1873)

One of the most important British philosophers of the nineteenth century, John Stuart Mill was born in London and educated by his father. As a child prodigy, Mill learned Greek at the age of three and Latin at the age of eight. When he was fourteen he had already received a thorough classical education. At the age of seventeen he began to work as a clerk at the East India Company and eventually became director of the company. In 1865 he was elected to Parliament. Mill wrote on many different subjects including Logic, Philosophy of Science, Philosophy of Religion, Political Philosophy, and Ethics. His principle works are *A System of Logic* (1843), *Utilitarianism* (1863), *On Liberty* (1859) and *The Subjection of Woman* (1869). Our present reading is from *Three Essays on Religion* (1874).

Vocabulary:

Benevolence:	goodness
Omnipotent:	all-powerful
Maleficent:	doing evil or harm
Capricious:	a tendency to change one's mind without reason
Despotic:	tyrannical
Intractableness:	not easily managed or controlled
Rectifying:	putting right or setting right
Pernicious:	causing harm

Predilections: preferences
Antithesis: opposite
Aberration: abnormality; mental disorder
Consecration: when something is made holy
Fetters: anything that confines or restrains

Concepts:

Omnipotent Creator:
Theory of Creation:
Principle of Good:
Nature:
Providence:

Questions:

1. *According to Mill, how do some define the goodness of God?*
2. *If God were omnipotent, what does Mill say the relationship between happiness and behavior would be?*
3. *What is an inescapable conclusion regarding the misery in the world?*
4. *What is Mill's argument against God being both all-good and all-powerful?*
5. *When are men's practical beliefs most inconsistent?*
6. *What do men believe is impressed upon nature?*
7. *Explain how Mill feels about Providence?*

If the maker of the world can do all that he wills, then he wills misery, and there is no escape from the conclusion. The more consistent of those who have deemed themselves qualified to ``vindicate the ways of God to man" have endeavored to avoid the alternative by hardening their hearts, and denying that misery is an evil. The goodness of God, they say, does not consist in willing the happiness of his creatures, but their virtue; and the universe, if not a happy, is a just, universe. But waving the objections to this scheme of ethics, it does not at all get rid of the difficulty. If the Creator of mankind willed that they should all be virtuous, his designs are as completely baffled as if he had willed that they should all be happy. The order of nature is constructed with even less regard to the requirements of justice than to those of benevolence. If the law of all creation were justice and the Creator omnipotent, then, in whatever amount suffering and happiness might be dispensed to the world, each person's share of them would be exactly proportioned to that person's good or evil deeds. No human being would have a worse lot than another, without worse deserts. Accident or favoritism would have no part in such a world, but every human life would be the playing out of a drama constructed like a perfect moral tale. No one is able to blind himself to the fact that the world we live in is totally different from this; insomuch as the necessity of redressing the balance has been deemed one of the strongest arguments for another life after death, this amounts to an admission that the order of things in this life is often an example of injustice, not justice. If it be said that God does not take sufficient account of pleasure and pain to make them the reward or punishment of the good or the wicked, but that virtue is itself the greatest good and vice the greatest evil, then these at least ought to be dispensed to all according to what they have done to deserve them. Instead, every kind of moral depravity is entailed upon multitudes by the fatality of their birth; through the fault of their parents, of society, or of uncontrollable circumstances, certainly through no fault of their own. Not even on the most distorted and contracted theory of good which ever was framed by religious or philosophical fanaticism, can the government of Nature be made to resemble the work of a being at once good and omnipotent.

The only admissible moral theory of Creation is that the Principle of Good cannot at once and altogether subdue the powers of evil, either physical or moral; could not place mankind in a world free from the necessity of an incessant struggle with the maleficent powers, or make them always victorious in that struggle, but could and did make them capable of carrying on the fight with vigor and with progressively increasing success. Of all the religious explanations of the order of nature, this alone is neither contradictory to itself, nor to the facts for which it attempts to account.

...And I venture to assert that such has really been, though often unconsciously, the faith of all who have drawn strength and support of any worthy kind from trust in a superintending Providence. There is no subject on which men's practical belief is more incorrectly indicated by the words they use to express it, than religion. Many have derived a base confidence from imagining themselves to be favorites of an omnipotent but capricious and despotic Deity. But those who have been in goodness by relying on the sympathizing support of a powerful and good Governor of the world, have, I am satisfied, never really believed that Governor to be, in the strict sense of the term, omnipotent. They have always saved his goodness at the expense of his power. They have believed, perhaps, that he could, if he willed, remove all the thorns from their individual path, but not without causing greater harm to someone else, or

frustrating some purpose of greater importance to the general well-being. They have believed that for any one thing, but not any combination of things: that his government, like human government, was a system of adjustments and compromises; that the world is inevitably imperfect, contrary to his intention. And since the exertion of all his power to make it as little imperfect as possible, leaves it no better than it is, they cannot but regard that power, though vastly beyond human estimate, yet as in itself not merely finite, but extremely limited.

...But even though unable to believe that Nature, as a whole, is a realization of the designs of perfect wisdom and benevolence, men do not willingly renounce the idea that some part of Nature, at least, must be intended as an exemplar, or type; that on some portion or other of the Creator's works, the image of the moral qualities which they are accustomed to ascribe to him, must be impressed; that if not all which is, yet something which is, must not only be a faultless model of what ought to be, but must be intended to be our guide and standard in rectifying the rest. It does not suffice them to believe, that what tends to good is to be imitated and perfected, and what tends to evil is to be corrected: they are anxious for some more definite indication of the Creator's designs; and being persuaded that this must somewhere be met within his works, undertake the dangerous responsibility of picking and choosing among them in quest of it. A choice which, except so far as directed by the general maxim that he intends all the good and none of the evil, must of necessity be perfectly arbitrary; and if it leads to any conclusions other than such as can be deduced from that maxim, must be, exactly in that proportion, pernicious.

It has never been settled by any accredited doctrine, what particular departments of the order of nature shall be reputed to be designed for our moral instruction and guidance; and accordingly each person's individual predilections, or momentary convenience, have decided what parts of the divine government the practical conclusions that he was desirous of establishing, should be recommended to approval as being analogous. One such recommendation must be as fallacious as another, for it is impossible to decide that certain of the Creator's works are more truly expressions of his character than the rest; and the only selection which does not lead to immoral results, is the selection of those which most conduce to the general good, in other words, of those which point to an end which, if the entire scheme is the expression of a single omnipotent and consistent will, is evidently not the end intended by it.

There is, however, one particular element in the construction of the world, which, to minds on the look-out for special indication of the Creator's will, has appeared, not without plausibility, peculiarly fitted to afford them. The active impulses of human and other animated beings. One can imagine such persons arguing that when the Author of Nature only made circumstances, he may not have meant to indicate the manner in which his rational creatures were to adjust themselves to those circumstances; but that when he implanted positive stimuli in the creatures themselves, stirring them up to a particular kind of action, it is impossible to doubt that he intended that sort of action to be practiced by them. This reasoning, followed out consistently, would lead to the conclusion that the Deity intended, and approves, whatever human beings do; since all that they do, being the consequence of some of the impulses with which their Creator must have endowed them, all must equally be considered as done in obedience to his will. As this practical conclusion was shrunk from, it was necessary to draw a distinction, and to pronounce that not the whole, but only parts of the active nature of mankind point to a special intention of the Creator in respect to their conduct. These parts it seemed natural to suppose, must be those in which the Creator's hand is manifested rather than the man's own: and hence the frequent antithesis between man as God made him, and man as he has made himself. Since what is done with deliberation seems more the man's own act, and he is held more completely responsible for it than for what he does from sudden impulse, the considerate part of human conduct is apt to be set down as man's share in the business, and the inconsiderate as God's. The result is the vein of sentiment so common in the modern world (though unknown to the philosophic ancients) which exalts instinct at the expense of reason; an aberration rendered still more mischievous by the opinion commonly held in conjunction with it, that every, or almost every, feeling or impulse which acts promptly without waiting to ask questions, is an instinct. Thus, almost every variety of unreflecting and uncalculating impulse receives a kind of consecration, except those which, though unreflecting at the moment, owe their origin to previous habits of reflection: these, being evidently not instinctive, do not meet with the favor accorded to the rest; so that all unreflecting impulses are invested with authority over reason, except the only ones which are most prob-

ably right. I do not mean, of course, that this mode of judgment is even pretended to be consistently carried out: life could not go on if it were not admitted that impulses must be controlled, and that reason ought to govern our actions. The pretension is not to drive Reason from the helm but rather to bind her by articles to steer only in a particular way. Instinct is not to govern, but reason is to practice some vague and unassignable amount of deference to instinct. Though the impression in favor of instinct as being a peculiar manifestation of the divine purposes, has not been cast into the form of a consistent general theory, it remains a standing prejudice, capable of being stirred up into hostility to reason in any case in which the dictate of the rational faculty has not acquired the authority of prescription.

I conceive that there is a radical absurdity in all these attempts to discover, in detail, what are the designs of Providence, in order when they are discovered to help Providence in bringing them about. Those who argue, from particular indications, that Providence intends this or that, either believe that the Creator can do all that he wills or that he cannot. If the first supposition is adopted—if Providence is omnipotent, Providence intends whatever happens, and the fact of its happening proves that Providence intended it. If so, everything which a human being can do is predestined by Providence and is a fulfillment of its designs. But if as is the more religious theory, Providence intends not all which happens, but only what is good, then indeed man has it in his power, by his voluntary actions, to aid the intentions of Providence; but he can only learn those intentions by considering what tends to promote the general good, and not what man has a natural inclination to; for, limited as, on this showing, the divine power must be, by inscrutable but insurmountable obstacles, who knows that man *could* have been created without desires which never are to be, and even which never ought to be, fulfilled? The inclinations with which man has been endowed, as well as any of the other contrivances which we observe in Nature, may be the expression not of the divine will, but of the fetters which impede its free action; and to take hints from these for the guidance of our own conduct may be falling into a trap laid by the enemy. The assumption that everything which infinite goodness can desire, actually comes to pass in this universe, or at least that we must never say or suppose that it does not, is worthy only of those whose slavish fears make them offer the homage of lies to a Being who, they profess to think, is incapable of being deceived and holds all falsehood in abomination.

From John Stuart Mill, *Three Essays on Religion*, 1874.

Evil as Privation

Augustine (354-430)

Augustine was born in a Roman province on the north coast of Africa in 354 to a pagan father and Christian mother. His mother, Monica, wielded a great deal of influence over him. Although he did not particularly excel at his early studies, he eventually became an expert in rhetoric when he moved to Carthage in 370. Carthage was a city of loose morals and Augustine gradually fell away from Christianity. He took a mistress and she bore him a son during his second year in Carthage.

During this time, Augustine rejected Christian morals and doctrines. What particularly troubled him was the inability of Christianity to explain how a good God could allow so much evil in the world. This problem led him to embrace the materialistic ideas of Manichaeism. This philosophy holds that the world is dominated by two eternal and opposed forces, good and evil, light and darkness.

In 383, Augustine traveled to Rome, where he opened his own school of rhetoric. Because he had so much trouble getting his students to pay their tuition, he eventually moved to Milan. This move proved to be a life changing event for Augustine for it was here that he was introduced to Platonic philosophy which spoke of a spiritual and transcendent conception of God, and the view that evil was a privation of goodness. This discovery, along with the influence of Ambrose, who was the bishop of Milan, and Augustine's own study of the New Testament, led to his conversion to Christianity in the summer of 386.

After his baptism by Ambrose in the autumn of 388, Augustine went back to Africa where his was ordained as a priest by the Bishop of Hippo. In 396, Augustine became the Bishop of Hippo.

Augustine wrote extensively and is credited with three of the most important theological and philosophical works ever written: The *Confessions* (the world's first autobiography), the *City of God* (the first philosophy of history), and *On the Trinity*.

Vocabulary:

Trinity:	the Godhead consisting of the Father, Son, and Holy Spirit
Immutable:	unchangeable
Omnipotent:	all-powerful
Privation:	diminishment of something; a reduction in value
Accident:	has no independent and self-sufficient existence, but exists only in another being, a substance or another accident. Accidents may change, disappear or be added, while substance remains the same
Augment:	to make greater

Concepts:

The Trinity:
Omnipotent:
Evil:
Free Will:

Questions:

1. *How does Augustine define evil?*
2. *Why is evil an accident?*
3. *Why can't something be totally evil?*
4. *Where does evil originate?*
5. *What role does our free will play in our evil actions?*

Enchiridion

Chapter 3:10
God Created All Things Good

By this Trinity, supremely and equally and immutably good, were all things created. But they were not created supremely, equally, nor immutably good. Still, each single created thing is good, and taken as a whole they are very good, because together they constitute a universe of admirable beauty.

Chapter 3:11
Evil Is The Privation Of Good

In this universe, even what is called evil, when it is rightly ordered and kept in its place, commends the good more eminently, since good things yield greater pleasure and praise when compared to the bad things. For the Omnipotent God, whom even the heathen acknowledge as the Supreme Power over all, would not allow any evil in his works, unless in his omnipotence and goodness, as the Supreme Good, he is able to bring forth good out of evil. What, after all, is anything we call evil except the privation of good? In animal bodies, for instance, sickness and wounds are nothing but the privation of health. When a cure is effected, the evils which were present (i.e., the sickness and the wounds) do not retreat and go elsewhere. Rather, they simply do not exist any more. For such evil is not a substance; the wound or the disease is a defect of the bodily substance which, as a substance, is good. Evil, then, is an accident, i.e., a privation of that good which is called health. Thus, whatever defects there are in a soul are privations of a natural good. When a cure takes place, they are not transferred elsewhere but, since they are no longer present in the state of health, they no longer exist at all.

Chapter 4:12
All Beings Were Made Good, But Not Being Made Perfectly Good, Are Liable To Corruption

All of nature, therefore, is good, since the Creator of all nature is supremely good. But nature is not supremely and immutably good as is the Creator of it. Thus the good in created things can be diminished and augmented. For good to be diminished is evil; still, however much it is diminished, something must remain of its original nature as long as it exists at all. For no matter what kind or however insignificant a thing may be, the good which is its "nature" cannot be destroyed without the thing itself being destroyed.

There is good reason, therefore, to praise an uncorrupted thing, and if it were indeed an incorruptible thing which could not be destroyed, it would doubtless be all the more worthy of praise. When, however, a thing is corrupted, its corruption is an evil because it is, by just so much, a privation of the good. Where there is no privation of the good, there is no evil. Where there is evil, there is a corresponding diminution of the good. As long, then, as a thing is being corrupted, there is good in it of which it is being deprived; and in this process, if something of its being remains that cannot be further corrupted, this will then be an incorruptible entity, and to this great good it will have come through the process of corruption. But even if the corruption is not arrested, it still does not cease having some good of which it cannot be further deprived. If, however, the corruption comes to be total and entire, there is no good left either, because it is no longer an entity at all. Wherefore corruption cannot consume the good without also consuming the thing itself. Every actual entity is therefore good; a greater good if it cannot be corrupted, a lesser good if it can be. Yet only the foolish and unknowing can deny that it is still good even when corrupted.

Whenever a thing is consumed by corruption, not even the corruption remains, for it is nothing in itself, having no subsistent being in which to exist.

Chapter 4:13
There Can Be No Evil Where There Is No Good

From this it follows that there is nothing to be called evil if there is nothing good. A good that wholly lacks an evil aspect is entirely good. Where there is some evil in a thing, its good is defective or deflectable. Thus there can be no evil where there is no good. This leads us to a surprising conclusion: that, since every being, in so far as it is a being, is good, if we then say that a defective thing is bad, it would seem to mean that we are saying that what is evil is good, that only what is good is ever evil and that there is no evil apart from something good.

This is because every actual entity is good. Nothing evil exists in itself, but only as an evil aspect of some actual entity. Therefore, there can be nothing evil except something good. Absurd as this sounds, nevertheless the logical connections of the argument compel us to it as inevitable.

At the same time, we must take warning lest we incur the prophetic judgment which reads: "Woe to those who call evil good and good evil: who call darkness light and light darkness; who call the bitter sweet and the sweet bitter." Moreover the Lord himself said: "An evil man brings forth evil out of the evil treasure of his heart." What, then, is an evil man but an evil entity, since man is an entity? Now, if a man is something good because he is an entity, what, then, is a bad man except an evil good? When, however, we distinguish between these two concepts, we find that the bad man is not bad because he is a man, nor is he good because he is wicked. Rather, he is a good entity in so far as he is a man, evil in so far as he is wicked.

Therefore, if anyone says that simply to be a man is evil, or that to be a wicked man is good, he rightly falls under the prophetic judgment: "Woe to him who calls evil good and good evil." For this amounts to finding fault with God's work, because man is an entity of God's creation. It also means that we are praising the defects in this particular man because he is a wicked person. Thus, every entity, even if it is a defective one, in so far as it is an entity, is good. In so far as it is defective, it is evil.

On Free Choice of the Will

Because the will is moved when it turns from an immutable good to a changeable one, you may perhaps ask how this movement arises. For the movement itself is certainly evil, although the free will must be numbered among the goods, because with it no one can live rightly. Even if this movement, the turning of the will from the Lord God, is with without a doubt a sin, we cannot say that God is the cause of the sin. This movement will not be from God, but what, then, is its origin? If I should answer your question by saying that I do not know, you would perhaps be disappointed; yet that would be the truth, for that which is nothing cannot be known. Only hold to your faith, since no good thing comes to your perception, understanding, or thought which is not from God. Nothing of any kind can be discovered which is not from God. Wherever you see measure, number, and order, you cannot hesitate to attribute all these to God, their Maker. When you remove measure, number, and order, nothing at all remains. Even if the beginning of some form were to remain, where you do not find order or measure or number (since wherever these exist, form is complete), you must remove even that very beginning of form which seems to be the artisan's raw material. If the completion of form is a good, there is some good even in the rudimentary beginning of form. Thus, if all good is completely removed, no vestige persists; indeed, nothing remains. Every good is from God. There is nothing of any kind that is not from God. Therefore, since the movement of turning away from good, which we admit to be sin, is a defective movement and since, moreover, every defect comes from nothing, see where this movement belongs: you may be sure that it does not belong to God.

Yet since this defect is voluntary, it lies within our power. You must not be willing to fear this defect, for if you do not desire it, it will not exist. What greater security can there be than to live a life where what you do not will cannot happen to you? Since a man cannot rise of his own will as he fell by his own will, let us hold with firm faith the right hand of God, Jesus Christ our Lord, which is stretched out to us. Let us wait for Him with steadfast hope; let us love Him with burning love.

From Augustine, *Enchiridion* and *On Free Choice of the Will*, trans. J.F. Shaw, 1892.

Soul-Making

Irenaeus (120-202)

Irenaeus was a Greek theologian and Bishop of Lyons. He was born in Asia Minor. Irenaeus was the earliest Father of the Church to systematize those Christian beliefs that would later be accepted as orthodox doctrine and is cited frequently by later theologians. Only two of his works survive, neither in the original Greek. The five-volume *Against Heresies* establishes Christian doctrine against the Gnostics and supplies much information on Gnosticism. The *Epideixix* is a concise exposition of Christian doctrine.

Iranaeus argues that human beings have the freedom of choice and it is this freedom that causes evil to exist. We are here to develop our souls so that we can have a loving relationship with God.

Vocabulary:

Indolent:	lazy
Surmise:	guess
Tenacious:	persistently
Nauseous:	to become sick; displaying strong disgust
Obstinately:	stubbornly

Concepts:

Soul-Making:

Zoe:

Bios:

Free Will:

Questions:

1. *What has man received from God and how has this affected his life?*
2. *What should man pursue in light of what he has received from God?*
3. *Who is responsible for man's disobedience towards God?*
4. *How does Hick understand Irenaeus' theodicy?*

Book IV: Chapter XXXIX.

Man is Endowed with the Faculty of Distinguishing Good and Evil; So That, Without Compulsion, He Has the Power, by His Own Will and Choice, to Perform God's Commandments, by Doing Which He Avoids the Evils Prepared for the Rebellious.

1. Man has received the knowledge of good and evil. It is good to obey God, and to believe in Him, and to keep His commandment, and this is the life of man; as not to obey God is evil, and this is his death. Since God, therefore, gave to man such mental power man knew both the good of obedience and the evil of disobedience, that the eye of the mind, receiving experience of both, may with judgment make choice of the better things; and that he may never become indolent or neglectful of God's command; and learning by experience that it is an evil thing which deprives him of life, that is, disobedience to God, may never attempt it at all, but that, knowing that what preserves his life, namely, obedience to God, is good, he may diligently keep it with all earnestness. Wherefore he has also had a twofold experience, possessing knowledge of both kinds, that with discipline he may make choice of the better things. But how, if he had no knowledge of the contrary, could he have had instruction in that which is good? For there is, thus a surer and an undoubted comprehension of matters submitted to us than the mere surmise arising from an opinion regarding them. For just as the tongue receives experience of sweet and bitter by means of tasting, and the eye discriminates between black and white by means of vision, and the ear recognizes the distinctions of sounds by hearing; so also does the mind, receiving through the

experience of both the knowledge of what is good, become more tenacious of its preservation, by acting in obedience to God: in the first place, casting away, by means of repentance, disobedience, as being something disagreeable and nauseous; and afterwards coming to understand what it really is, that it is contrary to goodness and sweetness, so that the mind may never even attempt to taste disobedience to God. But if any one does shun the knowledge of both these kinds of things, and the twofold perception of knowledge, he unawares divests himself of the character of a human being.

2. How, then, shall he be a God, who has not as yet been made a man? Or how can he be perfect who was but lately created? How, again, can he be immortal, who in his mortal nature did not obey his Maker? For it must be that thou, at the outset, should hold the rank of a man, and then afterwards partake of the glory of God. For thou dost not make God, but God thee. If, then, thou art God's workmanship, await the hand of thy Maker which creates everything in due time; in due time as far as thou art concerned, whose creation is being carried out. Offer to Him thy heart in a soft and tractable state, and preserve the form in which the Creator has fashioned thee, having moisture in thyself, lest, by becoming hardened, thou lose the impressions of His fingers. But by preserving the framework thou shall ascend to that which is perfect, for the moist clay which is in thee is hidden there by the workmanship of God. His hand fashioned thy substance; He will cover thee over, too, within and without with pure gold and silver, and He will adorn thee to such a degree, that even "the King Himself shall have pleasure in thy beauty." But if thou, being obstinately hardened, dost reject the operation of His skill, and show thyself ungrateful towards Him, because thou weft created a mere man, by becoming thus ungrateful to God, thou hast at once lost both His workmanship and life. For creation is an attribute of the goodness of God but to be created is that of human nature. If then, thou shall deliver up to Him what is thine, that is, faith towards Him and subjection, thou shall receive His handiwork, and shall be a perfect work of God.

3. If, however, thou wilt not believe in Him, and wilt flee from His hands, the cause of imperfection shall be in thee who didst not obey, but not in Him who called thee. For He commissioned messengers to call people to the marriage, but they who did not obey Him deprived themselves of the royal supper. The skill of God, therefore, is not defective, for He has power of the stones to raise up chil-

dren to Abraham; but the man who does not obtain it is the cause to himself of his own imperfection. Nor, in like manner, does the light fail because of those who have blinded themselves; but while it remains the same as ever, those who are thus blinded are involved in darkness through their own fault. The light does never enslave anyone by necessity; nor, again, does God exercise compulsion upon anyone unwilling to accept the exercise of His skill. Those persons, therefore, who have apostatized from the light given by the Father, and transgressed the law of liberty, have done so through their own fault, since they have been created free agents, and possessed of power over themselves.

4. But God, foreknowing all things, prepared fit habitations for both, kindly conferring that light which they desire on those who seek after the light of incorruption, and resort to it; but for the despisers and mockers who avoid and turn themselves away from this light, and who do, as it were, blind themselves, He has prepared darkness suitable to persons who oppose the light, and He has inflicted an appropriate punishment upon those who try to avoid being subject to Him. Submission to God is eternal rest, so that they who shun the light have a place worthy of their flight; and those who fly from

eternal rest, have a habitation in accordance with their fleeing. Now, since all good things are with God, they who by their own determination fly from God, do defraud themselves of all good things; and having been thus defrauded of all good things with respect to God, they shall consequently fall under the just judgment of God. For those persons who shun rest shall justly incur punishment, and those who avoid the light shall justly dwell in darkness. For as in the case of this temporal light, those who shun it do deliver themselves over to darkness, so that they do themselves become the cause to themselves that they are destitute of light, and do inhabit darkness; and, as I have already observed, the light is not the cause of such an unhappy condition of existence to them; so those who fly from the eternal light of God, which contains in itself all good things, are themselves the cause to themselves of their inhabiting eternal darkness, destitute of all good things, having become to themselves the cause of their consignment to an abode of that kind.

From Irenaeus, *Against Heresies*, Book IV, 39, 1-4.

Excerpts from John Hick:

John Hick is a professor of Philosophy at Claremont Graduate School. In his book *Evil and the God of Love* (1966), he presents Irenaeus' theodicy. He argues that according to the Irenaean tradition, Adam was not viewed as a free agent rebelling against God, but rather as a child developing maturity. The fall of humanity was caused by immaturity, not rebellion. God is still working with humanity in order to bring it from physical life (*bios*) to a state of spiritual life of self-realization in divine love (*zoe*). This life is a vale of soul-making.

There is thus to be found in Irenaeus the outline of an approach to the problem of evil which stands, in important respects, in contrast to the Augustinian type of theodicy. Instead of the doctrine that man was created finitely perfect and then incomprehensibly destroyed his own perfection and plunged into sin and misery, Irenaeus suggests that man was created as an imperfect, immature creature who was to undergo moral development and growth and finally be brought to the perfection intended for him by his Maker. Instead of the fall of Adam being presented, as in the Augustinian tradition, as an utterly malignant and catastrophic event, completely disrupting God's plan, Irenaeus pictures it as something that occurred in the childhood of the race, an understandable lapse due to

weakness and immaturity rather than an adult crime full of malice and pregnant with perpetual guilt. And instead of the Augustinian view of life's trials as a divine punishment for Adam's sin, Irenaeus sees our world of mingled good and evil as a divinely appointed environment for man's development towards the perfection that represents the fulfillment of God's good purpose for him…Irenaeus was the first great Christian theologian to think at all systematically along these lines, and, although he was far from working out a comprehensive theodicy, his hints are sufficiently explicit to justify his name being associated with the approach that we are studying in this part.

The world is seen, instead, as a place of "soul-making" in which free beings, grappling with the tasks and challenges of their existence in a common environment, may become "children of God" and "heirs of eternal life."

Hick, J., *Evil and the God of Love*, 1978.

The Problem of Evil Section Review

You should be familiar with the following terms and concepts

Theodicy
The Classical Argument of Evil
World Solution to the Problem of Evil
Maya
Dualism
Augustine's Definition of Evil
Moral Evil
Natural Evil
Free Will Defense
Christian Theology
Irenaen Theodicy
Bios
Zoe
Soul-Making
Metaphysical Evil
Eternal Harmony
John Stuart Mill's Argument
Happiness in Relation to Good Deeds
Unhappiness in Relation to Evil Deeds

Multiple Choice Example:

Which is the best explanation of the Metaphysical Evil Theodicy?

A. Only God is prefect. He cannot create another perfect being because the concept of perfection includes not being created. God has done the best he can by creating what he has. Natural evil is a necessary result of any creation because creation by definition cannot be perfect.

B. Only God is perfect. He can create another perfect being like himself. God has done the best he can by creating what he has. Natural evil is a necessary result of any creation.

C. Only God is prefect. He cannot create another perfect being. God has done the best he can by creating what he has. Natural evil is a necessary result of any creation.

D. Only God is prefect. He cannot create another perfect being because the concept of perfection includes not being created. God has done the best he can by creating what he has. Natural evil is not a necessary result of any creation.

Part IV
The Philosophy of Knowledge

Part IV

The Philosophy of Knowledge

> *"This alone cannot be detached from me. I am; I exist; this alone is certain."*
>   - ***Rene Descartes***
>
> *"Let us suppose the mind to be, as we say, white paper, void of all characters, without any ideas."*
>   - ***John Locke***
>
> *"To exist is one thing, and to be perceived is another."*
>   - ***George Berkeley***
>
> *"All the objects of human reason or enquiry may naturally be divided into two kinds, which are, Relations of Ideas, and Matters of Fact."*
>   - ***David Hume***

Introduction

THE PHILOSOPHY OF KNOWLEDGE

The philosophy of knowledge is also referred to as Epistemology. This English word is derived from two Greek words, *episteme*, which means knowledge, and *logos* which means words or study. It is an inquiry into the nature of knowledge and the justification of our beliefs. The major questions epistemology deals with are: What do we really know? How can we be certain that what we know is really true? How do we know anything?

Descartes raises the interesting and perplexing question of how do you know that you are dreaming? Now, to the average person this question may sound ridiculous. But when we think about it more deeply, we begin to realize that Descartes is asking, "How do we know that what we consider to be reality, is not simply a dream?" Isn't it true that we only know for certain that we have been dreaming when we wake up from the dream? Do you ever really know that you are dreaming when you are dreaming? If this is true, then how can we be certain that everything we have been experiencing in our lives is not really a dream and that maybe when we die, or think we are dead, we simply wake up from this dream? How do we know for certain that there is an objective reality outside of our own minds? When you take the time to think about it deeply, you will find these questions are not so easy to answer.

John Locke, George Berkeley and David Hume take for granted that there is an objective reality outside of our minds, but they all differ on how we obtain knowledge. Locke argues that our minds are blank slates (*tablus rasa*) at birth and that experience writes upon it. Berkeley rejects Locke's common sense notion of a material world and argues that to be is to be perceived (*esse est percipi*). Hume argues that while we can have certain knowledge (relation of ideas), we cannot have certain knowledge in our experience of the world (matters of fact).

Whereas Descartes is called a *rationalist* because he believed that all truth can be known by the mind alone by inquiring within itself, Locke, Berkeley and Hume are called *empiricists* because they believed that the source of all knowledge is experience.

The Cave

Plato

For Plato, the world of the Ideal Forms is the world of real being. This is not to say that the world we live in is unreal, but rather it is the world of becoming. It is less real, not in the sense of being an illusion, but in the sense of not having those qualities of eternity and necessity, that are the marks of true reality, as are found the realm of the Ideal Forms.

The best illustration of Plato's two-world view is his parable called the Myth of the Cave. It is a parable about bringing people from the less real to the truly real. It asks us to seriously evaluate that which we assume to be reality and question whether or not the world we live in might not only be a shadow of some much greater reality beyond our normal everyday experiences. To discern this greater reality is the pursuit of the philosopher and her pursuit of wisdom.

Vocabulary:

Subterranean:	under the earth
Fettered:	chained
Chafe:	to irritate by rubbing
Habituation:	to accustom by frequent exposure or repetition
Phantasms:	fantasies
Emulate:	to imitate
Opine:	to think; suppose

Perpetual: continuous
Surmise: guess; conjecture
Authentic: real

Concepts:

True Reality:
False Reality:
The Good:

Questions:

1. *Explain Plato's idea of the cave.*
2. *What is the main point to this analogy?*
3. *How would the prisoners think of reality?*
4. *How would they react to the prisoner who escaped into the "real" world?*
5. *What is the idea of good?*

The Myth of the Cave

Next, said I, compare our nature in respect to education and its lack of such an experience as this. Picture men dwelling in a sort of subterranean cavern with a long entrance open to the light on its entire width. Conceive them as having their legs and necks fettered from childhood, so that they remain in the same spot, able to look forward only, and prevented by the fetters from turning their heads. Picture further the light from a fire burning higher up and at a distance behind them, and between the fire and the prisoners and above them a road along which a low wall has been built, as the exhibitors of puppet shows have partitions before the men themselves, above which they show the puppets.

All that I see, he said.

See also, then, men carrying past the wall implements of all kinds that rise above the wall, and human images and shapes of animals as well, wrought in stone and wood and every material, some of these bearers presumably speaking and others silent.

A strange image you speak of, he said, and strange prisoners.

Like to us, I said. For, to begin with, tell me do you think that these men would have seen anything of themselves or of one another except the shadows cast from the fire on the wall of the cave that fronted them?

How could they, he said, if they were compelled to hold their heads unmoved through life?

And again, would not the same be true of the objects carried past them?

Surely.

If then they were able to talk to one another, do you not think that they would suppose that in naming the things that they saw they were naming the passing objects?

Necessarily.

And if their prison had an echo from the wall opposite them, when one of the passers-by uttered a sound, do you think that they would suppose anything else than the passing shadow to be the speaker?

By Zeus, I do not, he said.

Then, in every way, such prisoners would deem reality to be nothing else than the shadows of the artificial objects.

Quite inevitably, he said.

Consider, then, what would be the manner of the release and healing from these bonds and this folly if in the course of nature something of this sort should happen to them. When one was freed from his fetters and compelled to stand up suddenly and turn his head around and walk and to lift up his eyes to the light, and in doing all this felt pain and, because of the dazzle and glitter of the light, was unable to discern the objects whose shadows he formerly saw, what do you suppose would be his answer if someone told him that what he had seen before was all a cheat and an illusion, but that now, being nearer to reality and turned toward more real things, he saw more truly? And if also one should point out to him each of the passing objects and constrain him by questions to say what it is, do you not think that he would be at a loss and that he would regard what he formerly saw as more real than the things new pointed out to him?

Far more real, he said.

And, if he were compelled to look at the light itself, with the pain in his eyes, would he not turn away and flee to those things which he is able to discern and regard them as in every deed more clear and exact than the objects pointed out?

It is so, he said.

And if, said I, someone should drag him thence by force up the ascent which is rough and steep, and not let him go before he had drawn him out into the light of the sun, do you think that he would find it painful to be so haled along, and would chafe at it, and when he came into the light, that his eyes would be filled with its beams so that he would not be able to see even one of the things that we call real?

Why, no, not immediately, he said.

Then there would be need of habituation, I take it, to enable him to see the things higher up. And at first he would most easily discern the shadows and, after that, the likenesses or reflections in water of men and other things, and later, the things themselves, and from these he would go on to contemplate the appearances in the heavens itself, more easily by night, looking at the light of the stars and the moon, then by day the sun and the sun's light.

Of course.

And so, finally, I suppose, he would be able to look upon the sun itself and see its nature, not by reflections in water or phantasms of it in an alien setting, but in and by itself in its own place.

Necessarily, he said.

And at this point he would infer and conclude that thus it is that provides the seasons and the courses of the year and presides over all things in the visible region, and is in some sort the cause of all these things that they had seen. Obviously, he said, that would be the next step.

Well then, if he recalled to mind his first habitation and what passed for wisdom there, and his fellow bondsmen, do you not think that he would count himself happy in the change and pity them?

He would indeed.

And if there had been honors and commendations among them which they bestowed on one another and prizes for the man who is quickest to make out the shadows as they pass and best able to remember their customary precedences, sequences, and coexistences, and so most successful in guessing at what was to come, do you think he would be very keen about such rewards, and that he would envy and emulate those who were honored by these prisoners and lorded it among them, or that he would feel with Homer and greatly prefer while living on earth to be a serf of another, a landless man, and endure anything rather than opine with them and live that life?

Yes, he said, I think that he would choose to endure anything rather than such a life.

And consider this also, said I. If such a one should go down again and take his old place would he not get his eyes full of darkness, thus suddenly coming out of the sunlight?

He would indeed.

Now if he should be required to contend with these perpetual prisoners in "evaluating" these shadows while his vision was still dim and before his eyes were accustomed to the dark – and this time required for habituation would not be very short – would he not provoke laughter, and would it not be said of him that he returned from his journey aloft with his eyes ruined and that it was not worth while even to attempt the ascent? And if it were possible to lay hands on and to kill the man who tried to release them and lead them up, would they not kill him?

They certainly would, he said.

This image then, dear Glaucon, we must apply as a whole to all that has been said, likening the region revealed through sight to the habitation of the prison, and the light of the fire in it to the power of the sun. And if you assume that the ascent and the contemplation of the things above is the soul's ascension to the intelligible region, you will not miss my surmise, since that is what you desire to hear. But God knows whether it is true. But, at any rate, my dream, as it appears to me, is that in the region of the known, the last thing to be seen and hardly seen is the idea of good, and when seen it must point us to the conclusion that this is indeed, the cause for all things of all that is, right and beautiful, giving birth in the visible world to light, and the author of light and itself in the intelligible world being the authentic source of truth and reason, and that anyone who is to act wisely in private or public must have caught sight of this.

From Plato, *The Republic*, trans. Paul Shorey, 1930.

Cogito Ergo Sum

RENE DESCARTES (1596-1650)

Rene Descartes is recognized as the first great philosopher of the modern age. He was born in a small town in Touraine, France, and educated by the Jesuits. Descartes' primary interest throughout his life was with methodology, justification and certainty. His first work was entitled *Discourse on Method* (1637). In it he sought to establish the proper procedures by which a question could be investigated while avoiding the dangers of error and confusion.

In additions to his philosophical writings, he also wrote on mathematics. Linking geometry to algebra, he invented the Cartesian coordinate system and analytic geometry. In discovering that geometrical representations could be represented algebraically, Descartes opened the door to the possibility of representing the whole of nature mathematically.

His most famous work was entitled *Meditations on First Philosophy* (1641) which our present reading is from. This work was immediately recognized as a formidable challenge to the established philosophy and science of his time. Descartes challenged the foundation of knowledge. He argued that it should not be based upon accepted authority, but rather upon one's own rational intuitions. This signaled the beginning of the "modern" age of philosophy. Descartes was in pursuit of certain knowledge, that which could not be doubted. He employed the method of doubt to find that which he could not possible doubt. His conclusion is summed up in his famous phrase, "cogito ergo sum," which means "I think, therefore, I am." Descartes argued that when he thinks about the fact that he is thinking, he cannot be deceived.

Vocabulary:

Subsequently:	coming after
Prudence:	good judgment
Demented:	mentally impaired
Sirens:	any of several sea nymphs, represented as part bird and part woman, who lure sailors to their death on rocky coasts by seductive singing
Satyrs:	any of a class of minor woodland deities, usually represented as having pointed ears, short horns, the head and body of a man, and the legs of a goat and as being fond of riotous merriment.
Corporeal:	physical
Indubitable:	cannot be doubted, unquestionable
Fictitious:	not real, made up
Perpetually:	continually
Frivolity:	silliness
Patently:	clearly
Credulity:	gullibility
Intimacy:	closeness
Prejudice:	forming an opinion before the facts are fully known
Arduous:	difficult
Inextricable:	very complicated
Imprudently:	unwisely
Subtleties:	fine distinctions
Insubstantial:	not substantial, unimportant
Malicious:	intentionally harmful, mean
Feign:	to imagine, to make up

Concepts:

The Method of Doubt:

"Cogito Ergo Sum"

Innate Ideas:

Questions:

1. *What is Descartes in search of?*
2. *What method does he employ to achieve his goal?*
3. *Why does he doubt his beliefs?*
4. *Why does he doubt his senses?*
5. *Why does he posit the idea of an evil genius?*
6. *What is it that Descartes believes he can know with absolute certainty?*

MEDITATION ONE: CONCERNING THOSE THINGS THAT CAN BE CALLED INTO DOUBT

SEVERAL YEARS HAVE NOW PASSED since I first realized how many were the false opinions that in my youth I took to be true, and thus how doubtful were all the things that I subsequently built upon these opinions. From the time I became aware of this, I realized that for once I had to raze everything in my life, down to the very bottom, so as to begin again from the first foundations, if I wanted to establish anything firm and lasting in the sciences. But the task seemed so enormous that I waited for a point in my life that was so ripe that no more suitable a time for laying hold of these disciplines would come to pass. For this reason, I have delayed so long that I would be at fault were I to waste on deliberation the time that is left for action. Therefore, now that I have liberated my mind from all cares, and I have secured for myself some leisurely and carefree time, I withdraw in solitude. I will, in short, apply myself

181

earnestly and openly to the general destruction of my former opinions.

Yet, to this end it, will not be necessary that I show that all my opinions are false, which perhaps I could never accomplish anyway. But because reason now persuades me that I should withhold my assent no less carefully from things which are not plainly certain and indubitable than I would to what is patently false, it will be sufficient justification for rejecting them all, if I find a reason for doubting even the least of them. Nor, therefore, need one survey each opinion one after the other, a task of endless proportion. Rather — because undermining the foundations will cause whatever has been built upon them to fall down of its own accord — I will at once attack those principles which supported everything that I once believed.

Whatever I had admitted until now as most true I took in either from the senses or through the senses; however, I noticed that they sometimes deceived me. And it is a mark of prudence never to trust wholly in those things which have once deceived us.

But perhaps, although the senses sometimes deceive us when it is a question of very small and distant things, still there are many other matters which one certainly cannot doubt, although they are derived from the very same senses: that I am sitting here before the fireplace wearing my dressing gown: that I feel this sheet of paper in my hands, and so on. But how could one deny that these hands and that my whole body exist? Unless perhaps I should compare myself to insane people whose brains are so impaired by a stubborn vapor from a black bile that they continually insist that they are kings when they are in utter poverty, or that they are wearing purple robes when they are naked, or that they have a head made of clay, or that they are gourds, or that they are made of glass. But they are all demented, and I would appear no less demented if I were to take their conduct as a model for myself.

All of this would be well and good, were I not a man who is accustomed to sleeping at night, and to undergo in my sleep the very same things — or now and then even less likely ones — as do these insane people when they are awake. How often has my evening slumber persuaded me of such customary things as these: that I am here, clothed in my dressing gown, seated at the fireplace, when in fact I am lying undressed between the blankets! But right now I certainly am gazing upon this piece of paper with eyes wide awake. This head which I am moving is not heavy with sleep. I extend this hand consciously and deliberately and I feel it. These things would not be so distinct for one who is asleep. But this all seems as if I do not recall having been deceived by similar thoughts on other occasions in my dreams. As I consider these cases more intently, I see so plainly that there are no definite signs to distinguish being awake from being asleep that I am quite astonished, and this astonishment almost convinces me that I am sleeping.

Let us say, then, for the sake of argument, that we are sleeping and that such particulars as these are not true: that we open our eyes; move our heads; extend our hands. Perhaps we do not even have these hands, or any such body at all. Nevertheless, it really must be admitted that things seen in sleep are, as it were, like painted images, which could have been produced only in the likeness of true things. Therefore, at least these general things (eyes, head, hands, the whole body) are not imaginary things, but are true and exist. For, indeed, when painters wish to represent sirens and satyrs by means of bizarre and unusual forms, they surely cannot ascribe utterly new natures to these creatures. Rather, they simply intermingle the members of various animals. And even if they concoct something so utterly novel that its likes have never

been seen before (being utterly fictitious and false), certainly at the very minimum the colors from which the painters compose the things ought to be true. And for the same reason, although even these general things (eyes, head, hands, and the like) can be imaginary, still one must necessarily admit that at least other things that are even more simple and universal are true, from which, as from true colors, all these things — be they true or false — which in our thoughts are images of things, are constructed.

To this class seems to belong corporeal nature in general, together with its extension; likewise the shape of extended things, their quantity or size, their number; as well as the place where they exist, the time of their duration, and other such things.

Hence, perhaps we do not conclude improperly that physics, astronomy, medicine, and all the other disciplines that are dependent upon the consideration of composite things are all doubtful. But arithmetic, geometry, and other such disciplines — which deal of nothing but the simplest and most general things and which are indifferent as to whether these composite things do or do not exist — contain something certain and indubitable. For whether I be awake or asleep, two plus three makes five, and a square does not have more than four sides; nor does it seem possible that such obvious truths can fall under the suspicion of falsity.

All the same, a certain opinion of long standing has been fixed in my mind, namely that there exists a God who is able to do anything and by whom I, such as I am, have been created. How do I know that he did not bring it about that there be no earth at all, no heavens, no extended thing, no figure, no size, no place, and yet all these things should seem to me to exist precisely as they appear to do now? Moreover — for I judge that others sometimes make mistakes in matters that they believe they know most perfectly — how do I know that I am not deceived every time I add two and three, or count the sides of a square or perform an even simpler operation, if such can be imagined? But perhaps God has not willed that I be thus deceived, for it is said that he is good in the highest degree. Nonetheless, if it were repugnant to his goodness that he should have created me such that I be deceived all the time, it would seem, from this same consideration, to be foreign to him to permit me to be deceived occasionally. But we cannot make this last assertion.

Perhaps there are some who would rather deny such a powerful God, then believe that all other matters are uncertain. Let us not put these people off just yet; rather, let us grant that everything said here about God is fictitious. Now they suppose that I came to be what I am either by fate or by chance or by a continuous series of events or by some other way. But because being deceived and being mistaken seem to be imperfections, the less powerful they take the author of my being to be, the more probable it will be that I would be so imperfect as to be deceived perpetually. I have nothing to say in response to these arguments. At length I am forced to admit that there is nothing, among the things I once believed to be true, which it is not permissible to doubt — not for reasons of frivolity or a lack of forethought, but because of valid and considered arguments. Thus, I must carefully withhold assent no less from these things than from the patently false, if I wish to find anything certain.

But it is not enough simply to have made a note of this; I must take care to keep it before my mind. For long-standing opinions keep coming back again and again, almost against my will; they seize upon my credulity, as if it were bound over to them by long use and the claims of intimacy. Nor will I get out of the habit of assenting to them and believing in them, so long as I take them to be exactly what they are, namely, in some respects doubtful as by now is obvious, but nevertheless highly probable, so that it is much more consonant with reason to believe them than to deny them. Hence, it seems to me, I would do well to turn my will in the opposite direction, to deceive myself and pretend for a considerable period that they are wholly false and imaginary, until finally, as if with equal weight of prejudice on both sides, no bad habit should turn my judgment from the correct perception of things. For indeed I know that no danger or error will follow and that it is impossible for me to indulge in too much distrust, since I now am concentrating only on knowledge, not on action.

Thus, I will suppose not a supremely good God, the source of truth, but rather an evil genius, as clever and deceitful as he is powerful, who has directed his entire effort to misleading me. I will regard the heavens, the air, the earth, colors, shapes, sounds, and all external things as nothing but the deceptive games of my dreams, with which he lays snares for my credulity. I will regard myself as having no hands, no eyes, no flesh, no blood, no senses, but as nevertheless falsely believing that I possess all these things. I will remain resolutely fixed in this meditation, and, even if it be out of

my power to know anything true, certainly it is within my power to take care resolutely to withhold my assent to what is false, lest this deceiver, powerful and clever as he is, has an effect on me. But this undertaking is arduous, and laziness brings me back to my customary way of living. I am not unlike a prisoner who might enjoy an imaginary freedom in his sleep. When he later begins to suspect that he is sleeping, he fears being awakened and conspires slowly with these pleasant illusions. In just this way, I spontaneously fall back into my old beliefs, and dread being awakened, lest the toilsome wakefulness which follows upon a peaceful rest, have to be spent thence forward not in the light but among the inextricable shadows of the difficulties now brought forward.

MEDITATION TWO: CONCERNING THE NATURE OF THE HUMAN MIND: THAT THE MIND IS MORE KNOWN THAN THE BODY

Yesterday's meditation filled my mind with so many doubts that I can no longer forget about them—nor yet do I see how they are to be resolved. But, as if I had suddenly fallen into a deep whirlpool, I am so disturbed that I can neither touch my foot to the bottom, nor swim up to the top. Nevertheless, I will work my way up, and I will follow the same path I took yesterday, putting aside everything which admits of the least doubt, as if I had discovered it to be absolutely false. I will go forward until I know something certain — or, if nothing else, until I at least know for certain that nothing is certain. Archimedes sought only a firm and immovable point in order to move the entire earth from one place to another. Surely great things are to be hoped for if I am lucky enough to find at least one thing that is certain and indubitable.

Therefore, I will suppose that all I see is false. I will believe that none of those things that my deceitful memory brings before my eyes ever existed. I, thus, have no senses: body; shape; extension; movement; and place are all figments of my imagination. What then will count as true? Perhaps only this one thing: that nothing is certain.

But on what grounds do I know that there is nothing over and above all those which I have just reviewed, concerning which there is not even the least cause for doubt? Is there not a God (or whatever name I might call him) who instills these thoughts in me? But why should I think that, since perhaps I myself could be the author of these things?

Therefore, am I not at least something? But I have already denied that I have any senses and any body. Still, I hesitate; for what follows from that? Am I so tied to the body and to the senses that I cannot exist without them? But I have persuaded myself that there is nothing at all in the world: no heaven; no earth; no minds; no bodies. Is it not then true that I do not exist? But certainly I should exist, if I were to persuade myself of something. But there is a deceiver (I know not who he is) powerful and sly in the highest degree, who is always purposely deceiving me. Then there is no doubt that I exist, if he deceives me. And deceive me as he will, he can never bring it about that I am nothing so long as I shall think that I am something. Thus; it must be granted that, after weighing carefully and sufficiently everything, one must come to the considered judgment that the statement "I am, I exist" is necessarily true every time it is uttered by me or conceived in my mind.

But I do not yet understand well enough who I am — I, who now necessarily exists. And from this point on, I must take care lest I imprudently substitute something else in place of myself; and thus be mistaken even in that knowledge which I claim to be the most certain and evident of all. To this end, I shall meditate once more on what I once believed myself to be before having embarked upon these deliberations. For this reason, then, I will set aside whatever can be refuted even to a slight degree by the arguments brought forward, so that at length there shall remain precisely nothing but what is certain and unshaken.

What, therefore, did I formerly think I was? A man, of course. But what is a man? Might I not say a rational animal? No, because then one would have to inquire what an "animal" is and what "rational" means. And then from only one question we slide into many more difficult ones. Nor do I now have enough free time that I want to waste it on subtleties of this sort. But rather here I pay attention to what spontaneously and by my own nature came into my thought beforehand whenever I pondered what I was. Namely it occurred to me first that I have a face, hands, arms, and this entire mechanism of bodily members, the very same as are discerned in a corpse — which I referred to by the name "body." It also occurred to me that I eat, walk, feel and think; these actions I used to assign to the soul as their cause. But what this soul was I either did not think about or I imagined it was something terribly insubstantial — after the fashion of a wind, fire, or either — which has been poured into my coarser parts. I truly was not in doubt regarding the body;

rather I believed that I distinctly knew its nature, which, were I perhaps tempted to describe it such as I mentally conceived it, I would explain it thus: by "body," I understand all that is suitable for being bound by some shape; for being enclosed in some place, and thus for filling up space, so that it excludes every other body from that space; for being perceived by touch, sight, hearing, taste, or smell; for being moved in several ways, not surely by itself, but by whatever else that touches it. For I judged that the power of self-motion, and likewise of sensing or of thinking, in no way pertains to the nature of the body. Nonetheless, I used to marvel especially that such faculties were found in certain bodies.

But now what am I, when I suppose that some deceiver — omnipotent and, if I may be allowed to say it, malicious — takes all the pains he can in order to deceive me? Can I not affirm that I posses at least a small measure of all those traits which I already have said pertain to the nature of the body? I pay attention, I think, I deliberate — but nothing happens. I am wearied of repeating this in vain. But which of these am I to ascribe to the soul? How about eating or walking? These are surely nothing but illusions, because I do not have a body. How about sensing? Again, this also does not happen without a body, and I judge that I really did not sense those many things I seemed to have sensed in my dreams. How about thinking? Here I discover that thought is an attribute that really does not belong to me. This alone cannot be detached from me. I am; I exist; this is certain. But for how long? For as long as I think. Because perhaps it could also come to pass that if I should cease from all thinking I would then utterly cease to exist. I now admit nothing that is not necessarily true. I am, therefore, precisely only a thing that thinks; that is, a mind, or soul, or intellect, or reason — words the meaning of which I was ignorant before. Now, I am a true thing, and truly existing; but what kind of thing? I have said it already: a thing that thinks.

What then? I will set my imagination going to see if I am not something more. I am not that connection of members which is called the human body. Neither am I some subtle air infused into these members, not a wind, not a fire, not a vapor, not a breath — nothing that I imagine to myself, for I have supposed all these to be nothing. The assertion stands: the fact still remains that I am something. But perhaps it is the case that nevertheless, these very things which take to be nothing (because I am ignorant of them) in reality do not differ from that self

which I know. This I do not know. I shall not quarrel about it right now; I can make a judgment only regarding things which are known to me. I know that I exist; I ask now who is this "I" whom I know. Most certainly the knowledge of this matter, thus precisely understood, does not depend upon things that I do not yet know to exist. Therefore, it is not dependent upon any of those things that I feign in my imagination. But this word "feign" warns me of my error. For I would be feigning if I should "imagine" that I am something, because imagining is merely the contemplation of the shape or image of a corporeal thing. But I know now with certainty that I am, and at the same time it could happen that all these images — and, generally, everything that pertains to the nature of the body — are nothing but dreams. When these things are taken into account, I would speak no less foolishly were I to say: "I will imagine so that I might recognize more distinctly who I am," than were I to say: "Now I surely am awake, and I see something true, but because I do not yet see it with sufficient evidence, I will take the trouble of going to sleep so that my dreams might show this to me more truly and more evidently." Thus I know that none of what I can comprehend by means of the imagination pertains to this understanding that I have of myself. Moreover, I know that I must be most diligent about withdrawing my mind from these things so that it can perceive its nature as distinctly as possible.

But what then am I? A thing that thinks. What is that? A thing that doubts, understands, affirms, denies, wills, refuses, and which also imagines and knows.

Reprinted from *Descartes' Meditations on First Philosophy*, trans. Donald A. Cress, 1931.

Blank Slate

JOHN LOCKE (1632-1704)

Considered the greatest English philosopher of the modern period, John Locke was educated at Oxford University where he studied the classics, philosophy, and medicine. Locke wrote on a wide variety of subjects. His work *Two Treatises on Government* (1989) greatly influenced the founding fathers of the United States. His *Essay Concerning Human Understanding* (1689), where our reading comes from, is considered a classic in the theory of knowledge. It is the first systematic assault on Cartesian rationalism.

Locke argued that our knowledge must be derived from experience. He was an empiricist. Although he rejected Descartes' rationalism and his notion that we are born with innate ideas, Locke does believe that we have intuitive knowledge of our own existence and that God's existence can be demonstrated by reason.

According to Locke, our minds are a *tabula rasa*, or blank slate, at birth. It is like a blank computer screen, devoid of characters until it receives sense perceptions. All knowledge begins with sensory experience. The powers of the mind then operate upon this experience developing complex ideas from simpler ones. Contrary to the rationalist's claim of absolute knowledge, Locke held that, apart from the knowledge of the self, we know in degrees of certainty derived from inductive generalizations.

Vocabulary:

Innate:	to be born with
Koinai Ennoiai:	common thoughts
Speculative:	thoughtful

Maxims:	intentions
Apprehension:	mental understanding
Fancy:	imagination
Perpetually:	continuous
Solidity:	solid
Extension:	spread out, stretched out
Figure:	shape of an object
Corpuscles:	very small particles

Concepts:

Innate Principles:

Tabula Rasa:

Objects of Sensations:

Objects of Reflection:

Primary Qualities:

Secondary Qualities:

Abstraction:

Questions:

1. *What are Locke's arguments against Descartes' innate ideas?*
2. *According to Locke, where does our knowledge come from?*
3. *What are the differences between a sensation and a reflection?*
4. *How does Locke define "idea?"*
5. *What is the difference between primary and secondary qualities?*
6. *How does Locke define "abstraction?"*

BOOK I

Chapter I

1. It is an established opinion among some men, that there are in the understanding certain *innate principles*; some primary notions, *koinai ennoiai*, characters, as it were stamped upon the mind of man; which the soul receives in its very first being, and brings into the world with it. It would be sufficient to convince unprejudiced readers of the falseness of this supposition, if I should only show (as I hope I shall in the following parts of this Discourse) how men, barely by the use of their natural faculties, may attain to all the knowledge they have, without the help of any innate impressions; and may arrive at certainty, without any such original notions or principles. For I imagine anyone will easily grant that it would be impertinent to suppose the ideas of color innate in a creature to whom God hath given sight, and a power to receive them by the eyes from external objects: and no less unreasonable would it be to attribute several truths to the impressions of nature, and innate characters, when we may observe in ourselves faculties fit to attain as easy and certain knowledge of them as if they were originally imprinted on the mind.

But because a man is not permitted without censure to follow his own thoughts in the search of truth, when they lead him ever so little out of the common road, I shall set down the reasons that made me doubt of the truth of that opinion, as an excuse for my mistake, if I be in one; which I leave to be considered by those who, with me, dispose themselves to embrace truth wherever they find it.

2. There is nothing more commonly taken for granted than that there are certain *principles*, both *speculative* and *practical* (for they speak of both), universally agreed upon by all mankind: which, therefore, they argue, must needs be the constant impressions which the souls of men receive in their first beings, and which they bring into the world with them, as necessarily and really as they do any of their inherent faculties.

3. This argument, drawn from universal consent, has this misfortune in it, that if it were true in matter of fact, that there were certain truths wherein all mankind agreed, it would not prove them innate, if there can be any other way shown how men may come to that universal agreement, in the things they do consent in, which I presume may be done.

4. But, which is worse, this argument of universal consent, which is made use of to prove innate principles, seems to

me a demonstration that there are none such because there are none to which all mankind give an universal assent. I shall begin with the speculative, and instance in those magnified principles of demonstration, "Whatsoever, is, is," and "It is impossible for the same thing to be and not to be;" which, of all others, I think have the most allowed title to innate. These have so settled a reputation of maxims universally received, that it will no doubt be thought strange if any one should seem to question it. But yet I take liberty to say, that these propositions are so far from having an universal assent, that there are a great part of mankind to whom they are not so much as known.

5. For, first, it is evident, that all children and idiots have not the least apprehension or thought of them. And the want of that is enough to destroy that universal assent which must needs be the necessary concomitant of all innate truths: it seeming to me near a contradiction to say, that there are truths imprinted on the soul, which it perceives or understands not: imprinting, if it signify anything, being nothing else but the making of certain truths to be perceived. For to imprint anything on the mind without the mind's perceiving it, seems to me hardly intelligible. If, therefore, children and idiots have souls, have minds, with those impressions upon them, *they* must unavoidably perceive them, and necessarily know and assent to these truths; which since they do not, it is evident that there are no such impressions. For if they are not notions naturally imprinted, how can they be innate? And if they are notions imprinted, how can they be unknown? To say a notion is imprinted on the mind, and yet at the same time to say that the mind is ignorant of it, and never yet took notice of it, is to make this impression nothing. No proposition can be said to be in the mind which it never yet knew, which it was never yet conscious of. For if any one may, then, by the same reason, all propositions that are true, and the mind is capable ever of assenting to, may be said to be in the mind, and to be imprinted: since, if any one can be said to be in the mind, which it never yet knew, it must be only because it is capable of knowing it; and so the mind is of all truths it ever shall know. No, thus truths may be imprinted on the mind which it never did, nor ever shall know; for a man may live long, and die at last in ignorance of many truths which his mind was capable of knowing, and that with certainty. So that if the capacity of knowing be the natural impression contended for, all the truths a man ever comes to know will, by this account, be every one of them innate; and this great point

will amount to no more, but only to a very improper way of speaking; which, whilst it pretends to assert the contrary, says nothing different from those who deny innate principles. For nobody, I think, ever denied that the mind was capable of knowing several truths. The capacity, they say, is innate; the knowledge acquired. But then to what end such contest for certain innate maxims? If truths can be imprinted on the understanding without being perceived, I can see no difference there can be between any truths the mind is *capable* of knowing in respect of their original: they must all be innate or all adventitious: in vain shall a man go about to distinguish them. He, therefore, that talks of innate notions in the understanding, cannot (if he intend thereby any distinct sort of truths) mean such truths to be in the understanding as it never perceived, and is yet wholly ignorant of. For if these words "to be in the understanding" have any propriety, they signify to be understood. So that to be in the understanding, and not to be understood; to be in the mind and never to be perceived, is all one as to say anything is and is not in the mind or understanding. If, therefore, these two propositions, "Whatsoever is, is," and "It is impossible for the same thing to be and not to be," are by nature imprinted, children cannot be ignorant of them: infants,

and all that have souls, must necessarily have them in their understandings, know the truth of them, and assent to it...

BOOK II

Chapter I

1. Every man being conscious to himself that he thinks and that which his mind is applied about while thinking being the *ideas* that are there, it is past doubt that men have in their minds several ideas, — such as are those expressed by the words *whiteness, hardness, sweetness, thinking, motion, man, elephant, army, drunkenness*, and others: it is in the first place then to be inquired, *How he comes by them?*

I know it is a received doctrine, that men have native ideas, and original characters, stamped upon their minds in their very first being. This opinion I have at large, examined already; and, I suppose what I have said in the foregoing book will be much more easily admitted, when I have shown whence the understanding may get all the ideas it has; and by what ways and degrees they may come into the mind; — for which I shall appeal to everyone's own observation and experience.

2. Let us then suppose the mind to be, as we say, white paper, void of all characters, without any ideas: — How comes it to be furnished? Whence comes it by that vast store which the busy and boundless fancy of man has painted on it with an almost endless variety? Whence has it all the *materials* of reason and knowledge? To this I answer, in one word, from EXPERIENCE. In that all our knowledge is founded; and from that it ultimately derives itself. Our observation employed either, about external sensible objects, or about the internal operations of our minds perceived and reflected on by ourselves, is that which supplies our understandings with all the *materials* of thinking. These two are the fountains of knowledge, from whence all the ideas we have, or can naturally have, do spring.

3. First, our senses, conversant about particular sensible objects, do convey into the mind several distinct perceptions of things, according to those various ways where in those objects do affect them. And, thus, we come by those *ideas* we have of *yellow, white, heat, cold, soft, hard, bitter, sweet*, and all those which we call sensible qualities; which when I say the senses convey into the mind, I mean, they from external objects convey into the mind what produces there those perceptions. This great source of most of the ideas we have, depending wholly upon our senses, and derived by them to the understanding, I call SENSATION.

4. Secondly, the other fountain from which experience furnishes the understanding with ideas is, — the perception of the operations of our own mind within us, as it is employed about the ideas it has got; — which operations, when the soul comes to reflect on and consider, do furnish the understanding with another set of ideas, which could not be had from things without. And such are *perception, thinking, doubting, believing, reasoning, knowing, willing*, and all the different acting of our own minds; — which we, being conscious of, and observing in ourselves, do from these receive into our understandings as distinct ideas as we do from bodies affecting our senses. This source of ideas every man has wholly in himself, and though it be not sense, as having nothing to do with external objects, yet it is very like it, and might properly enough be called *internal sense*. But as I call the other Sensation, so I call this REFLECTION, the ideas it affords being such only as the mind gets by reflecting on its own operations within itself. By reflection then, in the following part of this discourse, I would be under-

stood to mean, that notice which the mind takes of its own operations, and the manner of them, by reason whereof there come to be ideas of these operations in the understanding. These two, I say, External material things, as the objects of SENSATION, and the operations of our own minds within, as the objects of REFLECTION, are to me the only originals from whence all our ideas take their beginnings. The term *operations* here I use in a large sense, as comprehending not barely the actions of the mind about its ideas, but some sort of passions arising sometimes from them, such as is the satisfaction or uneasiness arising from any thought.

5. The understanding seems to me not to have the least glimmering of any ideas which it doth not receive from one of these two. *External objects* furnish the mind with the ideas of sensible qualities, which are all those different perceptions they produce in us; and *the mind* furnishes the understanding with ideas of its own operations.

These, when we have taken a full survey of them, and their several modes, combinations, and relations, we shall find to contain all our whole stock of ideas; and that we have nothing in our minds which did not come in one of these two ways. Let anyone examine his own thoughts, and thoroughly search into his understanding; and then let him tell me, whether all the original ideas he has there, are any other than of the objects of his senses, or of the operations of his mind, considered as objects of his reflection. And how great a mass of knowledge so ever he imagines to be lodged there, he will, upon taking a strict view, see that he has not any idea in his mind but what one of these two have imprinted; — though perhaps, with infinite variety compounded and enlarged by the understanding, as we shall see hereafter.

6. He that attentively considers the state of a child, at his first coming into the world, will have little reason to think him stored with plenty of ideas, that are to be the matter of his future knowledge. It is by *degrees* he comes to be furnished with them. And though the ideas of obvious and familiar qualities imprint themselves before the memory begins to keep a register of time or order, yet it is often so late before some unusual qualities come in the way, that there are few men that cannot recollect the beginning of their acquaintance with them. And if it were worth while, no doubt a child might be so ordered as to have but a very few, even of the ordinary ideas, till he were grown up to a man. But all that are born into the world, being surrounded with bodies that perpetually and diversely affect them,

variety of ideas, whether care be taken of it or not, are imprinted on the minds of children. Light and colors are busy at hand everywhere, when the eye is but open; sounds and some tangible qualities fail not to solicit their proper senses, and force an entrance to the mind; — but yet, I think, it will be granted easily, that if a child were kept in a place where he never saw any other but black and white till he were a man, he would have no more ideas of scarlet or green, than he that from his childhood never tasted an oyster, or a pineapple, has of those particular relishes....

Chapter VIII

8. Whatsoever the mind perceives *in itself*, or is the immediate object of perception, thought, or understanding, that I call *idea*; and the power to produce any idea in our mind, I call *quality* of the subject wherein that power is. Thus a snowball having the power to produce those ideas in us, as they are in the snowball, I call qualities; and as they are sensations or perceptions in our understandings, I call them ideas; which *ideas*, if I speak of sometimes as in the things themselves, I would be understood to mean those qualities in the objects which produce them in us.

9. Qualities thus considered in bodies are, *First*, such as are utterly inseparable from all body, in what state soever it be; and such as in all the alterations and changes it suffers, all the force can be used upon it, it constantly keeps; and such as sense constantly finds in every particle of matter which has bulk enough to be perceived; and the mind finds inseparable from every particle of matter, though less than to make itself singly be perceived by our senses: Take a grain of wheat, divide it into two parts; each part has still solidity, extension, figure, and mobility: divide it again, and it retains still the same qualities; and so divide it on, till the parts become insensible; they must retain still each of them all those qualities. For division (which is all that a mill, or pestle, or any other body, does upon another, in reducing it to insensible parts) can never take away either solidity, extension, figure, or mobility from any body, but only makes two or more distinct separate masses of matter, of that which was but one before; all which distinct masses reckoned as so many distinct bodies, after division, make a certain number.

These I call *original* or *primary qualities* of body, which I think we may observe to produce simple ideas in us,. solidity, extension, figure, motion or rest and number.

10. *Secondly*, such qualities

which, in truth, are nothing in the objects themselves but powers to produce various sensations in us by their primary qualities, i.e. by the bulk, figure, texture, and motion of their insensible parts, as colors, sounds, tastes, etc. These I call *secondary qualities*. To these might be added a *third* sort, which are allowed to be barely powers; though they are as much real qualities in the subject as those which I, to comply with the common way of speaking, call qualities, but for distinction, secondary qualities. For the power in fire to produce a new color, or consistency in *wax* or *clay* — by its primary qualities, is as much a quality in fire, as the power it has to produce in *me* a new idea or sensation of warmth or burning, which I felt not before, — by the same primary qualities, the bulk, texture, and motion of its insensible parts....

13. ...let us suppose at present that the different motions and figures, bulk and number, of such particles, affecting the several organs of our senses, produce in us those different sensations which we have from the colors and smells of bodies; that a violet, by the impulse of such insensible particles of matter, of peculiar figures and bulks, and in different degrees and modifications of their motions, causes the ideas of the blue color, and sweet scent of that flower to be produced in our minds. It being no more impossible to conceive that God should annex such ideas to such motions, with which they have no similitude, than that he should annex the idea of pain to the motion of a piece of steel dividing our flesh, with which that idea hath no resemblance.

14. What I have said concerning colors and smells may be understood also of tastes and sounds, and other the like sensible qualities; which, whatever reality we by mistake attribute to them, are in truth nothing in the objects themselves, but powers to produce various sensations in us; and depend on those primary qualities, bulk, figure, texture, and motion of parts as I have said.

15. From whence I think it easy to draw this observation, — that the ideas of primary qualities of bodies are resemblances of them, and their patterns do really exist in the bodies themselves, but the ideas produced in us by these secondary qualities have no resemblance of them at all. There is nothing like our ideas, existing in the bodies themselves. They are, in the bodies we denominate from them, only a power to produce those sensations in us: and what is sweet, blue, or warm in idea, is but the certain bulk, figure, and motion of the insensible parts, in the bodies themselves, which we call so.

16. Flame is denominated hot and light; snow, white and cold; and manna, white and sweet, from the ideas they produce in us. Which qualities are commonly thought to be the same in those bodies that those ideas are in us, the one the perfect resemblance of the other, as they are in a mirror, and it would by most men be judged very extravagant if one should say otherwise. And yet he that will consider that the same fire that, at one distance produces in us the sensation of warmth, does, at a nearer approach, produce in us the far different sensation of pain, ought to bethink himself what reason he has to say — that this idea of warmth, which was produced in him by the fire, is *actually in the fire*; and his idea of pain, which the same fire produced in him the same way, is *not* in the fire. Why are whiteness and coldness in snow, and pain not, when it produces the one and the other idea in us; and can do neither, but yet the bulk, figure, number, and motion of its solid parts?

21. Ideas being thus distinguished and understood, we may be able to give an account how the same water, at the same time, may produce the idea of cold by one hand and of heat by the other: whereas it is impossible that the same water, if those ideas were really in it, should at the same time be both hot and cold. For, if we imagine *warmth*, as it is in our hands, to be nothing but a certain sort and degree of motion in the minute particles of our nerves or animal spirits, we may understand how it is possible that the same water may, at the same time, produce the sensations of heat in one hand and cold in the other; which yet *figure* never does, that never producing the idea of a square by one hand which has produced the idea of a globe by another. But if the sensation of heat and cold be nothing but the increase or diminution of the motion of the minute parts of our bodies, caused by the corpuscles of any other body, it is easy to be understood, that if that motion be greater in one hand than in the other; if a body be applied to the two hands, which has in its minute particles a greater motion than in those of one of the hands, and a less than in those of the other, it will increase the motion of the one hand and lessen it in the other; and so cause the different sensations of heat and cold that depend thereon....

When children have, by repeated sensations, got ideas fixed in their memories, they begin by degrees to learn the use of signs. And when they have got the skill to apply the organs of speech to the framing of articulate sounds, they begin to make use of words, to signify their ideas to others. These verbal signs they sometimes borrow from others, and sometimes make themselves, as one may observe among the new and unusual names children often give to things in the first use of language.

The use of words then begin to stand as outward marks of our internal ideas, and those ideas being taken from particular things, if every particular idea that we take in should have a distinct name, names must be endless. To prevent this, the mind makes the particular ideas received from particular objects to become general; which is done by considering them as they are in the mind such appearances, — separate from all other existences, and the circumstances of real existence, as time, place, or any other concomitant ideas. This is called ABSTRACTION, whereby ideas taken from particular beings become general representatives of all of the same kind; and their names generate names applicable to whatever exists conformable to such abstract ideas. Such precise, naked appearances in the mind, without considering how, whence, or with what others they came there, the understanding lays up (with names commonly annexed to them) as the standards to rank real existences into sorts, as they agree with these patterns, and to denominate them accordingly. Thus the same color being observed today in chalk or snow, which the mind yesterday received from milk, it considers that appearance alone, makes it a representative of all that kind; and having given it the name whiteness, it by that sound signifies the same quality where so ever to be imaged or met with; and thus universal, whether ideas or terms, are made....

From John Locke, *An Essay Concerning Human Understanding*, 1689.

To Be Is To Be Perceived

GEORGE BERKELEY (1685-1753)

Educated at Trinity College in Dublin, George Berkeley was an Irish philosopher and Anglican bishop. He traveled widely to both Yale and Harvard. Berkeley, California was named after him.

Berkeley is best known for his "philosophical idealism" or "immaterialist" doctrine. He held that the existence of sensible objects consists solely in their being perceived. His famous phrase is, "to be is to be perceived." His principle works are *A Treatise on the Principles of Knowledge* (1710) and *Three Dialogues between Hylas and Philonous* (1713), from which our present reading is taken. In this dialogue, Berkeley defends his idealistic position.

Hylas (from the Greek word for "matter") debates with Philonous (from the Greek "love of mind"). The interesting approach of Berkeley is that his idealism is not rationalistic, like Plato's traditional idealism. Berkeley assumes an empirical foundation. Although he agrees with Locke that all ideas originate in sense experience, he disagrees with Locke that primary and secondary qualities are different in nature. Berkeley holds that all we ever know is ideas. The only reality that exists is that which is perceived. To hold all of this ideal reality together, he posits a Divine mind who perceives all that exists.

Vocabulary:

Hylas:	from the Greek word for "matter"
Philonous:	from the Greek "love of mind"
Skeptical:	doubting; questioning

Paradoxes:	statements that seems contradictory, but may in fact not be
Repugnance:	extreme dislike
Peremptory:	cannot be denied, changed, delayed, opposed, etc.
Deducting:	taking away
Palate:	sense of taste
Tangible:	something that can be touched; having material properties
Subsistence:	existence; being
Vehement:	intense feeling or passion
Corporeal:	physical body; having a material nature
Obliges:	to compel
Indolence:	lazy; inactive; slow in developing;
Undulatory:	having a wave-like motion
Acute:	having a sharp point; keen or sharp of mind; severe
Accidents:	an attribute or quality that is not essential
Uncouth:	not known; strange; awkward
Substratum:	substance
Omnipresent:	present everywhere

Concepts:

"Esse Est Percipi":
Philosophical Idealism:
Berkeley's Proof for God's Existence:

Questions:

1. *According to Hylas, what is the most extravagant opinion that ever entered into the mind of man?*
2. *How does Hylas define sensible things?*
3. *Explain what Hylas means when he says that "to exist is one thing, and to be perceived is another"?*
4. *Explain how Hylas concludes that only sensations exist in our minds.*
5. *Explain how Hylas concludes that secondary and primary qualities have no existence without the mind.*
6. *Explain Berkeley's proof for the existence of God.*

Three Dialogues

HYLAS: YOU WERE REPRESENTED in last night's conversation as one who maintained the most extravagant opinion that ever entered into the mind of man, to wit, that there is no such thing as "material substance" in the world.

PHILONOUS: That there is no such thing as what philosophers call "material substance," I am seriously persuaded; but if I were made to see anything absurd or skeptical in this, I should then have the same reason to renounce this that I imagine I have now to reject the contrary opinion.

HYL.: What! Can anything be more fantastical, more repugnant to common sense or a more manifest piece of skepticism than to believe there is no such thing as matter?

PHIL.: Softly, good Hylas. What if it should prove that you, who hold there is, are, by virtue of that opinion, a greater skeptic and maintain more paradoxes and repugnances to common sense than I who believe no such thing?…

How comes it to pass then, Hylas, that you pronounce me a skeptic because I deny what you affirm, to wit, the existence of matter? Since, for aught you can tell, I am as peremptory in my denial as you in your affirmation.

HYL.: Hold, Philonous, I have been a little out in my definition; but every false step a man makes in discourse is not to be insisted on. I said, indeed, that a "skeptic" was one who doubted of everything, but I should have added: or who denies the reality and truth of things.

PHIL.: What things? Do you mean the principles and theorems of sciences? But these you know are universal intellectual notions, and consequently independent of matter; the denial therefore of this does not imply the denying them.

HYL.: I grant it. But are there no other things? What think you of distrusting the senses, of denying the real existence of sensible things or pretending to know nothing of them? Is not this sufficient to denominate a man a skeptic?

PHIL.: Shall we, therefore, examine which of us it is who denies the reality of sensible things or professes the greater ignorance of them, since, if I take you rightly, he is to be esteemed the greatest skeptic?

HYL.: That is what I desire.

PHIL.: What mean you by "sensible things?"

HYL.: Those things which are perceived by the senses. Can you imagine that I mean anything else?

PHIL.: Pardon me, Hylas, if I am desirous clearly to apprehend your notions, since this may much shorten our inquiry. Suffer me then to ask you this further question. Are those things only perceived by the senses which are perceived immediately? Or may those things properly be said to be "sensible" which are perceived immediately, or not without the intervention of others?

HYL.: I do not sufficiently understand you.

PHIL.: In reading a book, what I immediately perceive are the letters, but mediately, or by means of these, are suggested to my mind the notions of God, virtue, truth, etc. Now, that the letters are truly sensible things, or perceived by sense, there is no doubt; but I would like to know whether you take the things suggested by them to be so, too.

HYL.: No, certainly; it were absurd to think God or virtue sensible things, though they may be signified and suggested to the mind by the sensible marks with which they have an arbitrary connection.

PHIL.: It seems, then, that by "sensible things" you mean those only which can be perceived immediately by sense.

HYL.: Right.

PHIL.: Does it not follow from this that, though I see one part of the sky red, and another blue, and that my reason does, thence, evidently conclude there must be some cause of that diversity of colors, yet that cause cannot be said to be a sensible thing or perceived by the sense of seeing?

HYL.: It does.

PHIL.: In like manner, though, I hear a variety of sounds, yet I cannot be said to hear the causes of those sounds.

HYL.: You cannot.

PHIL.: And when by my touch I perceive a thing to be hot and heavy, I cannot say, with any truth or propriety, that I feel the cause of its heat or weight.

HYL.: To prevent any more questions of this kind, I tell you once for all that by "sensible things" I mean those only which are perceived by sense, and that in truth the senses perceive nothing which they do not perceive immediately, for they make no inferences. The deducing, therefore, of causes or occasions from effects and appearances, which alone are perceived by sense, entirely relates to reason.

PHIL.: This point then is agreed between us — that *sensible things are those only which are immediately perceived by sense*. You will further inform me whether we immediately perceive by sight anything besides light and colors and figures; or by hearing, anything but sounds; by the palate, anything besides tastes; by the smell, anything besides odors; or by the touch, more than tangible qualities.

HYL.: We do not.

PHIL.: It seems, therefore, that if you take away all sensible qualities, there remains nothing sensible?

HYL.: I grant it.

PHIL.: Sensible things, therefore, are nothing else but so many sensible qualities or combinations of sensible qualities?

HYL.: Nothing else.

PHIL.: Heat is then a sensible thing?

HYL.: Certainly.

PHIL.: Does the reality of sensible things consist in being perceived, or is it something distinct from their being perceived, and that bears no relation to the mind?

HYL.: To *exist* is one thing, and to be *perceived* is another.

PHIL.: I speak with regard to sensible things only; and of these I ask, whether by their real existence you mean a subsistence exterior to the mind and distinct from their being perceived?

HYL.: I mean a real absolute

being, distinct from and without any relation to their being perceived.

PHIL.: Heat, therefore, if it be allowed a real being, must exist without the mind?

HYL.: It must.

PHIL.: Tell me, Hylas, is this real existence equally compatible to all degrees of heat, which we perceive, or is there any reason why we should attribute it to some and deny it to others? And if there be, pray, let me know that reason.

HYL.: Whatever degree of heat we perceive by sense, we may be sure the same exists in the object that occasions it.

PHIL.: What! The greatest as well as the least?

HYL.: I tell you, the reason is plainly the same in respect of both: they are both perceived by sense; nay, the greater degree of heat is more sensibly perceived; and consequently, if there is any difference, we are more certain of its real existence than we can be of the reality of a lesser degree.

PHIL.: But is not the most vehement and intense degree of heat a very great pain?

HYL.: No one can deny it.

PHIL.: And is any unperceiving thing capable of pain or pleasure?

HYL.: No, certainly not.

PHIL.: Is your material substance a senseless being or a being endowed with sense and perception?

HYL.: It is senseless, without doubt.

PHIL.: It cannot, therefore, be the subject of pain?

HYL.: By no means.

PHIL.: Not, consequently, of the greatest heat perceived by sense, since you acknowledge this to be no small pain?

HYL.: I grant it.

PHIL.: What shall we say, then, of your external object: is it a material substance, or not?

HYL.: It is a material substance with the sensible qualities inhering in it.

PHIL.: How, then can a great heat exist in it, since you know it cannot exist in a material substance? I desire you would clear this point.

HYL.: Hold, Philonous, I fear I was out in yielding intense heat to be a pain. It should seem rather that pain is something distinct from heat, and the consequence or effect of it.

PHIL.: Upon putting your hand near the fire, do you perceive one simple uniform sensation or two distinct sensations?

HYL.: But one simple sensation.

PHIL.: Is not the heat immediately perceived?

HYL.: It is.

PHIL.: And the pain?

HYL.: True.

PHIL.: Seeing, therefore they are both immediately perceived at the same time, and the fire affects you only with one simple or uncompounded idea, it follows that this same simple idea is both the intense heat immediately perceived and the pain; and, consequently, that the intense heat, immediately perceived is nothing distinct from a particular sort of pain.

HYL.: It seems so.

PHIL.: Again, try in your thoughts, Hylas, if you can conceive a vehement sensation to be without pain or pleasure.

HYL.: I cannot.

PHIL.: Or can you frame to yourself an idea of sensible pain or pleasure, in general, abstracted from every particular idea of heat, cold, tastes, smells, etc.?

HYL.: I do not find that I can.

PHIL.: Does it not therefore, follow that sensible pain is nothing distinct from those sensations or ideas — in an intense degree?

HYL.: It is undeniable; and, to speak the truth, I begin to suspect a very great heat cannot exist but in a mind perceiving it.

PHIL.: What! Are you then in that skeptical state of suspense, between affirming and denying?

HYL.: I think I may be positive in the point. A very violent and painful heat cannot exist without the mind.

PHIL.: It has not, therefore, according to you, any real being?

HYL.: I have not denied there is any real heat in bodies. I only say there is no such thing as an intense real heat.

PHIL.: But did you not say before that all degrees of heat were equally real, or, if there was any difference, that the greater were undoubtedly more real than the lesser?

HYL.: True; but it was because I did not then consider the ground there is for distinguishing between them, which I now plainly see. And it is this: because intense heat is nothing else but a particular kind of painful sensation, and pain cannot exist but in a perceiving being, it follows that no intense heat can really exist in an unperceiving corporeal substance. But this is not reason why we should deny heat in an inferior degree to exist in such a substance.

PHIL.: But how shall we be able to discern those degrees of heat which exist only in the mind from those which exist without it?

HYL.: That is not a difficult matter. You know the least pain cannot exist unperceived; whatever, therefore, degree of heat is a pain, exists only in the mind. But as for all other degrees of heat nothing obliges us to think the same of them.

PHIL.: I think you granted before that no unperceiving being was capable of pleasure any more than of pain.

HYL.: I did.

PHIL.: And is not warmth, or a more gentle degree of heat than what causes uneasiness, a pleasure?

HYL.: So it seems.

PHIL.: Since, therefore, as well those degrees of heat that are not painful, as those that are, can exist only in a thinking substance, may we not conclude that external bodies are absolutely incapable of any degree of heat whatsoever?

HYL.: On second thought, I do not think it is so evident that warmth is a pleasure as that a great degree of heat is pain.

PHIL.: I do not pretend that warmth is as great a pleasure as heat is a pain. But if you grant it to be even a small pleasure, it serves to make good my conclusion.

HYL.: I could rather call it an "indolence." It seems to be nothing more than a privation of both pain and pleasure. And that such a quality or state as this may agree to an unthinking substance, I hope you will not deny.

PHIL.: If you are resolved to maintain that warmth, or a gentle degree of heat, is no pleasure, I know not how to convince you otherwise than by appealing to your own sense. But what think you of cold?

HYL.: The same that I do of heat. An intense degree of cold is a pain; for to feel a very great cold is to perceive a great uneasiness; it cannot, therefore, exist without the mind; but a lesser degree of cold may, as well as a lesser degree of heat.

PHIL.: Those bodies, therefore, upon whose application to our own we perceive a moderate degree of heat, must be concluded to have a moderate degree of heat or warmth in them; and those upon whose application we feel a like degree of cold must be thought to have cold in them.

HYL.: They must.

PHIL.: Can any doctrine be true that necessarily leads a man into an absurdity?

HYL.: Without doubt it cannot.

PHIL.: Is it not an absurdity to think that the same thing should be at the same time both cold and warm?

HYL.: It is.

PHIL.: Suppose now one of your hands is hot, and the other cold, and that they are both at once put into the same vessel of water, in an intermediate state, will not the water seem cold to one hand, and warm to the other?

HYL.: It will.

PHIL.: Ought we not, therefore, by your principles, to conclude it is really both cold and warm at the same time, that is, according to our own concession, to believe an absurdity?

HYL.: I confess it seems so.

PHIL.: Consequently, the principles themselves are false, since you have granted that no true principle leads to an absurdity.

HYL.: But, after all, can anything be more absurd than to say, *there is not heat in the fire*?

PHIL.: To make the point still clearer; tell me whether, in two cases exactly alike, we ought not to make the same judgment?

HYL.: We ought.

PHIL.: When a pin pricks your finger, does it not rend and divide the fibres of your flesh.

HYL.: It does.

PHIL.: And when a coal burns your finger, does it any more?

HYL.: It does not.

PHIL.: Since, therefore, you neither judge the sensation itself occasioned by the pin, nor anything like it to be in the pin, you should not, conformably to what you have now granted, judge the sensation occasioned by the fire, or anything like it, to be in the fire.

HYL.: Well, since it must be so, I am content to yield this point and acknowledge that heat and cold are only sensations existing in our minds. But there still remain qualities enough to secure the reality of external things.

PHIL.: But what will you say, Hylas, if it should appear that the case is the same with regard to all other sensible qualities, and that they can no more be supposed to exist without the mind than heat and cold?

HYL.: Then, indeed, you will have done something to the purpose; but this is what I despair of seeing proved.

PHIL.: Let us examine them in order. What think you of tastes — do they exist without the mind, or no?

HYL.: Can any man in his senses doubt whether sugar is sweet or wormwood bitter?

PHIL.: Inform me, Hylas. Is a sweet taste a particular kind of pleasure or pleasant sensation, or is it not?

HYL.: It is.

PHIL.: And is not bitterness some kind of uneasiness or pain?

HYL.: I grant it.

PHIL.: If therefore sugar and wormwood are unthinking corporeal substances existing without the mind, how can sweetness and bitterness, that is, pleasure and pain, agree to them?...

HYL.: I see it is to no purpose to hold out, so I give up the cause as to those mentioned qualities, though I profess it sounds oddly to say that sugar is not sweet.

PHIL.: But, for your further satisfaction, take this along with you: that which at other times seems sweet shall, to a distempered palate, appear bitter and nothing can be plainer than that diverse persons perceive different tastes in the same food, since that which one man delights in, another abhors. And how could this be if the taste was something really inherent in the food.

HYL.: I acknowledge I know not how.

PHIL.: In the next place, odors are to be considered. And with regard to these I would fain know whether what has been said of tastes does not exactly agree to them? Are there not so many pleasing or displeasing sensations?

HYL.: They are.

PHIL.: Can you then conceive it possible that they should exist in an unperceiving thing?

HYL.: I cannot.

PHIL.: Or can you imagine that filth and ordure affect those brute animals that feed on them out of choice with the same smells which we perceive in them?

HYL.: By no means.

PHIL.: May we not, therefore, conclude of smells, as of the other forementioned qualities, that they cannot exist in any but a perceiving substance or mind?

HYL.: I think so.

PHIL.: then as to sounds, what must we think of them, are they accidents really inherent in external bodies or not?

HYL.: That they inhere not in the sonorous bodies is plain from hence; because a bell struck in the exhausted receiver of an air-pump sends forth no sound. The air, therefore, must be thought the subject of sound.

PHIL.: What reason is there for that, Hylas?

HYL.: Because, when any motion is raised in the air, we perceive a sound greater or less, in proportion to the air's motion; but without some motion in the air we never hear any sound at all.

PHIL.: And granting that we never hear a sound but when some motion is produced in the air, yet I do not see how you can infer from thence that the sound itself is in the air.

HYL.: It is this very motion in the external air that produces in the mind the sensation of sound. For, striking on the drum of the ear, it causes a vibration which by the auditory nerves being communicated to the brain, the soul is thereupon affected with the sensation called "sound."

PHIL.: What! Is sound then a sensation?

HYL.: I tell you, as perceived by us it is a particular sensation in the mind.

PHIL.: And can any sensation exist without the mind?

HYL.: No, certainly.

PHIL.: How then can sound, being a sensation, exist in the air if by the "air" you mean a senseless substance existing without the mind?

HYL.: You must distinguish, Philonous, between sound as it is perceived by us, and as it is in itself; or (which is the same thing) between the sound we immediately perceive and that which exists without us. The former, indeed, is a particular kind of sensation, but the latter is merely a vibrative or undulatory motion in the air.

PHIL.: I thought I had already obviated that distinction by the answer I gave when you were applying it in a like case before. But, to say no more of that, are you sure then that sound is really nothing but motion?

HYL.: I am.

PHIL.: Whatever, therefore, agrees to real sound may with truth be attributed to motion?

HYL.: It may.

PHIL.: It is then good sense to speak of "motion" as of a thing that is *loud, sweet, acute,* or *grave.*

HYL.: I see you are resolved not to understand me. Is it not evident those accidents or modes belong only to sensible sound, or sound in the common acceptation of the word, but not to sound in the real and philosophic sense, which, as I just now told you, is nothing but a certain motion of the air?

PHIL.: It seems then there are two sorts of sound — the one vulgar, or that which is heard, the other philosophical and real?

HYL.: Even so.

PHIL.: And the latter consists in motion?

HYL.: I told you so before.

PHIL.: Tell me, Hylas, to which of the senses, think you, the idea of motion belongs? To the hearing?

HYL.: No, certainly; but to the sight and touch.

PHIL.: It should follow then that, according to you, real sounds may possibly be seen or *felt*, but never *heard*.

HYL.: Look you, Philonous, you may, if you please, make a jest of my opinion, but that will not alter the truth of things. I own, indeed, the inferences you draw me into sound something oddly, but common language, you know, is framed by, and for the use of, the vulgar. We must not, therefore, wonder if expressions adapted to exact philosophic notions seem uncouth and out of the way.

PHIL.: Is it come to that? I assure you I imagine myself to have gained no small point since you make so light of departing from common phrases and opinions, it being a main part of our inquiry to examine whose notions are widest of the common road and most repugnant to the general sense of the world. But can you think it on more than a philosophical paradox to say that "real sounds are never heard," and that the idea of them is obtained by some other sense? And is there nothing in this contrary to nature and the truth of things?

HYL.: To deal ingenuously, I do not like it. And, after the concessions already made, I had as well granted that sounds, too, have no real being without the mind..

I frankly own, Philonous, that it is in vain to stand out any longer. Colors, sounds, tastes, in a word, all those termed "secondary qualities," have certainly no existence without the mind. But, by this acknowledgment I must not be supposed to derogate anything from the reality of matter or external objects; seeing it is no more than several philosophers maintain, who nevertheless are the farthest imaginable from denying matter. For the clearer understanding of this you must know sensible qualities are by philosophers divided into "primary" and "secondary." The former are extension, figure, solidity, gravity, motion, and rest. And these they hold exist really in bodies. The latter are those above enumerated, or, briefly, all sensible qualities besides the primary, which they assert are only so many sensations or ideas existing nowhere but in the mind. But all this, I doubt not, you are already apprised of. For my part, I have been a long time sensible that there was such an opinion current among philosophers but was never thoroughly convinced of its truth till now.

PHIL.: You are still then of the opinion that *extension* and *figures* are inherent in external unthinking substances?

HYL.: I am

PHIL.: But what if the same arguments which are brought against secondary qualities will hold good against these also?

HYL.: Why, then, I shall be obliged to think they too exist only in the mind....

I acknowledge, Philonous, that,

upon a fair observation of what passes in my mind, I can discover nothing else but that I am a thinking being affected with a variety of sensations; neither is it possible to conceive how a sensation should exist in an unperceiving substance. But then, on the other hand, when I look on sensible things in a different view, considering them as so many modes and qualities, I find it necessary to suppose a material *substratum*, without which they cannot be conceived to exist.

PHIL.: "Material substratum" call you it? Pray, by which of your senses came you acquainted with that being?

HYL.: It is not itself sensible; its modes and qualities only being perceived by the senses.

PHIL.: I presume then it was by reflection and reason you obtained the idea of it?

HYL.: I do not pretend to any proper positive idea of it. However, I conclude it exists because qualities cannot be conceived to exist without a support.

PHIL.: It seems then you have only a relative notion of it, or that you conceive it not otherwise than by conceiving the relation it bears to sensible qualities?....

HYL.: Right.

PHIL.: Be pleased, therefore, to let me know wherein that relation consists.

HYL.: Is it not sufficiently expressed in the term "substratum" or "substance?"

PHIL.: If so, the word "substratum" should import that it is spread under the sensible qualities accidents?

HYL.: True.

PHIL.: And consequently under extension?

HYL.: I own it.

PHIL.: It is therefore somewhat in its own nature distinct from extension?

HYL.: I tell you extension is only a mode, and matter is something that supports modes. And is it not evident the thing supported is different from the thing supporting?

PHIL.: So that something distinct from, and exclusive of, extension is supposed to be the *substratum* of extension?

HYL.: Just so.

PHIL.: Answer me, Hylas, can a thing be spread without extension, or is not the idea of extension necessarily included in spreading?

HYL.: It is.

PHIL.: Whatsoever, therefore, you suppose spread under anything must have in itself an extension distinct from the extension of that thing under which it is spread?

HYL.: It must.

PHIL.: Consequently, every corporeal substance being the *substratum* of extension must have in itself another extension by which it is qualified to be a *substratum*, and so on to infinity? And I ask whether this be not absurd in itself and repugnant to what you granted just now, to wit, that the *substratum* was something distinct from and exclusive of extension?

HYL.: Aye, but, Philonous, you take me wrong. I do not mean that matter is *spread* in a gross literal sense under extension. The word "substratum" is used only to express in general the same thing with "substance."

PHIL.: Well then, let us examine the relation implied in the term "substance." Is it not that it stands under accidents?

HYL.: The very same.

PHIL.: But that one thing may stand under or support another, must it not be extended?

HYL.: It must.

PHIL.: Is not, therefore, this supposition liable to the same absurdity with the former?

HYL.: You still take things in a strict literal sense; that is not fair, Philonous.

PHIL.: I am not for imposing any sense on your words; you are at liberty to explain them as you please. Only, I beseech you, make me understand something by them. You tell me matter supports or stands under accidents. How? Is it as your legs support your body?

HYL.: No; that is the literal sense.

PHIL.: Pray let me know any sense, literal or not literal, that you understand it in. — How long must I wait for an answer, Hylas?

HYL.: I declare I know not what to say. I once thought I understood well enough what was meant by matter's supporting accidents. But now, the more I think on it, the less can I comprehend it; in short, I find that I know nothing of it.

PHIL.: It seems then you have no idea at all, neither relative nor positive, of matter? You know neither what it is in itself nor what relation it bears to accidents?

HYL.: I acknowledge it....

Other men may think as they please, but for your part you have nothing to reproach me with. My comfort is you are as much a skeptic as I am.

PHIL.: There, Hylas, I must beg leave to differ from you.

HYL.: What! Have you all along agreed to the premises, and do you now deny the conclusion and leave me to maintain those paradoxes by myself which you led me into? This surely is not fair.

PHIL.: I deny that I agreed with you in those notions that led to skepticism. You indeed said the *reality* of sensible things consisted in an *absolute existence* our of the minds of spirits, or distinct from their being perceived. And, pursuant to this notion of reality, you are obliged to deny sensible things any real existence; that is, according to your own definition, you profess yourself a skeptic. But I neither said nor thought the reality of sensible things was to be defined after that manner. To me it is evident, for the reasons you allow of, that sensible things cannot exist otherwise than in a mind or spirit. Whence I conclude, not that they have no real existence, but that, seeing they depend not on my thought and have an existence distinct from being perceived by me, *there must be some other mind wherein they exist.* As sure, therefore, as the sensible world really exists, so sure is there an infinite omnipresent Spirit, who contains and supports it.

HYL.: What! This is no more than I and all Christians hold; nay, and all others, too, who believe there is a God and that He knows and comprehends all things.

PHIL.: Aye, but here lies the difference. Men commonly believe that all things are known or perceived by God, because they believe the being of a God; whereas I, on the other side, immediately and necessarily conclude the being of a God, because all sensible things must be perceived by him.

HYL.: But so long as well all believe the same thing, what matter is it how we come by that belief?

PHIL.: But neither do we agree in the same opinion. For philosophers, though they acknowledge all corporeal beings to be perceived by God, yet they attribute to them an absolute subsistence distinct from their being perceived by any mind whatsoever which I do not. Besides, is there no difference between saying, *there is a God, therefore He perceives all things*, and saying, *sensible things do really exist; and if they really exist, they are necessarily perceived by an infinite mind: therefore, there is an infinite mind, or God*? This furnishes you with a direct and immediate demonstration, from a most evident principle, of the *being of a God*. Divines and philosophers had proved beyond all controversy, from the beauty and usefulness of the several parts of the creation, that it was the workmanship of God. But that — setting aside all help of astronomy and natural philosophy, all contemplation of the contrivance, order, and adjustment of things — an infinite mind should be necessarily inferred from the bare *existence* of the sensible world is an advantage peculiar to them only who have made this easy reflection, that the sensible world is that which we perceive by our several senses; and that nothing is perceived by the senses besides ideas; and that no idea or archetype of an idea can exist otherwise than in a mind.

From George Berkeley, *Three Dialogues Between Hylas and Philonous*, 1713.

Relations of Ideas and Matters of Fact

David Hume (1711-1776)

Like John Locke, Hume was an empiricist. He argued that the foundation of all our ideas was sensory experience. Hume thought that we can only have certain knowledge in the "relations of ideas." Examples of this certainty are analytic truth (the subject and the predicate are equal), tautologies, and mathematical truths. Regarding all other knowledge, which he termed "matters of fact," we can only obtain a high degree of probability. This type of knowledge is called synthetic truths (the predicate adds to the subject). As the consummate skeptic, Hume further argued that even the notion of probability is dubious because it is based upon the concept of cause and effect which is based upon an idea not an impression. One of Hume's most interesting ideas is his Empirical Criteria of Meaning which holds that all meaningful ideas must be traced back to an impression. If our ideas cannot be traced back to an impression, then they are meaningless.

Vocabulary:

Agitations:	disturbances
Sentiments:	feelings
Vivacity:	lively, spirited
Appellation:	an identifying name or title
Incongruous:	not harmonious
Transposing:	reversing in order or position
Augmenting:	increase in size or effect

Sublime:	exalted; noble; elevated or lofty in thought
Incumbent:	to develop or produce
Anatomize:	to examine in detail
Tincture:	a small amount
Propensity:	tendency

Concepts:

Relations of Ideas:

Matters of Fact:

Impressions:

Ideas:

Cause and Effect:

Analytic:

Synthetic:

Empirical Criteria of Meaning:

Questions:

1. *According to Hume, what is the difference between an impression and an idea?*
2. *Explain Hume's concept of the relations of ideas.*
3. *What level of certainty can we achieve in relations of ideas?*
4. *Explain Hume's concept of matters of fact.*
5. *What level of certainty can we achieve in matters of fact?*
6. *Explain Hume's concept of cause and effect.*

OF THE ORIGIN OF IDEAS

Everyone will readily allow that there is a considerable difference between the perceptions of the mind, when a man feels the pain of excessive heat, or the pleasure of moderate warmth, and when he afterwards recalls to his memory this sensation, or anticipates it by his imagination. These faculties may mimic or copy the perceptions of the senses; but they never can entirely reach the force and vivacity of the original sentiment. The utmost we say of them, even when they operate with greatest vigor, is, that they represent their object in so lively a manner, that we could almost say we feel or see it: But, except the mind be disordered by disease or madness, they never can arrive at such a pitch of vivacity, as to render these perceptions altogether undistinguishable. All the colors of poetry, however splendid, can never paint natural objects in such a manner as to make the description be taken for a real landscape. The most lively thought is still inferior to the dullest sensation.

We may observe a like distinction to run through all the other perceptions of the mind. A man in a fit of anger is actuated in a very different manner from one who only thinks of that emotion. If you tell me, that any person is in love, I easily understand your meaning, and form a just conception of his situation; but never can I mistake that conception for the real disorders and agitations of the passion. When we reflect on our past sentiments and affections, our thought is a faithful mirror, and copies its objects truly; but the colors which it employs are faint and dull, in comparison of those in which our original perceptions were clothed. It requires no nice discernment or metaphysical head to mark the distinction between them.

Here, therefore, we may divide all the perceptions of the mind into two classes or species, which are distinguished by their different degrees of force and vivacity. The less forcible and lively are commonly denominated Thoughts or Ideas. The other species want a name in our language, and in most others; I suppose, because it was not requisite for any, but philosophical purposes, to rank them under a general term or appellation. Let us, therefore, use a little freedom, and call them Impressions; employing that word in a sense somewhat different from the usual. By the term impression, then, I mean all our more lively perceptions, when we hear, or see, or feel, or love, or hate, or desire, or will. And impressions are distinguished from ideas, which are the less lively perceptions, of which we are conscious, when we reflect on any of those sensations or movements above mentioned.

Nothing, at first view, may seem more unbounded than the thought of man, which not only escapes all human power and authority, but is not even restrained within the limits of nature and reality. To form monsters, and joint incongruous shapes and appearances, costs the imagination no more trouble than to conceive the most natural and familiar objects. And while the body is confined to one planet, along which it creeps with pain and difficulty; the thought can in an instant transport us into the most distant regions of the universe; or even beyond the universe, into the unbounded chaos, where nature is supposed to lie in total confusion. What never was seen, or heard of, may yet be conceived; nor is anything beyond the power of thought, except what implies an absolute contradiction.

But though our thought seems to possess this unbounded liberty, we shall find, upon a nearer examination that it is really confined within very narrow limits, and that all this creative power of the mind amounts to no more than the faculty of compounding, transposing, augmenting, or diminishing the materials afforded us by the senses and experience. When we think of a golden mountain, we only join two consistent ideas, gold, and mountain, with which we were formerly acquainted. A virtuous horse we can conceive; because, from our own feeling, we can conceive virtue; and this we may unite to the figure and shape of a horse, which is an animal familiar to us. In short, all the materials of thinking are derived either from our outward or inward sentiment: the mixture and composition of these belongs alone to the mind and will. Or, to express myself in philosophical language, all our ideas or more feeble perceptions are copies of our impressions or more lively ones.

To prove this, the two following arguments will, I hope, be sufficient. First, when we analyze our thoughts or ideas, however compounded or sublime, we always find that they resolve themselves into such simple ideas as were copied from a precedent feeling or sentiment. Even those ideas, which, at first view, seem the widest of this origin, are found, upon a nearer scrutiny, to be derived from it. The idea of God, as meaning an infinitely intelligent, wise, and good Being, arises from reflecting on the operations of our own mind, and augmenting, without limit, those qualities of goodness and wisdom. We may prosecute this enquiry to what length we please; where we shall always find, that every idea which we examine is copied from a similar impression. Those who would assert that this position is not universally true nor without exception, have only one, and that an easy method of refuting it; by producing that idea, which, in their opinion, is not derived from this source. It will then be incumbent on us, if we would maintain our doctrine, to produce the impression, or lively perception, which corresponds to it.

Secondly, if it happens, from a defect of the organ, that a man is not susceptible of any species of sensation, we always find that he is as little susceptible of the correspondent ideas. A blind man can form no notion of colors; a deaf man of sounds. Restore either of them that sense in which he is deficient; by opening this new inlet for his sensations, you also open an inlet for the ideas; and he finds no difficulty in conceiving these objects....

Here, therefore, is a proposition, which not only seems, in itself, simple and intelligible; but, if a proper use were made of it, might render every dispute equally intelligible, and banish all that jargon, which has so long taken possession of metaphysical reasonings, and drawn disgrace upon them. All ideas, especially abstract ones, are naturally faint and obscure: the mind has but a slender hold of them: they are apt to be confounded with other resembling ideas; and

when we have often employed any term, though without a distinct meaning, we are apt to imagine it has a determinate idea annexed to it. On the contrary, all impressions, that is, all sensations, either outward or inward, are strong and determined. When we entertain, therefore, any suspicion that a philosophical term is employed without any meaning or idea (as is but too frequent), we need but enquire, from what impression is that supposed idea derived? And if it be impossible to assign any, this will serve to confirm our suspicion. By bringing ideas into so clear a light we may reasonably hope to remove all disputes, which may arise, concerning their nature and reality.

SKEPTICAL DOUBTS CONCERNING THE OPERATIONS OF THE UNDERSTANDING

Part I

All the objects of human reason or enquiry may naturally be divided into two kinds, which are Relations of Ideas, and Matters of Fact. Of the first kind are the sciences of Geometry, Algebra, and Arithmetic; and in short, every affirmation which is either intuitively or demonstratively certain. That the square of the hypotenuse is equal to the squares of the two sides is a proposition which expresses a relation between these figures. That three times five is equal to the half of thirty, expresses a relation between these numbers. Propositions of this kind are discoverable by the mere operation of thought, without dependence on what is anywhere existent in the universe. Though there never was a circle or triangle in nature, the truths demonstrated by Euclid would forever retain their certainty and evidence.

Matters of fact, which are the second objects of human reason, are not ascertained in the same manner; nor is our evidence of their truth, however great, of a like nature with the foregoing. The contrary of every matter of fact is still possible; because it can never imply a contradiction, and is conceived by the mind with the same facility and distinctness, as if ever so conformable to reality. That the sun will not rise tomorrow is no less intelligible a proposition, and implies no more contradiction than the affirmation, that it will rise. We should in vain, therefore, attempt to demonstrate its falsehood. Were it demonstratively false, it would imply a contradiction, and could never be distinctly conceived by the mind.

It may, therefore, be a subject worthy of curiosity, to enquire what is the nature of that evidence which assures us of any real existence and matters of fact, beyond the present testimony of our senses, or the records of our memory. This part of philosophy, it is observable, has been little cultivated, either by the ancients or moderns; and, therefore, our doubts and errors, in the prosecution of so important an enquiry, may be the more excusable; while we march through such difficult paths without any guide or direction. They may even prove useful, by exciting curiosity, and destroying that implicit faith and security, which is the bane of all reasoning and free enquiry. The discovery of defects in the common philosophy, if any such there be, will not, I presume, be a discouragement, but rather an incitement, as is usual, to attempt something more full and satisfactory than has yet been proposed to the public.

All reasonings concerning matters of fact seem to be founded on the relation of Cause and Effect. By means of that relation alone we can go beyond the evidence of our memory and senses. If you were to ask a man, why he believes any matter of fact, which is absent; for instance, that his friend is in the country, or in France; he would give you a reason; and this reason would be some other fact; as a letter received from him, or the knowledge of his former resolutions and promises. A man finding a watch or any other machine on a desert island would conclude that there had once been men on that island. All our reasonings concerning fact are of the same nature. And here it is between the present fact and that which is inferred from it. Were there nothing to bind them together, the inference would be entirely precarious. The hearing of an articulate voice and rational discourse in the dark assures us of the presence of some person: Why? Because they are the effects of the human make and fabric, and closely connected with it. If we anatomize all the other reasonings of this nature, we shall find that they are founded on the relation of cause and effect, and that this relation is either near or remote, direct or collateral. Heat and light are collateral effects of fire, and the one effect may justly be inferred from the other.

If we would satisfy ourselves, therefore, concerning the nature of that evidence, which assures us of matters of fact, we must enquire how we arrive at the knowledge of cause and effect....

This proposition, that causes and effects are discoverable, not by reason but by experience, will readily be admitted with regard to such objects, as we remember to have once been altogether unknown to us; since we must be conscious of the utter inability, which we then lay under, of foretelling what would arise from them. Present two smooth pieces of marble to a man who has no tincture of natural philosophy; he will never discover that they will adhere together in such a manner as to require great force to separate them in a direct line, while they make so small a resistance to a lateral pressure. Such events, as bear little analogy to the common course of nature, are also readily confessed to be known only by experience; nor does any man imagine that the explosion of gunpowder, or the attraction of a loadstone, could ever be discovered by arguments a priori. In like manner, when an effect is supposed to depend upon an intricate machinery or secret structure of parts, we make no difficulty in attributing all our knowledge of it to experience. Who will assert that he can give the ultimate reason, why milk or bread is proper nourishment for a man, not for a lion or a tiger?

But the same truth may not appear, at first sight, to have the same evidence with regard to events, which have become familiar to us from our first appearance in the world, which bear a close analogy to the whole course of nature, and which are supposed to depend on the simple qualities of objects, without any secret structure of parts. We are apt to imagine that we could discover these effects by the mere operation of our reason, without experience. We fancy, that were we brought all of a sudden into this world, we could at first have inferred that one billiard-ball would communicate motion to another upon impulse; and that we needed not to have waited for the event, in order to pronounce with certainty concerning it. Such is the influence of custom, that, where it is strongest, it not only covers our natural ignorance, but even conceals itself, and seems not to take place, merely because it is found in the highest degree.

But to convince us that all the laws of nature, and all the operations of bodies without exception, are known only by experience, the following reflections may, perhaps, suffice. Were any object presented to us, and were we required to pronounce concerning the effect, which will result from it, without consulting past observation; after what manner, I beseech you, must the mind proceed in this operation? It must invent or imagine some event, which it ascribes to the object as its effect; and it is plain that this invention must be entirely arbitrary. The mind can never possibly find the effect in the supposed cause, by the most accurate scrutiny and examination. For the effect is totally different from the cause, and con-

sequently can never be discovered in it. Motion in the second billiard-ball is a quite distinct event from motion in the first; nor is there anything in the one to suggest the smallest hint of the other. A stone or piece of metal raised into the air, and left without any support, immediately falls; but to consider the matter a priori, is there anything we discover in this situation which can beget the idea of a downward, rather than an upward, or any other motion, in the stone or metal?

And as the first imagination or invention of a particular effect, in all natural operations is arbitrary, where we consult not experience; so must we also esteem the supposed tie or connection between the cause and effect, which binds them together, and renders it impossible that any other effect could result from the operation of that cause. When I see, for instance, a billiard-ball moving in a straight line toward another; even suppose motion in the second ball should by accident be suggested to me, as the result of their contact or impulse; may I not conceive, that a hundred different events might as well follow from that cause? May not both these balls remain at absolute rest? May not the first ball return in a straight line, or leap off from the second in any line or direction? All these suppositions are consistent and conceivable. Why then should we give the preference to one, which is no more consistent or conceivable than the rest? All our reasonings a priori will never be able to show us any foundation for this preference.

In a word, then, every effect is a distinct event from its cause. It could not, therefore, be discovered in the cause, and the first invention or conception of it, a priori , must be entirely arbitrary. And even after it is suggested, the conjunction of it with the cause must appear equally arbitrary; since there are always many other effects, which, to reason, must seem fully as consistent and natural. In vain, therefore, should we pretend to determine any single event, or infer any cause of effect, without the assistance of observation and experience....

Part II

But we have not yet attained any tolerable satisfaction with regard to the question first proposed. Each solution still gives rise to a new question as difficult as the foregoing, and leads us on to further enquiries. When it is asked, what is the nature of all our reasonings concerning matter of fact? The proper answer seems to be, that they are founded on the relation of cause and effect.

When again it is asked, what is the foundation of all our reasonings and conclusions concerning that relation? It may be replied in one word, experience. But if we still carry on our sifting humor, and ask, what is the foundation of all conclusions from experience? This implies a new question, which may be of more difficult solution and explication. Philosophers, that give themselves airs of superior wisdom and sufficiency, have a hard task when they encounter persons of inquisitive dispositions, who push them from every corner to which they retreat, and who are sure at last to bring them to some dangerous dilemma. The best expedient to prevent this confusion is to be modest in our pretensions; and even to discover the difficulty ourselves before it is objected to us. By this means, we may make a kind of merit of our very ignorance.

I shall content myself, in this section, with an easy task, and shall pretend only to give a negative answer to the question here proposed. I say then, that, even after we have experience of the operations of cause and effect, our conclusions from that experience are not founded on reasoning, or any process of the understanding. This answer we must endeavor both to explain and to defend....

In reality, all arguments from

experience are founded on the similarity which we discover among natural objects, and by which we are induced to expect effects similar to those which we have found to follow from such objects. And though none but a fool or madman will ever pretend to dispute the authority of experience, or to reject that great guide of human life, it may surely be allowed a philosopher to have so much curiosity at least as to examine the principle of human nature, which gives this mighty authority to experience, and makes us draw advantage from that similarity which nature has placed among different objects. From causes which appear similar we expect similar effects. This is the sum of all our experimental conclusions. Now it seems evident that, if this conclusion were formed by reason, it would be as perfect at first, and upon one instance, as after ever so long a course of experience. But the case is far otherwise. Nothing so like as eggs; yet no one, on account of this appearing similarity, expects the same taste and relish in all of them. It is only after a long course of uniform experiments in any kind, that we attain a firm reliance and security with regard to a particular event. Now where is that process of reasoning which, from one instance, draws a conclusion, so different from that which it infers from a hundred instances that are no wise different from that single one? This question I propose as much for the sake of information, as with an intention of raising difficulties. I cannot find, I cannot imagine any such reasoning. But I keep my mind still open to instruction if anyone will vouchsafe to bestow it on me.

Should it be said that, from a number of uniform experiments, we infer a connection between the sensible qualities and the secret powers; this, I must confess, seems the same difficulty, couched in different terms. The question still recurs; on what process of argument this inference is founded? Where is the medium, the interposing ideas, which join propositions so very wide of each other? It is confessed that the color, consistence, and other sensible qualities of bread appear not, of themselves, to have any connection with the secret powers of nourishment and support. For otherwise we could infer these secret powers from the first appearance of these sensible qualities, without the aid of experience; contrary to the sentiment of all philosophers, and contrary to plain matter of fact. Here, then, is our natural state of ignorance with regard to the powers and influence of all objects. How is this remedied by experience? It only shows us a number of uniform effects, resulting from certain objects, and teaches us that those particular objects, at that particular time, were endowed with such powers and forces. When a new object, endowed with similar sensible qualities, is produced, we expect similar powers and forces, and look for a like effect. From a body of like color and consistence with bread we expect like nourishment and support. But this surely is a step or progress of the mind, which wants to be explained. When a man says, I have found, in all past instances, such sensible qualities conjoined with such secret powers: And when he says, Similar sensible qualities will always be conjoined with similar secret powers, he is not guilty of a tautology, nor are these propositions in any respect the same. You say that the one proposition is an inference from the other. But you must confess that the inference is not intuitive; neither is it demonstrative: Of what nature is it, then? To say it is experimental, is begging the question. For all inferences from experience suppose, as their foundation, that the future will resemble the past, and that similar powers will be conjoined with similar sensible qualities. If there be any suspicion that the course of nature may change, and that the past may be no rule for the future, all experience becomes useless, and can give rise to no inference or conclusion. It is impossible, therefore, that any arguments from experience can prove this resemblance of the past to the future; since all these arguments are founded on the supposition of that resemblance. Let the course of things be allowed hitherto ever so regular; that alone, without some new argument or inference, proves not that, for the future, it will continue so. In vain do you pretend to have learned the nature of bodies from your past experience? Their secret nature, and consequently all their effects and influence, may change, without any change in their sensible qualities. This happens sometimes, and with regard to some objects: Why may it [not] happen always, and with regard to all objects? What logic, what process of argument secures you against this supposition? My practice, you say, refutes my doubts. But you mistake the purport of my question. As an agent, I am quite satisfied in the point; but as a philosopher, who has some share of curiosity, I will not say skepticism, I want to learn the foundation of this inference. No reading, no enquiry has yet been able to remove my difficulty, or give me satisfaction in a matter of such importance. Can I do better than propose the difficulty to the public, even though, perhaps, I have small hopes of obtaining a solution? We shall, at least, by this means, be sensible of our ignorance, if we do not augment our knowledge.

I must confess that a man is guilty of unpardonable arrogance who concludes, because an argument has escaped his own investigation, that, therefore, it does not really exist. I must also confess that, though all the learned, for several ages, should have employed themselves in fruitless search upon any subject, it may still, perhaps, be rash to conclude positively that the subject must, therefore, pass all human comprehension. Even though we examine all the sources of our knowledge, and conclude them unfit for such a subject, there may still remain a suspicion, that the enumeration is not complete, or the examination not accurate. But with regard to the present subject, there are some considerations which seem to remove all this accusation of arrogance or suspicion of mistake.

It is certain that the most ignorant and stupid peasants — nay infants, nay even brute beasts — improve by experience, and learn the qualities of natural objects, by observing the effects which result from them. When a child has felt the sensation of pain from touching the flame of a candle, he will be careful not to put his hand near any candle; but will expect a similar effect from a cause which is similar in its sensible qualities and appearance. If you assert, therefore, that the understanding of the child is led into

this conclusion by any process of argument or ratiocination, I may justly require you to produce that argument; nor have you any pretense to refuse so equitable a demand. You cannot say that the argument is abstruse, and may possibly escape your enquiry; since you confess that it is obvious to the capacity of a mere infant. If you hesitate, therefore, a moment, or if, after reflection, you produce any intricate or profound argument, you, in a manner, give up the question, and confess that it is not reasoning which engages us to suppose the past resembling the future, and to expect similar effects from causes which are, to appearance, similar. This is the proposition which I intended to enforce in the present section. If I be right, I pretend not to have made any mighty discovery. And if I be wrong, I must acknowledge myself to be, indeed, a very backward scholar; since I cannot now discover an argument which, it seems, was perfectly familiar to me long before I was out of my cradle.

SKEPTICAL SOLUTION OF THESE DOUBTS
Part I

...Nature will always maintain her rights, and prevail in the end over any abstract reasoning whatsoever. Though we should conclude, for instance, as in the foregoing section, that, in all reasonings from experience, there is a step taken by the mind which is not supported by any argument or process of the understanding; there is no danger that these reasonings, on which almost all knowledge depends, will ever be affected by such a discovery. If the mind be not engaged by argument to make this step, it must be induced by some other principle of equal weight and authority; and that principle will preserve its influence as long as human nature remains the same. What that principle is may well be worth the pains of enquiry.

Suppose a person, though endowed with the strongest faculties of reason and reflection, to be brought on all of a sudden into this world; he would, indeed, immediately observe a continual succession of objects, and one event following another; but he would not be able to discover anything farther. He would not, at first, by any reasoning, be able to reach the idea of cause and effect; since the particular powers, by which all natural operations are performed, never appear to the senses; not is it reasonable to conclude, merely because one event, in one instance, precedes another, that therefore the one is the cause, the other the effect. Their conjunction may be arbitrary and casual. There may be no reason to infer the existence of one from the appearance of the other. And in a word, such a person, without more experience, could never employ his conjecture or reasoning concerning any matter of fact, or be assured of anything beyond what was immediately present to his memory and senses.

Suppose, again, that he has acquired more experience, and has lived so long in the world as to have observed familiar objects or events to be constantly conjoined together; what is the consequence of this experience? He immediately infers the existence of one object from the appearance of the other. Yet he has not, by all his experience, acquired any idea or knowledge of the secret power by which the one object produces the other; or is it, by any process of reasoning, he is engaged to draw this inference. But still he finds himself determined to draw it: and though he should be convinced that his understanding has no part in the operation, he would nevertheless continue in the same course of thinking. There is some other principle which determines him to form such a conclusion.

This principle is Custom or Habit. For wherever the repetition of any particular act or operation produces a propensity to renew the same act or operation, without being impelled by any reasoning or process of the understanding, we always say, that this propensity is the effect of Custom. By employing that word, we pretend not to have given the ultimate reason of such a propensity. We only point out a principle of human nature, which is universally acknowledged, and which is well known by its effects. Perhaps we can push our enquiries no farther, or pretend to give the cause of this cause; but must rest contented with it as the ultimate principle, which we can assign, of all our conclusions from experience. It is sufficient satisfaction, that we can go so far, without repining at the narrowness of our faculties because they will carry us no farther. And it is certain we here advance a very intelligible proposition at least, if not a true one, when we assert that, after the constant conjunction of two objects — heat and flame, for instance, weight and solidity — we are determined by custom alone to expect the one from the appearance of the other. This hypothesis seems even the only one which explains the difficulty, why we draw, from a thousand instances, an inference which we are not able to draw from one instance, that is, in no respect, different from them. Reason is incapable of any such variation. The conclusions which it draws from considering one circle are the same which it would form upon surveying all the circles in the universe. But no man, having seen only one body move after being impelled by another, could infer that every other body will move after a like impulse. All inferences from experience, therefore, are effects of custom, not of reasoning.

Custom, then, is the great guide of human life. It is that principle alone which renders our experience useful to us, and makes us expect, for the future, a similar train of events with those which have appeared in the past. Without the influence of custom, we should be entirely ignorant of every matter of fact beyond what is immediately present to the memory and senses. We should never know how to adjust means to ends, or to employ our natural powers in the production of any effect. There would be an end at once of all action, as well as of the chief part of speculation.

But here it may be proper to remark, that though our conclusions from experience carry us beyond our memory and senses, and assure us of matters of fact which happened in the most distant places and most remote ages, yet some fact must always be present to the senses or memory, from which we may first proceed in drawing these conclusions. A man, who should find in a desert country the remains of pompous buildings, would conclude that the country had, in ancient times, been cultivated by civilized inhabitants; but did nothing of this nature occur to him, he could never form such an inference. We learn the events of former ages from history; but then we must peruse the volumes in which this instruction is contained, and thence carry up our inferences from one testimony to another, till we arrive at the eyewitnesses and spectators of these distant events. In a word, if we proceed not upon some fact, present to the memory or senses, our reasonings would be merely hypothetical; and however the particular links might be connected with each other, the whole chain of inferences would have nothing to support it, nor could we ever, by its means, arrive at the knowledge of any real existence. If I ask why you believe any particular matter of fact, which you relate, you must tell me some reason; and this reason will be some other fact, connected with it. But as you cannot proceed after this manner, in infinitum, you must at least terminate in some fact, which is present to your memory or senses; or must allow that your belief is entirely without foundation.

What, then, is the conclusion of the whole matter? A simple one; though, it must be confessed, pretty remote from the common theories of philosophy. All belief of matters of fact or real existence is derived merely from some object, present to the memory or senses, and a customary conjunction between that and some other object. Or in other words; having found in many instances, that any two kinds of objects — flame or snow be presented anew to the senses, the mind is carried by custom to expect heat or cold, and to believe that such a quality does exist, and will discover itself upon a nearer approach. This belief is the necessary result of placing the mind in such circumstances. It is an operation of the soul, when we are so situated, as unavoidable as to feel the passion of love, when we receive benefits; or hatred, when we meet with injuries. All these operations are a species of natural instincts, which no reasoning or process of thought and understanding is able either to produce or to prevent.

From David Hume, *An Inquiry Concerning Human Understanding*, 1748.

The CopernicanRevolution

Immanuel Kant (1724-1804)

The Critique of Pure Reason (1781) is Kant's best known work. In this monumental work, he begins a Copernican-like revolution in the field of epistemology. He provides a synthesis of the competing theories of the rationalists and the empiricists. The rationalists, like Descartes, argued that reason alone is the ultimate source of knowledge, while the empiricists like Locke and Hume, argues that experience is the only source of knowledge. Are there innate ideas already in the mind that we are born with as Descartes held? Or is the mind a blank slate (tabula rasa) as Lock held?

Kant tells us that Hume "woke me from my dogmatic slumbers." Although Kant argues that all our knowledge begins with experience, he also argues that it does not necessarily follow that all our knowledge arises from experience. Kant sought to demonstrate that the rationalists had an invaluable insight, which had been lost in their speculation, that there is an a priori structure to the mind that causes us to know what we know.

Kant argued that this *a priori* structure of the human mind imposes interpretive categories on all our experience. We do not simply experience the world as the empiricists thought, but rather we interpret that sense data the experience gives to us. This is sometimes referred to as Kant's Copernican Revolution.

Vocabulary:

A priori:	before all experience
Supposition:	assumption
Intuition:	sense perception
Transcendental:	universal and necessary

Universality:	when something must always be
Genus:	a kind or class having common attributes
Cursory:	not thorough; hasty
Demurred:	to object; to disagree with
Apodeictic:	absolutely certain or necessarily true

Concepts:

A priori

A posteriori

A priori Synthetic Knowledge

Space

Time

Pure Knowledge

Empirical Knowledge

Transcendental Philosophy

Intuition

Analytic Judgment

Synthetic Judgment

Questions:

1. *What is the difference between pure and empirical knowledge?*
2. *What is the difference between analytic and synthetic judgments?*
3. *What are synthetic a priori judgments?*
4. *What does Kant mean when he says that space is a necessary condition for our perceptions?*
5. *What does Kant mean when he says that time is a necessary condition for our perceptions?*

Until now it has been assumed that all our knowledge must conform to objects. But all attempts to extend our knowledge of objects by establishing something in regard to them a priori, by means of concepts, have, on this assumption, ended in failure. We must, therefore, see whether we may not have more success in the tasks of metaphysics, if we suppose that objects must conform to our knowledge. This would agree better with what is desired, namely, that it should be possible to have knowledge of objects a priori, determining something in regard to them prior to their being given. We should then be proceeding in the same way as Copernicus' primary hypothesis. Failing to make progress in explaining the movements of the heavenly bodies on the supposition that they all revolved round the spectator, he considered whether he might not have better success if he made the spectator to revolve and the stars to remain at rest. A similar experiment can be tried in metaphysics, as regards the intuition of objects. If intuition must conform to the constitution of the objects, I do not see how we could know anything of the latter a priori; but if the object (as object of the senses) must conform to the constitution of our faculty of intuition, I have no difficulty in conceiving such a possibility.

INTRODUCTION. THE DISTINCTION BETWEEN PURE AND EMPIRICAL KNOWLEDGE

There can be no doubt that all our knowledge begins with experience. For how should our faculty of knowledge be awakened into action did not objects affecting our senses partly of themselves produce representations, partly arouse the activity of our understanding to compare these representations, and, by combining or separating them, work up the raw material of the sensible impressions into that knowledge of objects which is entitled experience? In respect to time, therefore, no knowledge of ours is before experience, but begins with it. But though all our knowledge begins with experience, it does not follow that it all arises out of experience.

THE IDEA OF TRANSCENDENTAL PHILOSOPHY

Experience is, beyond all doubt, the first product to which our understanding gives rise, in working up the raw material of sensible impressions. Experience is, therefore, our first instruction, and in its progress is so inexhaustible in new information, that in the interconnected lives of all future generations there will never be any lack of new knowledge that can be thus gathered. Nevertheless, it is by no means the sole field to which our understanding is confined.

For it may well be that even our empirical knowledge is made up of what we receive through impressions and of what our own faculty of knowledge (sensible impressions serving merely as the occasion) supplies from itself. If our faculty of knowledge makes any such addition, it may be that we are not in a position to distinguish it from the raw material, until with long practice of attention we have become skilled in separating it. This, then, is a question which at least calls for closer examination, and does not allow for any off-hand answer: — whether there is any knowledge that is thus independent of experience and even of all impressions of the senses. Such knowledge is entitled a priori, and distinguished from the empirical, which has its sources a posteriori, that is, in experience.

Experience tells us, indeed, what is, but not that it must necessarily be so, and not otherwise. It, therefore, gives us no true universality; and reason, which is so insistent upon this kind of knowledge, is, therefore, more stimulated by it than satisfied. Such universal modes of knowledge, which at the same time possess the character of inner necessity, must in themselves, independently of experience, be clear and certain. They are, therefore, entitled knowledge a priori; whereas, on the other hand, that which is borrowed solely from experience is, as we say, known only a posteriori, or empirically. Now we find, what is especially noteworthy, that even into our experiences there enter modes of knowledge which must have their origin a priori, and which perhaps serve only to give coherence to our sense-representations. For if we eliminate from our experiences everything which belongs to the senses, there still remain certain original concepts and certain judgments derived from them, which must have arisen completely a priori, independently of experience, inasmuch as they enable us to say, or at least lead us to believe that we can say, in regard to the objects which appear to the senses, more than mere experience would teach — giving to assertions true universality and strict necessity, such as mere empirical knowledge cannot supply.

The expression 'a priori' does not, however, indicate with sufficient precision the full meaning of our question. For it has been customary to say, even of much knowledge that is derived from empirical sources, that we have it or are capable of having it a priori, meaning thereby that we do not derive it immediately from experience, but from a universal rule — a rule which is itself, however, borrowed by us from experience. Thus we would say of a man who undermined the foundations of his house, that he might have known a priori that it would fall, that is, that he need not have waited for the experience of its actual falling. But still he could not know this completely a priori. For he had first to learn through experience that bodies are heavy, and therefore fall when their supports are withdrawn. In what follows, therefore, we shall understand by a priori knowledge, not knowledge independent of this or that experience, but knowledge absolutely independent of all experience. Opposed to it is empirical knowledge, which is knowledge possible only a posteriori, that is, through experience. A priori modes of knowledge are entitled pure when there is no admixture of anything empirical. Thus, for instance, the proposition, 'every alteration has its cause,' while an a priori proposition, is not a pure proposition, because alteration is a concept which can be derived only from experience.

WE ARE IN POSSESSION OF CERTAIN MODES OF A PRIORI KNOWLEDGE, AND EVEN THE COMMON UNDERSTANDING IS NEVER WITHOUT THEM

What we here require is a criterion by which to distinguish with certainty between pure and empirical knowledge.

Experience teaches us that a thing is so and so, but not that it cannot be otherwise. First, then, if we have a proposition which, in being thought is thought as necessary, it is an a priori judgment; and if, besides, it is not derived from any proposition except one which also has the validity of a necessary judgment, it is an absolutely a priori judgment. Secondly, experience never confers on its judgments true or strict but only assumed and comparative universality, through induction. We can properly only say, therefore, that so far as we have hitherto observed, there is no exception to this or that rule. If, then, a judgment is thought with strict universality, that is, in such manner that no exception is allowed as possible, it is not derived from experience, but is valid absolutely *a priori.*

Empirical universality is only an arbitrary extension of a validity holding in most cases to one which holds in all, for instance, in the proposition, 'all bodies are heavy.' When, on the other hand, strict universality is essential to a judgment, this indicates a special source of knowledge, namely, a faculty of a priori knowledge. Necessity and strict universality are thus sure criteria of a priori knowledge, and are inseparable from one another. But since in the employment of these criteria the contingency of judgments is sometimes more easily shown than their empirical limitation, or, as sometimes also happens, their unlimited universality can be more convincingly proved than their necessity, it is advisable to use the two criteria separately, each by itself being infallible.

Now it is easy to show that there actually are in human knowledge judgments which are necessary and, in the strictest sense universal, and which are, therefore, pure a priori judgments. If an example from the sciences be desired, we have only to look to any of the propositions of mathematics; if we seek an example from the understanding in its quite ordinary employment, the proposition, 'every alteration must have a cause,' will serve our purpose. In the latter case, indeed, the very concept of a cause so manifestly contains the concept of a necessity of connection with an effect and of the strict universality of the rule, that the concept would be altogether lost if we attempted to derive it, as Hume has done, from a repeated association of that which happens with that which precedes, and from a custom of connecting representations, a custom originating in this repeated association, and constituting, therefore, a merely subjective necessity. Even without appealing to such examples, it is possible to show that pure a priori princi-

ples are indispensable for the possibility of experience, and so to prove their existence a priori. For whence could experience derive its certainty, if all the rules, according to which it proceeds, were always themselves empirical, and, therefore, contingent? Such rules could hardly be regarded as first principles. At present, however, we may be content to have established the fact that our faculty of knowledge does have a pure employment, and to have shown what are the criteria of such an employment.

Such a priori origin is manifest in certain concepts, no less than in judgments. If we remove from our empirical concept of a body, one by one, every feature in it which is [merely] empirical, the colour, the hardness or softness, the weight, even the impenetrability, there still remains the space which the body (now entirely vanished) occupied, and this cannot be removed. Again, if we remove from our empirical concept of any object, corporeal or incorporeal, all properties which experience has taught us, we yet cannot take away that property through which the object is thought as substance or as inhering in a substance (although this concept of substance is more determinate than that of an object in general). Owing, therefore, to the necessity with which this concept of substance forces itself upon us, we have no option save to admit that it has its seat in our faculty of a priori knowledge.

THE DISTINCTION BETWEEN ANALYTIC AND SYNTHETIC JUDGMENTS

In all judgments in which the relation of a subject to the predicate is thought, this relation is possible in two different ways; either the predicate to the subject A, as something which is contained in this concept A; or outside the concept A, although it does indeed stand in connection with it. In the one case I entitle the judgment analytic, in the other, synthetic. Analytic judgments are, therefore, those in which the connection of the predicate with the subject is through identity; those in which this connection is thought without identity should be entitled synthetic. The former adds nothing to the predicate in the concept of the subject, but merely breaks it up into those constituent concepts that have all along been thought in it. The latter, on the other hand, add to the concept of the subject a predicate which has not been in any wise thought in it, and which no analysis could possibly extract from it. If I say, for instance, 'All bodies are extended,' this is an analytic judgment. For I do not require to go beyond the concept which I connect with 'body' in order to find extension as bound up with it. To meet with this predicate, I have merely to analyse the concept, that is, to become conscious to myself of the manifold which I always think in that concept. The judgment is, therefore, analytic. But when I say, 'All bodies are heavy,' the predicate is something quite different from anything that I think in the mere concept of body in general; and the addition of such a predicate, therefore, yields a synthetic judgment.

Judgments of experience, as such, are one and all synthetic. For it would be absurd to found an analytic judgment on experience. Since, in framing the judgment, I must not go outside my concept, there is no need to appeal to the testimony of experience in its support. That a body is extended is a proposition that holds a priori and is not empirical. For, before appealing to experience, I have already in the concept of body all the conditions required for my judgment. I have only to extract from it, in accordance with the principle of contradiction, the required predicate, and in so doing can at the same time become conscious of the necessity of the judgment — and that is what experience could never have taught me. On the other hand, though I do not include in the concept of a body in general the predicate 'weight,' none the less this concept indicates an object of experience through one of its parts, and I can add to that part other parts of this same experience, as in this way belonging together with the concept.

Thus it is evident: 1. that through analytic judgments our knowledge is not in any way extended, and that the concept which I already have is merely set forth and made intelligible to me; 2. that in synthetic judgments I must have, besides the concept of the subject, something else (X), upon which the understanding may rely, if it is to know that a predicate, not contained in this concept, nevertheless belongs to it. In the case of empirical judgments, judgments of experience, there is no difficulty whatsoever in meeting this demand. This X is the complete experience of the object which I think through the concept A — a concept which forms only one part of this experience.

From the start I can apprehend the concept of body analytically through the characters of extension, impenetrability, figure, etc., all of which are thought in the concept. Now, however, looking back on the experience from which I have derived this concept of body, and finding weight to be invariably connected with the above characters, I attach it as a predicate to the concept; and in doing so I attach it synthetically, and am, therefore, extending

my knowledge. The possibility of the synthesis of the predicate 'weight' with the concept of 'body' thus rests upon experience. While the one concept is not contained in the other, they yet belong to one another, though only contingently, as parts of a whole, namely, of an experience which is itself a synthetic combination of intuitions. But in a priori synthetic judgments this help is entirely lacking. [I do not here have the advantage of looking around in the field of experience.] Upon what, then, am I to rely, when I seek to go beyond the concept A, and to know that another concept B is connected with it? Through what is the synthesis made possible? Let us take the proposition, 'Everything which happens has its cause.' In the concept of 'something which happens,' I do indeed think an existence which is preceded by a time, etc., and from this concept analytic judgments may be obtained.

For though I do not include in the concept of a body in general the predicate 'weight,' the concept none the less indicates the complete experience through one of its parts; and to this part, as belonging to it, I can therefore add other parts of the same experience. By prior analysis I can apprehend the concept of body through the characters of extension, impenetrability, figure, etc., all of which are thought in this concept. To extend my knowledge, I then look back to the experience from which I have derived this concept of body, and find that weight is always connected with the above characters. Experience is thus the X which lies outside the concept A, and on which rests the possibility of the synthesis of the predicate 'weight' (B) with the concept (A).

But the concept of a 'cause' lies entirely outside the other concept, and signifies something different from 'that which happens,' and is not therefore in any way contained in this latter representation. How can I then predicate of that which happens something quite different, and to apprehend that the concept of cause, though not contained in it, yet belongs, and indeed necessarily belongs to it? What is the unknown = X which gives support to the understanding when it believes that it can discover outside the concept A a predicate B foreign to this concept, which it yet at the same time considers to be connected with it? It cannot be experience, because the suggested principle has connected the second representation with the first, not only with greater universality, but also with the character of necessity and, therefore, completely a priori and on the basis of mere concepts. Upon such synthetic judg-

ments all our a priori speculative knowledge must ultimately rest; analytic judgments are very important, and indeed necessary, but only for obtaining that clearness in the concepts which is requisite for such a sure and wide synthesis as will lead to a genuinely new addition to all previous knowledge.

A certain mystery lies here concealed; and only upon its solution can the advance into the limitless field of the knowledge yielded by pure understanding be made sure and trustworthy. What we must do is to discover, in all its proper universality, the ground of the possibility of a priori synthetic judgments, to obtain insight into the conditions which make each kind of such judgments possible, and to mark out all this knowledge, which forms a genus by itself, not in any cursory outline, but in a system, with completeness and in a manner sufficient for any use, according to its original sources, divisions, extent, and limits. So much, meantime, as regards what is peculiar in synthetic judgments.

If it had occurred to any of the ancients even to raise this question, this by itself would, up to our own time, have been a powerful influence against all systems of pure reason, and would have saved us so many of those vain attempts, which have been blindly undertaken without knowledge of what it is that requires to be done.

IN ALL THEORETICAL SCIENCES OF REASON SYNTHETIC A PRIORI JUDGMENTS ARE CONTAINED AS PRINCIPLES

1. All mathematical judgments, without exception, are synthetic. This fact, though incontestably certain and in its consequences very important, has hitherto escaped the notice of those who are engaged in the analysis of human reason, and is, indeed, directly opposed to all their conjectures. For as it was found that all mathematical inferences proceed in accordance with the principle of contradiction (which the nature of all apodeictic certainty requires), it was supposed that the fundamental propositions of the science can themselves be known to be true through that principle. This is an erroneous view. For though a synthetic proposition can indeed be discerned in accordance with the principle of contradiction, this can only be if another synthetic proposition is presupposed, and if it can then be apprehended as following from this other proposition; it can never be so discerned in and by itself. First of all, it has to be noted that mathematical propositions, strictly so called, are always judgments a priori, not empirical; because

they carry with them necessity, which cannot be derived from experience. If this be demurred to, I am willing to limit my statement to pure mathematics, the very concept of which implies that it does not contain empirical, but only pure a priori knowledge. We might, indeed, at first suppose that the proposition 7 & 5 = 12 is a merely analytic proposition, and follows by the principle of contradiction from the concept of a sum of 7 and 5. But if we look more closely we find that the concept of the sum of 7 and 5 contains nothing save the union of the two numbers into one, and in this no thought is being taken as to what that single number may be which combines both. The concept of 12 is, by no means, already thought in merely thinking this union of 7 and 5; and I may analyse my concept of such a possible sum as long as I please, still I shall never find the 12 in it. We have to go outside these concepts, and call in the aid of the intuition which corresponds to one of them, our five fingers, for instance, or, as Segner does in his Arithmetic, five points, adding to the concept of 7, unit by unit, the five given in intuition. For starting with the number 7, and for the concept of 5 calling in the aid of the fingers of my hand as intuition, I now add one by one to the number 7 the units which I previously took together to form the number 5, and with the aid of that figure [the hand] see the number 12 come into being. That 5 should be added to 7, I have indeed already thought in the concept of a sum = 7 & 5, but not that this sum is equivalent to the number 12. Arithmetical propositions are, therefore, always synthetic. This is still more evident if we take larger numbers. For it is then obvious that, however we might turn and twist our concepts, we could never, by the mere analysis of them, and without the aid of intuition, discover what [the number is that] is the sum. Just as little is any fundamental proposition of pure geometry analytic. That the straight line between two points is the shortest is a synthetic proposition. For my concept of straight contains nothing of quantity, but only of quality. The concept of the shortest is wholly an addition, and cannot be derived, through any process of analysis, from the concept of the straight line. Intuition, therefore, must here be called in; only by its aid is the synthesis possible.

What here causes us commonly to believe that the predicate of such apodeictic judgments is already contained in our concept, and that the judgment is, therefore, analytic, is merely the ambiguous character of the terms used. We are required to join in thought a certain predicate to a given concept, and this necessi-

ty is inherent in the concepts themselves. But the question is not what we ought to join in thought to the given concept, but what we actually think in it, even if only obscurely; and it is then manifest that, while the predicate is indeed attached necessarily to the concept, it is so in virtue of an intuition which must be added to the concept, not as thought in the concept itself. Some few fundamental propositions, presupposed by the geometrician, are, indeed, really analytic, and rest on the principle of contradiction. But, as identical propositions, they serve only as links in the chain of method and not as principles; for instance, a = a; the whole is equal to itself; or (a & b) a, that is, the whole is greater than its part. And even these propositions, though they are valid according to pure concepts, are only admitted in mathematics because they can be exhibited in intuition.

2. Natural science (physics) contains a priori synthetic judgments as principles. I need cite only two such judgments: that in all changes of the material world, the quantity of matter remains unchanged; and that in all communication of motion, action and reaction must always be equal. Both propositions, it is evident, are not only necessary, and therefore in their origin a priori, but also synthetic. For in the concept of matter I do

not think its permanence, but only its presence in the space which it occupies. I go outside and beyond the concept of matter, joining to it a priori in thought something which I have not thought in it. The proposition is not, therefore, analytic, but synthetic, and yet is thought a priori; and so likewise are the other propositions of the pure part of natural science.

3. Metaphysics, even if we look upon it as having hitherto failed in all its endeavours, is yet, owing to the nature of human reason, a quite indispensable science, and ought to contain a priori synthetic knowledge. For its business is not merely to analyse concepts which we make for ourselves a priori of things, and thereby to clarify them analytically, but to extend our a priori knowledge. And for this purpose we must employ principles which add to the given concept something that was not contained in it, and through a priori synthetic judgments venture out so far that experience is quite unable to follow us, as, for instance, in the proposition, that the world must have a first beginning, and such like. Thus, metaphysics consists, at least in intention, entirely of a priori synthetic propositions…

SPACE

By means of outer sense, a property of our mind, we represent to ourselves objects as outside us, and all without exception in space…Space is not an empirical concept which has been derived from outer experiences. For in order that certain sensations be referred to something outside of me (that is to something in another region of space from that in which I find myself), the representation of space must be presupposed. The representation of space cannot, therefore, be empirically obtained from the relations of outer appearance. On the contrary, this outer experience is itself possible at all only through that representation…Space is a necessary a priori representation, which underlies all outer intuitions. We can never represent to ourselves the absence of space.

TIME

Time is not an empirical concept that has been derived from any experience… Time is a necessary representation that underlies all intuitions… Appearances may one and all, vanish; but time (as the universal condition of their possibility) cannot itself be removed… Time is not a discursive, or what is called a general concept, but a pure form of sensible intuition…Time is the formal a priori condition of all appearances whatsoever…all objects of the senses are in time and necessarily stand in time-relations.

From Immanuel Kant, *Critique of Pure Reason* trans. Norman Kemp Smith, 1929.

IV. The Philosophy of Knowledge Review Section

Below is the review sheet for Part IV: The Philosophy of Knowledge. Included in this review are the terms and concepts you should be familiar with to prepare for the exam. I have also included an example of the multiple choice questions that you will have to answer. It will give you an idea of what type of questions to expect.

We will be reviewing each of these terms and concepts and the multiple choice question in class prior to the exam.

You should be familiar with the following terms and concepts:

Cognitive Realism
Cognitive Relativism
Analytic Truths
Synthetic Truths
Epistemology
Correspondence Theory of Truth
Coherency Theory of Truth
Pragmatic Theory of Truth
Cash Value
Empirically Adequate
Rationalists
Empiricists
Plato's Myth of the Cave

Descartes' Theory of Knowledge

Method of Doubt

"Cogito Ergo Sum"

Descartes Proof for God's existence

Discourse on Method

Criterion of Certainty

Innate Ideas

John Locke's Theory of Knowledge

"Tabula Rasa"

Objects of Sensation

Objects of Reflection

Primary Qualities

Secondary Qualities

Simple Ideas

Complex Ideas

Intuitive Knowledge

Reasoning

Probability and Faith

George Berkeley's Theory of Knowledge

'Esse Est Percipi"

Subjective Idealism

David Hume's Theory of Knowledge

Relations of Ideas

Matters of Fact

Impressions

Thoughts and Ideas

Empirical Criteria of Meaning

Causality

Custom / Habit

Immanual Kant's Theory of Knowledge
A priori
A posteriori
A priori synthetic knowledge
Space
Time Causality

Multiple Choice Example:

Which is the best explanation of George Berkeley's Theory of Knowledge?

A. George Berkeley was an empiricist. He was also called a subjective idealist. He basically argued that Locke's objects of sensation can be reduced to objects of reflection and that primary qualities can be reduced to secondary qualities. The reasons for this were that the only way we know about objects of sensation is through objects of reflection and the only way we know about primary qualities is through secondary qualities. Berkeley also argued that to be is to be perceived. This is what "esse est precipi" means. He also thought that God was the ultimate perceiver.

B. George Berkeley was a rationalist. He was also called a subjective idealist. He basically argued that Locke's objects of sensation can be reduced to objects of reflection and that primary qualities can be reduced to secondary qualities. The reasons for this were that the only way we know about objects of sensation is through objects of reflection and the only way we know about primary qualities is through secondary qualities. Berkeley also argued that to be is to be perceived. This is what "esse est precipi" means. He also thought that God was the ultimate perceiver.

C. George Berkeley was an empiricist. He was also called an objective idealist. He basically argued that Locke's objects of sensation can be reduced to objects of reflection and that secondary qualities can be reduced to primary qualities. The reasons for this were that the only way we know about objects of sensation is through objects of reflection and the only way we know about primary qualities is through secondary qualities. Berkeley also argued that to be is to be perceived.

This is what "esse est precipi" means. He also thought that God was the ultimate perceiver.

D. George Berkeley was an empiricist. He was also called a subjective idealist. He basically argued that Locke's objects of sensation cannot be reduced to objects of reflection and that primary qualities can be reduced to secondary qualities. The reasons for this were that the only way we know about objects of sensation is through objects of reflection and the only way we know about primary qualities is through secondary qualities. Berkeley also argued that to be is to be perceived. This is what "esse est precipi" means. He also thought that God was the ultimate perceiver.

Part V
Ethics

Part V

Ethics

> *"Every art and every scientific inquiry, and similarly, every action and purpose, may be said to aim at some good."*
>
> - *Aristotle*
>
> *"Nothing can possibly be conceived in the world, or even out of it, which can be called good, without qualification, except a Good Will."*
>
> - *Immanuel Kant*
>
> *" The creed which accepts as the foundation of morals, Utility, or the Greatest Happiness Principle, holds that actions are right in proportion as they tend to promote happiness, wrong as they tend to produce the reverse of happiness."*
>
> - *John Stuart Mill*

"Man is nothing else but what he makes of himself. Such is the first principle of existentialism."

- **John-Paul Sartre**

"Exploitation" does not belong to a depraved, or imperfect and primitive society: it belongs to the nature of the living being as a primary organic function; it is a consequence of the intrinsic Will to Power, which is precisely the Will to Life."

- **Friedrich Nietzsche**

Introduction

ETHICS

Ethics is the study of right or correct behavior. It is the analysis and investigation of moral concepts, principles and theories. It attempts to define concepts such as "right," "wrong," "good," "bad," "virtue," "values," and "ought." Some of the questions ethics deals with are; "Are there moral absolutes, or is right and wrong behavior simply relative to the individual and the circumstances they find themselves in?" "If there are moral absolutes, what are they based upon?" "How should people act?" "How should I live my life?"

There is a common fallacy that many people fall into when they study ethics. It is called the *Naturalistic Fallacy*. This occurs when we equate "is" with "ought." In other words, we argue that simply because people do, in fact, act a certain way, therefore, they should act that way, it is morally acceptable that they act this way. This is a fallacy because the essence of ethics is not to describe how people do, in fact, behave, but rather to determine how they ought to behave. For example, people do, in fact, commit murder, yet murder is universally prohibited.

Since philosophers first began to wrestle with the question of how human beings should act, there has been great debate. Aristotle argues that happiness is our chief goal in life and provides the ultimate evaluation of all human behavior. Kant argues that the categorical imperative is the ultimate moral principle we should follow. Mill argues that utilitarianism provides the ultimate moral principle we should follow.

In the end, each individual must decide for himself which moral principles he will follow. These readings are designed to help you become more familiar with what some of the great minds of the human race have concluded.

Moral theories can be divided into several categories as the following chart shows:

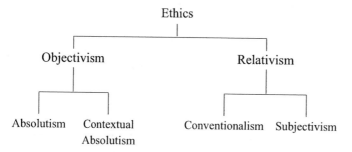

Objectivism: there are universally valid moral principles.

Absolutism: there is one universally valid moral principle we should follow.

Contextual Absolutism: there are several universally valid moral principles, and context determines which principle we should follow.

Relativism: there are no universally valid moral principles.

Conventionalism: there are no universally valid moral principles. Therefore, each society determines which moral principles to follow.

Subjectivism: there are no universally valid moral principles. Therefore, each individual determines which moral principles to follow.

The Ring of Gyges

Plato (427-347 B.C.)

The earliest philosopher for whom we still have extensive works, Plato immortalized his teacher, Socrates, in a series of dialogues. Many believe that Plato's greatest work is the *Republic*, which is a classic inquiry into political philosophy, centering on the concepts of justices and righteousness. In this work, Plato describes a utopia in which an aristocracy of philosopher-kings rule. Justice will only be realized when reason rules and the people are obedient to its commands.

In our present reading from the *Republic*, Socrates and Glaucon discuss the concept of justice and whether is it good in itself or only a necessary evil. Glaucon, puts forth the idea that because human beings are self-centered and power seeking, the more desirable situation is to experience the personal rewards of injustice, while others believe you to be just. He illustrates this point by telling the story of a shepherd named Gyges who finds a ring that makes the wearer become invisible. This allows him to escape the demands of societal justice, yet experience the rewards of injustice.

Vocabulary:

Multifarious: having great diversity

Concepts:

Justice:

Injustice:

Right:

Good:

Evil:

> ## *Questions:*
>
> 1. *What is the received account regarding the nature and origin of justice?*
> 2. *Briefly explain the story of Gyges.*
> 3. *According to Glaucon, what can no man do?*
> 4. *According to Glaucon, why are men just?*
> 5. *According to Glaucon, what do all men believe in their hearts about justice and injustice?*
> 6. *According to Glaucon, what is the highest reach of injustice?*
> 7. *Explain Socrates' example and how it relates to justice as a virtue and injustice as a vice.*

REPUBLIC

GLAUCON: They say that to do injustice is, by nature, good; to suffer injustice, evil; but that the evil is greater than the good. And so when men have both done and suffered injustice and have had experience of both, not being able to avoid the one and obtain the other, they think that they had better agree among themselves to have neither; hence, there arise laws and mutual covenants; and that which is ordained by law is termed by them lawful and just. This they affirm to be the origin and nature of justice:—it is a mean or compromise, between the best of all, which is to do injustice and not be punished, and the worst of all, which is to suffer injustice without the power of retaliation; and justice, being at a middle point between the two, is tolerated not as a good, but as the lesser evil, and honored by reason of the inability of men to do injustice. For no man who is worthy to be called a man would ever submit to such an agreement if he were able to resist; he would be mad if he did. Such is the received account, Socrates, of the nature and origin of justice.

Now that those who practice justice do so involuntarily and because they have not the power to be unjust will best appear if we imagine something of this kind: having given both to the just and the unjust power to do what they will, let us watch and see whither desire will lead them; then we shall discover in the very act the just and unjust man to be proceeding along the same road, following their interest, which all natures deem to be their good, and are only diverted into the path of justice by the force of law. The liberty which we are supposing may be most completely given to them in the form of such a power as is said to have been possessed by Gyges, the ancestor of Croesus the Lydian. According to the tradition, Gyges was a shepherd in the service of the king of Lydia; there was a great storm, and an earthquake made an opening in the earth at the place where he was feeding his flock. Amazed at the sight, he, descended into the opening, where, among other marvels, he beheld a hollow brazen horse, having doors, at which he stooping and looking in, saw a dead body of stature, as appeared to him, more than human, and having nothing on but a gold ring; this he took from the finger of the

dead and ascended. Now the shepherds met together, according to custom, that they might send their monthly report about the flocks to the king; into their assembly he came having the ring on his finger, and as he was sitting among them he chanced to turn the collet of the ring inside his hand, when instantly he became invisible to the rest of the company and they began to speak of him as if he were no longer present. He was astonished at this, and again touching the ring he turned the collet outwards and reappeared; he made several trials of the ring, and always with the same result—when he turned the collet inwards he became invisible, when outwards he reappeared. Whereupon he contrived to be chosen one of the messengers who were sent to the court; where as soon as he arrived he seduced the queen, and with her help conspired against the king and slew him, and took the kingdom. Suppose now that there were two such magic rings, and the just put on one of them and the unjust the other; no man can be imagined to be of such an iron nature that he would stand fast in justice. No man would keep his hands off what was not his own when he could safely take what he liked out of the market, or go into houses and lie with any one at his pleasure, or kill or release from prison whom he would, and in all respects be like a God among men. Then the actions of the just would be as the actions of the unjust; they would both come at last to the same point. And this we may truly affirm to be a great proof that a man is just, not willingly or because he thinks that injustice is any good to him individually, but of necessity, for wherever anyone thinks that he can safely be unjust, there he is unjust. For all men believe in their hearts that injustice is far more profitable to the individual than justice, and he who argues as I have been supposing, will say that they are right. If you could imagine anyone obtaining this power of becoming invisible, and never doing any wrong or touching what was another's, he would be thought by the lookers-on to be a most wretched idiot, although they would praise him to one another's faces, and keep up appearances with one another from a fear that they too might suffer injustice. Enough of this.

Now, if we are to form a real judgment of the life of the just and unjust, we must isolate them; there is no other way; and how is the isolation to be effected? I answer: Let the unjust man be entirely unjust, and the just man entirely just; nothing is to be taken away from either of them, and both are to be perfectly furnished for the work of their respective lives. First, let the unjust be like other distinguished masters of craft; like the skill-ful pilot or physician, who knows intuitively his own powers and keeps within their limits, and who, if he fails at any point, is able to recover himself. So let the unjust make his unjust attempts in the right way, and lie hidden if he means to be great in his injustice (he who is found out is nobody): for the highest reach of injustice is: to be deemed just when you are not. Therefore, I say, that in the perfectly unjust man we must assume the most perfect injustice; there is to be no deduction, but we must allow him, while doing the most unjust acts, to have acquired the greatest reputation for justice. If he has taken a false step he must be able to recover himself; he must be one who can speak with effect, if any of his deeds come to light, and who can force his way where force is required by his courage and strength, and command of money and friends. And at his side let us place the just man in his nobleness and simplicity, wishing, as Aechylus says, to be and not to seem good. There must be no seeming, for if he seems to be just he will be honored and rewarded, and then we shall not know whether he is just for the sake of justice or for the sake of honors and rewards; therefore, let him be clothed in justice only, and have no other covering; and he must be imagined in a state of life the opposite of the former. Let him be the best of men, and let him be thought the worst; then he will have been put to the proof; and we shall see whether he will be affected by the fear of infamy and its consequences. And let him continue, thus, to the hour of death; being just and seeming to be unjust. When both have reached the uttermost extreme, the one of justice and the other of injustice, let judgment be given which of them is the happier of the two.

Heavens! my dear Glaucon, I said, how energetically you polish them up for the decision, first one and then the other, as if they were two statues.

I do my best, he said. And now that we know what they are like there is no difficulty in tracing out the sort of life which awaits either of them. This I will proceed to describe; but as you may think the description a little too coarse, I ask you to suppose, Socrates, that the words which follow are not mine.—Let me put them into the mouths of the eulogists of injustice: they will tell you that the just man who is thought unjust will be scourged, racked, bound—will have his eyes burnt out; and, at last, after suffering every kind of evil, he will be impaled: Then he will understand that he ought to seem only, and not to be, just; the words of Aechylus may be more truly spoken of the unjust than of the just. For the unjust is pursuing a reality; he does not live with a view to appearances—he wants to be really unjust and not to seem only:

His mind has a soil deep and fertile.

Out of which spring his prudent counsels.

In the first place, he is thought just, and therefore bears rule in the city; he can marry whom he will, and give in marriage to whom he will; also he can trade and deal where he likes, and always to his own advantage, because he has no misgivings about injustice; and at every contest, whether in public or private, he gets the better of his antagonists, and gains at their expense, and is rich, and out of his gains he can benefit his friends, and harm his enemies, moreover, he can offer sacrifices, and dedicate gifts to the gods abundantly and magnificently, and can honor the gods or any man whom he wants to honor in a far better style than the just, and, therefore, he is likely to be dearer than they are to the gods. And thus, Socrates, gods and men are said to unite in making the life of the unjust better than the life of the just....

SOCRATES: "Now that we've gotten this far," I said, "let's go back to that statement made at the beginning, which brought us here: that it pays for a man to be perfectly unjust if he appears to be just. Isn't that what someone said?'

"Yes."

"Then since we've agreed what power, justice, and injustice each have, let's have a discussion with him."

"How?"

"By molding in word an image of the soul, so that the one who said that will realize what he was saying."

"What kind of image?"

"Oh, something like those natures the myths tell us were born in ancient times—the Chimaera, Scylla, Cerberus, and others in which many different shapes were supposed to have grown into one."

"So they tell us," he said.

"Then mold one figure of a colorful, many-headed beast with heads of wild and tame animals growing in a circle all around it; one that can change and grow all of them out of itself."

"That's a job for a skilled artist. Still, words mold easier than wax or clay, so consider it done."

"And another of a lion, and one of a man. Make the first by far the biggest.

"That's easier, and already done."

"Now joint the three together so that they somehow grow."

"All right."

"Next mold the image of one, the man, around them all, so that to someone who can't see what's inside, but looks only at the container, it appears to be a single animal man."

"I have."

"Then shall we inform the gentleman that when he says it pays for this man to be unjust, he's saying that it profits him to feast his multifarious beast and his lion and make them grow strong, but to starve and enfeeble the man in him so that he gets dragged wherever the animals lead him, and instead of making them friends and used to each other, to let them bite and fight and eat each other?"

"That's just what he's saying by praising injustice."

"The one who says justice pays, however, would be saying that he should practice and say whatever will give the most mastery to his inner man, who should care for the many-headed beast like a farmer, raising and domesticating its tame heads and preventing the wild ones from growing, making the lion's nature his partner and ally, and so raise them both to be friends to each other and to him."

"That's exactly what he means by praising justice."

"So in every way the commender of justice is telling the truth, the other a lie. Whether we examine pleasure, reputation, or profit, we find that the man who praises justice speaks truly, the one who disparages it disparages sickly and knows nothing of what he disparages."

"I don't think he does at all."

"Then let's gently persuade him—his error wasn't intended—by asking him a question: 'Shouldn't we say that the traditions of the beautiful and the ugly have come about like this: Beautiful things are those that make our bestial parts subservient to the human—or rather, perhaps, to the divine—part of our nature, while ugly ones are those that enslave the tame to the wild?' Won't he agree?"

"If he takes my advice."

"On this argument then, can it pay for a man to take money unjustly if that means making his best part a slave to the worst? If it wouldn't profit a man to sell his son or his daughter into slavery—to wild and evil men at that—even if he got a fortune for it, then if he has no pity on himself and enslaves the most godlike thing in him to the most godless and polluted, isn't he a wretch who gets bribed for gold into a destruction more horrible than Euriphyle's, who sold her husband's life for a necklace?"

"Much more horrible," said Glaucon.

"...everyone is better off being ruled by the godlike and intelligent; preferably if he has it inside, but if not, it should be imposed on him from without so that we may all be friends and as nearly alike as possible, all steered by the same thing."

"Yes, and we're right," he said.

"Law, the ally of everyone in the city, clearly intends the same thing, as does the rule of children, which forbids us to let them be free until we've instituted a regime in them as in a city. We serve their best part with a similar part in us, install a like guardian and ruler in them, and only then set them free."

"Clearly."

"Then how, by what argument, Glaucon, can we say that it pays for a man to be unjust or self-indulgent or to do something shameful to get more money or power if by doing so he makes himself worse?"

"We can't," he said.

"And how can it pay to commit injustice without getting caught and being punished? Doesn't getting away with it make a man even worse? Whereas if a man gets caught and punished, his beast-like part is taken in and tamed, his tame part is set free, and his whole soul acquires justice and temperance and knowledge. Therefore his soul recovers its best nature and attains a state more honorable than the state the body attains when it acquires health and strength and beauty, by as much as the soul is more honorable than the body."

"Absolutely."

"Then won't a sensible man spend his life directing all his efforts to this end?"

From, *The Dialogues of Plato*, trans. Benjamin Jowette, 1896.

Moral Conventionalism

Ruth Benedict (1887-1948)

One of the most influential American anthropologists, Ruth Benedict taught a Columbia University. Her best known work is *Patterns of Culture* (1934). In this work she develops the "idea-practice pattern of culture." According to her theory, human beings have a large repertoire of potential behavior. Based upon the history and environment that a particular culture experiences, certain behavior is chosen. Over time the culture develops a theory or religion in which these behaviors are favored. She defines social systems as communities with common beliefs and practices. Although the final social systems may vary greatly, Benedict argues that there is no basis for saying that one system is better than another. Normal and abnormal is simply culturally defined.

In our present reading, Benedict discusses several examples that she believes proves her thesis. Many examples are the result of her anthropological research of tribal behavior on an island in northwest Melanesia.

Vocabulary:

Catalepsy:	A condition in which consciousness and feeling may be lost and the muscles become rigid
Aberrant:	Deviating from what is normal or typical
Abnormality:	Something that is not normal
Megalomaniac:	A person suffering from delusions of grandeur
Phonetics:	The study of speech sounds
Treachery:	Betrayal of trust, loyalty, or faith
Exogamic:	The custom of marrying only outside one's own clan, tribe, etc.

Concepts:

Idea-Practice Pattern of Culture:

Normal and Abnormal:

Moral Goodness:

Questions:

1. How does Benedict define normal and abnormal?

2. How does Benedict define social systems?

3. What are the two factors that determine culturally acceptable behavior?

4. Describe the examples she gives to prove her thesis.

5. How does Benedict define morally good?

6. Do you think she has proven her thesis? Why or why not?

MODERN SOCIAL ANTHRO-POLOGY has become more and more a study of the varieties and common elements of cultural environment and the consequences of these in human behavior. For such a study of diverse social orders primitive peoples fortunately provide a laboratory not yet entirely vitiated by the spread of a standardized worldwide civilization. Dyaks and Hopis, Fijians and Yakuts are significant for psychological and sociological study because only among these simpler peoples has there been sufficient isolation to give opportunity for the development of localized social forms. In the higher cultures the standardization of custom and belief over a couple of continents has given a false sense of the inevitability of the particular forms that have gained currency, and we need to turn to a wider survey in order to check the conclusions we hastily base upon this near-universality of familiar customs. Most of the simpler cultures did not gain the wide currency of the one which, out of our experience, we identify with human nature, but this was for various historical reasons, and certainly not for any that gives us as its carriers a monopoly of social good or of social sanity. Modern civilization, from this point of view, becomes not a necessary pinnacle of human achievement but one entry in a long series of possible adjustments.

These adjustments, whether they are in mannerisms like the ways of showing anger, or joy, or grief in any society, or in major human drives like those of sex, prove to be far more variable than experience in any one culture would suggest. In certain fields, such as that of religion or of formal marriage arrangements, these wide limits of variability are well known and can be fairly described. In others it is not yet possible to give a generalized account, but that does not absolve us of the task of indicating the significance of the work that has been done and of the problems that have arisen.

One of these problems relates to the customary modern normal-abnormal categories and our conclusions regarding them. In how far are such categories culturally determined, or in how far can we with assurance regard them as absolute? In how far can we regard inability to function socially as diagnostic of abnormality, or in how far is it necessary to regard this as a function of the culture?

As a matter of fact, one of the most striking facts that emerges from a study of widely varying cultures is the ease with which our abnormal function in other cultures. It does not matter what kind of "abnormality" we choose for illustration — those which indicate extreme instability, or those which are more in the nature of character traits like sadism or delusions of grandeur or of persecution, there are well-described cultures in which these abnormal function at ease and with honor, and apparently without danger or difficulty to the society....

The most notorious of these is trance and catalepsy. Even a very mild mystic is aberrant in our culture. But most peoples have regarded even extreme psychic manifestations not only as normal and desirable, but even as characteristic of highly valued and gifted individuals. This was true even in our own cultural background in that period when Catholicism made the ecstatic experience the mark of sainthood. It is hard for us, born and brought up in a culture that makes no use of the experience, to realize how important a role it may play and how many individuals are capable of it, once it has been given an honorable place in any society....

Cataleptic and trance phenomena are, of course, only one illustration of the fact that those whom we regard as abnormal may function adequately in other cultures. Many of our culturally discarded traits are selected for elaboration in different societies. Homosexuality is an excellent example, for in this case our attention is not constantly diverted, as in the consideration of trance, to the interruption of routine activity which it implies. Homosexuality poses the problem very simply. A tendency toward this trait in our culture exposes an individual to all the conflicts to which all aberrants are always exposed, and we tend to identify the consequences of this conflict with homosexuality. But these consequences are obviously local and cultural. Homosexuals in many societies are not incompetent, but they may be such if the culture asks adjustments of them that would strain in any man's vitality. Wherever homosexuality has been given an honorable place in any society, those to whom it is congenial have filled adequately the honorable roles society assigns to them. Plato's *Republic* is, of course, the most convincing statement of such a reading of homosexuality. It is presented as one of the major means to the good life, and it was generally so regarded in Greece at that time.

The cultural attitude toward homosexuals has not always been on such a high ethical plane, but it has been very varied. Among many American Indian tribes there exists the institution of the berdache, as the French called them.

These men-women were men who at puberty or thereafter took the dress and the occupations of women. Sometimes they married other men and lived with them. Sometimes they were men with no inversion, persons of weak sexual endowment who chose this role to avoid the jeers of the women. The berdaches were never regarded as first-rate supernatural power, as similar men-women were in Siberia, but rather as leaders in women's occupations, good healers in certain diseases, or, among certain tribes, as the genial organizers of social affairs. In many cases, they were socially placed. They were not left exposed to the conflicts that visit the deviant who is excluded from participation in the recognized patterns of his society.

The most spectacular illustrations of the extent to which normality may be culturally defined are those cultures where an abnormality of our culture is the cornerstone of their social structure. It is not possible to do justice to these possibilities in a short discussion. A recent study of an island of northwest Melanesia by Fortune describes a society built upon traits which we regard as beyond the border of paranoia. In this tribe the exogamic groups look upon each other as prime manipulators of black magic, so that one marries always into an enemy group which remains for life one's deadly and unappeasable foes. They look upon a good garden crop as a confession of theft, for everyone is engaged in making magic to induce into his garden the productiveness of his neighbors'; therefore no secrecy in the island is so rigidly insisted upon as the secrecy of a man's harvesting of his yams. Their polite phrase at the acceptance of a gift is, "and if you now poison me, how shall I repay you this present?" Their preoccupation with poisoning is constant; no woman ever leaves her cooking pot for a moment untended. Even the great economic exchanges that are characteristic of this Melanesian culture area are quite altered in Dobu since they are incompatible with this fear and distrust that pervades the culture. They have even rigorous religiously enforced customs that forbid the sharing of seed even in one family group. Anyone else's food is deadly poison to you, so that communality of stores is out of the question. For some months before harvest the whole society is on the verge of starvation, but if one falls to the temptation and eats up one's seed yams, one is an outcast and a beachcomber for life. There is no coming back. It involves, as a matter of course, divorce and the breaking of all social ties.

Now in this society where no one may work with another and no one may share with another, Fortune describes the individual who was regarded by all his fellows as crazy. He was not one of those who periodically ran amok and, beside himself and frothing at the mouth, fell with a knife upon anyone he could reach. Such behavior they did not regard as putting anyone outside the pale. They did not even put the individuals who were known to be liable to these attacks under any kind of control. They merely fled when they saw the attack coming on and kept out of the way. "He would be all right tomorrow." But there was one man of sunny, kindly disposition who liked work and liked to be helpful. The compulsion was too strong for him to repress it in favor of the opposite tendencies of his culture. Men and women never spoke of him without laughing; he was silly and simple and definitely crazy. Nevertheless, to the ethnologist used to a culture that has, in Christianity, made his type the model of all virtue, he seemed a pleasant fellow....

Among the Kwakiutl it did not matter whether a relative had died in bed of disease, or by the hand of an enemy. In either case, death was an affront to be wiped out by the death of another person.

The fact that one had been caused to mourn was proof that one had been put upon. A chief's sister and her daughter had gone up to Victoria, and either because they drank bad whiskey or because their boat capsized they never came back. The chief called together his warriors, "Now I ask you, tribes, who shall wail? Shall I do it or shall another?" The spokesman answered, of course, "Not you, Chief. Let some other of the tribes." Immediately they set up the war pole to announce their intention of wiping out the injury, and gathered a war party. They set out, and found seven men and two children asleep and killed them. Then they felt good when they arrived at Sebaa in the evening.

The point which is of interest to us is that in our society those who on that occasion would feel good when they arrived at Sebaa that evening would be the definitely abnormal. There would be some, even in our society, but it is not a recognized and approved mood under the circumstances. On the Northwest Coast those are favored and fortunate to whom that mood under those circumstances is congenial, and those to whom it is repugnant are unlucky. This latter minority can register in their own culture only by doing violence to their congenial responses and acquiring others that are difficult for them. The person, for instance, who, like a Plains Indian whose wife has been taken from him, is too proud to fight, can deal with the Northwest Coast civilization only by ignoring its strongest bents. If he cannot achieve it, he is the deviant in that culture, their instance of abnormality.

This head-hunting that takes place on the Northwest Coast after a death is no matter of blood revenge or of organized vengeance. There is no effort to tie up the subsequent killing with any responsibility on the part of the victim for the death of the person who is being mourned. A chief whose son has died goes visiting wherever his fancy dictates, and he says to his host, "My prince has died today, and you go with him." Then he kills him. In this, according to their interpretation, he acts nobly because he has not been downed. He has thrust back in return. The whole procedure is meaningless without the fundamental paranoid reading of bereavement. Death, like all the other untoward accidents of existence, confounds man's pride and can only be handled in the category of insults.

Behavior honored upon the Northwest Coast is one which is recognized as abnormal in our civilization, and yet it is sufficiently close to the attitudes of our own culture to be intelligible to us

270

and to have a definite vocabulary with which we may discuss it. The megalomaniac paranoid trend is a definite danger in our society. It is encouraged by some of our major preoccupations, and it confronts us with a choice of two possible attitudes. One is to brand it as abnormal and reprehensible, and is the attitude we have chosen in our civilization. The other is to make it an essential attribute of ideal man, and this is the solution in the culture of the Northwest Coast.

These illustrations, which it has been possible to indicate only in the briefest manner, force upon us the fact that normality is culturally defined. An adult shaped to the drives and standards of either of these cultures, if he were transported into our civilization, would fall into our categories of abnormality. He would be faced with the psychic dilemmas of the socially unavailable. In his own culture, however, he is the pillar of society, the end result of socially inculcated mores, and the problem of personal instability in his case simply does not arise.

No one civilization can possibly utilize in its mores the whole potential range of human behavior. Just as there are great numbers of possible phonetic articulations, and the possibility of language depends on a selection and standardiza-

tion of a few of these in order that speech communication may be possible at all, so the possibility of organized behavior of every sort, from the fashions of local dress and houses to the dicta of a people's ethics and religion, depends upon a similar selection among the possible behavior traits. In the field of recognized economic obligations or sex taboos this selection is as non-rational and subconscious a process as it is in the field of phonetics. It is a process which goes on in the group for long periods of time and is historically conditioned by innumerable accidents of isolation or of contact of peoples. In any comprehensive study of psychology, the selection that different cultures have made in the course of history within the great circumference of potential behavior is of great significance.

Every society, beginning with some slight inclination in one direction or another, carries its preference farther and farther, integrating itself more and more completely upon its chosen basis, and discarding those types of behavior that are uncongenial. Most of those organizations of personality that seem to us most uncontrovertibly abnormal have been used by different civilizations in the very foundations of their institutional life. Conversely, the most valued traits of our normal individuals have been looked on in differently organized cultures as aberrant. Normality, in short, within a very wide range, is culturally defined. It is primarily a term for the socially elaborated segment of human behavior in any culture; and abnormality, a term for the segment that that particular civilization does not use. The very eyes with which we see the problem are conditioned by the long traditional habits of our own society.

It is a point that has been made more often in relation to ethics than in relation to psychiatry. We do not any longer make the mistake of deriving the morality of our locality and decade directly from the inevitable constitution of human nature. We do not elevate it to the dignity of a first principle. We recognize that morality differs in every society, and is a convenient term for socially approved habits. Mankind has always preferred to say, "It is morally good," rather than "It is habitual," and the fact of this preference is matter enough for a critical science of ethics. But historically the two phrases are synonymous.

The concept of the normal is properly a variant of the concept of the good. It is that which society has approved. A normal action is one which falls well within the limits of expected behavior for a particular society. Its variability among different peoples is essen- tially a function of the variability of the behavior patterns that different societies have created for themselves, and can never be wholly divorced from a consideration of culturally institutionalized types of behavior.

Each culture is a more or less elaborate working out of the potentialities of the segment it has chosen. Insofar as a civilization is well integrated and consistent within itself, it will tend to carry farther and farther, according to its nature, its initial impulse toward a particular type of action, and from the point of view of any other culture those elaborations will include more and more extreme and aberrant traits.

Each of these traits, in proportion as it reinforces the chosen behavior patterns of that culture, is for that culture normal. Those individuals to whom it is congenial either congenitally, or as the result of childhood sets, are accorded prestige in that culture, and are not visited with the social contempt or disapproval which their traits would call down upon them in a society that was differently organized. On the other hand, those individuals whose characteristics are not congenial to the selected type of human behavior in that community are the deviants, no matter how valued their personality traits may be in a contrasted civilization.

The Dobuan who is not easily susceptible to fear of treachery, who enjoys work and likes to be helpful, is their neurotic and regarded as silly. On the Northwest Coast the person who finds it difficult to read life in terms of an insult contest will be the person upon whom fall all the difficulties of the culturally un-provided for. The person who does not find it easy to humiliate a neighbor, nor to see humiliation in his own experience, who is genial and loving, may, of course, find some un-standardized way of achieving satisfactions in his society, but not in the major patterned responses that his culture requires of him. If he is born to play an important role in a family with many hereditary privileges, he can succeed only by doing violence to his whole personality. If he does not succeed, he has betrayed his culture; that is, he is abnormal.

I have spoken of individuals as having sets toward certain types of behavior, and of these sets as running sometimes counter to the types of behavior which are institutionalized in the culture to which they belong. From all that we know of contrasting cultures it seems clear that differences of temperament occur in every society. The matter has never been made the subject of investiga-

tion, but from the available material it would appear that these temperament types are very likely of universal recurrence. That is, there is an ascertainable range of human behavior that is found wherever a sufficiently large series of individuals is observed. But the proportion in which behavior types stand to one another in different societies is not universal. The vast majority of individuals in any group are shaped to the fashion of that culture. In other words, most individuals are plastic to the molding force of the society into which they are born. In a society that values trance, as in India, they will have supernormal experience. In a society that institutionalizes homosexuality, they will be homosexual. In a society that sets the gathering of possessions as the chief human objective, they will amass property. The deviants, whatever the type of behavior the culture has institutionalize, will remain few in number, and there seems no more difficulty in molding the vast malleable majority to the "normality" of what we consider an aberrant trait, such as delusions of reference, than to the normality of such accepted behavior patterns as acquisitiveness. The small proportion of the number of the deviants in any culture is not a function of the sure instinct with which that society has built itself upon the fundamental sanities, but of the universal fact that, happily, the majority of mankind quite readily take any shape that is presented to them...

From Ruth Benedict, "Anthropology and the Abnormal," (*The Journal of General Psychology* 10 (1934): 59-82.

Eudiamonia

Aristotle (384-322 B.C.)

Aristotle is one of the most important philosophers who ever lived. He was a student of Plato and tutor to Alexander the Great. He wrote on every major subject in philosophy including metaphysics, logic, philosophy of science, philosophy of psychology, aesthetics, politics, and ethics.

Although Aristotle was Plato's star student, he did not agree with Plato on every subject. Aristotle did not agree with Plato's idea of Forms. Plato thought that the Forms had independent existence. Aristotle thought that they had no existence independent of physical things. He was also more empirical than Plato, performing many experiments and inquiring into nature. After he broke away from Plato, he formed the Lyceum School of Philosophy in Athens.

Our present reading is from the *Nicomachean Ethics*. Aristotle begins by discussing the nature of ethics and its relationship to human existence. He then discussed the nature of virtue which he defines as character qualities that enable individuals to live well in communities. This state of well-being Aristotle calls happiness (*eudiamonia*).

Vocabulary

Ad infinitum:	for infinity; for ever
Comprehension:	understanding
Sardanapalus:	an Assyrian monarch who lived in great luxury
Paradox:	an apparent contradiction that upon closer inspection is revealed not to be a contradiction; a very difficult problem

275

Self-sufficient:	having the ability to sustain itself; having all one needs
Appetites:	desires
Theoretical:	having to do with theories or ideas; not necessarily practical
Temperance:	moderation; nothing in excess
Deficiency:	incomplete; lacking something
Licentious:	morally unrestrained, especially in sexual activities
Calypso:	name means "the concealer". She is a goddess with several functions, a complex character, and as an individual she represents the dual nature of the feminine as both light and dark in a subtle, integrated/harmonious/in accordance way. When coupled with Circe, Calypso primarily represents the light aspects of the Great Goddess
Iliad:	written by Homer, it is the story of the Trojan War

Concepts:

Happiness (eudiamonia):

The Good:

Virtue (arête):

Relative Mean:

Absolute Mean:

> ## *Questions:*
>
> *1. Why do you think Aristotle has ethics within the larger subject of politics?*
>
> *2. What do all human activities aim at? Why?*
>
> *3. Explain the three types of lives Aristotle identifies.*
>
> *4. How does Aristotle define happiness?*
>
> *5. How does one acquire virtue?*
>
> *6. How does the relative and absolute mean relate to virtue?*
>
> *7. Which property of the soul does virtue fall under?*
>
> *8. How does Aristotle define virtue?*
>
> *9. How does virtue lead to happiness?*

Nicomachean Ethics

BOOK I

All Human Activities Aim at Some Good

Chapter 1. EVERY ART AND EVERY scientific inquiry, and similarly every action and purpose, may be said to aim at some good. Hence the good has been well defined as that at which all things aim. But it is clear that there is a difference in ends; for the ends are sometimes activities and sometimes results beyond the mere activities. Where there are ends beyond the action, the results are naturally superior to the action.

As there are various actions, arts, and sciences it follows that the ends are also various. Thus health is the end of the medical art, a ship of shipbuilding, victory of strategy, and wealth of economics. It often happens that a number of such arts or sciences combine for a single enterprise, as the art of making bridles and all such other arts as furnish the implements of horsemanship combine for horsemanship, and horsemanship and every military action for strategy; and in the same way, other arts or sciences combine for others. In all these cases, the ends of the master arts or sciences, whatever they may be, are more desirable than those of the subordinate arts or sciences, as it is for the sake of the former that the latter are pursued. It makes no difference to the argument whether the activities themselves are the ends of the action, or something beyond the activities, as in the above-mentioned sciences.

If it is true that in the sphere of action there is some end which we wish for its own sake, and for the sake of which we wish everything else, and if we do not desire everything for the sake of something else (for, if that is so, the process will go on *ad infinitum*, and our desire will be idle and futile), clearly this end will be good and the supreme good. Does it not follow then that the knowledge of this good is of great importance for the conduct of life? Like archers who have a mark at which to aim, shall we not have a better chance of attaining what we want? If this is so, we must endeavor to comprehend, at least in outline, what this good is, and what science or faculty makes it its object.

It would seem that this is the most authoritative science. Such a kind is evidently the political, for it is that which determines what sciences are necessary in states, and what kinds should be studied, and how far they should be studied by each class of inhabitant. We see too that even the faculties held in highest esteem, such as strategy, economics, and rhetoric, are subordinate to it. Then since politics makes use of the other sciences and also rules what people may do and what they may not do, it follows that its end will comprehend the ends of the other sciences, and will therefore be the good of mankind. For even if the good of an individual is identical with the good of a state, yet the good of the state is evidently greater and more perfect to attain or to preserve. For though the good of an individual by himself is something worth working for, to ensure the good of a nation or a state is nobler and more divine.

These then are the objects at which the present inquiry aims, and it is in a sense a political inquiry....

The Science of the Good for Man Is Politics

Chapter 2. As every science and undertaking aims at some good, what is in our view the good at which political science aims, and what is the highest of all practical goods? As to its name there is, I may say, a general agreement. The masses and the cultured classes agree in calling it happiness, and conceive that "to live well" or "to do well" is the same thing as "to be happy." But as to what happiness is they do not agree, nor do the masses give the same account of it as the philosophers. The former take it to be something visible and palpable, such as pleasure, wealth, or honor; different people, however, give different definitions of it, and often even the same man gives different definitions at different times. When he is ill, it is health, when he is poor, it is wealth; if he is conscious of his own ignorance, he envies people who use grand language above his own comprehension. Some philosophers, on the other hand, have held that, besides these various goods, there is an absolute good which is the cause of goodness in them all. It would perhaps be a waste of time to examine all these opinions; will be enough to examine such as are most popular or as seem to be more or less reasonable.

Chapter 3. Men's conception of the good or of happiness may be read in the lives they lead. Ordinary or vulgar people conceive it to be a pleasure, and accordingly choose a life of enjoyment. For there are, we may say, three conspicuous types of life, the sensual, the political, and, thirdly, the life of thought. Now the mass of men present an absolutely slavish appearance, choosing the life of brute beasts, but they have ground for so doing because so many person in authority share the tastes of Sardanapalus. Cultivated and energetic people, on the other hand, identify happiness with honor, as honor is the general end of political life. But this seems too superficial an idea for our present purpose; for honor depends more upon the people who pay it than upon the person to whom it is paid, and the good we feel is something which is proper to a man himself and cannot be easily taken away from him. Men, too, appear to seek honor in order to be assured of their own goodness. Accordingly, they seek it at the hands of the sage and of those who know them well, and they seek it on the ground of their virtue; clearly then, in their judgment at any rate, virtue is better than honor. Perhaps, then, we might look on virtue rather than honor as the end of political life. Yet even this idea appears not quite complete; for a man may possess virtue and yet be asleep or inactive throughout life, and not only so, but he may experience the greatest calamities and misfortunes. Yet no one would call such a life a life of happiness, unless he were maintaining a paradox. But we need not dwell further on this subject, since it is sufficiently discussed in popular philosophical treatises. The third life is the life of thought, which we will discuss later.

The life of money making is a life of constraint; and wealth is obviously not the good of which we are in quest; for it is useful merely as a means to something else. It would be more reasonable to take the things mentioned before — sensual pleasure, honor, and virtue — as ends than wealth, since they are things desired on their own account. Yet these too are evidently not ends, although much argument has been employed to show that they are....

Characteristics of the Good

Chapter 5. But leaving this subject for the present, let us revert to the good of which we are in quest and consider what it may be. For it seems different in different activities or art; it is one thing in medicine, another in strategy, and so on. What is the good in each of these instances? It is presumably that for the sake of which all else is done. In medicine this is health, in strategy victory, in architecture a house, and so on. In every activity and undertaking it is the need, since it is for the sake of the end that all people do whatever else they do. If then there is an end for all our activity, this will be the good to be accomplished; and if there are several such ends, it will be these.

Our argument has arrived by a different path at the same point as before; but we must endeavor to make it still plainer. Since there are more ends than one, and some of these ends — for example, wealth, flutes, and instruments generally — we desire as means to something else, it is evident that not all are final ends. But the highest good is clearly something final. Hence if there is only one final end, this will be the object of which we are in search; and if there are more than one, it will be the most final. We call that which is sought after for its own sake more final than that which is sought after as a means to something else; we call that which is never desired as a means to something else more final than things that are desired both for themselves and as means to something else. Therefore, we call absolutely final that which is always desired for itself and never as a means to something else. Now happiness, more than anything else, answers to this description. For happiness we always desire for its own sake and never as means to something else, whereas honor, pleasure, intelligence, and every virtue we desire partly for their own sakes (for we should desire them independently of what might result from them), but partly also as means to happiness, because we suppose they will prove instruments of happiness. Happiness, on the other hand, nobody desires for the sake of these things, nor indeed as a means to anything else at all.

If we start from the point of view of self-sufficiency, we reach the same conclusion; for we assume that the final good is self-sufficient. By self-sufficiency we do not mean that a person leads a solitary life all by himself, but that he has parents, children, wife and friends and fellow citizens in general, as man is naturally a social being. Yet here it is necessary to set some limit; for if the circle must be extended to include ancestors, descendants, and friends' friends, it will go on indefinitely. Leaving this point, however, for future investigation, we call the self-sufficient that which, taken even by itself, makes life desirable and wanting nothing at all; and this is what we mean by happiness.

Again, we think happiness the most desirable of all things, and that not merely as one good thing among others. If it were only that, the addition of the smallest more good would increase its desirableness; for the addition would make an increase of goods, and the greater of two goods is always the more desirable. Happiness is something final and self-sufficient and the end of all action.

Chapter 6. Perhaps, however, it seems a commonplace to say that happiness is the supreme good; what is wanted is to define its nature a little more clearly. The best way of arriving at such a definition will probably be to ascertain the function of man. For, as with a flute player, a sculptor, or any artist, or in fact anybody who has a special function or activity, his goodness and excellence seem to lie in his function, so it would seem to be with man, if indeed he has a special function. Can it be said that, while a carpenter and a cobbler have special functions and activities, man, unlike them, is naturally functionless? Or, as the eye, the hand, the foot, and similarly each part of the body has a special function apart from all these? What, then, can this function be? It is not life; for life is apparently something that man shares with plants; and we are looking for something peculiar to him. We must exclude therefore the life of nutrition and growth. There is next what may be called the life of sensation. But this too, apparently, is shared by man with horses, cattle, and all other animals. There remains what I may call the active life of the rational part of man's being. Now this rational part is twofold; one part is rational in the sense of being obedient to reason, and the other in the sense of possessing and exercising reason and intelligence. The active life, too, may be conceived of in two ways, either as a state of character, or as an activity; but we mean by it the life of activity, as this seems to be the truer form of the conception.

The function of man then is activity of soul in accordance with reason, or not apart from reason. Now, the function of a man of a certain kind, and of a man who is good of that kind — for example, of a harpist and a good harpist — are in our view the same in kind. This is true of all people of all kinds without exception, the superior excellence being only an addition to the function; for it is the function of a harpist to play the harp, and of a good harpist to play the harp well. This being so, if we define the function of man as a kind of life, and this life as an activity of the soul or a course of action in accordance with reason, and if the function of a good man is such activity of a good and noble kind, and if everything is well done when it is done in accordance with its proper excellence, it follows that the good of man is activity of soul in accordance with virtue, or, if there are more virtues than one, in accordance with the best and most complete virtue. But we must add the words "in a complete life." For as one swallow or one day does not make a spring, so one day or a short time does not make a man blessed or happy....

Inasmuch as happiness is an activity of soul in accordance with perfect virtue, we must now consider virtue, as this will perhaps be the best way of studying happiness... Clearly it is human virtue we have to consider; for the good of which we are in search is, as we said, human good, and the happiness, human happiness. By human virtue or excellence we mean not that of the body, but that of the soul, and by happiness we mean an activity of the soul....

BOOK II

Moral virtues can best be acquired by practice and habit. They imply a right attitude toward pleasures and pains. A good man deliberately chooses to do what is noble and right for its own sake. What is right in matters of moral conduct is usually a mean between two extremes.

Chapter I. Virtue then is twofold, partly intellectual and partly moral, and intellectual virtue is originated and fostered mainly by teaching; it demands, therefore experience and time. Moral virtue on the other hand is the outcome of habit, and accordingly its name, *ethike*, is derived by a slight variation from *ethos*, habit. From this fact it is clear that moral virtue is not implanted in us by nature; for nothing that exists by nature can be transformed by habit. Thus a stone, that naturally tends to fall downwards, cannot be habituated or trained to rise upwards, even if we tried to train it by throwing it up ten thousand times. Nor again can fire be trained to sink downwards, nor anything else that follows one natural law be habituated or trained to follow another. It is neither by nature, then, nor in defiance of nature that virtues grow in us. Nature gives us the capacity to receive them, and that capacity is perfected by habit.

Again, if we take the various natural powers which belong to us, we first possess the proper faculties and afterwards display the activities. It is obviously so with the senses. Not by seeing frequently or hearing frequently do we acquire the sense of seeing or hearing; on the contrary, because we have the senses we make use of them; we do not get them by making use of them. But the virtues we get by first practicing them, as we do in the arts. For it is by doing what we ought to do when we study the arts that we learn the arts themselves; we become builders by building and harpists by playing the harp. Similarly, it is by doing just acts that we become just, by doing temperate acts

that we become temperate, by doing brave acts that we become brave. The experience of states confirms this statement, for it is by training in good habits that lawmakers make the citizens good. This is the object all lawmakers have at heart; if they do not succeed in it, they fail of their purpose; and it makes the distinction between a good constitution and a bad one.

Again, the causes and means by which any virtue is produced and destroyed are the same; and equally so in any part. For it is by playing the harp that both good and bad harpists are produced; and the case of builders and others is similar, for it is by building well that they become good builders and by building badly that they become bad builders. If it were not so, there would be no need of anybody to teach them; they would all be born good or bad in their several crafts. The case of the virtues is the same. It is by our actions in dealings between man and man that we become either just or unjust. It is by our actions in the face of danger and by our training ourselves to fear or to courage that we become either cowardly or courageous. It is much the same with our appetites and angry passions. People become temperate and gentle, others licentious and passionate, by behaving in one or the other way in particular circumstances. In a word, moral states are the results of activities like the states themselves. It is our duty therefore to keep a certain character in our activities, since our moral states depend on the differences in our activities. So the difference between one and another training in habits in our childhood is not a light matter, but important, or rather, all-important.

Chapter 2. Our present study is not, like other studies, purely theoretical in intention; for the object of our inquiry is not to know what virtue is but how to become good, and that is the sole benefit of it. We must, therefore, consider the right way of performing actions, for it is acts, as we have said, that determine the character of the resulting moral states.

That we should act in accordance with right reason is a common general principle, which may here be taken for granted. The nature of right reason, and its relation to the virtues generally, will be discussed later. But first of all it must be admitted that all reasoning on matters of conduct must be like a sketch in outline; it cannot be scientifically exact. We began by laying down the principle that the kind of reasoning demanded in any subject must be such as the subject matter itself allows; and questions of conduct and expediency no more admit of hard and fast rules than questions of health.

If this is true of general reasoning on ethics, still more true is it that scientific exactitude is impossible in treating of particular ethical cases. They do not fall under any art or law, but the actors themselves have always to take account of circumstances, as much as in medicine or navigation. Still, although such is the nature of our present argument, we must try to make the best of it.

The first point to be observed is that in the matters we are now considering deficiency and excess are both fatal. It is so, we see, in questions of health and strength. (We must judge of what we cannot see by the evidence of what we do see.) Too much or too little gymnastic exercise is fatal to strength. Similarly, too much or too little meat and drink is fatal to health, whereas a suitable amount produces, increases, and sustains it. It is the same with temperance, courage, and other moral virtues. A person who avoids and is afraid of everything and faces nothing becomes a coward; a person who is not afraid of anything but is ready to face everything becomes foolhardy. Similarly, he who enjoys every pleasure and abstains from none is licentious; he who refuses all pleasures, like a boor, is an insensible sort of person. For temperance and courage are destroyed by excess and deficiency but preserved by the mean.

Again, not only are the causes and agencies of production, increase, and destruction in moral states the same, but the field of their activity is the same also. It is so in other more obvious instances, as, for example, strength; for strength is produced by taking a great deal of food and undergoing a great deal of exertion, and it is the strong man who is able to take most food and undergo most exertion. So too, with the virtues. By abstaining from pleasures we become temperate, and, when we have become temperate, we are best able to abstain from them. So again with courage; it is by training ourselves to despise and face terrifying things that we become brave, and when we have become brave, we shall be best able to face them.

The pleasure or pain which accompanies actions may be regarded as a test of a person's moral state. He who abstains from physical pleasures and feels pleasure in so doing is temperate; but he who feels pain at so doing is licentious. He who faces dangers with pleasure, or at least without pain, is brave; but he who feels pain at facing them is a coward. For moral virtue is concerned with pleasures and pains. It is pleasure which makes us do what is base, and pain which makes us abstain from doing what is noble. Hence

the importance of having a certain training from very early days, as Plato says, so that we may feel pleasure and pain at the right objects; for this is true education....

Chapter 3. But we may be asked what we mean by saying that people must become just by doing what is just and temperate by doing what is temperate. For, it will be said, if they do what is just and temperate they are already just and temperate themselves, in the same way as, if they practice grammar and music, they are grammarians and musicians.

But is this true even in the case of the arts? For a person may speak grammatically either by chance or at the suggestion of somebody else; hence, he will not be a grammarian unless he not only speaks grammatically but does so in a grammatical manner, that is, because of the grammatical knowledge which he possesses.

There is a point of difference, too, between the arts and the virtues. The productions of art have their excellence in themselves. It is enough then that, when they are produced, they themselves should possess a certain character. But acts in accordance with virtue are not justly or temperately performed simply because they are in themselves just or temperate. The doer at the time of performing them must satisfy certain conditions; in the first place, he must know what he is doing; secondly, he must deliberately choose to do it and do it for his own sake; and thirdly, he must do it as part of his own firm and immutable character. If it be a question of art, these conditions, except only the condition of knowledge, are not raised; but if it be a question of virtue, mere knowledge is of little or no avail; it is the other conditions, which are the results of frequently performing just and temperate acts, that are not slightly but all-important. Accordingly, deeds are called just and temperate when they are such as a just and temperate person would do; and a just and temperate person is not merely one who does these deeds but one who does them in the spirit of the just and the temperate.

It may fairly be said that a just man becomes just by doing what is just, and a temperate man becomes temperate by doing what is temperate, and if a man did not so act, he would not have much chance of becoming good. But most people, instead of acting, take refuge in theorizing; they imagine that they are philosophers and that philosophy will make them virtuous; in fact, they behave like people who listen attentively to their doctors but never do anything that their doctors tell

them. But a healthy state of the soul will no more be produced by this kind of philosophizing than a healthy state of the body by this kind of medical treatment.

Chapter 4. We have next to consider the nature of virtue. Now, as the properties of the soul are three, namely, emotions, faculties, and moral states, it follows that virtue must be one of the three. By emotions I mean desire, anger, fear, pride, envy, joy, love, hatred, regret, ambition, pity — in a word, whatever feeling is attended by pleasure or pain. I call those faculties through which we are said to be capable of experiencing these emotions, for instance, capable of getting angry or being pained or feeling pity. And I call those moral states through which we are well or ill disposed in our emotions, ill disposed, for instance, in anger, if our anger be too violent or too feeble, and well disposed, if it be rightly moderate.

Now neither the virtues or the vices are emotions; for we are not called good or bad for our emotions but for our virtues or vices. We are not praised or blamed simply for being angry, but only for being angry in a certain way; but we are praised or blamed for our virtues or vices. Again, whereas we are angry or afraid without deliberate purpose, the virtues are matters of deliberate purpose, or require deliberate purpose. Moreover, we are said to be moved by our emotions, but by our virtues or vices we are not said to be moved but to have a certain disposition.

For these reasons the virtues are not faculties. For we are not called either good or bad, nor are we praised or blamed for having simple capacity for emotion. Also while Nature gives us our faculties, it is not Nature that makes us good or bad; but this point we have already discussed. If, then, the virtues are neither emotions nor faculties, all that remains is that they must be moral states.

Chapter 5. The nature of virtue has been now described in kind. But it is not enough to say merely that virtue is a moral state; we must also describe the character of that moral state.

We may assert then that every virtue or excellence puts into good condition that of which it is a virtue or excellence, and enables it to perform its work well. Thus excellence in the eye makes the eye good and its function good, for by excellence in the eye we see well. Similarly, excellence of the horse makes a horse excellent himself and good at racing, at carrying its rider and at facing the enemy. If, then, this rule is universally true, the virtue or excellence of a man will be such a moral state as makes a man good and able to perform his proper function well. How this will be the case we have already explained, but another way of making it clear will be to study the nature or character of virtue.

Now of everything, whether it be continuous or divisible, it is possible to take a greater, a smaller, or an equal amount, and this either in terms of the thing itself or in relation to ourselves, the equal being a mean between too much and too little. By the mean in terms of the thing itself, I understand that which is neither too much nor too little for us; but this is not one nor the same for everybody. Thus, if 10 be too much and 2 too little, we take 6 as a mean in terms of the thing itself; for 6 is as much greater than 2 as it is less than 10, and this is a mean in arithmetical proportion. But the mean considered relatively to ourselves may not be ascertained in that way. It does not follow that if 10 pounds of meat is too much and 2 too little for a man to eat, the trainer will order him 6 pounds, since this also may be too much or too little for him who is to take it; it will be too little, for example, for Milo but too much for a beginner in gymnastics. The same with running and wrestling; the right amount will vary with the individual. This being so, the skillful in any art avoids alike excess and deficiency; he seeks and chooses the mean, not the absolute mean, but the mean considered relatively to himself.

Every art then does its work well, if it regards the mean and judges the works it produces by the mean. For this reason we often say of successful works of art that it is impossible to take anything from them or to add anything to them, which implies that excess or deficiency is fatal to excellence but that the mean state ensures it. Good artists too, as we say, have an eye to the mean in their works. Now virtue, like Nature herself, is more accurate and better than any art; virtue, therefore, aims at the mean. I speak of moral virtue, since it is moral virtue which is concerned with emotions and actions, and it is in these we have excess and deficiency and the mean. Thus it is possible to go too far, or not far enough in fear, pride, desire, anger, pity, and pleasure and pain generally, and the excess and the deficiency are alike wrong; but to feel these emotions at the right times, for the right objects, towards the right persons, for the right motives, and in the right manner, is the mean or the best good, which signifies virtue. Similarly, there may be excess, deficiency, or the mean, in acts. Virtue is concerned with both emotions and actions, wherein excess is an error and deficiency a fault, while the mean is successful and praised, and success and praise are both characteristics of virtue.

It appears then that virtue is a kind of mean because it aims at the mean.

On the other hand, there are many different ways of going wrong; for evil is, in its nature, infinite, to use the Pythagorean phrase, but good is finite and there is only one possible way of going right. So the former is easy and the latter is difficult; it is easy to miss the mark but difficult to hit it. And so by our reasoning excess and deficiency are characteristics of vice and the mean is characteristic of virtue.

"For good is simple, evil manifold."

Chapter 6. Virtue, then, is a state of deliberate moral purpose, consisting in a mean relative to ourselves, the mean being determined by reason, or as a prudent man would determine it. It is a mean, firstly, as lying between two vices, the vice of excess on the one hand, the vice of deficiency on the other, and secondly, because, whereas the vices either fall short of or go beyond what is right in emotion and action, virtue discovers and chooses the mean. Accordingly, virtue, if regarded in its essence or theoretical definition, is a mean, though, if regarded from the point of view of what is best and most excellent, it is an extreme.

But not every action or every emotion admits of a mean. There are some whose very name implies wickedness, as, for example, malice, shamelessness, and envy among the emotions, and adultery, theft, and murder among the actions. All these and others like them are marked as intrinsically wicked, not merely the excesses or deficiencies of them. It is never possible then to be right in them; they are always sinful. Right or wrong in such acts as adultery does not depend on our committing it with the right woman, at the right time, or in the right manner; on the contrary, it is wrong to do it at all. It would be equally false to suppose that there can be a mean or an excess of deficiency in unjust, cowardly or licentious conduct; for, if that were so, it would be a mean of excess and deficiency, an excess of excess and a deficiency of deficiency. But as in temperance and courage there can be no excess or deficiency, because the mean there is in a sense an extreme, so too in these other cases there cannot be a mean or an excess or a deficiency, but however the acts are done, they are wrong. For in general an excess or deficiency does not have a mean, nor a mean an excess or deficiency....

Chapter 8. There are then three dispositions, two being vices, namely, excess and deficiency, and one virtue, which is the mean between them; and they are all in a sense mutually opposed. The extremes are opposed both to the mean and to each other, and the mean is opposed to the extremes. For as the equal if compared with the less is greater, but if compared with the greater is less, so the mean state, whether in emotion, or action, if compared with deficiency is excessive, but if compared with excess is deficient. Thus the brave man appears foolhardy compared with the coward, but cowardly compared with the foolhardy. Similarly, the temperate man appears licentious compared with the insensible man but insensible compared with the licentious; and the liberal man appears extravagant compared with the stingy man but stingy compared with the spendthrift. The result is that the extremes each denounce the mean as belonging to the other extreme; the coward calls the brave man foolhardy, and the foolhardy man calls him cowardly; and so on in other cases.

But while there is mutual opposition between the extremes and the mean, there is greater opposition between the two extremes than between extreme and the mean; for they are further removed from each other than from the mean, as the great is further from the small and the small from the great than either from the equal. Again, while some extremes show some likeness to the mean, as foolhardiness to courage and extravagance to liberality, there is the greatest possible dissimilarity between extremes. But things furthest removed from each other are called opposites; hence the further things are removed, the greater is the opposition between them.

In some cases it is deficiency and in others excess which is more opposed to the mean. Thus it is not foolhardiness, an excess, but cowardice, a deficiency, which is more opposed to courage, nor is it insensibility, a deficiency, but licentiousness, an excess, which is more opposed to temperance. There are two reasons why this should be so. One lies in the nature of the matter itself; for when one of two extremes is nearer and more like the mean, it is not this extreme but its opposite that we chiefly contrast with the mean. For instance, as foolhardiness seems more like and nearer to courage than cowardice, it is cowardice that we chiefly contrast with courage; for things further removed from the mean seem to be more opposite to it. This reason lies in the nature of the matter itself; there is a second which lies in our own nature. The things to which we ourselves are natural-

ly more inclined we think more opposed to the mean. Thus we are ourselves naturally more inclined to pleasures than to their opposites, and are more prone therefore to self-indulgence than to moderation. Accordingly we speak of those things in which we are more likely to run to great lengths as more opposed to the mean. Hence licentiousness, which is an excess, seems more opposed to temperance than insensibility.

Chapter 9. We have now sufficiently shown that moral virtue is a mean, and in what sense it is so; that it is a mean as lying between two vices, a vice of excess on the one side and a vice of deficiency on the other, and as aiming at the mean in emotion and action.

That is why it is so hard to be good; for it is always hard to find the mean in anything; it is not everyone but only a man of science who can find the mean or center of a circle. So too anybody can get angry — that is easy — and anybody can give or spend money, but o give it to the right person, to give the right amount of it, at the right time, for the right cause and in the right way, this is not what anybody can do, nor is it easy. That is why goodness is rare and praise worthy and noble. One then who aims at a mean must begin by departing from the extreme that is more contrary to the mean; he must act in the spirit of Calypso's advice,

> "Far from this spray and swell hold thou thy ship,"

for of the two extremes one is more wrong than the other. As it is difficult to hit the mean exactly, we should take the second best course, as the saying is, and choose the lesser of two evils. This we shall best do in the way described, that is, steering clear of the evil which is further from the mean. We must also note the weaknesses to which we are ourselves particularly prone, since different natures tend in different ways; and we may ascertain what our tendency is by observing our feelings of pleasure and pain. Then we must drag ourselves away towards the opposite extreme; for by pulling ourselves as far as possible from what is wrong we shall arrive at the mean, as we do when we pull a crooked stick straight.

In all cases we must especially be on our guard against the pleasant, or pleasure, for we are not impartial judges of pleasure. Hence our attitude towards pleasure must be like that of the elders of the people in the *Iliad* towards Helen, and we must constantly apply the words they use; for if we dismiss pleasure as they dismissed Helen, we shall be less likely to go wrong. By action of this kind, to put it summarily, we shall best succeed in hitting the mean.

Undoubtedly this is a difficult task, especially in individual cases. It is not easy to determine the right manner, objects, occasion and duration of anger. Sometimes we praise people who are deficient in anger, and call them gentle, and at other times we praise people who exhibit a fierce temper as high spirited. It is not however a man who deviates a little from goodness, but one who deviates a great deal, whether on the side of excess or of deficiency, that is blamed; for he is sure to call attention to himself. It is not easy to decide in theory how far and to what extent a man may go before he becomes blameworthy, but neither is it easy to define in theory anything else in the region of the senses; such things depend on circumstances, and our judgment of them depends on our perception.

So much, then, is plain, that the mean is everywhere praiseworthy, but that we ought to aim at one time towards an excess and at another towards a deficiency; for thus we shall most easily hit the mean, or in other words reach excellence.

From Aristotle, *Nicomachean Ethics*, trans. James E.C. Weldon, 1897

Categorical Imperative

Immanuel Kant (1724-1804)

Immanuel Kant was born and lived his entire life in the provincial city of Konigsberg in Prussia. His parents were deeply pietistic Lutherans. One of the greatest German philosophers who ever lived, he lived such a methodical life that it is said the citizens of Konigsberg set their clocks by his walks through the city.

In his greatest work, *The Critique of Pure Reason* (1781) he inaugurated a Copernican-like revolution in the theory of knowledge, as he brought together the rationalists and the empiricists. Kant wrote that David Hume "woke me from my dogmatic slumbers." Although he agreed with Hume that all our knowledge begins with experience, he also argued that not all our knowledge arises from experience. Kant argued that the mind is so constructed and empowered that it imposes interpretive categories on our experience, the way a computer program imposes a certain structure on the information we input. Kant refers to this structure of the mind as synthetic *a priori* knowledge.

In his classic work on ethics, *The Foundations of the Metaphysic of Morals*, which our present reading is from, Kant argues that the moral law is also synthetic *a priori* knowledge. His categorical imperative is "act only on the maxim that you could will to be a universal law of nature without contradiction." This imperative is given as a principle by which to judge all actions to determine if they are morally acceptable.

Kant offers a second formulation of the categorical imperative, "act so as to treat humanity, whether in your own person or in that of any other, as an end in themselves and never as merely a means to an end." This is based upon the dignity and profound worth of humanity because of their free will, moral autonomy, and rationality.

Vocabulary:

Precept:	general rule or principle
A priori:	before experience; not based upon experience
Rectify:	to make right
Maxim:	reason or intention
Import:	something important; consequences
Beneficent:	doing good
Gouty:	painful inflammation of the joints
Pathological:	any deviation from a healthy or normal condition
Propensions:	tendency
Inclination:	tendencies
Categorical:	absolute
Imperative:	command
Hypothetical:	presumed

Concepts:

Categorical Imperative:

First Formulation of Categorical Imperative:

Second Formulation of Categorical Imperative:

Maxim:

Duty:

Good Will:

Questions:

1. *Why is a good will the only thing that can possibly be conceived which is good without qualification?*
2. *Why has reason, not instinct, been made to guide the will?*
3. *Explain Kant's concept of moral worth.*
4. *Explain Kant's first formulation of the categorical imperative.*
5. *Explain Kant's second formulation of the categorical imperative.*

PREFACE

AS MY CONCERN HERE is with moral philosophy, I limit the question suggested to this: Whether it is not of the utmost necessity to construct a pure moral philosophy, perfectly cleared of everything which is only empirical, and which belongs to anthropology? For that such a philosophy must be possible is evident from the common idea of duty and of the moral laws. Everyone must admit that if a law is to have moral force, *i.e.* to be the basis of an obligation, it must carry with it absolute necessity; that, for example, the precept, "Thou shall not lie," is not valid for men alone, as if other rational beings had no need to observe it; and so with all the other moral laws properly so called; that, therefore, the basis of obligation must not be sought in the nature of man, or in the circumstances in the world in which he is placed, but *a priori* simply in the conception of pure reason; and although any other precept which is founded on principles of mere experience may be in certain respects universal, yet in as far as it rests even in the least degree on an empirical basis, perhaps only as to a motive, such a precept, while it may be a practical rule, can never be called a moral law....

THE GOOD WILL

Nothing can possibly be conceived in the world, or even out of it, which can be called good, without qualification, except a Good Will. Intelligence, wit, judgment, and the other *talents* of the mind, however they may be named, or courage, resolution, perseverance, as qualities of temperament, are undoubtedly good and desirable in many respects; but these gifts of nature may also become extremely bad and mischievous if the will which is to make use of them, and which, therefore, constitutes what is called *character,* is not good. It is the same with the *gifts of fortune.* Power, riches, honour, even health, and the general well-being and contentment with one's conditions which is called *happiness*, inspire pride, and often presumption, if there is not a good will to correct the influence of these on the mind, and with this also to rectify the whole principle of acting, and adapt it to its end. The sight of a being who is not adorned with a single feature of a pure and good will, enjoying unbroken prosperity, can never give pleasure to an imperial rational spectator. Thus, a good will appears to constitute the indispensable condition even of being worthy of happiness.

There are even some qualities which are of service to this good will itself, and may facilitate its action, yet which have no intrinsic unconditional value, but always presuppose a good will, and this qualifies the esteem that we justly have for them, and does not permit us to regard them as absolutely good. Moderation in the affections and passions, self-control, and calm deliberation are not only good in many respects, but even seem to constitute part of the intrinsic worth of the person; but they are far from deserving to be called good without qualification, although they have been so unconditionally praised by the ancients. For without the principles of a good will, they may become extremely bad; and the coolness of a villain not only makes him far more dangerous, but also directly makes him far more abominable in our eyes than he would have been without it.

A good will is good not because of what it performs or effects, not by its aptness for the attainment of some proposed end, but simply by virtue of the volition, that is, it is good in itself, and considered by itself to be esteemed much higher than all that can be brought about by it in favor of any inclination, nay, even of the sum total of all inclinations. Even if it should happen that, owing to special disfavor of fortune, or the niggardly provision of a step-motherly nature, this will should wholly lack power to accomplish its purpose, if with its greatest efforts, it should yet achieve nothing, and there should remain only the good will (not, to be sure, a mere wish, but the summoning of all means in our power), then, like a jewel, it would still shine by its own light, as a thing which has its whole value in itself. Its usefulness or fruitlessness can neither add to nor take away anything from this value. It would be, as it were, only the setting to enable us to handle it the more conveniently in common commerce, or to attract to it the attention of those who are not yet connoisseurs, but not to recommend it to true connoisseurs, or to determine its value.

WHY REASON WAS MADE TO GUIDE THE WILL

There is, however, something so strange in this idea of the absolute value of the mere will, in which no account is taken of its utility, that notwithstanding the thorough assent of even common reason to the idea, yet a suspicion must arise that it may perhaps really be the product of mere high-blown fancy, and that we may have misunderstood the purpose of nature in assigning reason as the governor of our will. Therefore, we will examine this idea from this point of view.

In the physical constitution of an organized being, that is, a being adapted suitable to the purposes of life, we assume it as a fundamental principle that no organ for any purpose will be found but what is also the fittest and best adapted for that purpose. Now in a being which has reason and a will, if the proper object of nature were its conservation, its welfare, in a word, its happiness, then nature would have hit upon a very bad arrangement in selecting the reason of the creature to carry out this purpose. For all the actions which the creature has to perform with a view to this purpose, and the whole rule of its conduct, would be far more surely prescribed to it by instinct, and that end would have been attained thereby much more certainly than it ever can be by reason. Should reason have been communicated to this favored creature over and above, it must only have served it to contemplate the happy constitution of its nature, to admire it, to congratulate itself thereon, and to feel thankful for it to the beneficent cause, but not that it should subject its desires to that weak and delusive guidance, and meddle bunglingly with the purpose of nature. In a word, nature would have taken care that reason should not break forth into practical exercise, nor have the presumption, with its weak insight, to think out for itself the plan of happiness, and of the means of attaining it. Nature would not only have taken on herself the choice of the ends, but also of the means, and with wise foresight would have entrusted both to instinct.

And, in fact, we find that the more

a cultivated reason applies itself with deliberate purpose to the enjoyment of life and happiness, so much the more does the man fail of true satisfaction. And from this circumstance there arises in many, if they are candid enough to confess it, a certain degree of misology, that is, hatred of reason, especially in the case of those who are most experienced in the use of it, because after calculating all the advantages they derive, I do not say from the invention of all the arts of common luxury, but even from the sciences (which seem to them to be after all only a luxury of the understanding), they find that they have, in fact, only brought more trouble on their shoulders, rather than gained in happiness; and they end by envying, rather than despising, the more common stamp of men who keep closer to the guidance of mere instinct, and do not allow their reason much influence on their conduct. And this we must admit, that the judgment of those who would very much lower the lofty eulogies of the advantages which reason gives us in regard to the happiness and satisfaction of life, or who would even reduce them below zero, is by no means morose or ungrateful to the goodness with which the world is governed, but that there lies at the root of these judgments the idea that our existence has a different and far nobler end,

for which, and not for happiness, reason is properly intended, and which must, therefore, be regarded as the supreme condition to which the private ends of man must, for the most part, be postponed.

For as reason is not competent to guide the will with certainty in regard to its objects and the satisfaction of all our wants (which it to some extent even multiplies), this being an end to which an implanted instinct would have led with much greater certainty; and since, nevertheless, reason is imparted to us as a practical faculty, i.e. as one which is to have influence on the will, therefore, admitting that nature generally in the distribution of her capacities has adapted the means to the end, its true destination must be to produce a will, not merely good as a means to something else, but good in itself, for which reason was absolutely necessary. This will then, though not indeed the sole and complete good, must be the supreme good and the condition of every other, even of the desire of happiness. Under these circumstances, there is nothing inconsistent with the wisdom of nature in the fact that the cultivation of the reason, which is requisite for the first and unconditional purpose, does in many ways interfere, at least in this life, with the attainment of the second, which is always conditional, namely, happiness.

Nay, it may even reduce it to nothing, without nature thereby failing in her purpose. For reason recognizes the establishment of a good will as its highest practical destination, and in attaining this purpose is capable only of a satisfaction of its own proper kind, namely, that from the attainment of an end, which end again is determined by reason only, notwithstanding that this may involve many a disappointment to the ends of inclination.

THE FIRST PROPOSITION OF MORALITY

(An action must be done from a sense of duty, if it is to have moral worth). We have then to develop the notion of a will which deserves to be highly esteemed for itself, and is good without a view to anything further, a notion which exists already in the sound natural understanding, requiring rather to be cleared up than to be taught, and which in estimating the value of our actions always takes the first place, and constitutes the condition of all the rest. In order to do this, we will take the notion of duty, which includes that of a good will, although implying certain subjective restrictions and hindrances. These, however, far from concealing it, or rendering it unrecognizable, rather bring it out by contrast, and make it shine forth so much the brighter.

I omit here all actions which are already recognized as inconsistent with duty although they may be useful for this or that purpose, for with these the question whether they are done from duty cannot arise at all, since they even conflict with it. I also set aside those actions which really conform to duty, but to which men have no direct inclination, performing them because they are impelled thereto by some other inclination. For in this case we can readily distinguish whether the action which agrees with duty is done from duty, or from a selfish view. It is much harder to make this distinction when the action accords with duty, and the subject has besides a direct inclination to it. For example, it is always a matter of duty that a dealer should not overcharge an inexperienced purchaser; and whenever there is much commerce the prudent tradesman does not overcharge, but keeps a fixed price for everyone, so that a child buys of him as well as any other. Men are thus honestly served; but this is not enough to make us believe that the tradesman has so acted from duty and from principles of honesty: his own advantage required it. It is out of the question in this case to suppose that he might besides have a direct inclination in favor of the buyers, so that, as it were, from love he should give no advantage to one over another. Accordingly the action was done neither from duty nor from direct inclination, but merely with a selfish view.

On the other hand, it is a duty to maintain one's life; and, in addition, everyone has also a direct inclination to do so. But on this account the often anxious care which most men take for it has no intrinsic worth, and their maxim has no moral import. They preserve their life *as duty requires*, no doubt, but not *because duty requires*. On the other hand, if adversity and hopeless sorrow have completely taken away the relish for life; if the unfortunate one, strong in mind, indignant at his fate rather than desponding or dejected, wishes for death, and yet preserves his life without loving it — not from inclination or fear, but from duty — then his maxim has a moral worth.

To be beneficent when we can is a duty; and besides this, there are many minds so sympathetically constituted that, without any other motive of vanity or self-interest, they find a pleasure in spreading joy around them, and can take delight in the satisfaction of others so far as it is their own work. But I maintain that in such a case an action of this kind, however proper, however amiable it may be, has nevertheless no true moral worth, but is on a level with other inclinations, *e.g.*

the inclination to honor, which, if it is happily directed to that which is in fact of public utility and accordant with duty, and consequently honorable, deserves praise and encouragement, but not esteem. For the maxim lacks the moral import, namely, that such actions be done *from duty*, not from inclination. Put the case that the mind of that philanthropist was clouded by sorrow of his own, extinguishing all sympathy with the lot of others, and that while he still has the power to benefit others in distress, he is not touched by their trouble because he is absorbed with his own; and now suppose that he tears himself out of this dead insensibility, and performs the action without any inclination to it, but simply from duty, then first has his action its genuine moral worth. Further still; if nature has put little sympathy in the heart of this or that man; if he, supposed to be an upright man, is by temperament cold and indifferent to the sufferings of others, perhaps because in respect of his own he is provided with the special gift of patience and fortitude, and supposes, or even requires, that others should have the same - and such a man would certainly not be the meanest product of nature — but if nature had not specially framed him for a philanthropist, would he not still find in himself a source from whence to give himself a far higher worth than that of a good-natured temperament could be? Unquestionably. It is just in this that the moral worth of the character is brought out which is incomparably the highest of all, namely, that he is beneficent, not from inclination, but from duty.

To secure one's own happiness is a duty, at least indirectly; for discontent with one's condition, under a pressure of many anxieties and amidst unsatisfied wants, might easily become a great *temptation to transgression* of duty. But here again, without looking to duty, all men have already the strongest and most intimate inclination to happiness, because it is just in this idea that all inclinations are combined in one total. But the precept of happiness is often of such a sort that it greatly interferes with some inclinations, and yet a man cannot form any definite and certain conception of the sum of satisfaction of all of them which is called happiness. It is not then to be wondered at that a single inclination, definite both as to what it promises and as to the time within which it can be gratified, is often able to overcome such a fluctuating idea, and that a gouty patient, for instance, can choose to enjoy what he likes, and to suffer what he may, since, according to his calculation, on this occasion at least, he has [only] not sacrificed the enjoyment of

the present moment to a possibly mistaken expectation of a happiness which is supposed to be found in health. But even in this case, if the general desire for happiness did not influence his will, and supposing that in his particular case health was not a necessary element in this calculation, there yet remains in this, as in all other cases, this law, namely, that he should promote his happiness not from inclination but from duty, and by this would his conduct first acquire true moral worth.

It is in this manner, undoubtedly, that we are to understand those passages of Scripture also in which we are commanded to love our neighbor, even our enemy. For love, as an affection, cannot be commanded, but beneficence for duty's sake may; even though we are not impelled to it by any inclination — nay, even repelled by a natural and unconquerable aversion. This is *practical* love, and not *pathological* — a love which is seated in the will, and not in the propensions of sense — in principles of action and not of tender sympathy; and it is this love alone which can be commanded.

THE SECOND PROPOSTION OF MORALITY

The second proposition is: That an action done from duty derives its moral worth, *not from the purpose* which is to be attained by it, but from the maxim by which it is determined, and ,therefore, does not depend on the realization of the object of the action, but merely on the *principle of volition* by which the action has taken place, without regard to any object of desire. It is clear from what precedes that the purposes which we may have in view in our actions, or their effects regarded as ends and springs of the will, cannot give to actions any unconditional or moral worth. In what, then, can their worth lie, if it is not to consist in the will and in reference to its expected effect? It cannot lie anywhere but in the principle of the will without regard to the ends which can be attained by the action. For the will stands between its *a priori* principle, which is formal, and its *a posteriori* spring, which is material, as between two roads, and as it must be determined by something, it follows that it must be determined by the formal principle of volition when an action is done from duty, in which case every material principle has been withdrawn from it.

THE THIRD PROPOSITION OF MORALITY

The third proposition , which is a consequence of the two preceding, I would express as thus: *Duty is the neces-sity of acting from respect for the law*. I may have *inclination* for an object as the effect of my proposed action, but I cannot have *respect* for it, just for this reason, that it is an effect and not an energy of will. Similarly, I cannot have respect for inclination, whether my own or another's; I can at most, if my own, approve it; if another's, sometimes even love it; *i.e.* look on it as favorable to my own interest. It is only what is connected with my will as a principle, by no means as an effect — what does not sub-serve my inclination, but overpowers it, or at least in case of choice excludes it from its calculation — in other words, simply the law of itself, which can be an object of respect, and hence a command. Now an action done from duty must wholly exclude the influence of inclination, and with it every object of the will, so that nothing remains which can determine the will except objectively the *law*, and subjectively pure respect for this practical law, and consequently the maxim that I should follow this law even to the thwarting of all my inclinations.

Thus, the moral worth of an action does not lie in the effect expected from it, nor in any principle of action which requires to borrow its motive from this expected effect. For all these effects — agreeableness of one's condition, and even the promotion of the happiness of others — could have been also brought about by other causes, so that for this there would have been no need of the will of a rational being; whereas it is in this alone that the supreme and unconditional good can be found. The pre-eminent good which we call moral can, therefore, consist in nothing else than the conception of law in itself, which certainly is only possible in a rational being, insofar as this conception, and not the expected effect, determines the will. This is a good which is already present in the person who acts accordingly, and we have not to wait for it to appear first in the result.

THE SUPREME PRINCIPLE OF MORALITY: THE CATEGORICAL IMPERATIVE

But what sort of law can that be, the conception of which must determine the will, even without paying any regard to the effect expected from it, in order that this will may be called good absolutely and without qualification? As I have deprived the will of every impulse which could arise to it from obedience to any law, there remains nothing but the universal conformity of its actions to law in general, which alone is to serve the will as a principle, *i.e.* I am never to act otherwise than so *that I could also will that my maxim should become a universal law.* here, now, it is the simple conformity to law in general, without assuming any particular law applicable to certain actions, that serves the will as its principle, and must so serve it, if duty is not to be a vain delusion and a chimerical notion. The common reason of men in its practical judgments perfectly coincides with this, and always has in view the principle here suggested. Let the question be, for example: May I, when in distress, make a promise with the intention not to keep it? I readily distinguish here between the two significations which the question may have: Whether it is prudent, or whether it is right, to make a false promise? The former may undoubtedly often be the case. I see clearly indeed that it is not enough to extricate myself from a present difficulty by means of this subterfuge, but it must be well considered whether there may not hereafter spring from this lie much greater inconvenience than that from which I now free myself, and as, with all my supposed *cunning*, the consequences cannot be so easily foreseen but that credit once lost may be much more injurious to me than any mischief which I seek to avoid at present, it should be considered whether it would not be more *prudent* to act herein according to a universal maxim, and to make it a habit to promise nothing except with the intention of keeping it. But it is soon clear to me that such a maxim will still only be based on the fear of consequences. Now it is a wholly different thing to be truthful from duty, and to be so from apprehension of injurious consequences. In the first case, the very notion of the action already implies a law for me; in the second case, I must first look about elsewhere to see what results may be combined with it which would affect myself. For to deviate from the principle of duty is beyond all doubt wicked; but to be unfaithful to my maxim of prudence may often be very advantageous to me, although to abide by it is certainly safer. The shortest way, however, and an unerring one, to discover the answer to this question whether a lying promise is consistent with duty, is to ask myself, "Should I be content that my maxim (to extricate myself from difficulty by a false promise) should hold good as a universal law, for myself as well as for other?" And should I be able to say to myself, "Every one may make a deceitful promise when he finds himself in a difficulty from which he cannot otherwise extricate himself?" Then I presently become aware that while I can will the lie, I can, by no means, will that lying should be a universal law. For with such a law there would be no promises at all, since it would be in vain to allege my

intention in regard to my future actions to those who would not believe this allegation, or if they over-hastily did so, would pay me back in my own coin. Hence, my maxim, as soon as it should be made a universal law, would necessarily destroy itself.

I do not, therefore, need any far-reaching penetration to discern what I have to do in order that my will may be morally good. Inexperienced in the course of the world, incapable of being prepared for all its contingencies, I only ask myself, "Canst thou also will that thy maxim should be a universal law?" If not, then it must be rejected, and that not because of a disadvantage accruing from myself or even to others, but because it cannot enter as a principle into a possible universal legislation, and reason extorts from me immediate respect for such legislation. I do not indeed as yet *discern* on what this respect is based (this the philosopher may inquire), but at least I understand his, that it is an estimation of the worth which far outweighs all worth of what is recommended by inclination, and that the necessity of acting from pure respect for the practical law is what constitutes duty, to which every other motive must give place, because it is the condition of a will being good in itself, and the worth of such a will is above everything.

Thus, then, without quitting the moral knowledge of common human reason, we have arrived at its principle. And although, no doubt, common men do not conceive it in such an abstract and universal form, yet they always have it really before their eyes, and use it as the standard of their decision....

Nor could anything be more fatal to morality than that we should wish to derive it from examples. For every example of it that is set before me must be first itself tested by principles of morality, whether it is worthy to serve as an original example, *i.e.* as a pattern, but by no means can it authoritatively furnish the conception of morality. Even the Holy One of the Gospels must first be compared with our ideal of moral perfection before we can recognize Him as such; and so He says of Himself, "Why call ye Me [whom you see] good; none is good [the model of good] but God only [whom ye do not see]." But whence have we the conception of God as the supreme good? Simply from the *idea* of moral perfection, which reason frames *a priori*, and connects inseparably with the notion of a free will. Imitation finds no place at all in morality, and examples serve only for encouragement, *i.e.* they put beyond doubt the feasibility of what the law commands, they make visible that which the practical rule expresses more generally, but they can never authorize us to set aside the true original which lies in reason, and to guide ourselves by examples.

From what has been said, it is clear that all moral conceptions have their seat and origin completely *a priori* in the reason, and that, moreover, in the commonest reason just as truly as in that which is in the highest degree speculative; that they cannot be obtained by abstraction from any empirical, and, therefore, merely contingent knowledge; that it is just this purity of their origin that makes them worthy to serve as our supreme practical principle, and that just in proportion as we add anything empirical, we detract from their genuine influence, and from the absolute value of actions; that it is not only of the greatest necessity, in a purely speculative point of view, but is also of the greatest practical importance, to derive these notions and laws from pure reason, to present them pure and unmixed, and even to determine the compass of this practical or pure rational knowledge, *i.e.* to determine the whole faculty of pure practical reason; and, in doing so, we must not make its principles dependent on the particular nature of human reason, though in speculative philosophy this may be permitted, or may even at times be necessary; but since moral laws ought to hold good for every rational creature, we must derive them from the general concept of a rational being. In this way, although for its *application* to man, morality has need of anthropology, yet, in the first instance, we must treat it independently as pure philosophy, *i.e.* as metaphysic, complete in itself (a thing which, in such distinct branches of science, is easily done); knowing well that unless we are in possession of this, it would not only be vain to determine the moral element of duty in right actions for purposes of speculative criticism, but it would be impossible to base morals on their genuine principles, even for common practical purposes, especially of moral instruction, so as to produce pure moral dispositions, and to engraft them on men's minds to the promotion of the greatest possible good in the world....

THE RATIONAL GROUND OF THE CATEGORICAL IMPERATIVE

...the question, how the imperative of *morality* is possible, is undoubtedly one, the only one, demanding a solution, as this is not at all hypothetical, and the objective necessity which it presents cannot rest on any hypothesis, as is the case with the hypothetical imperatives.

Only here we must never leave out of consideration that we *cannot* make out *by any example*, in other words empirically, whether there is such an imperative at all; but it is rather to be feared that all those which seem to be categorical may yet be at bottom hypothetical. For instance, when the precept is: thou shalt not promise deceitfully; and it is assumed that the necessity of this is not a mere counsel to avoid some other evil, so that it should mean: Thou shalt not make a lying promise, lest if it become known thou shouldst destroy the credit, but that an action of this kind must be regarded as evil in itself, so that the imperative of the prohibition is categorical; then we cannot show with certainty in any example that the will was determined merely by the law, without any other spring of action, although it may appear to be so. For it is always possible that fear of disgrace, perhaps also obscure dread of other dangers, may have a secret influence on the will. Who can prove by experience the nonexistence of a cause when all that experience tells us is that we do not perceive it? But in such a case the so-called moral imperative, which as such appears to be categorical and unconditional, would, in reality, be only a pragmatic precept, drawing our attention to our own interests, and merely teaching us to take these into consideration.

We shall, therefore, have to investigate *a priori* the possibility of a categorical imperative, as we have not, in this case, the advantage of its reality being given in experience, so that [the elucidation of] its possibility should be requisite only for its explanation, not for its establishment. In the meantime it may be discerned beforehand that the categorical imperative alone has the purport of a practical law: all the rest may indeed be called *principles* of the will but not laws, since whatever is only necessary for the attainment of some arbitrary purpose may be considered as in itself contingent, and we can at any time be free from the precept if we give up the purpose: on the contrary, the unconditional command leaves the will no liberty to choose the opposite; consequently it alone carries with it that necessity which we require in a law.

Secondly, in the case of this categorical imperative or law of morality, the difficulty (of discerning its possibility) is a very profound one. It is an a *priori* synthetical practical proposition; and as there is so much difficulty in discerning the possibility of speculative propositions of this kind, it may readily be supposed that the difficulty will be no less with the practical.

FIRST FORMULATION OF THE CATEGORICAL IMEPRATIVE: UNIVERSAL LAW

In this problem we will first inquire whether the mere conception of a categorical imperative may not perhaps supply us also with the formula of it, containing the proposition which alone can be a categorical imperative; for even if we know the tenor of such an absolute command, yet how it is possible will require further special and laborious study, which we postpone to the last section.

When I conceive a hypothetical imperative, in general I do not know beforehand what it will contain until I am given the condition. But when I conceive a categorical imperative, I know at once what it contains. For as the imperative contains besides the law only the necessity that the maxims shall conform to this law, while the law contains no conditions restricting it, there remains nothing but the general statement that the maxim of the action should conform to a universal law, and it is this conformity alone that the imperative properly represents as necessary.

There is therefore but one categorical imperative, namely, this: *Act only on that maxim whereby thou canst at the same time will that it should become a universal law without contradiction.*

Now if all imperatives of duty can be deduced from this one imperative as from their principle, then, although it should remain undecided whether what is called duty is not merely a vain notion, yet at least we shall be able to show what we understand by it and what this notion means.

Since the universality of the law according to which effects are produced constitutes what is properly called *nature* in the most general sense (as to form), that is the existence of things so far as it is determined by general laws, the imperative of duty may be expressed thus: Act as if the maxim of thy action were to become by they will a universal law of nature.

FOUR ILLUSTRATIONS

We will now enumerate a few duties, adopting the usual division of them into duties to ourselves and to others, and into perfect and imperfect duties.

1. A man reduced to despair by a series of misfortunes feels wearied of life, but is still so far in possession of his reason that he can ask himself whether it would not be contrary to his duty to himself to take his own life. Now he inquires whether the maxim of his action could become a universal law of nature. His maxim is: From self-love I adopt it as a principle to shorten my life when its longer duration is likely to bring more evil than satisfaction. It is asked then simply whether this principle founded on self-love can become a universal law of nature. Now we see, once that a system of nature of which it should be a law to destroy life by means of the very feeling whose special nature it is to impel to the improvement of life, would contradict itself, and therefore could not exist as a system of nature; hence that maxim cannot possibly exist as a universal law of nature, and consequently would be wholly inconsistent with the supreme principle of all duty.

2. Another finds himself forced by necessity to borrow money. He knows that he will not be able to repay it, but sees also that nothing will be lent to him, unless he promises stoutly to repay it in a definite time. He desires to make this promise, but he has still so much conscience as to ask himself, "Is it not unlawful and inconsistent with duty to get out of a difficulty in this way?" Suppose, however, that he resolves to do so, then the maxim of his action would be expressed thus: When I think myself in want of money, I will borrow money and promise to repay it, although I know that I never

can do so. Now this principle of self-love or of one's own advantage may perhaps be consistent with my whole future welfare; but the question is, Is it right? I change, then, the suggestion of self-love into a universal law, and state the question thus: "How would it be if my maxim were a universal law?" Then I see at once that it could never hold as a universal law of nature, but would necessarily contradict itself. For supposing it to be a universal law that everyone, when he thinks himself in a difficulty, should be able to promise whatever he pleases, with the purpose of not keeping his promise, the promise itself would become impossible, as well as the end that one might have in view of it, since no one would consider that anything was promised to him, but would ridicule all such statements as vain pretenses.

3. A third finds in himself a talent which, with the help of some culture, might make him a useful man in many respects. But he finds himself in comfortable circumstances, and prefers to indulge in pleasure rather than to take pains in enlarging and improving his happy natural capacities. He asks, however, whether his maxim of neglect of his natural gifts, besides agreeing with his inclination to indulgence, agrees also with what is called duty. He sees then that a system of nature could indeed subsist with such a universal law although men (like the South Sea islanders) should let their talents rest, and resolve to devote their lives merely to idleness, amusement, and propagation of their species — in a word, to enjoyment; but he cannot possibly *will* that this should be a universal law of nature, or be implanted in us as such by a natural instinct. For, as a rational being, he necessarily wills that his faculties be developed, since they serve him, and have been given him, for all sorts of possible purposes.

4. A fourth, who is in prosperity, while he sees that others have to contend with great wretchedness and that he could help them, thinks, "What concern is it of mine? Let everyone be as happy as Heaven pleases, or as he can make himself; I will take nothing from him nor even envy him, only I do not wish to contribute anything to his welfare or to his assistance in distress!" Now, no doubt if such a mode of thinking were a universal law, the human race might very well subsist, and doubtless even better than in a state in which everyone talks of sympathy and good-will, or even takes care occasionally to put it into practice, but, on the other side, also cheats when he can, betrays the rights of men, or otherwise violates them. But although it is possible

that a universal law of nature might exist in accordance with that maxim, it is impossible to *will* that such a principle should have the universal validity of a law of nature. For a will which resolved this would contradict itself, inasmuch as many cases might occur in which one would have need of the love and sympathy of others, and in which, by such a law of nature, sprung from his own will, he would deprive himself of all hope of the aid he desires.

These are a few of the many actual duties, or at least what we regard as such, which obviously fall into two classes on the one principle that we have laid down. We must be *able to will* that a maxim of our action should be a universal law. This is the canon of the moral appreciation of the action generally. Some actions are of such a character that their maxim cannot, without contradiction, be even *conceived* as a universal law of nature, far from it being possible that we should *will* that it *should* be so. In others this intrinsic impossibility is not found, but still it is impossible to *will* that their maxim should be raised to the universality of a law of nature, since such a will would contradict itself. It is easily seen that the former violate strict or rigorous (inflexible) duty; the latter only laxer (meritorious) duty. Thus, it has been completely shown by these examples how all duties depend as regards the nature of the obligation (not the object of the action) on the same principle.

SECOND FORMULATION OF THE CATEGORICAL IMPERATIVE: HUMANITY AS AN END IN ITSELF

. . . Now I say: man and generally any rational being *exists* as an end in himself, *not merely as a means* to be arbitrarily used by this or that will, but in all his actions, whether they concern himself or other rational beings, must be always regarded at the same time as an end. All objects of the inclinations have only a conditional worth; for if the inclinations and the wants founded on them did not exist, then their object would be without value. But the inclinations themselves being sources of want are so far from having an absolute worth for which they should be desired, that, on the contrary, it must be the universal wish of every rational being to be wholly free from them. Thus, the worth of any object which is to be *acquired* by our action is always conditional. Beings whose existence depends not on our will but on nature's, have nevertheless, if they are nonrational beings, only a relative value as means, and are, therefore, called *things*; rational beings, on the contrary, are called *persons*, because their very nature points them out as ends in themselves, that is as something which must not be used merely as means, and so far, therefore, restricts freedom of action (and is an object of respect). These, therefore, are not merely subjective ends whose existence has a worth *for us* as an effect of our action, but *objective ends*, that is things whose existence is an end in itself: an end moreover for which no other can be substituted, which they should subserve merely as means, for otherwise nothing whatsoever would possess *absolute worth*; but if all worth were conditioned and therefore contingent, then there would be no supreme practical principle of reason whatsoever.

If, then, there is a supreme practical principle or, in respect of the human will, a categorical imperative, it must be one which, being drawn from the conception of that which is necessarily an end for everyone because it is *an end in itself*, constitutes an *objective* principle of will, and can, therefore, serve as a universal practical law. The foundation of this principle is: *rational nature exists as an end in itself*. Man necessarily conceives his own existence as being so: so far then this is a *subjective* principle of human actions. But every other rational being regards its exis-

tence similarly, just on the same rational principle that holds for me: so that it is at the same time an objective principle, from which as a supreme practical law all laws of the will must be capable of being deduced. Accordingly the practical imperative will be as follows: *So act as to treat humanity, whether in thine own person or in that of any other, in every case as an end withal, never as means only. ...*

. . . Looking back now on all previous attempts to discover the principle of morality, we need not wonder why they all failed. It was seen that man was bound to laws by duty, but it was not observed that the laws to which he is subject are only those *of his own giving*, though at the same time they are *universal*, and that he is only bound to act in conformity with his own will; a will, however, which is designed by nature to give universal laws. For when one has conceived man only as subject to a law (no matter what), then this law required some interest, either by way of attraction or constraint, since it did not originate as a law from *his own* will, but his will was, according to a law, obliged by *something* else to act in a certain manner. Now by this necessary consequence all the labour spent in finding a supreme principle of *duty* was irrevocably lost. For men never elicited duty, but only a necessity of acting from a certain interest. Whether this interest was private or otherwise, in any case the imperative must be conditional, and could not by any means be capable of being a moral command. I will, therefore, call this the principle of *Autonomy* of the will. I contrast with every other which I accordingly reckon as *Heteronomy*.

From Immanuel Kant, *The Foundations of the Metaphysic of Morals*, trans. T.K. Abbott, 1873.

Utilitarianism

John Stuart Mill (1806-1873)

In this work, taken from *Utilitarianism* (1861), Mill argues that the principle of utilitarianism is the fundamental principle by which we should make our moral decisions. The principle of utilitarianism states that we should always act to create the greatest amount of happiness for the greatest number of people, as per a disinterested spectator.

Vocabulary:

Epicureans:	philosophers who believed that pleasure was the goal of life
Stoics:	philosophers who believed in fixed natural laws and that man should remain indifferent to the external world, passions and desires
Gainsaid:	denied
Imputation:	when we attribute something, some quality, to some person
Inculcate:	to teach persistently and earnestly
Appellation:	an identifying name or title
Intrinsic:	belong to a thing by its very nature
Sustenance:	anything that sustains

Tribunal:	a court of justice
Suffrage:	the right to vote
Homogeneous:	of the same kind or nature
Heterogeneous:	of a different kind or nature
Enunciation:	pronouncement; clear declaration
Superfluous:	unimportant; unneccessary

Concepts:

Utilitarianism:

Happiness:

Pleasure:

Mental Pleasure:

Physical Pleasure:

Questions:

1. *Explain Mill's concept of utilitarianism.*
2. *How does Mill define happiness?*
3. *What are the three major differences between physical and mental pleasure?*
4. *What sort of proof does Mill use to justify utilitarianism?*

Utilitarianism

The creed which accepts as the foundation of morals, Utility, or the Greatest Happiness Principle, holds that actions are right in proportion as they tend to promote happiness, wrong as they tend to produce the reverse of happiness. By happiness is intended pleasure, and the absence of pain; by unhappiness, pain, and the privation of pleasure. To give a clear view of the moral standard set up by the theory, much more requires to be said; in particular, what things it includes in the ideas of pain and pleasure; and to what extent this is left an open question. But these supplementary explanations do not affect the theory of life on which this theory of morality is grounded – namely, that pleasure, and freedom from pain, are the only things desirable as ends; and that all desirable things (which are as numerous in the utilitarian as in any other scheme) are desirable either for the pleasure inherent in themselves, or as means to the promotion of pleasure and the prevention of pain.

Now, such a theory of life excites in many minds, and among them in some of the most estimable in feeling and purpose, habitual dislike. To suppose that life has (as they express it) no higher end than pleasure – no better and nobler object of desire and pursuit – they designate as utterly mean and groveling; as a doctrine worthy of only swine, to whom the followers of Epicurus were, at a very early period, contemptuously likened; and modern holders of the doctrine are occasionally made the subject of equally polite comparisons by its German, French, and English assailants.

When thus attacked, the Epicureans have always answered, that it is not they, but their accusers, who represent human nature in a degrading light; since the accusation supposes human beings to be capable of no pleasure except those of which swine are capable. If this supposition were true, the charge could not be gainsaid, but would then be no longer an imputation. For if the sources of pleasure were precisely the same to human beings and swine, the rule of life which is good enough for the one would be good enough for the other. The comparison of the Epicurean life to that of beasts is felt as degrading, precisely because a beast's pleasures do not satisfy a human being's conception of happiness. Human beings have faculties more elevated than the animal appetites, and when once made conscious of them, do not regard anything as happiness which does not include their gratification. I do not, indeed, consider the Epicureans to have been by any means faultless in drawing out their scheme of consequences from the utilitarian principle. To do this in any sufficient manner, many Stoics, as well as Christians elements require to be included. But there is no known Epicurean theory of life which does not assign to the pleasures of the intellect, of feelings and imagination, and of the moral sentiments, a much higher value as pleasure than to those of mere sensation. I must be admitted, however, that utilitarian writers in general have placed the superiority of mental over bodily pleasures chiefly in the greater permanency, safety, uncostliness, etc., of the former – that is, in their circumstantial advantages rather than in their intrinsic nature. And on all these points utilitarians have fully proved their case; but they might have taken the other, and, as it may be called, higher ground, with entire consistency. It is quite compatible with the principle of utility to recognize the fact that some kinds of pleasure are more desirable and more valuable than others. It would be absurd that while, in estimating all other things, quality is considered as well as quantity, the estimation of pleasures should be supposed to depend on quantity alone.

If I am asked, what I mean by difference of quality in pleasures, or what makes one pleasure more valuable than another, merely as a pleasure, except its being greater in amount, there is but one possible answer. Of two pleasures, if there be one which all or almost all who have experience of both give a decided preference, irrespective of any feeling of moral obligation to prefer it, that is the more desirable pleasure. If one of the two is placed so far above the other by those who are competently acquainted with both, even though knowing it to be attended with a great amount of discontent, and would not resign it for any quantity of the other pleasure which their nature is capable of, we are justified in ascribing to the preferred enjoyment a superiority in quality, so far outweighing quantity as to render it, in comparison, of small account.

Now it is an unquestioned fact that those who are equally acquainted with, and equally capable of appreciating and enjoying both, do give a most marked preference to the higher faculties. Few human beings would consent to be changed into any of the lower animals, for a promise of the fullest allowance of the beast's pleasures. No intelligent human being would consent to be a fool. No educated person an ignoramus, no person of feeling and conscience would be selfish and base, even though they should be persuaded that the fool, the dunce, or the rascal is better satisfied with his lot than they are with theirs. They would not resign what they possess more than he for the most complete satisfaction of all the desires which they have in common with him. If they ever fancy they would, it is only in cases of unhappiness so extreme, that to escape from it they would exchange their lot for almost any other, however undesirable in their own eyes. A being of higher faculties requires more to make him happy. He is capable of more acute suffering and certainly accessible to it at more points than one of an inferior type. But in spite of these liabilities, he can never really wish to sink into what he feels to be a lower grade of existence. We may give what explanation we please of this unwillingness. We may attribute it to pride, a name which is given indiscriminately to some of the most, and to some the least, estimable feelings of which humankind are capable. We may refer it to the love of liberty and personal independence, an appeal to which the Stoics made a most effective means of inculcation. We may refer it to the love of power, love of excitement, both of which do really enter into and contribute to it. But its most appropriate appellation is a sense of dignity, which all human beings possess in one form or another. In some, though by no means in all, this is in proportion to their higher faculties, and which is so essential a part of their happiness that nothing conflicts with it other than a momentary object of desire.

Whoever supposes that this preference takes place at a sacrifice of happiness – that the superior being, in anything like equal circumstances, is not happier than the inferior – confounds the two very different ideas, of happiness, and contentment. It is indisputable that the being whose capacities of enjoyment are low has the greatest chance of having them fully satisfied. A highly endowed being will always feel that any happiness which he can look for, as the world is constituted, is imperfect. But he can learn to bear its imperfections, if they are at all bearable. They will not make him envy the being who is indeed unconscious of the imperfections, but only because he feels not at all the good which those imperfections qualify. It is better to be a human being dissatisfied than a pig satisfied. It is better to be Socrates dissatisfied than a fool satisfied. And if the fool or the pig are of a different opinion, it is only because they only know their own side of the question. The other party knows both sides.

It may be objected that many who are capable of the higher pleasures occasionally, under the influence of temptation, postpone them to the lower. But this is quite compatible with a full appreciation of the intrinsic superiority of the higher. Men often, from infirmity of character, make their election for the nearer good, though they know it to be the less valuable, and this no less the case when the choice is between two bodily pleasures than when it is between bodily and mental. They pursue sensual indulgences to the injury of health, though perfectly aware that health is the greater good. It may be further objected, that many who begin with youthful enthusiasm for everything noble, as they advance in years sink into indolence and selfishness. But I do not believe that those who undergo this very common change voluntarily choose the lower description of pleasures in preference to the higher. I believe that before they devote themselves exclusively to the one, they have already become incapable of the other. Capacity for the nobler feelings is in most natures a very tender plant, easily killed, not only by hostile influences, but also by mere want of sustenance. In the majority of young persons it speedily dies away if the occupations to which their position in life has devoted them, and the society into which it has thrown them, are not favorable to keeping that higher capacity exercised. Men lose their high aspirations as they lose their intellectual tastes because they have not time nor opportunity for indulging them. They addict themselves to inferior pleasures, not because they deliberately prefer them, but because they are either the only ones to which they have access, or the only ones which they are any longer capable of enjoying. It may be questioned whether anyone who has remained equally susceptible to both classes of pleasures, ever knowingly and calmly preferred the lower. In all ages, many have failed to combine both.

From this verdict of the only competent judges, I apprehend that there can be no appeal. On a question of which of two pleasures is the best to have, or which of two modes of existence is the most grateful to feelings, apart from its moral attributes and from its consequences, the judgment of those who are qualified by knowledge of both must be admitted as final. And if those qualified differ, then that of the majority must be admitted as final. And there needs to be less hesitation to accept this judgment respecting the quality of pleasure, since there is no other tribunal to be referred to even on the question of quantity. What means are there of determining which is the acutest of two pains, or the most intense of two pleasurable sensations, except the general suffrage of those who are familiar with both? Neither pains nor pleasures are homogeneous, and pain is always heterogeneous with pleasure.

What is there to decide whether a particular pleasure is worth purchasing at the cost of a particular pain, except the feelings and judgments of the experienced? When therefore, those feelings and judgments declare the pleasures derived from the higher faculties to be preferable in kind, apart from the question of intensity, to those of which the animal nature, disjoined from the higher faculties, is susceptible, they are entitled on this subject to the same regard.

I dwelt on this point, as being a necessary part of a perfectly just conception of utility or happiness, considered as the directive rule of human conduct. But it is by no means an indispensable condition to the acceptance of the utilitarian standard. For that standard is not the agent's own greatest happiness, but the greatest amount of happiness all together. And, if it may possibly be doubted whether a noble character is always the happier for its

nobleness, there can be no doubt that it makes other people happier and the world in general is immensely better by it. Utilitarianism, therefore, could only attain its end by the general cultivation of nobleness of character, even if each individual were only benefited by the nobleness of others, and his own, so far as happiness is concerned, were sheer deduction from the benefit, the bare enunciation of such an absurdity as this last, renders refutation superfluous.

According to the greatest happiness principle, as above explained, the ultimate end, with reference to and for the sake of which all other things are desirable (whether we are considering our own good or that of other people), is an existence exempt as far as possible from pain, and as rich as possible in enjoyments, both in point of quantity and quality. The test of quality, and the rule for measuring it against quantity, being the preference felt by those who in their opportunities of experience, to which must be added their habits of self-consciousness and self-observation, are best furnished with the means of comparison. This being according to the utilitarian opinion, the end of human action, is necessarily also the standard of morality, which may accordingly be defined, the rules and precepts for human conduct, by the observation of which an existence such as has been described might be, to the greatest extent possible, secured to all humankind.

From John Stuart Mill, *Utilitarianism*, 1861.

Beyond Good and Evil

Friedrich Nietzsche (1844-1900)

Friedrich Nietzsche was born in Germany into a puritanical, religious family. Growing up as the son of a minister, he became one of the most influential and outspoken critics of religion, particularly of Christianity and traditional morality.

After studying at the University of Bonn and the University of Leipzig, he became professor of Philosophy at the University of Basel. His works include: *Thus Spoke Zarathustra* (1884); *Beyond Good and Evil* (1886); *The Genealogy of Morals* (1887); *The Antichrist* (1888); and *The Will to Power* (1906).

It was Nietzsche who coined the phrase, "God is Dead." Although many have discounted his work, Nietzsche's works have influenced many of France's and Germany's most important thinkers such as; Thomas Mann, Hermann Hesse, Karl Jaspers, Martin Heidegger, Sigmund Freud and Jean-Paul Sartre.

Nietzsche argued that the fundamental creative force in all creation is the will to power. All individuals seek to fulfill their desires, affirm themselves, flourish and dominate others. Since we are unequal in our talents and abilities, the fittest will survive and dominate those who are weaker and less talented. Nietzsche's great disdain for Christianity is that it seeks to frustrate this natural will to power by its basic belief that all human beings are of equal worth. He labeled Christianity "slave morality" and "the ethics of resentment" because he believed it was the invention of jealous priests who were envious and resentful of the power of the nobility.

Our present readings are taken from *Beyond Good and Evil, The Genealogy of Morals,* and *The Twilight of the Idols.*

Vocabulary:

Tedious:	long and tiresome; wearisome
Soporific:	tending to cause sleep
Advocates:	supporters
Ensnaring:	trapping
Calamity:	disaster
Cant:	insincere statements, especially praise; monotonous speech
Taruffism:	cantism (see above)
Insinuate:	to suggest something, usually negative
Interrogating:	questioning
Ponderous:	considering something
Mediocre:	below average
Incarnated:	put into concrete form
Pathos:	evoking pity, sorrow, or compassion
Appropriation:	authorization for a specific purpose
Obtrusion:	to push out of the way
Antithesis:	opposite
Mendicant:	a beggar
Derivatively:	to undergo change from an original source
Retaliation:	revenge
Refinement:	to make clearer
Unemancipated:	not free
Ascendancy:	the state of being dominant
Impious:	not religious
Paltry:	extremely small; worthless
Egregious:	a great error or wrong
Veneration:	worship
Astuteness:	keen discernment

Sojourn: long journey
Idiosyncrasy: individual or particular habit or manner

Concepts:

The Will to Power:
Master-Morality:
Slave Morality:
Christianity:
Beyond Good and Evil:
The Ethics of Resentment:
The Death of God:
Nobility:

Questions:

1. *How does Nietzsche describe "general welfare?"*
2. *According to Nietzsche, what is life?*
3. *How does Nietzsche describe exploitation?*
4. *How does Nietzsche describe the master-morality?*
5. *How does Nietzsche describe the slave-morality?*
6. *According to Nietzsche, who is beyond good and evil?*
7. *How does Nietzsche describe Christianity?*

I HOPE TO BE FORGIVEN for discovering that all moral philosophy hitherto has been tedious and has belonged to the soporific appliances — and that "virtue," in my opinion, has been more injured by the *tediousness* of its advocates than by anything else; at the same time, however, I would not wish to overlook their general usefulness. It is desirable that as few people as possible should reflect upon morals, and consequently it is *very* desirable that morals should not some day become interesting! But let us not be afraid! Things still remain today as they have always been: I see no one in Europe who has (or discloses) an idea of the fact that philosophizing concerning morals might be conducted in a dangerous, captious, and ensnaring manner - that *calamity* might be involved therein. ...No new thought, nothing of the nature of a finer turning or better expression of an old thought, not even a proper history of what has been previously thought on the subject: an *impossible* literature, taking it all in unless one knows how to leaven it with some mischief. In effect, the old English vice called *cant*, which is *moral Taruffism*, has insinuated itself also into these moralists (whom one must certainly read with an eye to their motives if one *must* read them), concealed this time under the new form of the scientific spirit; moreover, there is not absent from them a

secret struggle with the pangs of conscience, from which a race of former Puritans must naturally suffer, in all their scientific tinkering with morals. (Is not a moralist the opposite of a Puritan? That is to say, as a thinker who regards morality as questionable, as worthy of interrogation, in short, as a problem? Is moralizing not — immoral?) In the end, they all want *English* morality to be recognized as authoritative, inasmuch as mankind, or the "general utility," or "the happiness of the greatest number," — no! The happiness of *England*, will be best served thereby. They would like, by all means, to convince themselves that the striving after *English* happiness, I mean after *comfort* and *fashion* (and in the highest instance, a seat in Parliament), is at the same time the true path of virtue; in fact, that insofaras there has been virtue in the world hitherto, it has just consisted in such striving. Not one of those ponderous, conscience-stricken herding-animals (who undertake to advocate the cause of egoism as conducive to the general welfare) wants to have any knowledge or inkling of the facts that the "general welfare" is no ideal, no goal, no notion that can be at all grasped, but is only a nostrum, — that what is fair to one *may not* at all be fair to another, that the requirement of one morality for all is really a detriment to higher men, in short, that there is a *distinction of rank* between man and man, and consequently between morality and morality. They are an unassuming and fundamentally mediocre species of men, these utilitarian Englishmen, ... Every elevation of the type "man," has hitherto been the work of an aristocratic society — and so will it always be — a society believing in a long scale of gradations of rank and differences of worth among human beings, and requiring slavery in some form or other. Without the *pathos of distance,* such as grows out of the incarnated difference of classes, out of the constant out looking and down looking of the ruling caste on subordinates and instruments, and out of their equally constant practice of obeying and commanding, of keeping down and keeping at a distance — that other more mysterious pathos could never have arisen, the longing for an ever new widening of distance within the soul itself, the formation of ever higher, rarer, further, more extended, more comprehensive states, in short, just the elevation of the type "man," the continued "self-surmounting of man," to use a moral formula in a super moral sense. To be sure, one must not resign oneself to any humanitarian illusions about the history of the origin of an aristocratic society (that is to say, of the preliminary condition for the elevation of the type "man"): the truth is hard. Let us acknowledge unprejudiced how every higher civilization hitherto has *originated*! Men

with a still natural nature, barbarians in every terrible sense of the word, men of prey, still in possession of unbroken strength of will and desire for power, threw themselves upon weaker, more moral, more peaceful races (perhaps trading or cattle-rearing communities), or upon old mellow civilizations in which the final vital force was flickering out in brilliant fireworks of wit and depravity. At the commencement, the noble caste was always the barbarian caste: their superiority did not consist first of all in their physical, but in their psychical power — they were more *complete* men (which at every point also implies the same as "more complete beasts").

To refrain mutually from injury, from violence, from exploitation, and put one's will on a par with that of others, this may result in a certain rough sense in good conduct among individuals when the necessary conditions are given (namely, the actual similarity of the individuals in amount of force and degree of worth, and their co-relation within one organization). As soon, however, as one wished to take this principle more generally, and if possible even as the *fundamental principle of society*, it would immediately disclose what it really is — namely, a will to the *denial* of life, a principle of dissolution and decay. Here one must think profoundly to the very basis and resist all sentimental weakness: life itself is essentially appropriation, injury, conquest of the strange and weak, suppression, severity, obtrusion of peculiar forms, incorporation, and at the least, putting it mildly, exploitation; — but why should one for ever use precisely these words on which for ages a disparaging purpose has been stamped? Even the organization within which, as was previously supposed, the individuals treat each other as equal — it takes place in every healthy aristocracy — must itself, if it be a living and not a dying organization, do all that towards other bodies, which the individuals within it refrain from doing to each other: it will have to be the incarnated Will to Power, it will endeavor to grow, to gain ground, attract to itself and acquire ascendancy — not owing to any morality or immorality, but because it *lives*, and because life *is* precisely Will to Power. On no point, however, is the ordinary consciousness of Europeans more unwilling to be corrected than on this matter; people now rave everywhere, even under the guise of science, about coming conditions of society in which "the exploiting character" is to be absent: — that sounds to my ears as if they promised to invent a mode of life which should refrain from all organic functions. "Exploitation" does not belong to a depraved, or imperfect and primitive society: it belongs to the *nature* of the living being as a primary organic function; it is a consequence of the intrinsic Will to Power, which is precisely the Will to Life. — Granting that as a theory this is a novelty — as a reality it is the *fundamental* fact of all history: let us be so far honest towards ourselves!

In a tour through the many finer and coarser moralities which have hitherto prevailed or still prevail on the earth, I found certain traits recurring regularly together and connected with one another, until finally two primary types revealed themselves to me, and a radical distinction was brought to light. There is *master-*morality and *slave*-morality; — and I would at once add, however, that in all higher and mixed civilizations, there are also attempts at the reconciliation of the two moralities; but one finds still oftener the confusion and mutual misunderstanding of them, indeed, sometimes their close juxtaposition — even in the same man, within one soul. The distinctions of moral values have either originated in a ruling caste, pleasantly conscious of being different from the ruled — or among the ruled class, the slaves and dependents of all sorts. In the first case, when it is the rulers who determine the conception "good," it is the exalted, proud disposition which is regarded as the distinguishing feature and that which determines the order of rank. The noble type of man separates from himself the beings in which the opposite of this exalted, proud disposition displays itself: he despises them. Let it at once be noted that in this first kind of morality the antithesis "good" and "bad" means practically the same as "noble" and "despicable"; — the antithesis "good" and "*evil*" is of a different origin. The cowardly, the timid, the insignificant, and those thinking merely of narrow utility are despised; moreover, also, the distrustful, with their constrained glances, the self-abasing, the dog-like kind of men who let themselves be abused, the mendicant flatterers, and, above all, the liars: — it is a fundamental belief of all aristocrats that the common people are untruthful. "We truthful ones" — the nobility in ancient Greece called themselves. It is obvious that everywhere the designations of moral value were at first applied to *men*, and were only derivatively and at a later period, applied to *actions*; it is a gross mistake, therefore, when historians of morals start with questions like, "Why have sympathetic actions been praised?" The noble type of man regards himself as a determiner of values; he does not require to be approved of; he passes the judgment: "What is injurious to me is injurious in itself"; he knows that it is he himself only who confers honor on things; he is a creator of values. He honors whatever he recognizes in himself: such morality is self-glorification. In the foreground there is the feeling of plenti-

tude, of power, which seeks to overflow, the happiness of high tension, the consciousness of a wealth which would faint give and bestow: — the noble man also helps the unfortunate, but not — or scarcely — out of pity, but rather from an impulse generated by the super-abundance of power. The noble man honors in himself the powerful one, him also who has power over himself, who knows how to speak and how to keep silence, who takes pleasure in subjecting himself to severity and hardness, and has reverence for all that is severe and hard. "Wotan placed a hard heart in my breast," says an Old Scandinavian Saga: it is thus rightly expressed from the soul of a proud Viking. Such a type of man is even proud of not being made for sympathy; the hero of the Saga, therefore, adds warningly: "He who has not a hard heart when young, will never have one." The noble and brave who think thus are the furthest removed from the morality which sees precisely in sympathy, or in acting for the good of others, or in *disinterestedness*, the characteristic of the moral; faith in oneself, pride in oneself, a radical enmity and irony towards "selflessness," belong as definitely to noble morality, as do a careless scorn and precaution in presence of sympathy and the "warm heart." — It is the powerful who *know* how to honor; it is their art, their domain for invention. The profound reverence for age

327

and for tradition — all law rests on this double reverence, — the belief and prejudice in favor of ancestors and unfavorable to newcomers, is typical in the morality of the powerful; and if, reversely, men of "modern ideas" believe almost instinctively in "progress" and the "future," and are more and more lacking in respect for old age, the ignoble origin of these "ideas" has complacently betrayed itself thereby. A morality of the ruling class, however, is more especially foreign and irritating to present-day taste in the sternness of its principle that one has duties only to one's equals; that one may act towards beings of a lower rank, towards all that is foreign, just as seems good to one, or "as the heart desires," and in any case "beyond good and evil": it is here that sympathy and similar sentiments can have a place. The ability and obligation to exercise prolonged gratitude and prolonged revenge — both only within the circle of equals, — artfulness in retaliation, *refinement* of the idea in friendship, a certain necessity to have enemies (as outlets for the emotions of envy, quarrelsomeness, arrogance — in fact, in order to be a good *friend*): all these are typical characteristics of the noble morality, which, as has been pointed out, is not the morality of "modern ideas," and is, therefore, at present difficult to realize, and also to unearth and disclose — It is otherwise with the second type of morality, *slave-morality*. Supposing that the abused, the oppressed, the suffering, the unemancipated, the weary, and those uncertain of themselves, should moralize, what will be the common element in their moral estimates? Probably a pessimistic suspicion with regard to the entire situation of man will find expression, perhaps a condemnation of man, together with his situation. The slave has an unfavorable eye for the virtues of the powerful; he has a skepticism and distrust, a *refinement* of distrust of everything "good" that is there honored — he would fain persuade himself that the very happiness there is not genuine. On the other hand, those *qualities* which serve to alleviate the existence of sufferers are brought into prominence and flooded with light; it is here that sympathy, the kind, helping hand, the warm heart, patience, diligence, humility, and friendliness attain to honor; for here these are the most useful qualities, and almost the only means of supporting the burden of existence. Slave-morality is essentially the morality of utility. Here is the seat of the origin of the famous antithesis "good" and "evil": — power and dangerousness are assumed to reside in the evil, a certain dreadfulness, subtlety, and strength, which do not admit of being despised. According to slave-morality, therefore, the "evil" man arouses fear: according to master-morality, it is precisely the "good" man who arouses fear and seeks to arouse it, while the bad man is regarded as the despicable being. The contrast attains its maximum when, in accordance with the logical consequences of slave-morality, a shade of depreciation — it may be slight and well-intentioned — at last attaches itself even to the "good" man of this morality; because, according to the servile mode of thought, the good man must in any case be the *safe* man: he is good-natured, easily deceived, perhaps a little stupid, *un bonhomie*. Everywhere that slave-morality gains the ascendancy, language shows a tendency to approximate the significance of the words "good" and "stupid." ...

What then, alone, can our teaching be? — That no one gives man his qualities, neither God, society, his parents, his ancestors, nor himself. ...No one is responsible for the fact that he exists at all, that he is constituted as he is, and that he happens to be in certain circumstances and in particular environments. The fatality of his being cannot be divorced from the fatality of all that which has been and will be. This is not the result of an individual attention, of a will, of an aim, there is no attempt at attaining to any "ideal man," or "ideal happiness" or "ideal morality" with him — it is absurd to wish him to be careering towards some sort of purpose. *We* invented the concept "purpose," in reality purpose is altogether lacking. One is necessary, one is a piece of fate, one belongs to the whole, one is in the whole — there is nothing that could judge, measure, compare, and condemn our existence, for that would mean judging, measuring, comparing and condemning the whole. *But there is nothing outside the whole!* The fact that no one shall any longer be made responsible, that the nature of existence may not be traced to a *causa prima*, that the world is an entity neither as a sensorial nor as a spirit — *this alone is the great deliverance* — thus alone is the innocence of becoming restored. ...The concept "God" has been the greatest objection to existence hitherto. ... We deny God, we deny responsibility in God: thus, alone do we save the world.

* * * * *

I regard Christianity as the most fatal and seductive lie that has ever yet existed — as the greatest and most impious lie: I can *discern* the last sprouts and branches of its ideal beneath every form of disguise, I decline to enter into any compromise or false position in reference to it — I urge people to declare open war with it.

The morality of paltry people as the measure of all things: this is the most repugnant kind of degeneracy that civilization has ever yet brought into existence. And this *kind of ideal* is hanging still, under the name of "God," over men's heads!!

However modest one's demands may be concerning intellectual cleanliness, when one touches the New Testament one cannot help experiencing a sort of inexpressible feeling of discomfort; for the unbounded cheek with which the least qualified people will have their say in its pages, in regard to the greatest problems of existence, and claim to sit in judgment on such matters, exceeds all limits. The impudent levity with which the most unwieldy problems are spoken of here (life, the world, God, the purpose of life), as if they were not problems at all, but the most simple things which these little bigots *know all about*!!

This was the most fatal form of insanity that has ever yet existed on earth: — when these little lying abortions of bigotry began laying claim to the words "God," "last judgment," "truth," "love," "wisdom," "Holy Spirit," and thereby distinguishing themselves from the rest of the world; when such men began to transvalue values to suit themselves, as though they were the sense, the salt, the standard, and the measure of all things; then all that one should do is this: build lunatic asylums for their incarceration. To *persecute* them was an egregious act of antique folly: this was taking them too seriously, it was making them serious.

The *law*, which is the fundamental-

ly realistic formula of certain self-preservative measures of a community, forbids certain actions that have a definite tendency to jeopardize the welfare of that community: it does *not* forbid the attitude of mind which gives rise to these actions — for in the pursuit of other ends the community requires these forbidden actions, namely, when it is a matter of opposing its *enemies*. The moral idealist now steps forward and says: "God sees into men's hearts: the action itself counts for nothing; the reprehensible attitude of mind from which it proceeds must be extirpated. ..." In normal conditions men laugh at such things; it is only in exceptional cases, when a community lives *quite* beyond the need of waging war in order to maintain itself, that an ear is lent to such things. Any attitude of mind is abandoned, the utility of which cannot be conceived.

This was the case, for example, when Buddha appeared among a people that were both peaceable and afflicted with great intellectual weariness.

This was also the case in regard to the first Christian community (as also the Jewish), the primary condition of which was the absolutely *apolitical* Jewish society. Christianity could grow only upon the soil of Judaism — that is to say, among a people that had already renounced the political life, and which led a sort of parasitic existence within the Roman sphere of government. Christianity goes a step *farther*: it allows men to "emasculate" themselves even more; the circumstances actually favor their doing so. — *Nature is expelled* from morality when it is said, "Love ye your enemies:" for *Nature's* injunction, "Ye shall *love* your neighbor and *hate* your enemy," has now become senseless in the law (in instinct); now, even *the love a man feels for his neighbor* must first be based upon something (*a sort of love of God*). *God* is introduced everywhere, and *utility* is withdrawn; the natural *origin* of morality is denied everywhere: the *veneration of Nature*, which lies in *acknowledging a natural morality*, is *destroyed* to the roots. ...

Whence comes the *seductive charm* of this emasculate ideal of man? Why are we not *disgusted* by it, just as we are disgusted at the thought of a eunuch? ...The answer is obvious: it is not the voice of the eunuch that revolts us, despite the cruel mutilation of which it is the result; for, as a matter of fact, it has grown sweeter. ...And owing to the very fact that the "male organ" has been amputated from virtue, its voice now has a feminine ring, which, formerly, was not to be discerned.

On the other hand, we have only to think of the terrible hardness, dangers, and accidents to which a life of manly virtues leads ... to perceive how the most robust type of man was fascinated and moved by the voluptuous ring of this "goodness" and "purity." ...

The *Astuteness of moral castration.* — How is war waged against the virile passions and valuations? No violent physical means are available; the war must, therefore, be one of ruses, spells, and lies — in short, a "spiritual war."

First recipe: One appropriates virtue in general, and makes it the main feature of one's ideal; the older ideal is denied and declared to be *the reverse of all ideals*. Slander has to be carried to a fine art for this purpose.

Second recipe: One's own type is set up as a general *standard*; and this is projected into all things, behind all things, and behind the destiny of all things — as God.

Third recipe: The opponents of one's ideal are declared to be the opponents of God; one arrogates to oneself a *right* to great pathos, to power, and a right to curse and to bless.

Fourth recipe: All suffering, all gruesome, terrible, and fatal things are declared to be the results of opposition *to one's* ideal — all suffering is *punishment* even in the case of one's adherents (except it be a trial, etc).

Fifth recipe: One goes so far as to regard Nature as the reverse of one's ideal, and the lengthy sojourn amid natural conditions is considered a great trial of patience

— a sort of martyrdom; one studies contempt, both in one's attitudes and one's looks towards all "natural things."

Sixth recipe: The triumph of anti-naturalism and ideal castration, the triumph of the world of the pure, good, sinless, and blessed, is projected into the future as the consummation, the finale, the great hope, and the "Coming of the Kingdom of God."

I hope that one may still be allowed to laugh at this artificial hoisting up of a small species of man to the position of an absolute standard of all things.

To what extent psychologists have been corrupted by the moral idiosyncrasy! — Not one of the ancient philosophers had the courage to advance the theory of the non-free will (that is to say, the theory that denies morality); — not one had the courage to identify the typical feature of happiness, of every kind of happiness ("pleasure"), with the will to power: for the pleasure of power was considered immoral; — not one had the courage to regard virtue as a *result of immorality* (as a result of a will to power) in the service of a species (or of a race, or of a *polis*); for the will to power was considered immoral.

In the whole of moral evolution, there is no sign of truth: all the conceptual elements which come into play are fictions; all the psychological tenets are false; all the forms of logic employed in this department

of prevarication are sophisms. The chief feature of all moral philosophers is their total lack of intellectual cleanliness and self-control: they regard "fine feelings" as arguments: their heaving breasts seem to them the bellows of godliness. ...

This "virtue" made wholly abstract was the highest form of seduction; to make oneself abstract means to *turn one's back on the world.*

The moment is a very remarkable one: the Sophists are within sight of the first *criticism* of morality, the first knowledge of *morality*: — they classify the majority of moral valuations (in view of their dependence upon local conditions) together; — they lead one to understand that every form of morality is capable of being upheld dialectically: that is to say, they guessed that all the fundamental principles of a morality must be *sophistical* — a proposition which was afterwards proved in the grandest possible style by the ancient philosophers from Plato onwards (up to Kant); — they postulate the primary truth that there is no such thing as a "moral *per se*," a "good *per se*," and that it is madness to talk of "truth" in this respect.

From *The Complete Works of Nietzsche*, ed. Oscar Levy, 1910.

EXISTENTIALISM

Jean-Paul Sartre (1905-1980)

Jean-Paul Sartre was a French philosopher, playwright, and novelist. He was born in Paris in 1905 and was the son of a navel officer. His mother was the cousin of the famous theologian and jungle doctor, Albert Schweitzer. Orphaned at a young age, Sartre was raised by his grandfather. During World War II he joined the French Army, was captured by the Germans, and spent eight months in a prison camp. After the war, Sartre's plays (*No Exit*, 1944; *The Flies*, 1946; *The Condemned of Altona*, 1960)); novels (*Nausea*, 1938), and philosophical works (*Being and Nothingness*, 1943) set him apart as one of Europe's greatest philosophers.

In our present essay, taken from *Existentialism* (1947), Sartre defines atheistic existentialism and sets forth its basic principles. He says that human beings are condemned to be free; that since there is no God to give us our essence, we must create our own essence (existence precedes essence); we are completely responsible for our actions; human lives are characterized by anguish, forlornness and despair. Existentialism, according to Sartre, is a celebration of optimism and is future oriented as we realize that we are creators of our own values.

Vocabulary:

Surrealism:	modern movement in art and literature characterized by an irrational, fantastic arrangement of material
Envisage:	to imagine
Fascism:	a system of government characterized by rigid one-

	party dictatorship, forcible suppression of opposition, etc.
Bourgeois:	capitalist a social class opposed to the proletariat or working class
Dubious:	doubtful
Essence:	that which makes something what it is
Efficacy:	the power to produce desired effects
Collaborationist:	a person who cooperates with an enemy invader
Proletariat:	working class opposed to the bourgeois or capitalists

Concepts:

Existentialism:

Existence precedes essence:

Subjectivity:

Anguish:

Forlornness:

Despair:

Questions:

1. Explain Sartre's concept of existence preceding essence?

2. How does Sartre define subjectivity?

3. Explain Sartre's concepts of anguish, forlornness and despair.

4. What is the point of the story of the boy faced with the choice of fighting in the war or staying home with his mother?

5. Briefly explain existentialism.

WHAT IS MEANT by the term *existentialism*?

Most people who use the word would be rather embarrassed if they had to explain it, since, now that the word is all the rage, even the work of a musician or painter is being called existentialist...It seems that for want of an ad vanguard doctrine analogous to surrealism, the kind of people who are eager for scandal and flurry turn to this philosophy which in other respects does not at all serve their purposes in this sphere.

Actually, it is the least scandalous, the most austere of doctrines. It is intended strictly for specialists and philosophers. Yet it can be defined easily. What complicates matters is that there are two kinds of existentialists; first, those who are Christian, among whom I would include Jaspers and Gabriel Marcel, both Catholic; and on the other hand, the atheistic existentialists, among whom I class Heidegger, and then the French existentialists and myself. What they have in common is that they think that existence precedes essence, or, if you prefer, that subjectivity must be the starting point.

Just what does that mean? Let us consider some object that is manufactured, for example, a book or a paper-cutter: here is an object which has been made by an artisan whose inspiration came from a concept. He referred to the concept of what a paper-cutter is and likewise to a known method of production, which is part of the concept, something which is, by and large, a routine. Thus, the paper-cutter is at once an object produced in a certain way and, on the other hand, one having a specific use; and one cannot postulate a man who produces a paper-cutter but does not know what it is used for. Therefore, let us say that, for the paper-cutter, essence — that is, the ensemble of both the production routines and the properties which enable it to be both produced and defined — precedes existence. Thus, the presence of the paper-cutter or book in front of me is determined. Therefore, we have here a technical view of the world whereby it can be said that production or essence precedes existence.

When we conceive God as the Creator, He is generally thought of as a superior sort of artisan. Whatever doctrine we may be considering, whether one like that of Descartes or that of Leibnitz, we always grant that will more or less follows understanding or, at the very least, accompanies it, and that when God creates He knows exactly what He is creating. Thus, the concept of man in the mind of God is comparable to the concept of paper-cutter in the mind of the manufacturer, and, following certain techniques and a conception, God produces man, just as the artisan, following a definition and a technique, makes a paper-cutter. Thus, the individual man is the realization of a certain concept in the divine intelligence.

In the eighteenth century, the atheism of the *philosophes* discarded the idea of God, but not so much for the notion that essence precedes existence. To a certain extent, this idea is found everywhere; we find it in Diderot, in Voltaire, and even in Kant. Man has a human nature; this human nature, which is the concept of the human, is found in all men, which means that each man is a particular example of a universal concept, man. In Kant, the result of this universality is that the wild-man, the natural man, as well as the bourgeois, are circumscribed by the same definition and have the same basic qualities. Thus, here too the essence of man precedes the historical existence that we find in nature.

Atheistic existentialism, which I represent, is more coherent. It states that if God does not exist, there is at least one being in whom existence precedes essence, a being who exists before he can be defined by any concept, and that this being is man, or, as Heidegger says, human reality. What is meant here by saying that existence precedes essence? It means that, first of all, man exists, turns up, appears on the scene, and, only afterwards, defines himself. If man, as the existentialist conceives him, is indefinable, it is because at first he is nothing. Only afterward will he be something, and he himself will have made what he will be. Thus, there is no human nature, since there is no God to conceive it. Not only is man what he conceives himself to be, but he is also only what he wills himself to be after this thrust toward existence.

Man is nothing else but what he makes of himself. Such is the first principle of existentialism. It is also what is called subjectivity, the name we are labeled with when charges are brought against us. But what do we mean by this, if not that man has a greater dignity than a stone or table? For we mean that man first exists, that is, that man first of all is the being in the future. Man is at the start a plan which is aware of itself, rather than a patch of moss, a piece of garbage, or a cauliflower; nothing exists prior to this plan; there is nothing in heaven; man will be what he will have planned to be. Not what he will want to be. Because by the word "will" we generally mean a conscious decision, which is subsequent to what we have already made of ourselves. I may want to belong to a political party, write a book, get married; but all that is only a manifestation of an earlier, more spontaneous choice that is called "will." But if existence really does precede essence, man, is responsible for what he is. Thus, existentialism's first move is to make every man aware of what he is and to make the full responsibility of his existence rest on him. And when we say that a man is responsible for himself, we do not only mean that he is responsible for his own individuality, but that he is responsible for all men.

The word subjectivism has two meanings, and our opponents play on the two. Subjectivism means, on the one hand, that an individual chooses and makes himself; and, on the other, that it is impossible for man to transcend human subjectivity. The second of these is the essential meaning of existentialism. When we say that man chooses his own self, we mean that every one of us does likewise; but we also mean by that that in making this choice he also chooses all men. In fact, in creating the man that we want to be, there is not a single one of our acts which does not at the same time create an image of man as we think he ought to be. To choose to be this or that is to affirm at the same time the value of what we choose, because we can never choose evil. We always choose the good, and nothing can be good for us without being good for all.

If, on the other hand, existence precedes essence, and if we grant that we exist and fashion our image at one and the same time, the image is valid for everybody and for our whole age. Thus, our responsibility is much greater than we might have supposed, because it involves all mankind. If I am a workingman and choose to join a Christian trade-union rather than be a communist, and if by being a member I want to show that the best thing for man is resignation, that the kingdom of man is not of this world, I am not only involving my own case — I want to be resigned for everyone. As a result, my action has involved all humanity. To take a more individual matter, if I want to marry, to have children, even if this marriage depends solely on my own circumstances or passion or wish, I am involving all humanity in monogamy and not merely myself. Therefore, I am responsible for myself and for everyone else. I am creating a certain image of man of my own choosing. In choosing myself, I choose man.

This helps us understand what the actual content is of such rather grandiloquent words as anguish, forlornness, despair. As you will see, it's all quite simple.

First, what is meant by anguish? The existentialists say at once that man is anguish. What that means is this: the man who involves himself and who realizes that he is not only the person he chooses to be, but also a law-maker who is, at the same time, choosing all mankind as well as himself, cannot help escape the feeling of his total and deep responsibility. Of course, there are many people who are not anxious; but we claim that they are hiding their anxiety, that they are fleeing from it. Certainly, many people believe that when they do something, they themselves are the only ones involved, and when some-one says to them, "What if everyone acted that way?" they shrug their shoulders and answer, "Everyone doesn't act that way." But really, one should always ask himself, "What would happen if everybody looked at things that way?" There is no escaping this disturbing thought except by a kind of double-dealing. A man who lies and makes excuses for himself by saying "not everybody does that," is someone with an uneasy conscience, because the act of lying implies that a universal value is con-ferred upon the lie.

Anguish is evident even when it conceals itself. This is the anguish that Kieregaard called the anguish of Abraham. You know the story: an angel has ordered Abraham to sacrifice his son; if it really were an angel who has come and said, "You are Abraham, you shall sacrifice your son," everything would be all right. But everyone might first wonder, "Is it really an angel, and am I really Abraham? What proof do I have?"...

Now, I'm not being singled out as an Abraham, and yet at every moment I'm obliged to perform exemplary acts. For every man, everything happens as if all mankind had its eyes fixed on him and were guiding itself by what he does. And every man ought to say to himself, "Am I really the kind of man who has the right to act in such a way that humanity might guide itself by my actions?" And if he does not say that to himself, he is masking his anguish.

There is no question here of the kind of anguish which would lead to qui-etism, to inaction. It is a mater of a simple sort of anguish that anybody who has had responsibilities is familiar with. For example, when a military officer takes the responsibility for an attack and sends a certain number of men to death, he choos-es to do so, and in the main he alone makes the choice. Doubtless, orders come from above, but they are too broad; he interprets them, and on this interpretation depend the lives of ten or fourteen or twenty men. In making a decision he can-not help having a certain anguish. All leaders know this anguish. That doesn't keep them from acting; on the contrary, it is the very condition of their action. For it implies that they envisage a number of possibilities, and when they choose one, they realize that it has value only because it is chosen. We shall see that this kind of anguish, which is the kind that existentialism describes, is explained, in addition, by a direct responsibility to the other men whom it involves. It is not a curtain separating us from action, but is part of action itself.

When we speak of forlornness, a term Heidegger was fond of, we mean only that God does to exist and that we have to face all the consequences of this. The existentialist is strongly opposed to a certain kind of secular ethics which would like to abolish God with the least possible expense. About 1880, some French teachers tried to set up a secular ethics which went something like this: God is a useless and costly hypothesis; we are discarding it; but meanwhile, in order for there to be an ethics, a society, a civilization, it is essential that certain values be taken seriously and that they be considered as having an *a priori* existence. It must be obligatory, *a priori*, to be honest, not to lie, not to beat your wife, to have children, etc., etc. So we're going to try a little device which will make it possible to show that values exist all the same, inscribed in a heaven of ideas, though otherwise God does not exist. In other words — and this, I believe, is the tendency of everything called reformism in France — nothing will be changed if God does not exist. We shall find ourselves with the same norms of honesty, progress, and humanism, and we shall have made of God an outdated hypothesis which will peacefully die off by itself.

The existentialist, on the contrary, thinks it very distressing that God does not exist, because all possibility of finding values in a heaven of ideas disappears along with Him; there can be no longer an *a priori* good, since there is no infinite and perfect consciousness to think it. Nowhere is it written that the good exists, that we must be honest, that we must not lie; because the fact is we are on a plane where there are only men. Dostoyevsky said, "If God didn't exist, everything would be possible." That is the very starting point of existentialism. Indeed, everything is permissible if God does not exist, and as a result man is forlorn, because neither within him nor without does he find anything to cling to. He can't start making excuses for himself.

If existence really does precede essence, there is no explaining things away by reference to a fixed and given human nature. In other words, there is no determinism, man is free, man is freedom.

On the other hand, if God does not exist, we find no values or commands to turn to which legitimize our conduct. So, in the bright realm of values, we have no excuse behind us, no justification before us. We are alone, with no excuses.

That is the idea I shall try to convey when I say that man is condemned to be free. Condemned, because he did not create himself, yet, in other respects is free; because, once thrown into the world, he is responsible for everything he does. The existentialist does not believe in the power of passion. He will never agree that a sweeping passion is a ravaging torrent which fatally leads a man to certain acts and is, therefore, an excuse. He thinks that man is responsible for his passion.

The existentialist does not think that man is going to help himself by finding in the world some omen by which to orient himself. Because he thinks that man will interpret the omen to suit himself. Therefore, he thinks that man, with no support and no aid, is condemned every moment to invent man. Ponge, in a very fine article, has said, "Man is the future of man." That's exactly it. But if it is taken to mean that this future is recorded in heaven, that God sees it, then it is false, because it would really no longer be a future. If it is taken to mean that, whatever a man may be, there is a future to be

forged, a virgin future before him, then this remark is sound. But then we are forlorn.

To give you an example which will enable you to understand forlornness better, I shall cite the case of one of my students who came to see me under the following circumstances: his father was on bad terms with his mother, and, moreover, was inclined to be a collaborationist; his older brother had been killed in the German offensive of 1940, and the young man, with somewhat immature but generous feelings, wanted to avenge him. His mother lived alone with him, very much upset by the half-treason of her husband and the death of her older son; the boy was her only consolation.

The boy was faced with the choice of leaving for England and joining the Free French Forces — that is, leaving his mother behind — or remaining with his mother and helping her to carry on. He was fully aware that the woman lived only for him and that his going-off — and perhaps his death — would plunge her into despair. He was also aware that every act that he did for his mother's sake was a sure thing, in the sense that it was helping her to carry on, whereas every effort he made toward going off and fighting was an uncertain move which might run aground and prove completely useless;

for example, on his way to England he might, while passing through Spain, be detained indefinitely in a Spanish camp; he might reach England, or Algiers and be stuck in an office at a desk job. As a result, he was faced with two very different kinds of action: one, concrete, immediate, but concerning only one individual; the other concerned an incomparably vaster group, a national collectivity, but for that very reason was dubious, and might be interrupted en route. And, at the same time, he was wavering between two kinds of ethics. On the one hand, an ethics of sympathy, of personal devotion; on the other, a broader ethics, but one whose efficacy was more dubious. He had to choose between the two.

Who could help him choose? Christian doctrine? No. Christian doctrine says, "Be charitable, love your neighbor, take the more rugged path, etc., etc." But which is the more rugged path? Whom should he love as a brother? The fighting man or his mother? Which does the greater good; The vague act of fighting in a group, or the concrete one of helping a particular human being to go on living? Who can decide *a priori*? Nobody. No book of ethics can tell him. The Kantian ethics says, "Never treat any person as a means, but as an end." Very well, if I stay with my mother, I'll treat her as an end

and not as a means; but by virtue of this very fact, I'm running the risk of treating the people around me who are fighting, as means; and conversely, if I go to join those who are fighting, I'll be treating them as an end, and, by doing that, I run the risk of treating my mother as a means.

If values are vague, and if they are always too broad for the concrete and specific case that we are considering, the only thing left for us is to trust our instincts. That's what this young man tried to do; and when I saw him, he said, "In the end, feeling is what counts. I ought to choose whichever pushes me in one direction. If I feel that I love my mother enough to sacrifice everything else for her — my desire for vengeance, for action, for adventure — then I'll stay with her. If, on the contrary, I feel that my love for my mother isn't enough, I'll leave."

But how is the value of a feeling determined? What gives his feeling for his mother value? Precisely the fact that he remained with her. I may say that I like so-and-so well enough to sacrifice a certain amount of money for him, but I may say so only if I've done it. I may say, "I love my mother well enough to remain with her" if I have remained with her. The only way to determine the value of this affection is, precisely, to perform an act which confirms and defines it. But, since I require this affection to justify my act, I find myself caught in a vicious circle....

As for despair, the term has a very simple meaning. It means that we shall confine ourselves to reckoning only with what depends upon our will, or on the ensemble of probabilities which make our action possible. When we want something, we always have to reckon with probabilities. I may be counting on the arrival of a friend. The friend is coming by rail or streetcar; this supposes that the train will arrive on schedule, or that the streetcar will not jump the track. I am left in the realm of possibility; but possibilities are to be reckoned with only to the point where my action comports with the ensemble of these possibilities, and no further. The moment the possibilities I am considering are not rigorously involved by my action, I ought to disengage myself from them, because no God, no scheme, can adapt the world and its possibilities to my will. When Descartes said, "Conquer yourself rather than the world," he meant essentially the same thing.

The Marxists to whom I have spoken reply, "You can rely on the support of others in your action, which obviously has certain limits because you're not going to live forever. That means: rely on both what others are doing elsewhere to help you, in China, in Russia, and what they will do later on, after your death, to carry on the action and lead it to its fulfillment, which will be the revolution. You even *have* to rely upon that, otherwise you're immortal." I reply at once that I will always rely on fellow fighters insofar as these comrades are involved with me in a common struggle, in the unity of a party or a group in which I can more or less make my weight felt; that is, one whose ranks I am in as a fighter and whose movements I am aware of at every moment. In such a situation, relying on the unity and will of the party is exactly like counting on the fact that the train will arrive on time or that the car won't jump the track. But, given that man is free and that there is no human nature for me to depend on, I cannot count on men whom I do not know by relying on human goodness or man's concern for the good of society. I don't know what will become of the Russian revolution; I may make an example of it to the extent that at the present time it is apparent that the proletariat plays a part in Russia that it plays in no other nation. But I can't swear that this will inevitably lead to a triumph of the proletariat. I've got to limit myself to what I see.

Given that men are free, and that tomorrow they will freely decide what man will be, I cannot be sure that, after my death, fellow fighters will carry on my work to bring it to its maximum perfection. Tomorrow, after my death, some men may decide to set up Fascism, and the others may be cowardly and muddled enough to let them do it. Fascism will then be the human reality, so much the worse for us.

Actually, things will be as man will have decided they are to be. Does that mean that I should abandon myself to quietism? No. First, I should involve myself; then, act on the old saying, "Nothing ventured, nothing gained." Nor does it mean that I shouldn't belong to a party, but rather that I shall have no illusions and shall do what I can. For example, suppose I ask myself, "Will socialization, as such, ever come about?" I know nothing about it. All I know is that I'm going to do everything in my power to bring it about. Beyond that, I can't count on anything. Quietism is the attitude of people who say, "Let others do what I can't do." The doctrine I am presenting is the very opposite of quietism, since it declares, "There is no reality except in action." Moreover, it goes further, since it adds, "Man is nothing else than his plan; he exists only to the extent that he fulfills himself; he is, therefore, nothing else than the ensemble of his acts, nothing else than his life."

From Jean-Paul Sartre, *Existentialism*, trans. by Bernard Frechtman, 1947.

Moral Dilemmas

1. Jack Smith and his son, Jason, are imprisoned in a concentration camp in Nazi Germany during World War II. Jason has been sentenced to death for attempting to escape. The commandant of the camp orders Jason to stand against the wall. The commandant then gives Mr. Smith the gun with one bullet and orders him to kill his son. If he refuses to kill his son, the commandant tells Mr. Smith that not only will his son die, but also another innocent young man.

What should Mr. Smith do?

2. Jane met Omar at the university. Omar was a graduate student from Iran. They fell in love and married. After establishing themselves in their careers, they decided to have children. Jane was a devout Baptist and wanted to raise the children as Christians. Omar was a devout Moslem and wanted to raise the children as Moslems.

How should they resolve this dispute?

3. A passenger ship, the Fatal Attraction, capsizes in the ocean, killing all but 40 survivors. The survivors crowd into a lifeboat meant to hold only 20 people. Captain Heartless, who is also saved, takes command of the lifeboat. He tells the survivors that the lifeboat contains only enough food for 20 people for 3 days. He further explains that it will take at least five days of hard rowing to get to land. If all stay on the boat, all will die, according to the captain. He says he will pick the strongest to stay because they can row

the best and have the best chance of surviving. He argues that it is better for 20 people to live than all to die. The rest will have to be pushed overboard into the shark-infested ocean. Finally, the captain's orders are carried out. Some people jump overboard willingly, others are pushed. Five days later the lifeboat is rescued with all on board alive. Shortly after, Captain Heartless is put on trial for murder.

If you were on the jury, would you find the captain guilty of murder?

4. Professor Scared notices that Betty is cheating on one of his exams. He calls her into his office and confronts her about her cheating. She does not deny that she has cheated, but she argues that it is not immoral because she had a mutual agreement with her friend Susan to help her on the exam. Plus she argues that cheating isn't harming anyone and how can something be immoral if it harms no one? Finally, she hints that if Professor Scared does anything about this, she will spread a false rumor that he tried to sexually harass her and is simply punishing her now for refusing his advances. Professor Scared comes up for tenure next year.

What should the professor do?

5. While you and your mother are taking a pleasure boat trip, your mother and a world-famous brain surgeon fall overboard. Neither of them can swim and you have time to save only one. Your mother is 85 years old and needs constant help and expensive medical care. The doctor is young and, undoubtedly, will save many lives in his career.

Whom do you save?

6. You go to see one of your best friends whose wife was recently brutally raped and murdered. While you are consoling him he confesses to you that he killed the man who did this to his wife. A few days later you find out that an innocent man has been charged with the murder of your friend's wife. The D.A. is asking for the death penalty if

he is found guilty. You ask your friend to go to the police and give himself up, but he refuses and reminds you that you promised not to tell anyone about his secret.

What should you do?

7. You find out that your roommate is selling cocaine. You know her and she is an excellent student and a great friend. You talk with her about what she is doing and she tells you that she believes that drugs should be legal and the laws against drug use are unjust. She also explains to you that she desperately needs the money from the sale of the drugs to pay for the cost of college and to support her sick mother who lives alone at home.

What should you do?

8. One of your friends asks you for a job recommendation that he needs very badly in order to support his family. You do not think he is qualified for the job, or that he is of good character.

Would you lie in your letter of recommendation for him or refuse to write the letter?

9. Sally is a senior in high school. She finds out she is pregnant and she wants to have an abortion. She goes to the school nurse and tells her about her situation and asks for help in finding out about where she can get an abortion and how much it costs. Sally is from a loving family and you happen to be good friends with her mother.

Should you as the school nurse, tell her mother about Sally's plans?

10. Sandy and Joe, both college students, have been living together for six months. They decide to get married after they learn that Sandy is pregnant. In order to get married,

they must have blood tests. The blood test reveals that Joe has AIDS. He claims that he got it by sharing hypodermic needles with his heroin-addict friends. Although Sandy is shocked, she is relieved that she doesn't have the incurable and deadly disease. They call off the wedding and Sandy decides to go back home and live with her parents. Several weeks later, Sandy learns from a friend that Joe has been sleeping with every woman he can without telling them about his disease.

What should Sandy do?

11. Ralph and Mary have been married for twenty-five years. They have three children who are now high school age. Ralph is a business man who works long hours and usually gets home late at night. One day, while Mary is cleaning in Ralph's office at home, she comes across homosexual pornography. She is surprised and confronts Ralph about this material. Ralph admits that he is gay and has a long-standing homosexual affair. Ralph tells Mary that he does not want a divorce for the kids' sakes.

What should Mary do?

12. Tom and Paula Brown have been happily married for ten years and desperately want a child but cannot have one because Mrs. Brown is infertile. One of their friends, Mrs. Smith, has two healthy children and offers to be a surrogate mother for the Browns for a fee of ten thousand dollars plus expenses. The Browns agree and Mrs. Smith is artificially inseminated with sperm from Mr. Brown. When Mrs. Smith finally gives birth to a healthy baby boy, she changes her mind and refuses to give the baby over to the Browns. She also refuses the ten thousand dollars and wants to pay for the expenses herself. The Browns remind her of the agreement they had, but Mrs. Smith now argues that engaging in a contract to sell a baby is immoral. The Browns argue that this situation is more like adoption-- which is moral.

Who do you think is right?
What should be done?

13. Betty is a sixteen year old girl who is raped one night on her way home from work. She finds out she is pregnant as a result of the rape. She doesn't know what to do. Her parents are devout Catholics and do not believe in abortion, yet she doesn't know if she wants to go through with the pregnancy and raise the child herself. A pro-life clinic tells her that she could give the baby up for adoption. Her friends tell her that she should have an abortion. She doesn't know if she can deal with the trauma of giving birth to this child that is the result of a rape.

What should she do?

14. Lisa is twenty-nine years old and three months pregnant. Her father is diagnosed as having Parkinson's disease, a brain disease causing uncontrollable shaking of the hands and head. An experimental medical procedure has been introduced whereby fetal brain tissue is transplanted from aborted fetuses into the brain of Parkinson's patients. The procedure has been remarkably successful in alleviating the symptoms. Lisa's father asks her to abort the fetus so that the brain tissue can be transplanted into his brain and perhaps cure him of his disease. Lisa hates the idea of abortion, but her father tells her that she could always have another baby. He also offers her ten thousand dollars if she agrees to help him.

What should Lisa do?
Is Lisa's father making a fair request?

15. Mary and Fred have been married for forty years. At the age of seventy, Mary finds out she has Alzheimer's disease, an incurable brain-degenerative illness that leads to progressive senility and death. Mary tells Fred that she does not want to see the day of her own degeneration through senility and incontinence, and she asks Fred to promise to allow her to die before her condition gets too much worse. Eventually Mary begins to deteriorate to the point where she doesn't even recognize Fred or her children. Fred,

remembering his promise to Mary, gives her an overdose of sleeping pills and she dies. He is found out and charged with murder.

How would you vote if you were on the jury?
Did Fred do the right thing?

16. You and your best friend, Sam, join the army together. You are both assigned to the same battalion and sent into battle. During a assault on the enemy, Sam is shot in the chest and critically wounded. You both know that medical assistance is impossible as the enemy is advancing toward your position. The enemy is known for its extremely cruel torture of captives. You cannot carry Sam to safety and if you stay, you will be captured. Sam begs you to kill him before the enemy gets to him.

What should you do?

V. Ethics Section Review

Below is the review sheet for Part V: Ethics. Included in this review are the terms and concepts you should be familiar with to prepare for the exam. I have also included an example of the multiple choice questions that you will have to answer. It will give you an idea of what type of questions to expect.

We will be reviewing each of these terms and concepts and the multiple choice question in class prior to the exam.

You should be familiar with the following terms and concepts:

Ethics Chart

Deontological ethics

Teleological ethics

Divine Command Theory

Ring of Gyges

Absolute power corrupts absolutely

Ruth Benedict's Moral Theory

History and environment

Social systems

Idea-practice pattern of culture

Ethnocentricity

Normal / abnormal

Diversity thesis

Dependency thesis
Aristotle's Moral Theory
Eudiamonia / happiness
Arête / virtue
Relative / Absolute Mean
The Golden Mean
Wisdom
Justice
Courage
Moderation
Ethics part of Politics
Kant's Moral Theory
Prerequisites
Categorical Imperative
Moral worth
Duty
Intention
1st formulation
2nd formulation
Mill's Moral Theory
Utilitarianism
Greatest Happiness Principle
Formulation of principle
Happiness defined
Pleasure
Different kinds
Quality / quantity
Greater Permanence
Safer

Less costly

Empirical proof

Act / rule utilitarianism

Nietzsche's Moral Theory

Will to power

Slave morality

Master morality

Sartre's Moral Theory

Existentialism

Existence precedes essence

Subjectivity

Anguish

Forlornness

Despair

Multiple Choice Example:

Which statement best describes Aristotle's moral theory?

A. Aristotle believed that the purpose of human existence was to be happy. His concept of happiness includes having wealth, fame, and a good family. We are to develop virtues to insure that we will achieve happiness. His virtues are wisdom, justice, courage and moderation. These virtues are the relative mean between two extremes.

B. Aristotle believed that the purpose of human existence was to be happy. His concept of happiness includes having wealth, fame, a good family, and luck. We are to develop virtues to insure that we will achieve happiness. His virtues are wisdom, justice, courage and moderation. These virtues are the relative mean between two extremes.

C. Aristotle believed that the purpose of human existence was to be happy. His concept of happiness includes having wealth, fame, and a good family. We are to develop virtues to give us a better chance of achieving happiness because there is no way to insure happiness. His virtues are wisdom, justice, courage and moderation. These virtues are the relative mean between two extremes.

D. Aristotle believed that the purpose of human existence was to be happy. His concept of happiness includes having wealth, fame, and a good family. We are to develop virtues to give us a better chance of achieving happiness because there is no way to insure happiness. His virtues are wisdom, justice, courage and moderation. These virtues are the relative mean between two extremes, not the absolute mean.

Part VI
Abortion

SUPREME COURT DECISION:
ROE v. WADE

Roe v. Wade is one of the most controversial decisions in the last century. The Court ruled that a woman has the right to an abortion up through the first six months of pregnancy and possibly beyond. Justice Harry A. Blackmun argued for the majority opinion that there is a right to privacy implied in the Constitution's Bill of Rights. Liberty cannot be protected without a right to privacy that includes rights relating to marriage, procreation, contraception, and child rearing. A woman's decision whether or not to terminate her pregnancy is a private decision protected by the Constitution.

The majority conceded that it could not determine whether the fetus is a person. Nevertheless, the state has a legitimate interest in protecting the potential life of the fetus and the health of the woman. Because modern medical science has progressed, an abortion in the first trimester is safer than childbirth and, therefore, should be allowed. During the second trimester, the state has the right to regulate the abortion to protect the health of the woman. In the third trimester, when the fetus reaches viability, individual states may prohibit abortion to protect the potential life of the fetus, except in cases where the mother's health is involved.

Justices Byron White and William Rehnquist disagreed with the majority decision. They argued that to allow a woman to have an abortion for any reason she wishes at the expense of the life of the fetus puts a greater value on a woman's convenience than on human life. They also argued that there is no right to privacy in the Constitution. They concluded that it would be more democratic for individual states to decide this issue than have the Court's view imposed upon them.

Vocabulary:

Antisepsis:	ability to keep something entirely clean and free from germs
Dilatation and Curettage:	a surgical procedure in which the uterine lining is scraped for diagnostic or therapeutic purposes
Amici:	friends
Appellant:	one who appeals a court decision
Supra:	above
Inferentially:	drawn from an inference or conclusion
Interposing:	putting in between, as a barrier

Concepts:

Right of personal privacy:
Tri-mester system:
Compelling points:
Viability:

> ## Questions:
>
> 1. What were the three reasons the court gave to explain historically the enactment of criminal abortion laws in the 19th century?
> 2. How did the court conclude that the word "person" in the U.S. Constitution does not apply to the fetus?
> 3. What is the compelling point and its reasoning during the first trimester?
> 4. What is the compelling point and its reasoning during the third trimester?
> 5. What are the reasons given by Justice Byron White in his dissenting opinion?

Majority Opinion in *Roe v. Wade*

Justice Harry A. Blackmun

It is apparent that common law, at the time of the adoption of our Constitution, and throughout the major portion of the 19th century, abortion was viewed with less disfavor than under most American statutes currently in effect. Phrasing it another way, a woman enjoyed a substantially broader right to terminate a pregnancy than she does in most states today. At least with respect to the early stage of pregnancy, and very possibly without such a limitation, the opportunity to make this choice was present in this country well into the 19th century. Even later, the law continued for some time to treat less punitively an abortion procured in early pregnancy. ...

Three reasons have been advanced to explain historically the enactment of criminal abortion laws in the 19th century and to justify their continued existence.

It has been argued occasionally that these laws were the product of a Victorian social concern to discourage illicit sexual conduct. Texas, however, does not advance this justification in the present case, and it appears that no court or commentator has taken the argument seriously. ...

A second reason is concerned with abortion as a medical procedure. When most criminal abortion laws were first enacted, the procedure was a hazardous one for the woman. This was particularly true prior to the development of antisepsis. Antiseptic techniques, of course, were based on discoveries by Lister, Pasteur, and others first announced in 1867, but were not generally accepted and employed until about the turn of the century. Abortion mortality was high. Even after 1900, and perhaps until as late as the development of antibiotics in the 1940s, standard modern techniques such as dilatation and curettage were not nearly so safe as they are today. Thus it has been argued that a state's real concern in enacting a criminal abortion law was to protect the pregnant woman, that is, to restrain her from submitting to a procedure that places her life in serious jeopardy.

Modern medical techniques have altered this situation. Appellant and various *amici* refer to medical data indicating that abortion in early pregnancy, that is, prior to the end of first trimester, although not without its risk, is now relatively safe.

Mortality rates for women undergoing early abortions, where the procedure is legal, appear to be as low as or lower than the rates for normal childbirth. Consequently, any interest of the State in protecting the woman from an inherently hazardous procedure, except when it would be equally dangerous for her to forgo it, has largely disappeared. Of course, important state interests in the area of health and medical standards do remain. The State has a legitimate interest in seeing to it that abortion, like any other medical procedure, is performed under circumstances that insure maximum safety for the patient. This interest obviously extends at least to the performing physician and his staff, to the facilities involved, to the availability of after-care, and to adequate provision for any complication or emergency that might arise. The prevalence of high mortality rates at illegal "abortion mills" strengthens, rather than weakens, the state's interest in regulating the conditions under which abortions are performed. Moreover, the risk to the woman increases as her pregnancy continues. Thus, the State retains a definite interest in protecting the woman's own health and safety when an abortion is performed at a late stage of pregnancy.

The third reason is the State's interest — some phrase it in terms of duty

— in protecting prenatal life. Some of the argument for this justification rests on the theory that a new human life is present from the moment of conception. The State's interest and general obligation to protect life then extends, it is argued, to prenatal life. Only when the life of the pregnant mother herself is at stake, balanced against the life she carries within her, should the interest of the embryo or fetus not prevail. Logically, of course, a legitimate state interest in this area needs not stand nor fall on acceptance of the belief that life begins at conception or at some other point prior to live birth. In assessing the state's interest, recognition may be given to the less rigid claim that as long as at least potential life is involved, the State may assert interests beyond the protection of the pregnant woman alone.

Parties challenging state abortion laws have sharply disputed in some courts the contention that a purpose of these laws, when enacted, was to protect prenatal life. Pointing to the absence of legislative history to support the contention, they claim that most state laws were designed solely to protect the woman. Because medical advances have lessened this concern, at least with respect to abortion in early pregnancy, they argue that with respect to such abortions the laws

can no longer be justified by any state interest. There is some scholarly support for this view of original purpose. the few state courts called upon to interpret their laws in the late 19th and early 20th centuries did focus on the State's interest in protecting the woman's health rather than in preserving the embryo and fetus. ...

The Constitution does not explicitly mention any right of privacy. In a line of decisions, however, going back perhaps as far as *Union Pacific R. Co. v. Botsford* (1891), the Court has recognized that a right of personal privacy, or a guarantee of certain areas or zones of privacy, does exist under the Constitution. In varying contexts the Court or individual Justices have indeed found at least the roots of that right in the First Amendment, ...in the Fourth and Fifth Amendments ... in the penumbras of the Bill of Rights ... in the Ninth Amendment ... or in the concept of liberty guaranteed by the first section of the Fourteenth Amendment. ...These decisions make it clear that only personal rights that can be deemed "fundamental" or "implicit in the concept of ordered liberty," ... are included in this guarantee of personal privacy. They also make it clear that the right has some extension to activities relating to marriage, ... procreation, ... contraception, ... family relationships, ... and child rearing and education. ...

This right of privacy, whether it be founded in the Fourteenth Amendment's concept of personal liberty and restrictions upon state action, as we feel it is, or, as the District Court determined, in the Ninth Amendment's reservation of rights to the people, is broad enough to encompass a woman's decision whether or not to terminate her pregnancy. ...

... [A]ppellant and some *amici* argue that the woman's right is absolute and that she is entitled to terminate her pregnancy at whatever time, in whatever way, and for whatever reason she alone chooses. With this we do not agree. Appellants' arguments that Texas either has no valid interest at all in regulating the abortion decision, or no interest strong enough to support any limitation upon the woman's sole determination, is unpersuasive. The Court's decisions recognizing a right of privacy also acknowledge that some state regulation in areas protected by that right is appropriate. As noted above, a state may properly assert important interests in safe-guarding health, in maintaining medical standards, and in protecting potential life. At some point in pregnancy, these respective interests become sufficiently compelling to sustain regulation of the factors that govern the abortion decision. The privacy right involved, therefore, cannot be said to be absolute. ...

We, therefore, conclude that the right of personal privacy includes the abortion decision, but that this right is not unqualified and must be considered against important state interests in regulation.

We note that those federal and state courts that have recently considered abortion law challenges have reached the same conclusion. ...

Although the results are divided, most of these courts have agreed that the right of privacy, however based, is broad enough to cover the abortion decision; that the right, nonetheless, is not absolute and is subject to some limitations; and that at some point the state interests as to protection of health, medical standards, and prenatal life, become dominant. We agree with this approach. ...

The appellee and certain *amici* argue that the fetus is a "person" within the language and meaning of the Fourteenth Amendment. In support of this they outline at length and in detail the well-known facts of fetal development. If this suggestion of personhood is established, the appellant's case, of course, collapses, for the fetus' right to life is then guaranteed specifically by the

Amendment. The appellant conceded as much on reargument. On the other hand, the appellee conceded on reargument that no case could be cited that holds that a fetus is a person within the meaning of the fourteenth Amendment. ...

All this, together with our observation, *supra*, that throughout the major portion of the 19th century prevailing legal abortion practices were far freer than they are today, persuades us that the word "person," as used in the Fourteenth Amendment, does not include the unborn. ...Indeed, our decision in *United States v. Vuitch* (1971) inferentially is to the same effect, for we therefore would not have indulged in statutory interpretation favorable to abortion in specified circumstances if the necessary consequence was the termination of life entitled to Fourteenth Amendment protection.

...As we have intimated above, it is reasonable and appropriate for a state to decide that at some point in time, another interest, that of health of the mother or that of potential human life, becomes significantly involved. The woman's privacy is no longer sole and any right of privacy she possesses must be measured accordingly.

Texas urges that, apart from the Fourteenth Amendment, life begins at conception and is present throughout pregnancy, and that, therefore, the State has a compelling interest in protecting that life after conception. We need not resolve the difficult question of when life begins. When those trained in the respective disciplines of medicine, philosophy, and theology are unable to arrive at any consensus, the judiciary, at this point in the development of man's knowledge, is not in a position to speculate as to the answer.

It should be sufficient to note briefly the wide divergence of thinking on this most sensitive and difficult question. There has always been strong support for the view that life does not begin until live birth. This was the belief of the Stoics. It appears to be the predominant, though not the unanimous, attitude of the Jewish faith. It may be taken to represent also the position of a large segment of the Protestant community, insofar as that can be ascertained; organized groups that have taken a formal position on the abortion issue have generally regarded abortion as a matter for the conscience of the individual and her family. As we have noted, the common law found greater significance in quickening. Physicians and their scientific colleagues have regarded that event with less interest and have tended to focus either upon conception or upon live birth or upon the interim point at which the fetus becomes "viable," that is, potentially able to live outside the mother's womb, albeit with artificial aid. Viability is usually placed at about seven months (28 weeks) but may occur earlier, even at 24 weeks. ...

In areas other than criminal abortion the law has been reluctant to endorse any theory that life, as we recognize it, begins before live birth or to accord legal rights to the unborn except in narrowly defined situations and except when the rights are contingent upon live birth. ...In short, the unborn have never been recognized in the law as persons in the whole sense.

In view of all this, we do not agree that, by adopting one theory of life, Texas may override the rights of the pregnant woman that are at stake. We repeat, however, that the state does have an important and legitimate interest in preserving and protecting the health of the pregnant woman, whether she be a resident of the State or a nonresident who seeks medical consultation and treatment there, and that it has still *another* important and legitimate interest in protecting the potentiality of human life. These interests are separate and distinct. Each grows in substantiality as the woman approaches term and, at a point during pregnancy, each becomes "compelling."

With respect to the State's important and legitimate interest in the health of the mother, the "compelling" point, in the light of present medical knowledge, is at approximately the end of the first trimester. This is so because of the now established medical fact ... that until the end of the first trimester mortality in abortion is less than mortality in normal childbirth. It follows that, from this point, a state may regulate the abortion procedure to the extent that the regulation reasonably relates to the preservation and protection of maternal health. Examples of permissible state regulation in this area are requirements as to the qualifications of the person who is to perform the abortion; as to the licensure of that person; as to the facility in which the procedure is to be performed, that is, whether it must be a hospital or may be a clinic or some other place of less-than-hospital status; as to the licensing of the facility; and the like.

This means, on the other hand, that, for the period of pregnancy prior to this "compelling" point, the attending physician, in consultation with his patient, is free to determine, without regulation by the State, that in his medical judgment the patient's pregnancy should be terminated. If that decision is reached, the judgment may be effectuated by an abortion free of interference by the State.

With respect to the State's important and legitimate interest in potential life, the "compelling" point is at viability. This is so because the fetus then presumably has the capability of meaningful life outside the mother's womb. State regulation protective of fetal life after viability thus has both logical and biological justifications. If the State is interested in protecting fetal life after viability, it may go so far as to proscribe abortion during that period except when it is necessary to preserve the life or health of the mother. ...

To summarize and repeat:

1. A state criminal abortion statute for the current Texas type, that excepts from criminality only a *life saving* procedure on behalf of the mother, without regard to pregnancy state and without recognition of the other interests involved, is violative of the Due Process Clause of the Fourteenth Amendment.

(a) For the stage prior to approximately the end of the first trimester, the abortion decision and its effectuation must be left to the medical judgment of the pregnant woman's attending physician.

(b) For the stage subsequent to approximately the end of the first trimester, the State, in promoting its interest in the health of the mother, may, if it chooses, regulate the abortion procedure in ways that are reasonably related to maternal health.

(c) For the stage subsequent to viability, the State, in promoting its interest in the potentiality of human life, may, if it chooses, regulate, and even proscribe, abortion except where it is necessary, in appropriate medical judgment, for the preservation of the life or health of the mother.

2. The State may define the term "physician," as it has been employed [here], to mean only a physician currently licensed by the State, and may proscribe any abortion by a person who is not a physician as so defined.

...The decision leaves the State free to place increasing restrictions on abortion as the period of pregnancy lengthens, so long as those restrictions are tailored to the recognized state interests. The decision vindicates the right of the physician to administer medical treatment according to his professional judgment up to the points where important state interests provide compelling justifications for intervention. Up to those points the abortion decision in all its aspects is inherently, and primarily, a medical decision, and basic responsibility for it must rest with the physician. If an individual practitioner abuses the privilege of exercising proper medical judgment, the usual remedies, judicial and intra-professional, are available. ...

Dissenting Opinion in *Roe v. Wade*

Justice Byron R. White

At the heart of the controversy in these cases are those recurring pregnancies that pose no danger whatsoever to the life or health of the mother but are nevertheless unwanted for any one or more of a variety of reasons — convenience, family planning, economics, dislike of children, the embarrassment of illegitimacy, etc. The common claim before us is that for any one of such reasons, or for no reason at all, and without asserting or claiming any threat to life or health, any woman is entitled to an abortion at her request if she is able to find a medical advisor willing to undertake the procedure.

The Court, for the most part, sustains this position: during the period prior to the time the fetus becomes viable, the Constitution of the United States values the convenience, whim, or caprice of the putative mother more than the life or potential life of the fetus; the Constitution, therefore, guarantees the right to an abortion as against any state law or policy seeking to protect the fetus from an abortion not prompted by more compelling reasons of the mother.

With all due respect, I dissent. I find nothing in the language or history of the Constitution to support the Court's judgment. The Court simply fashions and announces a new constitutional right for pregnant mothers and, with scarcely any reason or authority for its action, invests that right with sufficient substance to override most existing state abortion statutes. The upshot is that the people and the legislatures of the 50 States are constitutionally disentitled to weigh the relative importance of the continued existence and development of the fetus on the one hand against a spectrum of possible impacts on the mother on the other hand. As an exercise of raw judicial power, the Court perhaps has authority to do what it does today; but in my view its judgment is an improvident and extravagant exercise of the power of judicial review which the Constitution extends to this Court.

The Court apparently values the convenience of the pregnant mother more than the continued existence and development of the life or potential life which she carries. Whether or not I might agree with that marshaling of values, I can in no event join the Court's judgment because I find no constitutional warrant for imposing such an order of priorities on the people and legislatures of the States. In a sensitive area such as this, involving as it does issues over which reasonable men may easily and heatedly differ, I cannot accept the Court's exercise of its clear power of choice by interposing a constitutional barrier to state efforts to protect human life and by investing mothers and doctors with the constitutionally protected right to exterminate it. This issue, for the most part, should be left with the people and to the political processes the people have devised to govern their affairs.

It is my view, therefore, that the Texas statute is not constitutionally infirm because it denies abortions to those who seek to serve only their convenience rather than to protect their life or health. ...

From the U.S. Supreme Court, 410 U.S. 113, 1973.

The Abortion Issue

Joe Mixie (1956-)

Joe Mixie teaches Philosophy at Sacred Heart University located in Fairfield, CT. He is the author of *The Existence of God* (2004), *The Atheist Trap* (1994), and several articles.

In this article, Mixie explains the conservative, liberal and moderate positions on abortion. For conservatives, life begins at the moment of conception. Therefore, abortion is the taking of a human life. Conservatives usually allow for abortion only when the mother's life is in danger as per the conditions of The Principle of Double Effect. The liberal position on abortion is that only those who possess the five personhood characteristics have full moral rights, which includes the right to life. Prior to the attainment of these personhood characteristics, there is no "person" in the moral sense and, therefore, no right to life. Since fetuses do not possess these characteristics, their termination is not immoral. The moderate position is that just because a fetus may be a person, it does not necessarily follow that its termination is always immoral. Moderates argue that the "right to life" really means the right not to be killed unjustly. Each case needs to be analyzed to make this determination.

Vocabulary:

Proponents:	those supporting a position
Spermatozoa:	male sperm
Oocyte:	female eggs
Ovulate:	to produce and discharge female eggs

Discontinuity:	not continuous
Viability:	the ability of the fetus to live outside the mother's womb
Untenable:	unacceptable

Concepts:

Principle of Double Effect:

Five Personhood Characteristics:

Good Samaritan:

The Right to Life:

Questions:

1. *What are the strengths and weaknesses of the conservative position on abortion?*
2. *What are the strengths and weaknesses of the liberal position on abortion?*
3. *What are the strengths and weaknesses of the moderate position on abortion?*
4. *Why does Thomson use such imaginative examples?*
5. *What is Warren's position on infanticide?*

The Abortion Issue

There is no other issue in our society today that stirs up emotions like the issue of abortion. Yet, there is little understanding of the underlying philosophical arguments for the different positions on this issue. It is very important for proponents on all sides of this issue to understand, or at least try to understand, the reasoning of their opponent's position. With greater dialogue comes greater understanding, and with greater understanding comes the possibility of genuine and sincere debate and, perhaps, changing of positions. We will begin with an explanation of the conservative position. Then we will consider the liberal position, and finally we will consider the moderate position.

The Conservative Position

The conservative position on abortion is that human life begins at the moment of conception. Conservatives argue that this position is justified by the biological fact that at the moment of conception all the genetic material is present for the formation of a new individual life. Prior to this moment, when eggs and sperm are separate, there is no new individual human life.

This position is most forcefully argued for by John T. Noonan, Jr., in his article entitled "An Almost Absolute Value in History." He says, "The positive argument for conception as the decisive moment of humanization is that at conception the new being receives the genetic code. It is this genetic information which determines his characteristics, which is the biological carrier of the possibility of human wisdom, which makes him a self-evolving being. A being with a human genetic code is a man" (Noonan 1970, 52).

The main question this position is trying to answer is, "When is the appropriate point at which to make a moral distinction of what constitutes a new human life?" All moral judgments must rest upon distinctions. The more justified the moral judgment is, the less arbitrary the distinction must be. Therefore, if the distinctions are not to appear arbitrary, they should relate to some real difference in probabilities. Regarding the abortion debate, Noonan writes, "There is a kind of continuity in all life, but the earlier stages of the elements of human life possess tiny probabilities of development. Consider for example, the spermatozoa in any normal ejaculate: There are about 200,000,000 in any single ejaculate, of which one has a chance of development into a zygote. Consider the oocyte which may become ova: There are 100,000 to 1,000,000 oocytes in a female infant, of which a maximum of 390 are ovulated. But once spermatozoon and ovum meet and the conceptus is formed, such studies as have been made show that roughly in only 20 percent of the cases will spontaneous abortion occur. In other words, the chances are about 4 out of 5 that this new being will develop. At this stage in the life of the being there is a sharp shift in probabilities, an immense jump in potentiality. To make a distinction between the rights of spermatozoa and the rights of the fertilized ovum is to respond to an enormous shift in possibilities" (Noonan 1970, 53).

Because the moment of conception is the point in time when all the genetic material necessary for a new human life is present, conservatives argue that this is the most morally defensible point in time when a distinction can be made. Some might ask what a change in biological probabilities has to do with establishing humanity. "The argument from probabilities is not aimed at establishing humanity but at establishing an objective discontinuity which may be taken into account in moral discourse. As life itself is a matter of probabilities, as most moral reasoning is an estimate of probabilities, so it seems in accord with the structure of reality and the nature of moral thought to found a moral judgment on the change in probabilities at concep-

tion" (Noonan 1970, 54). The conservatives are trying to justify drawing a moral distinction between the conceptus, when sperm and eggs meet and all the genetic information for a new individual is present in one organism, and when the sperm and eggs are separate and the genetic information for a new individual is not present in one organism. Because the moment of conception represents an enormous jump in probabilities, conservatives argue that this is the best point in time to make the moral distinction regarding when a new life with full moral rights begins. To grant full moral rights to sperm and eggs separately is not morally justified.

What other alternatives have philosophers and theologians presented as an alternative to the moment of conception as the point where humanity becomes realized? Historically there have been four: viability; experience; the feelings of adults; and societal membership.

Viability means that the fetus can live outside the mother's womb. Some have argued that this is the best criterion for determining when humanity is realized because the fetus is no longer totally dependent upon the mother for survival. Critics of this position point out that although it may be true that at the point of viability the fetus is no longer completely dependent upon the mother for survival, the fetus is still completely dependent upon some type of "stand-in" mother for survival. The fetus is by no means self-sufficient at this point and neither are infants and young children. Viability also depends upon the current state of technology and varies in different racial groups. Opponents point out the dubious outcome of this position by arguing that it leads to the conclusion that humanity will ultimately depend upon technology and also implies that some racial groups become human before others. Both conclusions seem untenable

A second distinction has been attempted in terms of experience. According to this position, humanity depends on the formation of experience, such as having lived, suffered, possessing memories, etc. Those who do not possess these experiences are considered not to be human or less than fully human. Opponents of this position point out that the fetus is already experiencing and reacting, for example it is responsive to touch and brain waves can be detected after eight weeks. Plus there is the difficulty of dealing with those who have their memory erased through injury. Do they become less human as a result of lost experiences?

A third distinction is made by appealing to the feelings of adults. For example, we do not usually have funerals for fetuses, whereas we do have funerals for the youngest of children who die. Opponents of this position point out that feelings are notoriously an unreliable guide to base the humanity of others upon. While we may mourn the death of a ten years old boy more than his 90-year old grandfather, this has more to do with unrealized potentiality and promise than with any indication of the humanity of either. It is also pointed out that feelings can be the basis for uncompromising prejudice and great injustice, as with racial, religious, or sexual discrimination.

A fourth distinction is made by appeal to societal membership. It is argued that only those who are perceived as members of society are entitled to full human rights and privileges, the primary right being the right to life. One only needs to look at our history to see the potential for abuse that this distinction can lead too. When society decides who is human this distinction often reflects the deepest prejudices. Examples of such consequences abound, such as slavery and forms of discrimination.

When all alternative positions have been analyzed, conservatives argue that the moment of conception provides the best time when a morally defensible distinction can be made. All other positions are morally untenable.

So, does this mean that conservatives do not allow abortion under any circumstances? The answer is no. Conservatives usually allow abortions in those cases when the mother's life would be in danger if the pregnancy were to continue. This exception is not inconsistent with the position that new human life begins at the moment of conception because it appeals to the moral principle called the Principle of Double Effect. The Principle of Double Effect says that in those cases where an action will produce two effects, one being intentional and having good results, and one being unintentional and having bad results, the action is morally justified because the *intended* effect will have good results. For example, suppose a young woman is married, gets pregnant, and is then involved in a terrible car accident. The doctors tell her that due to her injuries her life will be in jeopardy if she continues the pregnancy. Here, the Principle of Double Effect would allow this woman to terminate her pregnancy. The good intended effect is that her life will be saved. The bad unintended effect is that the fetus will not live. If it were possible to remove the fetus and have it survive such as at viability, then the termination of the fetus would be unjustified.

This principle is also used in other moral dilemmas, such as during times of war. Suppose your enemy is using missiles to attack you and they are located in civilian areas. Are you justified in destroying the missiles even though there is a risk that civilians might be hurt? According to the Principle of Double Effect your intended good effect is to destroy the missiles to keep your country safe, while the unintended bad effect might be the harming of civilians in your enemy's country. Therefore, you are justified in destroying the enemy missiles.

In cases of rape and incest, the conservative position is rather difficult for many people to accept because it does not allow for abortion. Although this position might appear rather harsh, it is consistent with the position that new human life begins at the moment of conception. Regardless of how a human being is conceived, whether from loving parents or a violent rape, once conceived all human beings have full moral rights and this includes a right to life. A person's right to life is superior to all other rights. It is important to note that reported abortions resulting from rape and incest are roughly 2% to 3% of the 1.4 million annually reported abortions.

The Liberal Position

The liberal position on abortion is that only a person has full moral rights, which includes the right to life, and the fetus does not fulfill the requirements of personhood. This position is most forcefully argued for by Mary Anne Warren in her article entitled, "Abortion Is Morally Permissible." Warren criticizes the conservative position by arguing that it is not biological or genetic humanity that is the important point in the abortion issue, but personhood in the moral sense. She says, "I suggest that the traits which are most central to the concept of personhood, or humanity in the moral sense, are, very roughly, the following: 1) Consciousness (of objects and events external and/or internal to the being), and in, particular, the capacity to feel pain; 2) Reasoning (the developed capacity to solve new and relatively complex problems); 3) Self-motivated activity (activity which is relatively independent of either genetic or direct external control); 4) The capacity to communicate, by whatever means, messages of an indefinite variety of types, that is, not just with an indefinite number of possible contents, but on indefinitely many possible topics; 5) The presence of self-concepts and self-awareness, either individual or racial, or both" (Warren 1973, 79).

It is not biological humanity that provides a moral distinction for the liberal position, but rather the attainment of certain personhood characteristics. It is the possession of these characteristics that bestow moral rights upon an individual. Warren continues, "In searching for such criteria, it is useful to look beyond the set of people with whom we are acquainted, and ask how we would decide whether a totally alien being was a person or not. (For we have no right to assume that genetic humanity is necessary for personhood.) Imagine a space traveler who lands on an unknown planet and encounters a race of beings utterly unlike any he has ever seen or heard of. If he wants to be sure of behaving morally towards these beings, he has to somehow decide whether they are people, and hence have full moral rights, or whether they are the sort of thing which he need not feel guilty about treating as, for example, a source of food" (Warren 1973, 82).

Someone might ask whether there is a relationship between fetal development and the right to life because we know that as the fetus develops it begins to develop more of the personhood characteristics, for example the fetus has the ability to feel pain after eight weeks. Warren's answer is a resounding no! There is no relationship between fetal development and the right to life. "Thus, in the relevant respects, a fetus, even a fully developed one, is considerably less person-like than is the average mature mammal, indeed the average fish. And I think that a rational person must conclude that if the right to life of a fetus is to be based upon its resemblance to a person, then it cannot be said to have any more right to life than, let us say, a newborn guppy (which also seems to be capable of feeling pain), and that a right of that magnitude could never override a woman's right to obtain an abortion, at any stage of her pregnancy" (Warren 1973, 84).

According to the liberal position, only persons have full moral rights, including the right to life. If a being does not possess the five personhood characteristics, then they do not possess full moral rights. It is important to note that although the five personhood characteristics are acquired over time, that is, not all at once, the acquisition of full moral rights, including the right to life, is acquired all at once and not progressively. Beings cannot possess some personhood rights sooner than others, but they are acquired all at once when all five of the characteristics are acquired.

Someone might ask whether there is a relationship between potential personhood and the right to life because we know that full fledged members of the moral community, that is those with full moral rights, come from fetuses. Warren's response is that potential persons have potential rights and actual persons have actual rights. The greatest right of a potential person, the right to life, is less important than the minimal rights of an actual person, for example, the right not to be inconvenienced.

Someone might ask if infanticide is morally acceptable based upon the five personhood characteristics set forth by Warren. It is interesting to note that because of her strong stance on the relationship between the five personhood characteristics and the acquisition of full moral rights, she was asked this question. Warren argues that although killing a newborn infant is not murder, "it does not follow, however, that infanticide is permissible" (Warren 1975, 45). She gives two reasons. Her first is that there are people who would like to have the infant and would be willing to care for it, therefore, its destruction is unnecessary. Her second reason is that even if there are no other people who would want to care for the infant, we as a society would rather have our taxes pay for orphanages than have the infant killed. Although some might argue that these same two conditions could also hold for fetuses, Warren argues that there is a crucial difference, "so long as the fetus is unborn, its preservation, contrary to the wishes of the pregnant woman, violates her rights to freedom, happiness, and self-determination. Her rights override the rights of those who would like the fetus preserved, just as if someone's life or limb is threatened by a wild animal, his right to protect himself by destroying the animal overrides the rights of those who would prefer that the animal not be harmed" (Warren 1975, 46).

Once the fetus is born, however, Warren argues that "its preservation no longer violates any of its mother's rights, even if she wants it destroyed, because she is free to put it up for adoption" (Warren 1975, 47). Although the moment of birth does not mark any sharp discontinuity regarding the possession of the right to life, it does mark the end of the mother's right to determine the fate of the infant.

It might disturb some to know that for unwanted or defective infants who are born into a society which cannot afford or is unwilling to care for them, Warren argues that their destruction is permissible.

The Moderate Position

As we have seen, the debate between conservatives and liberals on the abortion issues is thought to turn on whether the fetus is a person. That is, it seems reasonable to think that if the fetus is a person, abortion is morally impermissible, and if the fetus is not a person, abortion is morally permissible.

The conservative argument is based upon two critical premises. First is the idea that the fetus is a moral person with a right to life. The second has to do with the strength of the right to life relative to other rights. It is claimed that one person's right to life necessarily outweighs another person's right to control her own body.

Instead of trying to show that the fetus is not a person, Judith Jarvis Thomson in her article entitled "A Defense of Abortion," tries to show that it is not necessarily true that one person's right to life outweighs another person's right to control what happens to her body when these rights come into conflict. She does this by producing an example in which a person's right to control what happens to her body outweighs another person's right to life. Suppose you wake up one morning and find that a famous violinist's circulatory system has been plugged into your's, so that your kidneys can be used to extract poison from his blood as well as from your own. He needs to remain plugged into you for nine months. If you unplug him, he will die because there is no other person who has the right blood type (Thomson 1971, 48). Here is a situation in which the violinist's right to life comes into conflict with your right to control what happens to your own body. Is it morally permissible for you to unplug the violinist, given that you know he will die when you do so?

Now the fact that you were hooked up to the violinist against your will reflects the situation of rape. A young girl is raped against her will, as you were hooked up against your will. If you argue that you have the right to unhook yourself even though someone will die as a result, then why doesn't the young girl who was raped have the right to "unhook" herself even though someone will die? This brings up an interesting point because according to the conservative position, abortion is not morally permissible even in cases of rape.

According to the moderate position, abortion is morally permissible under certain circumstances, such as rape, incest, and where the mother's life is in danger. But what about the cases where a woman voluntarily indulges in intercourse, knowing of the chance she might become pregnant, and then she does become pregnant. Is she not in part

responsible for the presence, in fact the very existence, of the unborn person inside of her? Even though she did not invite the unborn person in, she certainly seems to have at least a partial responsibility for its being there and doesn't this give the fetus a right to the use of her body?

Again Thomson provides some thought provoking examples for us to consider. "If the room is stuffy, and I therefore open a window to air it, and a burglar climbs in, it would be absurd to say, "Ah, now he can stay, she's given him a right to the use of her house – for she is partially responsible for his presence there, having voluntarily done what enabled him to get in, in full knowledge that there are such things as burglars, and that burglars burgle." It would be still more absurd to say this if I had had bars installed outside my windows, precisely to prevent burglars from getting in, and a burglar got in only because of a defect in the bars. It remains equally absurd if we imagine it is not a burglar who climbs in, but an innocent person who blunders or falls in. Again, suppose it were like this: people-seeds drift about in the air like pollen, and if you open your window, one may drift in and take root in your carpets or upholstery. You don't want children, so you fix up your windows with fine mesh screens, the very best you can buy. As can happen, and on very, very rare occasions does happen, one of the screens is defective and a seed drifts in and takes root. Does the person-plant who now develops have a right to use your house? Surely not – despite the fact that you voluntarily opened your window, you knowingly kept carpets and upholstered furniture, and you knew that screens were sometimes defective. Someone may argue that you are responsible for its rooting, that it does have a right to your house because, after all, you could have lived out your life with bare floors and no furniture, or with sealed windows and doors. But this won't do – for by the same token anyone can avoid a pregnancy due to rape by having a hysterectomy, or anyway by never leaving home without a reliable army (Thomson 1971, 60).

Thomson provides these examples to help us think deeply about just what are the appropriate moral responsibilities for a woman who practices all the realistic safe guards while engaging in consensual sexual relations and becomes pregnant. Her position is that there are times when an unborn person does have a right to use its mother's body and there are times when it does not. If the unborn person does have a right to use its mother's body, then killing it would be unjust.

If it does not have a right to use its mother's body, then killing it would not be unjust. This leads Thomson to conclude that "the right to life consists not in the right to be killed, but rather in the right not to be killed unjustly" (Thomson 1971, 58).

Thomson makes one other point that is important to consider and that is the difference between the "Good Samaritan" and the "Minimally Decent Samaritan." Recall the story of the Good Samaritan: Jesus said: "A man was going down from Jerusalem to Jericho, when he fell into the hands of robbers. They stripped him of his clothes, beat him and went away, leaving him half dead. A priest happened to be going down the same road, and when he saw the man, he passed by on the other side. So too, a Levite, when he came to the place and saw him, passed by on the other side. But a Samaritan, as he traveled, came where the man was; and when he saw him, he took pity on him. He went to him and bandaged his wounds, pouring on oil and wine. Then he put the man on his own donkey, took him to an inn and took care of him. The next day he took out two silver coins and gave them to the innkeeper. 'Look after him,' he said, 'and when I return, I will reimburse you for any extra expense you may have (Luke 10:30-35).

The Good Samaritan helped the man even at cost to himself. Thomson feels that this would reflect a woman who becomes pregnant as the result of rape or incest and decides to continue with her pregnancy. She is going above and beyond what most people would think is necessary, similar to the Good Samaritan. Although she bears no responsibility in becoming pregnant, she is still willing to continue because of the unborn person she now carries. A Minimally Decent Samaritan would be the woman who engages in voluntary a sexual relationship, gets pregnant, and then decides to continue with the pregnancy. She is a minimally decent Samaritan because although she may not necessarily want to be pregnant, she realizes she does bear some responsibility in the pregnancy and is willing to accept the consequences of her actions.

Summary

We have examined the conservative, liberal, and moderate positions on the issue of abortion. We have seen that each approaches this very difficult question from a different perspective. Armed with the strength of biology, the conservatives argue that a new human life begins at the moment of conception. Therefore, it has a right to life which can only be taken in cases of self-defense. Arguing that it is not genetic humanity that is crucial, but personhood, the liberal position holds that certain personhood characteristics must be attained to possess full moral rights, which includes the right to life. Prior to the attainment of this status, no moral rights are possessed, including the right to life. The new life can be terminated for any reason. The moderate position is between the conservative and the liberal positions and argues that there are circumstances when abortion is morally permissible, such as rape, incest, and when the life of the mother is threatened, and there are circumstances when it is not, such as inconvenience. The important point to keep in mind, according to the moderate position is that the right to life does not mean the right not to be killed, but rather, the right not to be killed unjustly.

Which of these positions is correct? This question must be answered by each of us individually, and collectively as a society.

References:

Noonan, John, Jr. 1970. "An Almost Absolute Value in History." *The Morality of Abortion: Legal and Historical Perspectives.* Cambridge, MA: Harvard

University Press.

Thomson, Judith, J. 1971. "A Defense of Abortion." *Philosophy and Public Affairs.*" Vol. 1. No. 1 pp. 47-66.

Warren, Mary Anne. 1973. "On the Moral and Legal Status of Abortion." *The Monist.* Vol. 57. No. 1 pp. 56-72.

Section VI: Contemporary Ethiccal Issues: Abortion Section Review

Below is the review sheet for Part VI: Contemporary Ethical Issues: Abortion. Included in this review are the terms and concepts you should be familiar with to prepare for the exam. I have also included an example of the multiple choice questions that you will have to answer. It will give you an idea of what type of questions to expect.

We will be reviewing each of these terms and concepts and the multiple choice question in class prior to the exam.

You should be familiar with the following terms and concepts:

Roe v. Wade
(1973)
Historical prologue
3 reasons for strict abortion laws
Right to Privacy
Trimester system
Compelling points
Reasons for compelling points
Doe v. Boulton
Justice Harry Blackmun
Justice Byron White

Abortion
Conservative Position
John Noonan
Moment of conception
Possibility / probability
Principle of Double Effect
Liberal Position
Mary Ann Warren
5 personhood characteristics
Fetal development and Right to Life
Potential personhood and Right to Life
Moral community
Postscript on infanticide
Moderate Position
Judith Jarvis Thomson
Right to life
Good Samaritan
Minimally decent Samaritan

Multiple Choice Example:

Which statements best describe the historical thinking behind the Roe v. Wade decision?

A. The majority opinion was written by Harry Blackmun. It begins with a historical prologue that discusses why women enjoyed a greater freedom to terminate their pregnancies for most of U.S. history. It then gives three reasons why this changed in the 19th century. The reasons given are that the laws were the product of Victorian morality, the concern for abortion as a medical procedure and the state's interest in protecting potential life. The Constitution does not explicitly mention any right to privacy, but the court has recognized a right of personal privacy. The court concluded that the word "persons" in the 14th Amendment does include the unborn.

B. The majority opinion was written by Byron White. It begins with a historical prologue that discusses why women enjoyed a greater freedom to terminate their pregnancies for most of U.S. history. It then gives three reasons why this changed in the 19th century. The reasons given are that the laws were the product of Victorian morality, the concern for abortion as a medical procedure, and the state's interest in protecting potential life. The Constitution does not explicitly mention any right to privacy, but the court has recognized a right of personal. The court concluded that the word "persons" in the 14th Amendment does not include the unborn.

C The majority opinion was written by Harry Blackmun. It begins with a historical prologue that discusses why women enjoyed a greater freedom to terminate their pregnancies for most of U.S. history. It then gives three reasons why this changed in the 19th century. The reasons given are that the laws were the product of Victorian morality, the concern for abortion as a medical procedure, and the state's interest in protecting potential life. The Constitution does not explicitly mention any right to privacy, but the court has recognized a right of personal privacy. The court concluded that the word "persons" in the 14th Amendment does not include the unborn.

D. The majority opinion was written by Harry Blackmun. It begins with a historical prologue that discusses why women enjoyed less freedom to terminate their pregnancies for most of U.S. history. It then gives three reasons why this changed in the 19th century. The reasons given are that the laws were the product of Victorian morality, the concern for abortion as a medical procedure, and the state's interest in protecting potential life. The Constitution does not explicitly mention any right to privacy, but the court has recognized a right of personal privacy. The court concluded that the word "persons" in the 14th Amendment does not include the unborn.

Part VII
Political Philosophy

Part VII

Political Philosophy

> *"In the state of nature, the life of man is solitary, poor, nasty, brutish, and short."*
> - **Thomas Hobbes**
>
> *"The great and chief end, therefore, of men's uniting into commonwealths, and putting themselves under government, is the preservation of their property; to which, in the state of nature, there are many things wanting."*
> - **John Locke**
>
> *"I regard utility as the ultimate appeal on all ethical questions; but it must be utility in the largest sense, grounded on the permanent interests of man as a progressive being."*
> - **John Stuart Mill**
>
> *"We hold these truths to be self-evident, that all men are created equal, that they are endowed by their Creator with certain unalienable rights, that among these are Life, Liberty, and the Pursuit of Happiness."*
> - **The Declaration of Independence**

Introduction

POLITICAL PHILOSOPHY

Political Philosophy deals with questions such as the origin and justification of government, the justifiable extent of authority the state has over the individual, analysis of the different types of political systems, and defining crucial concepts such as "justice," "rights," "authority," "liberty," "law," etc.

Which is the best political system? Is it democracy, socialism, or communism? How do governments justify taxing their citizens, drafting them into a war where they might be killed, and establishing different kinds of law which all its citizens must obey or be subject to punishment? Surely you must have asked these same questions if you have ever paid taxes, received a speeding ticket, or been drafted into the army.

Throughout human history, many different kinds of answers have been given to these questions. We will consider three of these answers. First we will consider Thomas Hobbes' answer. He believed that because the state of nature was so brutal and life threatening, government arose out of the individual's self-interest. Therefore, the government had complete power and authority over the individual, much like an overpowering animal has, hence the term *leviathan*.

John Locke believed that the justification of government was that it reflected the will of the majority of the people. A democracy should have no trouble serving the people because the people elect the government. The limits of government would be set by the individual's natural rights and the voice of the majority. The United States democracy is based in large part upon the ideas of John Locke.

John Stuart Mill argued that the basis of government is utilitarianism. This is where the greatest amount of happiness is created for the greatest number of people. Mill argued that, although representative government would fulfill this condition, it must also be checked against the "tyranny of the majority," that is the exploitation of the minority by the majority.

Finally, we will consider our own Declaration of Independence and the United States Constitution, often called the greatest political documents ever written. How do these documents compare with the great political documents of human history?

Leviathan

THOMAS HOBBES (1588-1679)

Educated at Oxford University, Thomas Hobbes is one of the major figures in what has come to be called the "social contract" school of political theory. Deeply moved by the social unrest of the English civil war (1640-1660), he was convinced of the necessity of a strong central government.

In his most famous work, *Leviathan* (1651), he argued that all people are egoists in pursuit of their own self gratification. Because of the conditions of the "state of nature" in which life is "solitary, poor, nasty, brutish, and short," people are unable to obtain this gratification because of the constant fear of their safety. In this state of anarchy, the prudent person concludes that it is in everyone's self interest to give up some of their freedoms for the protection of the state. To ensure that society's laws are obeyed, Hobbes proposes a strong central government or "Leviathan."

Vocabulary:

Felicity:	the state of being happy
Machination:	the act of plotting; a crafty scheme
Prudence:	wisdom
Delectation:	enjoyment
Wiles:	a tricks or schemes
Subsist:	to remain alive; to continue to exist
Augmentation:	an increase in size or effect
Commodious:	spacious and roomy
Impediments:	obstacles

Covenant:	agreement
Pertinent:	directly relating to the matter at hand
Equity:	fairness and justice
Theorems:	propositions that can be deduced from the premises of a system
Husbandry:	thrifty management, as of resources

Concepts:

Social Contract:

State of Nature:

Anarchy:

Minimal of Morality:

Leviathan:

Right of Nature:

Law of Nature:

Contract:

Grace:

Justice:

Injustice:

Common Wealth:

Sovereign:

Questions:

1. *How does Hobbes describe the State of Nature?*
2. *What is a Social Contract?*
3. *What is the difference between the Right of Nature and the Law of Nature?*
4. *How does Hobbes define a contract?*
5. *What is the Leviathan and what is its purpose?*

OF THE NATURAL CONDITION OF MANKIND AS CONCERNING THEIR FELICITY AND MISERY

NATURE HAS MADE men so equal, in the faculties of the body, and mind; as that though there be found one man manifestly stronger in body, or of quicker mind than another, yet when all is reckoned together, the difference between man and man is not so considerable, as that one man can thereupon claim to himself any benefit to which another may not also claim. For as to the strength of body, the weakest has strength enough to kill the strongest, either by secret machination, or by confederacy with others.

And as to the faculties of the mind, I find yet a greater equality amongst men, than that of strength. For prudence, is but experience. That which may perhaps make such equality incredible, is but a vain conceit of one's own wisdom, which almost all men think they have in a greater degree, than the vulgar. For such is the nature of men, that howsoever they may acknowledge many others to be more witty, or more eloquent, or more learned; yet they will hardly believe there be many so wise as themselves. But this proves rather that men are in that point equal, than unequal. For there is not ordinarily a greater sign of the equal distribution of any thing, than that every man is content with his share.

From this equality of ability, arises equality of hope in the attaining of our ends. And therefore if any two men desire the same thing, which nevertheless they cannot both enjoy, they become enemies. In the way to their end, which is principally their own conservation, endeavor to destroy, or subdue one another.

And from this diffidence of one another, there is no way for any man to secure himself.

Again, men have no pleasure, but on the contrary a great deal of grief, in keeping company, where there is no power able to over-awe them all. For every man looks at his companion as a value, at the same rate he sets upon himself: and upon all signs of contempt, or undervaluing, natural endeavors, as far as he dares, to extort a greater value from his companions, by damage; and from others, by the example.

So that in the nature of man, we find three principal causes of quarrel. First, competition; second, diffidence; third, glory.

The first, makes men invade for gain; the second, for safety; and the third, for reputation. The first uses violence, to make themselves masters of other men's persons, wives, children, and cattle; the second, defends them; the third, for trifles, as a word, a smile, a different option, and any other sign of undervalue, either direct in their persons, or by reflection in their kindred, their friends, their nation, their profession, or their name.

Hereby it is manifest, that during the time men live without a common power to keep them all in awe, they are in that condition which is called war; and such a war, as is of every man, against every man. For war, consists not in battle only, or the act of fighting; but in a tract of time, wherein the will to contend by battle is sufficiently known: and therefore the notion of *time*, is to be considered in the nature of war; as it is in the nature of weather. For as the nature of foul weather, lies not in the shower or two of rain; but in an inclination thereto of many days together: so the nature of war, consists not in actual fighting; but in the known disposition thereto, during all the time there is no assurance to the contrary. All other time is PEACE.

Whatsoever, therefore, is consequent to a time of war, where every man is enemy to every man; the same is consequent to the time, wherein men live without other security, than what their own strength, and their own invention shall furnish them with. In such condition, there is no place for industry; because the fruit thereof is uncertain: and consequently no cultivation of the earth; no naviga-

tion, nor use of the commodities that may be imported by sea; no commodious building; no instruments of moving, and removing, such things as require much force; no knowledge of the face of the earth; no account of time; no arts; no letters; no society; and which is worst of all, continual fear, and danger of violent death; and the life of man is solitary, poor, nasty, brutish, and short.

It may seem strange to some man, that has not well weighed these things; that nature should thus dissociate, and render men apt to invade, and destroy one another. Let him therefore consider with himself, when taking a journey, he arms himself, and seeks to go well accompanied; when going to sleep, he locks his doors; when even in his house he locks his chests; and this when he knows there be laws, and public officers, armed, to revenge all injuries that shall be done him; what opinion he has of his fellow-subjects, when he rides armed; of his fellow citizens, when he locks his doors; and of his children, and servants, when he locks his chests. Does he not there as much accuse mankind by his actions, as I do by my words? The desires, and other passions of man, are in themselves no sin. No more are the actions, that proceed from those passions, till they know a law that forbids them: which till laws be made they cannot know: nor can any law be made, till they have agreed upon the person that shall make it.

It may be thought, there was never such a time, nor condition of war as this; and I believe it was never generally so, over all the world: but there are many places, where they live so now. For the savage people in many places of America, except the government of small families, the concord, whereof, depends on natural lust, have no government at all; and live at this day in that brutish manner, as I said before. Howsoever, it may be perceived what manner of life there would be, where there were no common power to fear, by the manner of life, which men that have formerly lived under a peaceful government, use to degenerate into, in a civil war.

But though there had never been any time, wherein particular men were in a condition of war one against another; yet in all times, kings, and persons of sovereign authority, because of their independency, are in continual jealousies, and in the state and posture of gladiators; having their weapons pointing, and their eyes fixed on one another; that is, their forts, garrisons, and guns upon the frontiers of their kingdoms; and continual spies upon their neighbors; which is a posture of war.

To this war of every man, against every man, this also is consequent; that nothing can be unjust. The notions of right and wrong, justice and injustice have there no place. Where there is no common power, there is no law: where no law, no injustice. Force, and fraud, are in war the two cardinal virtues. Justice, and injustice are none of the faculties neither of the body, nor mind. If they were, they might be in a man that were alone in the world, as well as his senses, and passions. They are qualities, that relate to men in society, not in solitude. It is consequent also to the same condition, that there be no propriety, no dominion, no *mine* and *thine* distinct; but only that to be every man's, that he can get; and for so long, as he can keep it. And thus much for the ill condition, which man by mere nature is actually placed in; though with a possibility to come out of it, consisting partly in the passions, partly in his reason.

The passions that incline men to peace, are fear of death; desire of such things as are necessary to commodious living; and a hope by their industry to obtain them. And reason suggests convenient articles of peace, upon which men may be drawn to agreement. These articles, are they, which otherwise are called the Laws of Nature: whereof I shall speak more particularly, in the two following chapters.

OF THE FIRST AND SECOND NATURAL LAWS AND OF CONTRACTS

The right of nature, which writers commonly call *jus naturale*, is the liberty each man hath, to use his own power, as he will himself, for the preservation of his own nature; that is to say, of his own life; and consequently, of doing any thing, which in his own judgment, and reason, he shall conceive to be the aptest means thereunto.

By LIBERTY, is understood, according to the proper signification of the word, the absence of external impediments: which impediments, may oft take away part of a man's power to do what he would; but cannot hinder him from using the power left him, according as his judgment, and reason shall dictate to him.

A LAW OF NATURE, *lex naturalis*, is a precept or general rule, found out by reason, by such a man is forbidden to do that, which is destructive of his life, or takes away the means of preserving the same; and to omit that, by which he thinks it may be best preserved. For though they that speak of this subject, use to confound *jus*, and *lex*, *right* and *law*: yet they ought to be distinguished; because RIGHT, consists in liberty to do, or to forbear; whereas LAW, determines, and binds to one of them: so that law, and right, differ as much, as obligation, and liberty; which in one and the same matter are inconsistent.

And because the condition of man, as hath been declared in the precedent chapter, is a condition of war of every one; in which case every one is governed by his own reason; and there is nothing he can make use of, that may not be a help unto him, in preserving his life against his enemies; it follows, that in such a condition, every man has a right to every thing; even to one another's body. And therefore, as long as this natural right of every man to every thing endures, there can be no security to any man, how strong or wise so ever he be, of living out the time, which nature ordinarily allows men to live. And consequently it is a precept, or general rule of reason, *that every man, ought to endeavor peace, as far as he has hope of obtaining it; and when he cannot obtain it, that he may see, and use, all helps, and advantages of war.* The first branch of which rule, contains the first, and fundamental law of nature; which is, *to seek peace, and follow it.* The second, the sum of the right of nature; which is, *by all means we can, to defend ourselves.*

From this fundamental law of nature, by which men are commanded to endeavor peace, is derived this second law; *that a man be willing, when others are so too, as far-forth, as for peace, and defense of himself he shall think it necessary, to lay down this right to all things; and be contented with so much liberty against other men, as he would allow other men against himself.* For as long as every man holds this right, of doing any thing he likes; so long are all men in the condition of war. But if other men will not lay down their right, as well as he; then there is no reason for any one, to divest himself of his: for that were to expose himself to prey, which no man is bound to, rather than to dispose himself to peace. This is that law of the Gospel; *whatsoever you require that others should do to you, that do ye to them.* And that law of all men, *quod tibi fieri non vis, alteri ne feceris* (What you do not want done to you, do not do to others).

To *lay down* a man's *right* to any thing, is to *divest* himself of the *liberty*, of hindering another of the benefit of his own right to the same. For he that renounces or passes away his right, gives not to any other man a right which he had not before; because there is nothing to which every man had not right by nature: but only stands out of his way that he may enjoy his own original right, without hindrance from him; not without hindrance from another. So that the effect which rebounds to one man, by another man's defect of right, is but so much diminution of impediments to the use of his own right original.

Right is laid aside, either by simply renouncing it; or by transferring it to another. By *simply* RENOUNCING; when he cares not to whom the benefit thereof redounds. By TRANSFERRING; when he intends the benefit thereof to some certain person, or persons. And when a man hath in either manner abandoned, or granted away his right; then is he said to be OBLIGED, or BOUND, not to hinder those, to whom such right is granted, or abandoned, from the benefit of it: and that he *ought*, and it is his DUTY, not to make void that voluntary act of his own: and that such hindrance is INJUSTICE, and INJURY, as being *sine jure*, the right being before renounced, or transferred. So that *injury*, or *injustice*, in the controversies of the world, is somewhat like to that, which in the disputations of scholars is called *absurdity*. For as it is there called an absurdity, to contradict what one maintained in the beginning: so in the world, it is called injustice, and injury, voluntarily to undo that, which from the beginning he had voluntarily done. The way by which a man either simply renounces, or transfers his right, is a declaration, or signification, by some voluntary and sufficient sign, or signs, that he doth so renounce, or transfer; or hath so renounced, or transferred the same, to him that accepts it. And these signs are either words only, or actions only; or, as it happens most often, both words, and actions. And the same are the BONDS, by which men are bound, and obliged: bonds, that have their strength, not from their own nature, for nothing is more easily broken than a man's word, but from fear of some evil consequence upon the rupture.

When so ever a man transfers his right, or renounces it; it is either in consideration of some right reciprocally transferred to himself; or for some other good he hopes for thereby. For it is a voluntary act: and of the voluntary acts of every man, the object is some *good to himself.* And therefore there be some rights, which no man can be understood by any words, or other signs, to have abandoned, or transferred. At first a man cannot lay down the right of resisting them, that assault him by force, to take away his life; because he cannot be understood to aim thereby, at any good to himself. The same may be said of wounds, and chains, and imprisonment; both because there is no benefit consequent to such patience; as there is to the patience of suffering another to be wounded, or imprisoned: as also because a man cannot tell, when he sees men proceed against him by violence, whether they intend his death or not. And lastly the motive, and

end for which this renouncing, and transferring of right is introduced, is nothing else but the security of a man's person, in his life, and in the means of so preserving life, as not to be weary of it. And therefore if a man by words, or other signs, seem to despoil himself of the end, for which those signs were intended; he is not to be understood as if he meant it, or that it was his will; but that he was ignorant of how such words and actions were to be interpreted.

The mutual transferring of right, is that which men call CONTRACT.

There is a difference between transferring of right to the thing; and transferring, that which is delivered of the thing itself. For the thing may be delivered together with the translation of the right; as in buying and selling with ready-money; or exchange of goods, or lands: and it may be delivered some time after.

Again, one of the contractors, may deliver the thing contracted for on his part, and leave the other to perform his part at some determinate time after, and in the mean time be trusted; and then the contract on his part, is called PACT, or COVENANT: or both parts may contract now, to perform hereafter: in which cases, he that is to perform in time to come, being trusted, his performance is called *keeping of promise*, or faith; and the failing of performance, if it be voluntary, *violation of faith.*

When the transferring of right, is not mutual: but one of the parties transfers, in hope to gain thereby friendship, or service from another, or from his friends; or in hope to gain the reputation of charity, or magnanimity; or to deliver his mind from the pain of compassion; or in hope of reward in heaven, this is not contract, but GIFT, FREE-GIFT, GRACE: these words signify one and the same thing.

Signs of contract, are either *express*, or *by inference*. Express, are words spoken with understanding of what they signify: and such words are either of the time *present*, or *past*; as, I give, *I grant, I have given, I have granted, I will that this be yours*: or of the future; as, *I will give, I will grant*: which words of the future are called PROMISE.

If a covenant be made, wherein neither of the parties perform presently, but trust one another; in the condition of mere nature, which is a condition of war of every man against every man, upon any reasonable suspicion, it is void: but if there be a common power set over them both, with right and force sufficient to compel performance, it is not void. For he that performs first, has no assurance the other will perform after; because the bonds of words are too weak to bridle men's ambition, avarice anger, and other passions, without the fear of some coercive power; which in the condition of mere nature, where all men are equal, and judges of the justness of their own fears, cannot possibly be supposed. And therefore he which performs first, does but betray himself to his enemy; contrary to the right, he can never abandon, of defending his life and means of living.

But in a civil estate where there is a power set up to constrain those that would otherwise violate their faith, that fear is no more reasonable: and for that cause, he which by the covenant is to perform first, is obliged so to do.

The cause of fear, which makes such a covenant invalid must be always something arising after the covenant made; as some new fact, or other sign of the will not to perform: else it cannot make the covenant void. For that which could not hinder a man from promising, ought not to be admitted as a hindrance of performing.

OF THE CAUSES, GENERATION, AND DEFINITION OF A COMMONWEALTH

The final cause, end, or design of men, who naturally love liberty, and dominion over others, in the introduction of that restraint upon themselves, in which we see them live in common-wealths, is the foresight of their own preservation, and of a more contented life thereby; that is to say, of getting themselves out from that miserable condition of war, which is necessarily consequent, as hath been shown in chapter XIII, to the natural passions of men, when there is no visible power to keep them in awe, and tie them by fear of punishment to the performance of their covenants, and observation of those laws of nature set down in the fourteenth and fifteenth chapters.

For the laws of nature, as justice, equity, modesty, mercy, and, in sum, doing to others, as we would be done to, of themselves, without the terror of some power, to cause them to be observed, are contrary to our natural passions, that carry us to partiality, pride, revenge, and the like. And covenants, without the sword, are but words and of no strength to secure a man at all. Therefore notwithstanding the laws of nature, which everyone hath then kept, when he has the will to keep them, when he can do it safely, if there be no power erected, or not great enough for our security; every man will, and may lawfully rely on his own strength and art, for caution against all other men. And in all places, where men have lived by small families, to rob and spoil one another, has been a trade, and so far from being reput-

ed against the law of nature, that the greater spoils they gained, the greater was their honor; and men observed no other laws therein, but the laws of honor; that is, to abstain from cruelty, leaving to men their lives, and instruments of husbandry. And as small families did then; so now do cities and kingdoms which are but greater families, for their own security, enlarge their dominions, upon all pretences of danger, and fear of invasion, or assistance that may be given to invaders, and endeavor as much as they can, to subdue, or weaken their neighbors, by open force, and secret arts, for want of other caution, justly; and are remembered for it in after ages with honor.

It is true, that certain living creatures, as bees, and ants, live sociably one with another, which are therefore by Aristotle numbered amongst political creatures; and yet have no other direction than their particular judgments and appetites; nor speech, whereby one of them can signify to another, what he thinks expedient for the common benefit: and therefore some man may perhaps desire to know, why mankind cannot do the same. To which I answer,

First, that men are continually in competition for honor and dignity, which these creatures are not; and consequently amongst men there arises on that ground, envy and hatred, and finally war; but amongst these not so.

Secondly, that amongst these creatures, the common good difference not from the private; and being by nature inclined to their private, they procure thereby the common benefit. But man, whose joy consists in comparing himself with other men, can relish nothing but what is eminent.

Third, that these creatures, having not, as man, the use of reason, do not see, nor think they see any fault, in the administration of their common business; whereas amongst men, there are very many, that think themselves wiser, and abler to govern the public, better than the rest; and these strive to reform and innovate, one this way, another that way; and thereby bring it into distraction and civil war.

Fourthly, that these creatures, though they have some use of voice, in making known to one another their desires, and other affections; yet they want that art of words, by which some men can represent to others, that which is good, in the likeness of evil; and evil, in the likeness of good; and augment, or diminish the apparent greatness of good and evil; discontenting men, and troubling their peace at their pleasure.

Fifthly, irrational creatures cannot distinguish between *injury*, and *damage*; and therefore as long as they be at ease, they are not offended with their fellows: whereas man is then most troublesome, when he is most at ease: for then it is that he loves to show his wisdom, and control the actions of them that govern the commonwealth.

Lastly, the agreement of these creatures is natural; that of men, is by covenant only, which is artificial: and therefore it is no wonder if there be somewhat else required, besides covenant, to make their agreement constant and lasting; which is a common power, to keep them in awe, and to direct their actions to the common benefit.

The only way to erect such a common power, as may be able to defend them from the invasion of foreigners, and the injuries of one another, and thereby to secure them in such sort, as that by their own industry, and by the fruits of the earth, they may nourish themselves and live contentedly; is, to confer all their power and strength upon one man, or upon one assembly of men, that may reduce all their wills, by plurality of voices, unto one will: which is as much as to say, to appoint one man, or assembly of men, to bear their person; and every one to own, and acknowledge himself to be author of whatsoever he that so bears their person, shall act, or cause to be acted, in those things which concern the common peace and safety; and therein to submit their wills, every one to his will, and their judgments, to his judgment. This is more than consent, or concord; it is a real unity of them all, in one and the same person, made by covenant of every man with every man, in such manner, as if every man should say to every man, *I authorize and give up my right of governing myself, to this man, or to this assembly of men, on this condition, that thou give up thy right to him, and authorize all his actions in like manner.* This done, the multitude so united in one person, is called a COMMONWEALTH, in Latin CIVITAS. This is the generation of that great LEVIATHAN, or rather, to speak more reverently, of that *mortal god,* to which we owe under the *immortal God,* our peace and defense. For by this authority, given him by every particular man in the commonwealth, he hath the use of so much power and strength conferred on him, that by terror thereof, he is enabled to perform the wills of them all, to peace at home, and mutual aid against their enemies abroad. And in him consists the essence of the commonwealth; which, to define it, is one person, of whose acts a great multitude, by mutual covenants one with another, have made themselves every one the author, to the end he may use the strength and means of them all, as he shall think expedient, for their peace and common defense.

And he that carries this person, is called SOVEREIGN, and said to have sovereign power; and every one besides, his SUBJECT.

From Thomas Hobbes, *Leviathan,* 1651.

Natural Rights

JOHN LOCKE (1632-1704)

In his work, the *Second Treatise of Civil Government* (1690), Locke sought to limit the power of the King and give greater power to the elected branch of government. Locke argued that human nature and the state of nature were not as pessimistic as Hobbes described them. For Locke, the state of nature is still one where our natural rights are enjoyed even though this is an inferior state because of a lack of cooperation and common laws Government arises out of a social contract where the individual is bound by the laws of a central authority that represents the will of the majority. Locke's major contribution to political philosophy is his idea that the will of the majority and the natural rights of life, liberty, and property limit the authority of government. When the government ceases to represent the will of the people and infringes upon their natural rights, it loses its legitimacy and revolution is justified.

Vocabulary:

Annexed:	attached or incorporated into
Jurisdiction:	authority or control
Commonwealth:	a country or nation of people
Promulgated:	made known or put into effect
Prerogative:	a right or privilege

Concepts:

State of Nature:

Common Law:

Natural Rights:

Social Contract:

Will of the Majority:

Revolution:

Questions:

1. How does Locke's ideas of the State of Nature compare with Hobbes'?
2. How does government come into existence?
3. What are the ends of political society and government?
4. What is the extent of legislative power?
5. When is revolution legitimate?

OF THE BEGINNING OF POLITICAL SOCIETIES

MEN BEING BY NATURE ALL FREE, equal, and independent, no one can be put out of his estate and subjected to the political power of another without his own consent, which is done by agreeing with other men, to join and unite into a community for their comfortable, safe, and peaceful living, one among another, in a secure enjoyment of their properties, and a greater security against any that are not of it. This any number of men may do, because it injures not the freedom of the rest; they are left, as they were, in the liberty of the state of nature. When any number of men have so consented to make one community or government, they are thereby presently incorporated, and make one body politic, wherein the majority have a right to act and [include] the rest.

For, when any number of men have, by the consent of every individual, made a community, they have thereby made that community one body, with a power to act as one body, which is only by the will and determination of the majority. ...

And thus every man, by consenting with others to make one body politic under one government, puts himself under an obligation to everyone of that society to submit to the determination of the majority, and to be [included] by it; or else this original compact, whereby he with others incorporates into one society, would signify nothing, and be no compact if he be left free and under no other ties than he was in before in the state of nature. For what appearance would there be of any compact? ...For where the majority cannot include the rest, there they cannot act as one body, and consequently will be immediately dissolved again.

Whosoever therefore out of a state of nature unites into a community, must be understood to give up all the power necessary to the ends for which they unite society to the majority of the community, unless they expressly agreed in any number greater than the majority. And this is done by barely agreeing to unite into one political society, which is all the compact that is, or needs be, between the individuals that enter into or make up a commonwealth. And thus, that which begins and actually constitutes any political society is nothing but the consent of any number of freemen capable of a majority, to unite and incorporate into such a society. And this is that, and that only,

which did or could give beginning to any lawful government in the world. ...

Every man that hath any possession of enjoyment of any part of the dominions of any government doth thereby give his tacit consent, and is as far forth obliged to obedience to the laws of that government, during such enjoyment, as any one under it, whether this his possession be of land to him and his heirs, or a lodging only for a week; or whether it be barely travelling freely on the highway; and, in effect, it reaches as far as the very being of anyone within the territories of that government.

To understand this better, it is fit to consider that every man, when he at first incorporates himself into any commonwealth, he, by his uniting himself thereunto, annexes also, and submits to the community those possessions which he has, or shall acquire, that do not already belong to any other government. For it would be a direct contradiction for anyone to enter into society with others for the securing and regulating of property, and yet to suppose his land, whose property is to be regulated by the laws of the society, should be exempt from the jurisdiction of that government to which he himself, the proprietor of the land, is subject. By the same act, therefore, whereby anyone unites his person, which was before free to any commonwealth, by the same he unites his possessions, which were before free, to it also; and they become, both of them, person and possession, subject to the government and dominion of that commonwealth as long as it hath a being. Whoever therefore from thenceforth, by inheritance, purchase, permission, or otherwise enjoys any part of the land so annexed to, and under the government of that commonwealth, must take it with the condition it is under; that is, of submitting to the government of the commonwealth, under whose jurisdiction it is, as far forth as any subject of it.

But since the government has a direct jurisdiction only over the land and reaches the possessor of it (before he has actually incorporated himself in the society) only as he dwells upon and enjoys that, the obligation anyone is under by virtue of such enjoyment to submit to the government begins and ends with the enjoyment; so that whenever the owner, who has given nothing but such a tacit consent to the government, will, by donation, sale or otherwise, quit the said possession, he is at liberty to go and incorporate himself into any other commonwealth, or agree with others to begin a new one in any part of the world they can find free and un-possessed; whereas he that has once, by actual agreement and any express declaration, given his consent to be of any commonwealth, is perpetually and indispensably obliged to be, and remain unalterably a subject to it, and can never be again in the liberty of the state of nature, unless by any calamity the government he was under comes to be dissolved; or else by some public act cuts him off from being any longer a member of it.

But submitting to the laws of any country, living quietly, and enjoying privileges and protection under them makes not a man a member of that society; this is only a local protection and homage due to and from all those who, not being in a state of war, come within the territories belonging to any government, to all parts whereof the force of its law extends. But this no more makes a man a member of that society than it would make a man a subject to another in whose family he found it convenient to abide for some time. ...Nothing can make any man [a citizen] but his actually entering into it by positive engagement and express promise and compact.

OF THE ENDS OF POLITICAL SOCIETY AND GOVERNMENT

If man in the state of nature be so free as has been said; if he be absolute lord of his own person and possessions; equal to the greatest and subject to no body, why will he part with his freedom? Why will he give up this empire, and subject himself to the dominion and control of any other power? To which 'tis obvious to answer, that though in the state of nature he hath such a right, yet the enjoyment of it is very uncertain and constantly exposed to the invasion of others; for all being kings as much as he, every man his equal, and the greater part no strict observers of equity and justice, the enjoyment of the property he has in this state is very unsafe, very insecure. This makes him willing to quit this condition which, however free, is full of fears and continual dangers; and 'tis not without reason that he seeks out and is willing to join in society with others who are already united, or have a mind to unite for the mutual preservation of their lives, liberties, and estates, which I call by the general name, property.

The great and chief end, therefore, of men's uniting into commonwealths, and putting themselves under government, is the preservation of their property; to which in the state of nature there are many things wanting.

First, there wants an established, settled, known law, received and allowed by common consent to be the standard of right and wrong, and the common measure to decide all controversies between them. For though the law of nature be plain and intelligible to all rational creatures, yet men, being biased by their interest, as well as ignorant for want of study of it, are not apt

to allow of it as a law binding to them in the application of it to their particular cases.

Secondly, in the state of nature there wants a known and indifferent judge, with authority to determine all differences according to the established law. For everyone in that state being both judge and executioner of the law of nature, men being partial to themselves, passion and revenge is very apt to carry them too far, and with too much heat in their own cases, as well as negligence and unconcern, make them too remiss in other men's eyes.

Thirdly, in the state of nature there often wants power to back and support the sentence when right, and to give it due execution. They who by any injustice offended, will seldom fail where they are able by force to make good their injustice. Such resistance many times makes the punishment dangerous, and frequently destructive to those who attempt it.

Thus mankind notwithstanding all the privileges of the state of nature, being but in an ill condition while they remain in it, are quickly driven into society. Hence it comes to pass, that we seldom find any number of men live any time together in this state. The inconveniences that they are therein exposed to by the irregular and uncertain exercise of the power every man has of punishing the transgressions of others, make them take sanctuary under the established laws of government, and therein seek the preservation of their property. This makes them so willing to give up their power of punishing to be exercised by such alone as shall be appointed to it amongst them, and by such rules as the community, or those authorized by them to that purpose, shall agree on. And in this we have the original right and rise of both the legislative and executive power as well as of the governments and societies themselves.

For in the state of nature to omit the liberty he has of innocent delights, a man has two powers.

The first is to do whatsoever he thinks fit for the preservation of himself and others within the permission of the law of nature; by which law, common to them all, he and all the rest of mankind are one community, make up one society distinct from all other creatures and were it not for the corruption and viciousness of degenerate men, there would be no need of any other, no necessity that men should separate from this great and natural community, and associate into less combinations.

The other power a man has in the state of nature is the power to punish the crimes committed against that law. Both these he gives up when he joins in a private, if I may so call it, or particular political society, and incorporates into any commonwealth separate from the rest of mankind.

The first power, *viz.* of doing whatsoever he thought fit for the preservation of himself and the rest of mankind, he gives up to be regulated by laws made by the society, so far forth as the preservation of himself and the rest of that society shall require; which laws of the society in many things confine the liberty he had by the law of nature.

Secondly, the power of punishing he wholly gives up, and engages his natural force (which he might employ before the execution of the law of nature, by his own single authority, as he thought fit) to assist the executive power of the society as the law thereof shall require. For being now in a new state, wherein he is to enjoy many conveniences from the labor, assistance, and society of others in the same community, as well as protection from its whole strength, he is to part also with as much of his natural liberty, in providing for himself, as the good, prosperity, and safety of the society shall require, which is not only necessary but just, since the other members of the society do the like.

But though men when they enter into society give up the equality, liberty, and executive power they had in the state of nature into the hands of the society, to be so far disposed of by the legislative as the good of the society shall require, yet it being only with an intention in everyone the better to preserve himself, his liberty and property (for no rational creature can be supposed to change his condition with an intention to be worse), the power of the society or legislative constituted by them can never be supposed to extend farther than the common good, but is obliged to secure everyone's property by providing against those three defects above-mentioned that made the state of nature so unsafe and uneasy. And so, whoever has the legislative or supreme power of any commonwealth, is bound to govern by established standing laws, promulgated and known to the people, and not by extemporary decrees, by indifferent and upright judges, who are to decide controversies by those laws; and to employ the force of the community at home only in the execution of such laws, or abroad to prevent or redress foreign injuries and secure the community from inroads and invasion. And all this to be directed to no other end but the peace, safety, and public good of the people.

OF THE EXTENT OF THE LEGISLATIVE POWER

These are the bounds which the trust that is put in them by the society and the law of God and nature have set to the legislative power of every commonwealth, in all forms of government.

First, They are to govern by promulgated established laws, not to be varied in particular cases, but to have one rule for rich and poor, for the favourite at Court, and the countryman at plough.

Secondly, These laws also ought to be designed for no other end ultimately but the good of the people.

Thirdly, They must not raise taxes on the property of the people without the consent of the people given by themselves or their deputies. And this properly concerns only such governments where the legislative is always in being, or at least where the people have not reserved any part of the legislative to deputies, to be, from time to time, chosen by themselves.

Fourthly, The legislative neither must, nor can, transfer the power of making laws to anybody else, or place it anywhere but where the people have...

THE LEGITIMACY OF REVOLUTION

The reason why men enter into society is the preservation of their property; and the end why they choose and authorize a legislative is that there may be laws made and rules set as guards and fences to the properties of all the members of the society to limit the power and moderate the dominion of every part and member of the society; for since it can never be supposed to be the will of the society that the legislative should have a power to destroy that which every one designs to secure by entering into society, and for which the people submitted themselves to legislators of their own making. Whenever the legislators endeavor to take away and destroy the property of the people, or to reduce them to slavery under arbitrary power, they put themselves into a state of war with the people who are thereupon absolved from any further obedience, and are left to the common refuge which God has provided for all men against force and violence. When so ever, therefore, the legislative shall transgress this fundamental rule of society, and either by ambition, fear, folly, or corruption, endeavor to grasp themselves, or put into the hands of any other, an absolute power over the lives, liberties, and estates of the people, by this breach of trust they forfeit the power the people had put into their hands for quite contrary ends. It devolves to the people, who have a right to resume their original liberty and, by the establishment of a new legislative, such as they shall think fit, provide for their own safety and security, which is the end for which they are in society. What I have said here concerning the legislative in general holds true also concerning the supreme executor, who having a double trust put in him — both to have a part in the legislative and the supreme execution of the law — acts against both

when he goes about to set up his own arbitrary will as the law of the society. ...

Here, it is like, the common question will be made: who shall be judge whether the prince or legislative act contrary to their trust? This, perhaps, ill-affected and factious men may spread amongst the people, when the prince only makes use of his due prerogative. To this I reply: The people shall be judge; for who shall be judge whether his trustee or deputy acts well and according to the trust reposed in him but he who deputes him and must, by having deputed him, have still a power to discard him when he fails in his trust? If this be reasonable in particular cases of private men, why should it be otherwise in that of the greatest moment where the welfare of millions is concerned, and also where the evil, if not prevented, is greater and the redress very difficult, dear, and dangerous? ...

To conclude, the power that every individual gave the society when he entered into it, can never revert to the individuals again as long as the society lasts, but will always remain in the community, because without this there can be no community, no commonwealth, which is contrary to the original agreement; so also when the society hath placed the legislative in any assembly of men to continue in them and their successors, with direction and authority for providing such successors, the legislative can never revert to the people whilst that government lasts, because having provided a legislative with power to continue for ever, they have given up their political power to the legislative and cannot resume it. But if they have set limits to the duration of their legislative, and made this supreme power in any person or assembly only temporary; or else when by the miscarriages of those in authority it is forfeited; upon the forfeiture, or at the determination of the time set, it reverts to the society, and the people have a right to act as supreme, and continue the legislative in themselves; or place it in a new form, or new hands as they think good.

From John Locke, *Second Treatise on Civil Government*, 1690.

Tyranny of the Majority

JOHN STUART MILL (1806-1873)

In this essay, Mill agrees with John Locke in favoring a representational democracy. But he does not accept Locke's idea of natural rights, which he refers to as "nonsense on stilts." The only justifiable bases for government is utilitarianism which promotes the greatest amount of happiness for the citizens through its commitment to individual liberty. Mill is the first political philosopher to bring up the concept of the tyranny of the majority. This occurs when the majority exploits a minority within the society. Mill argues that this form of tyranny can be every bit as diabolical as any other form of tyranny. Mill argues that the only legitimate reason for government limiting individual liberty is to protect others from harm. Mill also speaks of the freedom of speech, thought, press, assembly and life-style.

Vocabulary

Latent:	present but invisible or inactive; lying hidden
Conspicuous:	obvious
Tyranny:	exploitation
Antagonistic:	acting in opposition
Harpies:	reckless, greedy people
Efficaciously:	effectively
Predominates:	dominating influences
Infirmities:	defects; weaknesses

Axiomatic:	self-evident
Usurping:	overthrowing
Despotism:	the rule of a tyrant or evil ruler
De jure:	by right or legal establishment
Automatons:	machine-like

Concepts:

Tyranny of the Majority:

Liberty:

Utilitarianism:

Harm Principle:

Patriot:

---

1. *What is the purpose of this essay?*
2. *How does Mill define a patriot?*
3. *How does the patriot limit the power of government?*
4. *How did the idea of a democratically elected government seem to cure tyranny?*
5. *What does Mill mean by the tyranny of the majority?*
6. *When is government justified in interfering with our liberty?*
7. *Does Mill argee with natural rights? Why or why not?*
8. *What freedoms does Mill discuss?*

CHAPTER I. INTRODUCTORY

THE SUBJECT OF THIS ESSAY is not the so-called Liberty of the Will, so unfortunately opposed to the misnamed doctrine of Philosophical Necessity, but Civil, or Social Liberty: the nature and limits of the power which can be legitimately exercised by society over the individual. This is a question seldom stated, and hardly ever discussed, in general terms, but which profoundly influences the practical controversies of the age by its latent presence, and is likely soon to make itself recognized as the vital question of the future. It is so far from being new, that, in a certain sense, it has divided mankind, almost from the remotest ages; but in the stage of progress into which the more civilized portions of the species have now entered, it presents itself under new conditions, and requires a different and more fundamental treatment.

The struggle between Liberty and Authority is the most conspicuous feature in the portions of history with which we are earliest familiar, particularly in that of Greece, Rome, and England. But in old times this contest was between subjects, or some classes of subjects, and the Government. By liberty, was meant protection against the tyranny of the political rulers. The rulers were conceived (except in some of the popular governments of Greece) as in a necessarily antagonistic position to the people whom they ruled. They consisted of a governing One, or a governing tribe or caste, who derived their authority from inheritance or conquest, who, at all events, did not hold it at the pleasure of the governed, and whose supremacy men did not venture, perhaps did not desire, to contest, whatever precautions might be taken against its oppressive exercise. Their power was regarded as necessary, but also as highly dangerous; as a weapon which they would attempt to use against their subjects, no less than against external enemies. To prevent the weaker members of the community from being preyed upon by innumerable vultures, it was needful that there should be an animal of prey stronger than the rest, commissioned to keep them down. But as the king of the vultures would be no less bent upon preying on the flock than any of the minor harpies, it was indispensable to be in a perpetual attitude of defense against his beak and claws. The aim, therefore, of patriots was to set limits to the power which the ruler should be suffered to exercise over the community; and this limitation was what they meant by liberty. It was attempted in two ways. First, by obtaining a recognition of certain immunities, called political liberties or rights, which it was to be regarded as a breach of duty in the ruler to infringe, and which if he did infringe, specific resistance, or general rebellion, was held to be justifiable. A second, and generally a later expedient, was the establishment of constitutional checks, by which the consent of the community, or of a body of some sort, supposed to represent its interests, was made a necessary condition to some of the more important acts of the governing power. To the first of these modes of limitation, the ruling power, in most European countries, was compelled, more or less, to submit. It was not so with the second; and, to attain this, or when already in some degree possessed, to attain it more completely, became everywhere the principal object of the lovers of liberty. And so long as mankind were content to combat one enemy by another, and to be ruled by a master, on condition of being guaranteed more or less efficaciously against his tyranny, they did not carry their aspirations beyond this point.

A time, however, came, in the progress of human affairs, when men ceased to think it a necessity of nature that their governors should be an independent power, opposed in interest to themselves. It appeared to them much better that the various magistrates of the State should be their tenants or delegates, revocable at their pleasure. In that way alone, it seemed, could they have complete security that the powers of government would never be abused to their disadvantage. By degrees this new demand for elective and temporary rulers became the prominent object of the exertions of the popular party, wherever any such party existed; and superseded, to a considerable extent, the previous efforts to limit the power of rulers. As the struggle proceeded for making the ruling power emanate from the periodical choice of the ruled, some persons began to think that too much importance had been attached to the limitation of the power itself. That (it might seem) was a resource against rulers whose interests were habitually opposed to those of the people. What was now wanted was, that the rulers should be identified with the people; that their interest and will should be the interest and will of the nation. The nation did not need to be protected against its own will. There was no fear of its tyrannizing over itself. Let the rulers be effectually responsible to it, promptly removable by it, and it could afford to trust them with power of which it could itself dictate the use to be made. Their power was but the nation's own power, concentrated, and in a form convenient for exercise. This mode of thought, or rather perhaps of feeling, was common among the last generation of European liberalism in the Continental section of which it still apparently predominates. Those who admit no limit to what a government may do, except in the case of such governments as they think ought not to exist, stand out as brilliant exceptions among the political thinkers of the Continent. A similar tone of sentiment might by this time have been prevalent in our own country, if the circumstances which for a time encouraged it, had continued unaltered.

But, in political and philosophical theories, as well as in persons, success discloses faults and infirmities which failure might have concealed from observation. The notion, that the people have no need to limit their power over themselves, might seem axiomatic, when popular government was a thing only dreamed about, or read of as having existed at some distant period of the past. Neither was that notion necessarily disturbed by such temporary aberrations as those of the French Revolution, the worst of which were the work of a usurping few, and which, in any case, belonged, not to the permanent working of popular institutions, but to a sudden and convulsive outbreak against monarchical and aristocratic despotism. In time, however, a democratic republic came to occupy a large portion of the earth's surface, and made itself felt as one of the most powerful members of the community of nations; and elective and responsible government became subject to the observations and criticisms which wait upon a great existing fact. It was now perceived that such phrases as 'self-government,' and 'the power of the people over themselves,' do not express the true state of the case. The 'people' who exercise the power are not always the same people with those over whom it is exercised; and the 'self-government' spoken of is not the government of each by himself, but of each by all the rest. The will of the people, moreover, practically means the will of the most numerous or the most active part of the people; the majority, or those who succeed in making themselves accepted as the majority; the people, consequently may desire to oppress a part of their number; and precautions are as much needed against this as against any other abuse of power. The limitation, therefore, of the power of government over individuals loses none of its importance when the holders of power are regularly accountable to the community, that is, to the strongest party therein. This view of things, recommending itself equally to the intelligence of thinkers and to the inclination of those important classes in European society to whose real or supposed interests democracy is adverse, has had no difficulty in establishing itself, and in political speculations "the tyranny of the majority" is now generally included among the evils against which society requires to be on its guard.

Like other tyrannies, the tyranny of the majority was at first, and is still vulgarly, held in dread, chiefly as operating through the acts of the public authorities. But reflecting persons perceived that when society is itself the tyrant — society collectively over the separate individuals who compose it — its means of tyrannizing are not restricted to the acts which it may do by the hands of its political functionaries. Society can and does execute its own mandates: and if it issues wrong mandates instead of right, or any mandates at all in things with which it ought not to meddle, it practices a social tyranny more formidable than many kinds of political oppression, since, though not usually upheld by such extreme penalties, it leaves fewer means of escape, penetrating much more deeply into the details of life, and enslaving the soul itself. Protection, therefore, against the tyranny of the magistrate is not enough: there needs protection also against the tyranny of the prevailing opinion and feeling; against the tendency of society to impose, by other means than civil penalties, its

own ideas and practices as rules of conduct on those who dissent from them; to fetter the development, and, if possible, prevent the formation, of any individuality not in harmony with its ways, and compels all characters to fashion themselves upon the model of its own. There is a limit to the legitimate interference of collective opinion with individual independence and to find that limit, and maintain it against encroachment, is as indispensable to a good condition of human affairs as protection against political despotism.

The object of this essay is to assert one very simple principle, as entitled to govern absolutely the dealings of society with the individual in the way of compulsion and control, whether the means used be physical force in the form of legal penalties, or the moral coercion of public opinion. That principle is, that the sole end for which mankind are warranted, individually or collectively, in interfering with the liberty of action of any of their number, is self-protection. That the only purpose for which power can be rightfully exercised over any member of a civilized community, against his will, is to prevent harm to others. His own good, either physical or moral, is not a sufficient warrant. He cannot rightfully be compelled to do or forbear because it will be better for him to do so, because it will make him happier, because, in the opinions of others, to do so would be wise, or even right. These are good reasons for remonstrating with him, or reasoning with him, or persuading him, or entreating him, but not for compelling him, or visiting him with any evil in case he do otherwise. To justify that, the conduct from which it is desired to deter him must be calculated to produce evil to someone else. The only part of the conduct of any one, for which he is amenable to society, is that which concerns others. In the part which merely concerns himself, his independence is, of right, absolute. Over himself, over his own body and mind, the individual is sovereign.

It is, perhaps, hardly necessary to say that this doctrine is meant to apply to human beings in the maturity of their faculties. We are not speaking of children or of young persons below the age which the law may fix as that of manhood or womanhood. Those who are still in a state to require being taken care of by others must be protected against their own actions as well as against external injury. For the same reason, we may leave out of consideration those backward states of society in which the race itself may be considered as in its nonage. The early difficulties in the way of spontaneous progress are so great, that there is seldom any choice of means for overcoming them; and a ruler full of the spirit of improvement is warranted in the use of any expedients that will attain an end, perhaps otherwise unattainable. Despotism is a legitimate mode of government in dealing with barbarians, provided the end be their improvement, and the means justified by actually affecting that end.

Liberty, as a principle, has no application to any state of things anterior to the time when mankind became capable of being improved by free and equal discussion. Until then, there is nothing for them but implicit obedience to an Akbar or a Charlemagne, if they are so fortunate as to find one. But as soon as mankind has attained the capacity of being guided to their own improvement by conviction or persuasion (a period long since reached in all nations with whom we need here concern ourselves), compulsion, either in the direct form or in that of pains and penalties for noncompliance, is no longer admissible as a means to their own good, and justifiable only in the security of others.

It is proper to state that I forego any advantage which could be derived to my argument from the idea of abstract right as a thing independent of utility. I regard utility as the ultimate appeal on all ethical questions; but it must be utility in the largest sense, grounded on the permanent interests of man as a progressive being. Those interests, I contend, authorize the subjection of individual spontaneity to external control, only in respect to those actions of each, which concern the interest of other people. If anyone does an act hurtful to others, there is a prima facie case for punishing him by law, or, where legal penalties are not safely applicable, by general disapprobation. There are also many positive acts for the benefit of others, which he may rightfully be compelled to perform; such as, to give evidence in a court of justice; to bear his fair share in the common defense, or in any other joint work necessary to the interest of the society of which he enjoys the protection; and to perform certain acts of individual beneficence, such as saving a fellow-creature's life, or interposing to protect the defenseless against ill-usage, things which whenever it is obviously a man's duty to do, he may rightfully be made responsible to society for not doing. A person may cause evil to others not only by his actions but by his inaction, and in neither case he is justly accountable to them for the injury. The latter case, it is true, requires a much more cautious exercise of compulsion than the former. To make anyone answerable for doing evil to others, is the rule; to make him answerable for not preventing evil, is, comparatively speaking, the exception. Yet there are many cases clear enough and grave enough to justify that exception. In all things which regard the external relations of the individual, he is *de jure* amenable to those whose interests are concerned, and if need be, to society as their protector. There are often good reasons for not holding him to the responsibility; but these reasons must arise from the special expediencies of the case: either because it is a kind of case in which he is, on the whole, likely to act better when left to his own discretion than when controlled in any way in which society has it in its power to control him; or because the attempt to exercise control would produce other evils, greater than those which it would prevent. When such reasons as these preclude the enforcement of responsibility, the conscience of the agent himself should step into the vacant judgment-seat, and protect those interests of others which have no external protection; judging himself all the more rigidly, because the case does not admit of his being made accountable to the judgment of his fellow creatures.

But there is a sphere of action in which society, as distinguished from the individual, has, if any, only an indirect interest; comprehending all that portion of a person's life and conduct which affects only himself, or, if it also affects others, only with their free, voluntary, and undeceived consent and participation. When I say only himself. I mean directly, and in the first instance: for whatever affects himself, may affect others through himself, and the objection which may be grounded on this contingency will receive consideration in the sequel. This, then, is the appropriate region of human liberty. It comprises, first, the inward domain of consciousness; demanding liberty of conscience, in the most comprehensive sense; liberty of thought and feeling; absolute freedom of opinion and sentiment on all subjects, practical or speculative, scientific, moral, or theological. The liberty of expressing and publishing opinions may seem to fall under a different principle, since it belongs to that part of the conduct of an individual which concerns other people; but, being almost of as much importance as the liberty of thought itself, and resting in great part on the same reasons, is practically inseparable from it. Secondly, the principle requires liberty of tastes and pursuits; of framing the plan of our life to suit our own character; of doing as we like, subject to such consequences as may follow; without impediment from our fellow-creatures, so long as what we do does not harm them, even though they

should think our conduct foolish, perverse, or wrong. Thirdly, from this liberty of each individual, follows the liberty, within the same limits, of combination among individuals; freedom to unite for any purpose not involving harm to others: the persons combining being supposed to be of full age, and not forced or deceived.

No society in which these liberties are not, on the whole, respected, is free, whatever may be its form of government; and none is completely free in which they do not exist absolute and unqualified. The only freedom which deserves the name is that of pursuing our own good in our own way, so long as we do not attempt to deprive others of their freedom or impede their efforts to obtain it. Each is the proper guardian of his own health, whether bodily, or mental and spiritual. Mankind are greater gainers by suffering each other to live as seems good to themselves, than by compelling each to live as seems good to the rest.

Though this doctrine is anything but new, and, to some persons, may have the air of a truism, there is no doctrine which stands more directly opposed to the general tendency of existing opinion and practice. Society has expended fully as much effort in the attempt (according to its lights) to compel people to conform to its notions of personal and of social excellence.

CHAPTER II. OF THE LIBERTY OF THOUGHT AND DISCUSSION

The time, it is to be hoped, is gone by when any defense would be necessary of the 'liberty of the press' as one of the securities against corrupt or tyrannical government. No argument, we may suppose, can now be needed against permitting a legislature or an executive, not identified in interest with the people, to prescribe opinions to them, and determine what doctrines or what arguments they shall be allowed to hear. This aspect of the question, besides, has been so often and so triumphantly enforced by preceding writers, that it needs not be specially insisted on in this place. Though the law of England, on the subject of the press, is as servile to this day as it was in the time of the Tudors, there is little danger of its being actually put in force against political discussion, except during some temporary panic, when fear of insurrection drives ministers and judges from their propriety; and, speaking generally, it is not, in constitutional countries, to be apprehended that the government, whether completely responsible to the people or not, will often attempt to control the expression of opinion , except when in doing so it makes itself the organ of the general intolerance of the public. Let us suppose, therefore, that the government is entirely at one with the people, and never thinks of exerting any power of coercion unless in agreement with what it conceives to be their voice. But I deny the right of the people to exercise such coercion, either by themselves or by their government. The power itself is illegitimate. The best government has no more title to it than the worst. It is as noxious, or more noxious, when exerted in accordance with public opinion, than when in opposition to it. If all mankind minus one were of one opinion, and only one person were of the contrary opinion , mankind would be no more justified in silencing that one person, than he, if he had the power, would be justified in silencing mankind. Were an opinion a personal possession of no value except to the owner; if to be obstructed in the enjoyment of it were simply a private injury, it would make some difference whether the injury was inflicted only on a few persons or on many. But the peculiar evil of silencing the expression of an opinion is, that it is robbing the human race; posterity as well as the existing generation; those who dissent from the opinion, still more than those who hold it. If the opinion is right, they are deprived of the opportunity of exchanging error for truth: If wrong, they lose, what is almost as great a benefit, the clearer perception and livelier impression of truth, produced by its collision with error.

As it is useful that, while mankind is imperfect, there should be different opinions, so is it that there should be different experiments of living; that free scope should be given to varieties of character, short of injury to others; and that the worth of different modes of life should be proved practically, when anyone thinks fit to try them. It is desirable, in short, that, in things which do not primarily concern others, individuality should assert itself. Where, not the person's own character, but the traditions or customs of other people are the rule of conduct, there is wanting one of the principal ingredients of human happiness, and quite the chief ingredient of individual and social progress.

In maintaining this principle, the greatest difficulty to be encountered does not lie in the appreciation of means towards an acknowledged end, but in the indifference of persons in general to the end itself. If it were felt that the free development of individuality is one of the leading essentials of well-being, that it is not only a coordinate element with all like that is designated by the terms civiliza-tion, instruction, education, culture, but is itself a necessary part and condition of all those things; there would be no danger that liberty should be undervalued, and the adjustment of the boundaries between it and social control would present no extraordinary difficulty. But the evil is that individual spontaneity is hardly recognized by the common modes of thinking as having any intrinsic worth or deserving any regard on its own account.

He who lets the world, or his own portion of it, choose his plan of life for him, has no need of any other faculty than the ape-like one of imitation. He who chooses his plan for himself, employs all his faculties. He must use observation to see, reasoning and judgment to foresee activity to gather materials for decision, discrimination to decide, and when he has decided, firmness and self-control to hold to his deliberate decision. And these qualities he requires and exercises exactly in proportion as the part of his conduct which he determines according to his own judgment and feelings is a large one. It is possible that he might be guided in some good path, and kept out of harm's way, without any of these things. But what will be his comparative worth as a human being? It really is of importance, not only what men do, but also what manner of men they are that do it. Among the works of man, which human life is rightly employed in perfecting and beautifying, the first in importance surely is man himself. Supposing it were possible to get houses built, corn grown, battles fought, causes tried, and even churches erected and prayers said, by machinery — by automatons in human form — it would be a considerable loss to exchange for these automatons even the men and women who at present inhabit the more civilized parts of the world, and who assuredly are but starved specimens of what nature can and will produce. Human nature is not a machine to be built after a model, and set to do exactly the work prescribed for it, but a tree, which requires to grow and develop itself of all sides, according to the tendency of the inward forces which make it a living thing. ...

From John Stuart Mill, *On Liberty*, 1859.

THE DECLARATION OF INDEPENDENCE (1776)

Drafted by Thomas Jefferson between June 11 and June 28, 1776, the Declaration of Independence is at once the nation's most cherished symbol of liberty and Jefferson's most enduring monument. Here, in exalted and unforgettable phrases, Jefferson expressed the convictions in the minds and hearts of the American people. The political philosophy of the Declaration was not new; its ideals of individual liberty had already been expressed by John Locke and the Continental philosophers. What Jefferson did was to summarize this philosophy in "self-evident truths" and set forth a list of grievances against the King in order to justify before the world the breaking of ties between the colonies and the mother country.

Vocabulary:

Transient:	not permanent; passing away
Usurpation:	the unlawful or violent seizure of a government or throne
Evinces:	to shows plainly; makes manifest
Despotism:	rule-by anyone who acts like a tyrant; an absolute ruler
Sufferance:	the power or capacity to tolerate pain
Candid:	open; honest or frank
Annihilation:	destruction
Convulsions:	any violent disturbances
Emigration:	to leave one country to settle in another

Magnanimity:	being noble in mind and spirit; generous to overlook an injury
Consanguinity:	close association; connection
Acquiesce:	to agree or consent without protest

Concepts:

Unalienable Rights:

Questions:

1. *Why was the Declaration of Independence necessary?*
2. *What are unalienable rights?*
3. *What were some of the things that King George III was doing that upset the colonists?*
4. *Do you feel that the Declaration was necessary? Why or why not?*

The Declaration of Independence of the Thirteen Colonies In CONGRESS, July 4, 1776

The unanimous Declaration of the thirteen united States of America,

When in the course of human events, it becomes necessary for one people to dissolve the political bands which have connected them with another, and to assume among the powers of the earth, the separate and equal station to which the Laws of Nature and of Nature's God entitle them, a decent respect to the opinions of mankind requires that they should declare the causes which impel them to the separation.

We hold these truths to be self-evident, that all men are created equal, that they are endowed by their Creator with certain unalienable Rights, that among these are Life, Liberty and the Pursuit of Happiness. —That to secure these rights, governments are instituted among men, deriving their just powers from the consent of the governed, —That whenever any Form of Government

428

becomes destructive of these ends, it is the right of the people to alter or to abolish it, and to institute new government, laying its foundation on such principles and organizing its powers in such form, as to them shall seem most likely to effect their safety and happiness. Prudence, indeed, will dictate that governments long established should not be changed for light and transient causes; and accordingly all experience hath shewn, that mankind are more disposed to suffer, while evils are sufferable, than to right themselves by abolishing the forms to which they are accustomed. But when a long train of abuses and usurpations, pursuing invariably the same object evinces a design to reduce them under absolute despotism, it is their right, it is their duty, to throw off such government, and to provide new guards for their future security. —Such has been the patient sufferance of these Colonies; and such is now the necessity which constrains them to alter their former systems of government. The history of the present King of Great Britain [George III] is a history of repeated injuries and usurpations, all having in direct object the establishment of an absolute tyranny over these States. To prove this, let facts be submitted to a candid world.

He has refused his assent to Laws, the most wholesome and necessary for the public good.

He has forbidden his governors to pass laws of immediate and pressing importance, unless suspended in their operation till his assent should be obtained; and when so suspended, he has utterly neglected to attend to them.

He has refused to pass other laws for the accommodation of large districts of people, unless those people would relinquish the right of representation in the Legislature, a right inestimable to them and formidable to tyrants only.

He has called together legislative bodies at places unusual, uncomfortable, and distant from the depository of their public records, for the sole purpose of fatiguing them into compliance with his measures.

He has dissolved Representative Houses repeatedly, for opposing with manly firmness his invasions on the rights of the people.

He has refused for a long time, after such dissolutions, to cause others to be elected; whereby the Legislative powers, incapable of annihilation, have returned to the people at large for their exercise; the State remaining in the mean time exposed to all the dangers of invasion from without, and convulsions within.

He has endeavoured to prevent the population of these States; for that purpose obstructing the laws for naturalization of foreigners; refusing to pass others to encourage their migrations hither, and raising the conditions of new appropriations of lands.

He has obstructed the Administration of Justice, by refusing his assent to laws for establishing judiciary powers.

He has made judges dependent on his will alone, for the tenure of their offices, and the amount and payment of their salaries.

He has erected a multitude of new offices, and sent hither swarms of officers to harass our people, and eat out their substance.

He has kept among us, in times of peace, standing armies without the consent of our legislatures.

He has affected to render the Military independent of and superior to the civil power.

He has combined with others to subject us to a jurisdiction foreign to our constitution and unacknowledged by our laws; giving his assent to their acts of pretended legislation:

For Quartering large bodies of armed troops among us:

For protecting them, by a mock trial, from punishment for any murders which they should commit on the inhabitants of these States:

For cutting off our trade with all parts of the world:

For imposing taxes on us without our consent:

For depriving us, in many cases, of the benefits of trial by Jury:

For transporting us beyond seas to be tried for pretended offences:

For abolishing the free system of English Laws in a neighbouring province, establishing therein an arbitrary government, and enlarging its boundaries so as to render it at once an example and fit instrument for introducing the same absolute rule into these Colonies:

For taking away our Charters, abolishing our most valuable laws, and altering fundamentally the forms of our governments:

For suspending our own Legislatures, and declaring themselves invested with power to legislate for us in all cases whatsoever.

He has abdicated government here, by declaring us out of his protection and waging war against us.

He has plundered our seas, ravaged our coasts, burnt our towns, and destroyed the lives of our people.

He is at this time transporting

large Aarmies of foreign mercenaries to complete the works of death, desolation and tyranny, already begun with circumstances of cruelty and perfidy scarcely paralleled in the most barbarous ages, and totally unworthy the Head of a civilized nation.

He has constrained our fellow citizens taken captive on the high seas to bear Arms against their country, to become the executioners of their friends and brethren, or to fall themselves by their hands.

He has excited domestic insurrections amongst us, and has endeavoured to bring on the inhabitants of our frontiers, the merciless Indian savages, whose known rule of warfare, is an undistinguished destruction of all ages, sexes and conditions.

In every stage of these oppressions we have petitioned for redress in the most humble terms: Our repeated petitions have been answered only by repeated injury. A prince whose character is thus marked by every act which may define a tyrant, is unfit to be the ruler of a free people.

Nor have we been wanting in attentions to our British brethren. We have warned them from time to time of attempts by their legislature to extend an unwarrantable jurisdiction over us. We have reminded them of the circumstances of our emigration and settlement here. We have appealed to their native justice and magnanimity, and we have conjured them by the ties of our common kindred to disavow these usurpations, which, would inevitably interrupt our connections and correspondence. They too have been deaf to the voice of justice and of consanguinity. We must, therefore, acquiesce in the necessity, which denounces our separation, and hold them, as we hold the rest of mankind, Enemies in War, in Peace Friends.

We, therefore, the Representatives of the United States of America, in General Congress, assembled, appealing to the Supreme Judge of the world for the rectitude of our intentions, do, in the name, and by the authority of the good people of these Colonies, solemnly publish and declare, that these United Colonies are, and of right ought to be Free and Independent States; that they are absolved from all allegiance to the British Crown, and that all political connection between them and the State of Great Britain, is and ought to be totally dissolved; and that as Free and Independent States, they have full power to levy war, conclude peace, contract alliances, establish commerce, and to do all other acts and things which Independent States may of right do. And for the support of this Declaration, with a firm reliance on the protection of divine Providence, we mutually pledge to each other our lives, our fortunes and our sacred honor.

The signers of the Declaration represented the new states as follows:

New Hampshire:

Josiah Bartlett, William Whipple, Matthew Thornton

Massachusetts:

John Hancock, Samual Adams, John Adams, Robert Treat Paine, Elbridge Gerry

Rhode Island:

Stephen Hopkins, William Ellery

Connecticut:

Roger Sherman, Samuel Huntington, William Williams, Oliver Wolcott

New York:

William Floyd, Philip Livingston, Francis Lewis, Lewis Morris

New Jersey:

Richard Stockton, John Witherspoon, Francis Hopkinson, John Hart, Abraham Clark

Pennsylvania:

Robert Morris, Benjamin Rush, Benjamin Franklin, John Morton, George Clymer, James Smith, George Taylor, James Wilson, George Ross

Delaware:

Caesar Rodney, George Read, Thomas McKean

Maryland:

Samuel Chase, William Paca, Thomas Stone, Charles Carroll of Carrollton

Virginia:

George Wythe, Richard Henry Lee, Thomas Jefferson, Benjamin Harrison, Thomas Nelson, Jr., Francis Lightfoot Lee, Carter Braxton

North Carolina:

William Hooper, Joseph Hewes, John Penn

South Carolina:

Edward Rutledge, Thomas Heyward, Jr., Thomas Lynch, Jr., Arthur Middleton

Georgia:

Button Gwinnett, Lyman Hall, George Walton

From *The Declaration of Independence*, 1776.

THE UNITED STATES CONSTITUTION

The United States Constitution was framed by a convention of delegates from twelve of the thirteen original states in Philadelphia in May, 1787, Rhode Island failing to send a delegate. George Washington presided over the session, which lasted until September 17, 1787. The draft (originally a preamble and seven Articles) was submitted to all thirteen states and was to become effective when ratified by nine states. It went into effect on the first Wednesday in March, 1789, having been ratified by New Hampshire, the ninth state to approve, on June 21, 1788.

Vocabulary:

Adjournment:	a suspension until a later stated time
Appellate:	having power to review decisions of lower courts
Apportionment:	a proportionate distribution
Attainder:	the loss of all civil rights by a person sentenced for a serious crime
Concurrence:	having the same opinion; agreement
Bill of Credit:	A bill of credit is some sort of paper medium by which value is exchanged between the government and individuals. Money is a bill of credit, but a bill of credit need not be money. An interest-bearing certificate that was issued by Missouri, and usable in the payment of taxes, was thus ruled to be an unconstitutional bill of credit.

Corruption of Blood: Corruption of Blood was part of ancient English penalty for treason. It was usually part of a Bill of Attainder, which normally sentenced the accused to death. The corruption of blood would forbid the accused's family from inheriting his property. Such bills and punishments were often inflicted upon Tories by colonial governments immediately following independence.

Deprive: the taking of something away from; divest. 2. To keep from the possession of something.

Domestic Tranquility: One of the concerns of the Framers was that the government prior to that under the Constitution was unable, by force or persuasion, to quell rebellion or quarrels amongst the states. The government watched in horror as Shay's Rebellion transpired just before the Convention, and some states had very nearly gone to war with each other over territory (such as between Pennsylvania and Connecticut over Wilkes-Barre). One of the main goals of the Convention, then, was to ensure the federal government had powers to squash rebellion and to smooth tensions between states.

Double Jeopardy: Double jeopardy is a term used in law. Double jeopardy is forbidden by the Constitution. Double jeopardy is what would happen if someone were to be charged with a crime and be found innocent, and then be charged with that crime a second time. For example, if you are charged with stealing a car, and a jury finds you innocent, you cannot be charged with stealing the car again.

Emolument:	the product (as salary or fees) of an employment
Enumerate:	to determine the number of, to count, to list
Excise:	a tax on the manufacture, sale, or consumption of goods within a country
Ex post facto:	Formulated, enacted, or operating retroactively
Habeas Corpus:	A writ issued to bring a party before a court to prevent unlawful restraint
Impartial:	Not partial or biased; unprejudiced.
Impeachment:	In the U.S. and Great Britain proceeding by a legislature for the removal from office of a public official charged with misconduct in office. Impeachment comprises both the act of formulating the accusation and the resulting trial of the charges; it is frequently but erroneously taken to mean only the removal from office of an accused public official. An impeachment trial may result in either an acquittal or in a verdict of guilty. In the latter case the impeached official is removed from office; if the charges warrant such action, the official is also remanded to the proper authorities for trial before a court.
Impost:	tax; duty
Infringe:	violate, transgress, encroach, trespass
Jurisdiction:	the power, right, or authority to interpret and apply the law, the limits or territory within which authority may be exercised
Letter of Marque:	A letter of marque was issued by a nation to a privateer or mercenary to act on the behalf of that nation for the purpose of retaliating against another

nation for some wrong, such as a border incursion or seizure.

Nobility,
Title of Nobility:

is technically a station in society that is had simply by being born into the right family. The class of persons, well-characterized by the aristocracy of Great Britain, were considered to be higher in status and power because of the family name. A title of nobility indicated that status, where a person was a king, queen, prince, princess, count, countess, duke, duchess, baron, or baroness; these titles were granted by the monarch at some point in the family history and passed from parent to child. The Framers wished to ensure that no such system of heredity developed in the United States and specifically prohibited any state or the federal government from granting any title of nobility.

Ordain:

To order by or as if by decree

Poll Tax:

A poll tax has had two historical meanings. The older is that of a fee that had to be paid to satisfy taxpayer requirements in voting laws. In some places, only people who could demonstrate a financial tie to a community were permitted to vote in that community. For those who did not otherwise own property or pay taxes, this sort of poll tax was sufficient to allow voting. More recently, however, a poll tax is a tax that must be paid by anyone wishing to cast a vote. Poll taxes of this sort were generally low, perhaps a dollar or two, but high enough to make voting uneconomical

	for poor people. The 24th Amendment bars both of these types of poll taxes
Post Road:	a road over which mail is carried
Posterity:	future generations; all of a person's descendents.
Pro tempore:	for the time being; temporarily
Quarter:	to provide with shelter
Quorum:	the number of members required to be present for business to be legally conducted
Redress:	to set right, remedy or rectify; to make amends for; satisfaction for wrong done
Reprisal:	an act taken by a nation, short of war, to gain redress for an action taken against that nation. For example, seizing a ship in retaliation for a seized ship.
Republic:	a government having a chief of state who is not a monarch and is usually a president
Suffrage:	a vote; the right or privilege of voting; franchise
Treason:	the offense of attempting to overthrow the government of one's country or of assisting its enemies in war
Welfare:	health, happiness, or prosperity; well-being

Concepts:

Domestic Tranquility
Double Jeopardy
Habeas Corpus
Impeachment
Suffrage
Welfare

> ## *Questions:*
>
> *1. When was the U.S. Constitution ratified?*
> *2. Which states ratified the U.S. Constitution?*
> *3. In your opinion, which is the most important Article of the U.S.*
>   *Constitution? Why?*
> *4. What is the "Bill of Rights?"*
> *5. In your opinion, which is the most important Amendment to the*
>   *Constitution? Why?*

(See Note 1)

We the People of the United States, in Order to form a more perfect Union, establish Justice, insure domestic Tranquility, provide for the common defence, promote the general Welfare, and secure the Blessings of Liberty to ourselves and our Posterity, do ordain and establish this Constitution for the United States of America.

Article. I.

Section 1.

All legislative Powers herein granted shall be vested in a Congress of the United States, which shall consist of a Senate and House of Representatives.

Section 2.

Clause 1: The House of Representatives shall be composed of Members chosen every second Year by the People of the several States, and the Electors in each State shall have the Qualifications requisite for Electors of the most numerous Branch of the State Legislature.

Clause 2: No Person shall be a Representative who shall not have attained to the Age of twenty five Years, and been seven Years a Citizen of the United States, and who shall not, when elected, be an Inhabitant of that State in which he shall be chosen.

Clause 3: Representatives and direct Taxes shall be apportioned among the several States which may be included within this Union, according to their respective Numbers, which shall be determined by adding to the whole Number of free Persons, including those bound to Service for a Term of Years, and excluding Indians not taxed, three fifths of all other Persons. *(See Note 2)* The actual Enumeration shall be made within three Years after the first Meeting of the Congress of the United States, and within every subsequent Term of ten Years, in such Manner as they shall by Law direct. The Number of Representatives shall not exceed one for every thirty Thousand, but each State shall have at Least one Representative; and until such enumeration shall be made, the State of New Hampshire shall be entitled to chuse three, Massachusetts eight, Rhode-Island and Providence Plantations one, Connecticut five, New-York six, New Jersey four, Pennsylvania eight, Delaware one, Maryland six, Virginia ten, North Carolina five, South Carolina five, and Georgia three.

Clause 4: When vacancies happen in the Representation from any State, the Executive Authority thereof shall issue Writs of Election to fill such Vacancies.

Clause 5: The House of Representatives shall chuse their Speaker and other Officers; and shall have the sole Power of Impeachment.

Section 3.

Clause 1: The Senate of the United States shall be composed of two Senators from each State, chosen by the Legislature thereof, *(See Note 3)* for six Years; and each Senator shall have one Vote.

Clause 2: Immediately after they shall be assembled in Consequence of the first Election, they shall be divided as equally as may be into three Classes. The Seats of the Senators of the first Class shall be vacated at the Expiration of the second Year, of the second Class at the Expiration of the fourth Year, and of the third Class at the Expiration of the sixth Year, so that one third may be chosen every second Year; and if Vacancies happen by Resignation, or otherwise, during the Recess of the Legislature of any State, the Executive thereof may make temporary Appointments until the next Meeting of the Legislature, which shall then fill such Vacancies. *(See Note 4)*

Clause 3: No Person shall be a Senator who shall not have attained to the Age of thirty Years, and been nine Years a Citizen of the United States, and who shall not, when elected, be an Inhabitant of that State for which he shall be chosen.

Clause 4: The Vice President of the United States shall be President of the Senate, but shall have no Vote, unless they be equally divided.

Clause 5: The Senate shall chuse their other Officers, and also a President pro tempore, in the Absence of the Vice President, or when he shall exercise the Office of President of the United States.

Clause 6: The Senate shall have the sole Power to try all Impeachments. When sitting for that Purpose, they shall be on Oath or Affirmation. When the President of the United States is tried, the Chief Justice shall preside: And no Person shall be convicted without the Concurrence of two thirds of the Members present.

Clause 7: Judgment in Cases of Impeachment shall not extend further than to removal from Office, and disqualification to hold and enjoy any Office of honor, Trust or Profit under the United States: but the Party convicted shall nevertheless be liable and subject to Indictment, Trial, Judgment and Punishment, according to Law.

Section. 4.

Clause 1: The Times, Places and Manner of holding Elections for Senators and Representatives, shall be prescribed in each State by the Legislature thereof; but the Congress may at any time by Law make or alter such Regulations, except as to the Places of chusing Senators.

Clause 2: The Congress shall assemble at least once in every Year, and such Meeting shall be on the first Monday in December, *(See Note 5)* unless they shall by Law appoint a different Day.

Section. 5.

Clause 1: Each House shall be the Judge of the Elections, Returns and Qualifications of its own Members, and a Majority of each shall constitute a Quorum to do Business; but a smaller Number may adjourn from day to day, and may be authorized to compel the Attendance of absent Members, in such Manner, and under such Penalties as each House may provide.

Clause 2: Each House may determine the Rules of its Proceedings, punish its Members for disorderly Behaviour, and, with the Concurrence of two thirds, expel a Member.

Clause 3: Each House shall keep a Journal of its Proceedings, and from time to time publish the same, excepting such Parts as may in their Judgment require Secrecy; and the Yeas and Nays of the Members of either House on any question shall, at the Desire of one fifth of those Present, be entered on the Journal.

Clause 4: Neither House, during the Session of Congress, shall, without the Consent of the other, adjourn for more than three days, nor to any other Place than that in which the two Houses shall be sitting.

Section. 6.

Clause 1: The Senators and Representatives shall receive a Compensation for their Services, to be ascertained by Law, and paid out of the Treasury of the United States. *(See Note 6)* They shall in all Cases, except Treason, Felony and Breach of the Peace, be privileged from Arrest during their Attendance at the Session of their respective Houses, and in going to and returning from the same; and for any Speech or Debate in either House, they shall not be questioned in any other Place.

Clause 2: No Senator or Representative shall, during the Time for which he was elected, be appointed to any civil Office under the Authority of the United States, which shall have been created, or the Emoluments whereof shall have been increased during such time; and no Person holding any Office under the United States, shall be a Member of either House during his Continuance in Office.

Section. 7.

Clause 1: All Bills for raising Revenue shall originate in the House of Representatives; but the Senate may propose or concur with Amendments as on other Bills.

Clause 2: Every Bill which shall have passed the House of Representatives and the Senate, shall, before it becomes a Law, be presented to the President of the United States; If he approves he shall sign it, but if not he shall return it, with his Objections to that House in which it shall have originated, who shall enter the Objections at large on their Journal, and proceed to reconsider it. If after such Reconsideration two thirds of that House shall agree to pass the Bill, it shall be sent, together with the Objections, to the other House, by which it shall likewise be reconsidered, and if approved by two thirds of that House, it shall become a Law. But in all such Cases the Votes of both Houses shall be determined by yeas and Nays, and the Names of the Persons voting for and against the Bill shall be entered on the Journal of each House respectively. If any Bill shall not be returned by the President within ten Days (Sundays excepted) after it shall have been presented to him, the Same shall be a Law, in like Manner as if he had signed it, unless the Congress by their Adjournment prevent its Return, in which Case it shall not be a Law.

Clause 3: Every Order, Resolution, or Vote to which the Concurrence of the Senate and House of Representatives may be necessary (except on a question of Adjournment) shall be presented to the President of the United States; and before the Same shall take Effect, shall be approved by him, or being disapproved by him, shall be repassed by two thirds of the Senate and House of Representatives, according to the Rules and Limitations prescribed in the Case of a Bill.

Section. 8.

Clause 1: The Congress shall have Power to lay and collect Taxes, Duties, Imposts and Excises, to pay the Debts and provide for the common Defence and general Welfare of the United States; but all Duties, Imposts and Excises shall be uniform throughout the United States;

Clause 2: To borrow Money on the credit of the United States;

Clause 3: To regulate Commerce with foreign Nations, and among the several States, and with the Indian Tribes;

Clause 4: To establish an uniform Rule of Naturalization, and uniform Laws on the subject of Bankruptcies throughout the United States;

Clause 5: To coin Money, regulate the Value thereof, and of foreign Coin, and fix the Standard of Weights and Measures;

Clause 6: To provide for the Punishment of counterfeiting the Securities and current Coin of the United States;

Clause 7: To establish Post Offices and post Roads;

Clause 8: To promote the Progress of Science and useful Arts, by securing for limited Times to Authors and Inventors the exclusive Right to their respective Writings and Discoveries;

Clause 9: To constitute Tribunals inferior to the supreme Court;

Clause 10: To define and punish Piracies and Felonies committed on the high Seas, and Offences against the Law of Nations;

Clause 11: To declare War, grant Letters of Marque and Reprisal, and make Rules concerning Captures on Land and Water;

Clause 12: To raise and support Armies, but no Appropriation of Money to that Use shall be for a longer Term than two Years;

Clause 13: To provide and maintain a Navy;

Clause 14: To make Rules for the Government and Regulation of the land and naval Forces;

Clause 15: To provide for calling forth the Militia to execute the Laws of the Union, suppress Insurrections and repel Invasions;

Clause 16: To provide for organizing, arming, and disciplining the Militia, and for governing such Part of them as may be employed in the Service of the United States, reserving to the States respectively, the Appointment of the Officers, and the Authority of training the Militia according to the discipline prescribed by Congress;

Clause 17: To exercise exclusive Legislation in all Cases whatsoever, over such District (not exceeding ten Miles square) as may, by Cession of particular States, and the Acceptance of Congress, become the Seat of the Government of the United States, and to exercise like Authority over all Places purchased by the Consent of the Legislature of the State in which the Same shall be, for the Erection of Forts, Magazines, Arsenals, dock-Yards, and other needful Buildings;—And

Clause 18: To make all Laws which shall be necessary and proper for carrying into Execution the foregoing Powers, and all other Powers vested by this Constitution in the Government of the United States, or in any Department or Officer thereof.

Section. 9.

Clause 1: The Migration or Importation of such Persons as any of the States now existing shall think proper to admit, shall not be prohibited by the Congress prior to the Year one thousand eight hundred and eight, but a Tax or duty may be imposed on such Importation, not exceeding ten dollars for each Person.

Clause 2: The Privilege of the Writ of Habeas Corpus shall not be suspended, unless when in Cases of Rebellion or Invasion the public Safety may require it.

Clause 3: No Bill of Attainder or ex post facto Law shall be passed.

Clause 4: No Capitation, or other direct, Tax shall be laid, unless in Proportion to the Census or Enumeration herein before directed to be taken. *(See Note 7)*

Clause 5: No Tax or Duty shall be laid on Articles exported from any State.

Clause 6: No Preference shall be given by any Regulation of Commerce or Revenue to the Ports of one State over those of another; nor shall Vessels bound to, or from, one State, be obliged to enter, clear, or pay Duties in another.

Clause 7: No Money shall be drawn from the Treasury, but in Consequence of Appropriations made by Law; and a regular Statement and Account of the Receipts and Expenditures of all public Money shall be published from time to time.

Clause 8: No Title of Nobility shall be granted by the United States; And no Person holding any Office of Profit or Trust under them, shall, without the Consent of the Congress, accept of any present, Emolument, Office, or Title, of any kind whatever, from any King, Prince, or foreign State.

Section. 10.

Clause 1: No State shall enter into any Treaty, Alliance, or Confederation; grant Letters of Marque and Reprisal; coin Money; emit Bills of Credit; make any Thing but gold and silver Coin a Tender in Payment of Debts; pass any Bill of Attainder, ex post facto Law, or Law impairing the Obligation of Contracts, or grant any Title of Nobility.

Clause 2: No State shall, without the Consent of the Congress, lay any Imposts or Duties on Imports or Exports, except what may be absolutely necessary for executing it's inspection Laws: and the net Produce of all Duties and Imposts, laid by any State on Imports or Exports, shall be for the Use of the Treasury of the United States; and all such Laws shall be subject to the Revision and Control of the Congress.

Clause 3: No State shall, without the Consent of Congress, lay any Duty of Tonnage, keep Troops, or Ships of War in time of Peace, enter into any Agreement or Compact with another State, or with a foreign Power, or engage in War, unless actually invaded, or in such imminent Danger as will not admit of delay.

Article. II.

Section. 1.

Clause 1: The executive Power shall be vested in a President of the United States of America. He shall hold his Office during the Term of four Years, and, together with the Vice President, chosen for the same Term, be elected, as follows

Clause 2: Each State shall appoint, in such Manner as the Legislature thereof may direct, a Number of Electors, equal to the whole Number of Senators and Representatives to which the State may be entitled in the Congress; but no Senator or Representative, or Person holding an Office of Trust or Profit under the United States, shall be appointed an Elector.

Clause 3: The Electors shall meet in their respective States, and vote by Ballot for two Persons, of whom one at least shall not be an Inhabitant of the same State with themselves. And they shall make a List of all the Persons voted for, and of the Number of Votes for each; which List they shall sign and certify, and transmit sealed to the Seat of the Government of the United States, directed to the President of the Senate. The President of the Senate shall, in the Presence of the Senate and House of Representatives, open all the Certificates, and the Votes shall then be counted. The Person having the greatest Number of Votes shall be the President, if such Number be a Majority of the whole Number of Electors appointed; and if there be more than one who have such Majority, and have an equal Number of Votes, then the House of Representatives shall immediately chuse by Ballot one of them for President; and if no Person have a Majority, then from the five highest on the List the said House shall in like Manner chuse the President. But in chusing the President, the Votes shall be taken by States, the Representation from each State having one Vote; A quorum for this Purpose shall consist of a Member or Members from two thirds of the States, and a Majority of all the States shall be necessary to a Choice. In every Case, after the Choice of the President, the Person having the greatest Number of Votes of the Electors shall be the Vice President. But if there should remain two or more who have equal Votes, the Senate shall chuse from them by Ballot the Vice President. *(See Note 8)*

Clause 4: The Congress may determine the Time of chusing the Electors, and the Day on which they shall give their Votes; which Day shall be the same throughout the United States.

Clause 5: No Person except a natural born Citizen, or a Citizen of the United States, at the time of the Adoption of this Constitution, shall be eligible to the Office of President; neither shall any Person be eligible to that Office who shall not have attained to the Age of thirty five Years, and been fourteen Years a Resident within the United States.

Clause 6: In Case of the Removal of the President from Office, or of his Death, Resignation, or Inability to discharge the Powers and Duties of the said Office, *(See Note 9)* the Same shall devolve on the Vice President, and the Congress may by Law provide for the Case of Removal, Death, Resignation or Inability, both of the President and Vice President, declaring what Officer shall then act as President, and such Officer shall act accordingly, until the Disability be removed, or a President shall be elected.

Clause 7: The President shall, at stated Times, receive for his Services, a Compensation, which shall neither be increased nor diminished during the Period for which he shall have been elected, and he shall not receive within that Period any other Emolument from the United States, or any of them.

Clause 8: Before he enter on the Execution of his Office, he shall take the following Oath or Affirmation:—"I do solemnly swear (or affirm) that I will faithfully execute the Office of President of the United States, and will to the best of my Ability, preserve, protect and defend the Constitution of the United States."

Section. 2.

Clause 1: The President shall be Commander in Chief of the Army and Navy of the United States, and of the Militia of the several States, when called into the actual Service of the United States; he may require the Opinion, in writing, of the principal Officer in each of the executive Departments, upon any Subject relating to the Duties of their respective Offices, and he shall have Power to grant Reprieves and Pardons for Offences against the United States, except in Cases of Impeachment.

Clause 2: He shall have Power, by and with the Advice and Consent of the Senate, to make Treaties, provided two thirds of the Senators present concur; and he shall nominate, and by and with the Advice and Consent of the Senate, shall appoint Ambassadors, other public Ministers and Consuls, Judges of the supreme Court, and all other Officers of the United States, whose Appointments are not herein otherwise provided for, and which shall be established by Law; but the Congress may by Law vest the Appointment of such inferior Officers, as they think proper, in the President alone, in the Courts of Law, or in the Heads of Departments.

Clause 3: The President shall have Power to fill up all Vacancies that may happen during the Recess of the Senate, by granting Commissions which shall expire at the End of their next Session.

Section. 3.

He shall from time to time give to the Congress Information of the State of the Union, and recommend to their Consideration such Measures as he shall judge necessary and expedient; he may, on extraordinary Occasions, convene both Houses, or either of them, and in Case of Disagreement between them, with Respect to the Time of Adjournment, he may adjourn them to such Time as he shall think proper; he shall receive Ambassadors and other public Ministers; he shall take Care that the Laws be faithfully executed, and shall Commission all the Officers of the United States.

Section. 4.

The President, Vice President and all civil Officers of the United States, shall be removed from Office on Impeachment for, and Conviction of, Treason, Bribery, or other high Crimes and Misdemeanors.

Article. III.

Section. 1.

The judicial Power of the United States, shall be vested in one supreme Court, and in such inferior Courts as the Congress may from time to time ordain and establish. The Judges, both of the supreme and inferior Courts, shall hold their Offices during good Behaviour, and shall, at stated Times, receive for their Services, a Compensation, which shall not be diminished during their Continuance in Office.

Section. 2.

Clause 1: The judicial Power shall extend to all Cases, in Law and Equity, arising under this Constitution, the Laws of the United States, and Treaties made, or which shall be made, under their Authority;—to all Cases affecting Ambassadors, other public

Ministers and Consuls;—to all Cases of admiralty and maritime Jurisdiction;—to Controversies to which the United States shall be a Party;—to Controversies between two or more States;—between a State and Citizens of another State; *(See Note 10)*—between Citizens of different States, —between Citizens of the same State claiming Lands under Grants of different States, and between a State, or the Citizens thereof, and foreign States, Citizens or Subjects.

Clause 2: In all Cases affecting Ambassadors, other public Ministers and Consuls, and those in which a State shall be Party, the supreme Court shall have original Jurisdiction. In all the other Cases before mentioned, the supreme Court shall have appellate Jurisdiction, both as to Law and Fact, with such Exceptions, and under such Regulations as the Congress shall make.

Clause 3: The Trial of all Crimes, except in Cases of Impeachment, shall be by Jury; and such Trial shall be held in the State where the said Crimes shall have been committed; but when not committed within any State, the Trial shall be at such Place or Places as the Congress may by Law have directed.

Section. 3.

Clause 1: Treason against the United States, shall consist only in levying War against them, or in adhering to their Enemies, giving them Aid and Comfort. No Person shall be convicted of Treason unless on the Testimony of two Witnesses to the same overt Act, or on Confession in open Court.

Clause 2: The Congress shall have Power to declare the Punishment of Treason, but no Attainder of Treason shall work Corruption of Blood, or Forfeiture except during the Life of the Person attainted.

Article. IV.

Section. 1.

Full Faith and Credit shall be given in each State to the public Acts, Records, and judicial Proceedings of every other State. And the Congress may by general Laws prescribe the Manner in which such Acts, Records and Proceedings shall be proved, and the Effect thereof.

Section. 2.

Clause 1: The Citizens of each State shall be entitled to all Privileges and Immunities of Citizens in the several States.

Clause 2: A Person charged in any State with Treason, Felony, or other Crime, who shall flee from Justice, and be found in another State, shall on Demand of the executive Authority of the State from which he fled, be delivered up, to be removed to the State having Jurisdiction of the Crime.

Clause 3: No Person held to Service or Labour in one State, under the Laws thereof, escaping into another, shall, in Consequence of any Law or Regulation therein, be discharged from such Service or Labour, but shall be delivered up on Claim of the Party to whom such Service or Labour may be due. *(See Note 11)*

Section. 3.

Clause 1: New States may be admitted by the Congress into this Union; but no new State shall be formed or erected within the Jurisdiction of any other State; nor any State be formed by the Junction of two or more States, or Parts of States, without the Consent of the Legislatures of the States concerned as well as of the Congress.

Clause 2: The Congress shall have Power to dispose of and make all needful Rules and Regulations respecting the Territory or other Property belonging to the United States; and nothing in this Constitution shall be so construed as to Prejudice any Claims of the United States, or of any particular State.

Section. 4.

The United States shall guarantee to every State in this Union a Republican Form of Government, and shall protect each of them against Invasion; and on Application of the

Legislature, or of the Executive (when the Legislature cannot be convened) against domestic Violence.

Article. V.

The Congress, whenever two thirds of both Houses shall deem it necessary, shall propose <u>Amendments</u> to this Constitution, or, on the Application of the Legislatures of two thirds of the several States, shall call a Convention for proposing Amendments, which, in either Case, shall be valid to all Intents and Purposes, as Part of this Constitution, when ratified by the Legislatures of three fourths of the several States, or by Conventions in three fourths thereof, as the one or the other Mode of Ratification may be proposed by the Congress; Provided that no Amendment which may be made prior to the Year One thousand eight hundred and eight shall in any Manner affect the first and fourth Clauses in the Ninth Section of the first Article; and that no State, without its Consent, shall be deprived of its equal Suffrage in the Senate.

Article. VI.

Clause 1: All Debts contracted and Engagements entered into, before the Adoption of this Constitution, shall be as valid against the United States under this Constitution, as under the Confederation.

Clause 2: This Constitution, and the Laws of the United States which shall be made in Pursuance thereof; and all Treaties made, or which shall be made, under the Authority of the United States, shall be the supreme Law of the Land; and the Judges in every State shall be bound thereby, any Thing in the Constitution or Laws of any State to the Contrary notwithstanding.

Clause 3: The Senators and Representatives before mentioned, and the Members of the several State Legislatures, and all executive and judicial Officers, both of the United States and of the several States, shall be bound by Oath or Affirmation, to support this Constitution; but no religious Test shall ever be required as a Qualification to any Office or public Trust under the United States.

Article. VII.

The Ratification of the Conventions of nine States, shall be sufficient for the Establishment of this Constitution between the States so ratifying the Same.

done in Convention by the Unanimous Consent of the States present the Seventeenth Day of September in the Year of our Lord one thousand seven hundred and Eighty seven and of the Independence of the United States of America the Twelfth In witness whereof We have hereunto subscribed our Names,

(Signatures of Representatives)

NOTES

Note 1: This text of the Constitution follows the engrossed copy signed by Gen. Washington and the deputies from 12 States. The small superior figures preceding the paragraphs designate Clauses, and were not in the original and have no reference to footnotes.

The Constitution was adopted by a convention of the States on September 17, 1787, and was subsequently ratified by the several States, on the following dates: Delaware, December 7, 1787; Pennsylvania, December 12, 1787; New Jersey, December 18, 1787; Georgia, January 2, 1788; Connecticut, January 9, 1788; Massachusetts, February 6, 1788; Maryland, April 28, 1788; South Carolina, May 23, 1788; New Hampshire, June 21, 1788.

Ratification was completed on June 21, 1788.

The Constitution was subsequently ratified by Virginia, June 25, 1788; New York, July 26, 1788; North Carolina, November 21, 1789; Rhode Island, May 29, 1790; and Vermont, January 10, 1791.

In May 1785, a committee of Congress made a report recommending an alteration in the Articles of Confederation, but no action was taken on it, and it was left to the State Legislatures to proceed in the matter. In January 1786, the Legislature of Virginia passed a resolution providing for the appointment of five commissioners, who, or any three of them, should meet such commissioners as might be appointed in the other States of the Union, at a time and place to be agreed upon, to take into consideration the trade of the United States; to consider how far a uniform system in their commercial regulations may be necessary to their common interest and their permanent harmony; and to report to the several States such an act, relative to this great object, as, when ratified by them, will enable the United States in Congress effectually to provide for the same. The Virginia commissioners, after some correspondence, fixed the first Monday in September as the time, and the city of Annapolis as the place for the meeting, but only four other States were represented, viz: Delaware, New York, New Jersey, and Pennsylvania; the commissioners appointed by Massachusetts, New Hampshire, North Carolina, and Rhode Island failed to attend. Under the circumstances of so partial a representation, the commissioners present agreed upon a report, (drawn by Mr. Hamilton, of New York,) expressing their unanimous conviction that it might essentially tend to advance the interests of the Union if the States by which they were respectively delegated would concur, and use their endeavors to procure the concurrence of the other States, in the appointment of commissioners to meet at Philadelphia on the Second Monday of May following, to take into consideration the situation of the United States; to devise such further provisions as should appear to them necessary to render the Constitution of the Federal Government adequate to the exigencies of the Union; and to report such an act for that purpose to the United States in Congress assembled as, when agreed to by them and afterwards confirmed by the Legislatures of every State, would effectually provide for the same.

Congress, on the 21st of February, 1787, adopted a resolution in favor of a convention, and the Legislatures of those States which had not already done so (with the exception of Rhode Island) promptly appointed delegates. On the 25th of May, seven States having convened, George Washington, of Virginia, was unanimously elected President, and the consideration of the proposed constitution was commenced. On the 17th of September, 1787, the Constitution as engrossed and agreed upon was signed by all the members present, except Mr. Gerry of Massachusetts, and Messrs. Mason and Randolph, of Virginia. The president of the convention transmitted it to Congress, with a resolution stating how the proposed Federal Government should be put in operation, and an explanatory letter. Congress, on the 28th of September, 1787, directed the Constitution so framed, with the resolutions and letter concerning the same, to "be transmitted to the several Legislatures in order to be submitted to a convention of delegates chosen in each State by the people thereof, in conformity to the resolves of the convention."

On the 4th of March, 1789, the day which had been fixed for commencing the operations of Government under the new Constitution, it had been ratified by the conventions chosen in each State to consider it, as follows: Delaware, December 7, 1787; Pennsylvania, December 12, 1787; New Jersey, December 18, 1787; Georgia, January 2, 1788; Connecticut, January 9, 1788; Massachusetts, February 6, 1788; Maryland, April 28, 1788; South Carolina, May 23, 1788; New Hampshire, June 21, 1788; Virginia, June 25, 1788; and New York, July 26, 1788.

The President informed Congress, on the 28th of January, 1790, that North Carolina had ratified the Constitution November 21, 1789; and he informed Congress on the 1st of June, 1790, that Rhode Island had ratified the Constitution May 29, 1790. Vermont, in convention, ratified the Constitution January 10, 1791, and was, by an act of Congress approved February 18, 1791, "received and admitted into this Union as a new and entire member of the United States."

Note 2: The part of this Clause relating to the mode of apportionment of representatives among the several States has been affected by Section 2 of amendment XIV, and as to taxes on incomes without apportionment by amendment XVI.

Note 3: This Clause has been affected by Clause 1 of amendment XVII.

Note 4: This Clause has been affected by Clause 2 of amendment XVIII.

Note 5: This Clause has been affected by amendment XX.

Note 6: This Clause has been affected by amendment XXVII.

Note 7: This Clause has been affected by amendment XVI.

Note 8: This Clause has been superseded by amendment XII.

Note 9: This Clause has been affected by amendment XXV.

Note 10: This Clause has been affected by amendment XI.

Note 11: This Clause has been affected by amendment XIII.

Note 12: The first ten amendments to the Constitution of the United States (and two others, one of which failed of ratification and the other which later became the 27th amendment) were proposed to the legislatures of the several States by the First Congress on September 25, 1789. The first ten amendments were ratified by the following States, and the notifications of ratification by the Governors thereof were successively communicated by the President to Congress: New Jersey, November 20, 1789; Maryland, December 19, 1789; North Carolina, December 22, 1789; South Carolina, January 19, 1790; New Hampshire, January 25, 1790; Delaware, January 28, 1790; New York, February 24, 1790; Pennsylvania, March 10, 1790; Rhode Island, June 7, 1790; Vermont, November 3, 1791; and Virginia, December 15, 1791.

Ratification was completed on December 15, 1791.

The amendments were subsequently ratified by the legislatures of Massachusetts, March 2, 1939; Georgia, March 18, 1939; and Connecticut, April 19, 1939.

Note 13: Only the 13th, 14th, 15th, and 16th articles of amendment had numbers assigned to them at the time of ratification.

Note 14: This sentence has been superseded by section 3 of amendment XX.

Note 15: See amendment XIX and section 1 of amendment XXVI.

Note 16: Repealed by section 1 of amendment XXI.

Amendments to the Constitution

The Bill of Rights (Amendments 1-10)

Amendment [I.]

Congress shall make no law respecting an establishment of religion, or prohibiting the free exercise thereof; or abridging the freedom of speech, or of the press; or the right of the people peaceably to assemble, and to petition the Government for a redress of grievances.

Amendment [II.]

A well regulated Militia, being necessary to the security of a free State, the right of the people to keep and bear Arms, shall not be infringed.

Amendment [III.]

No Soldier shall, in time of peace be quartered in any house, without the consent of the Owner, nor in time of war, but in a manner to be prescribed by law.

Amendment [IV.]

The right of the people to be secure in their persons, houses, papers, and effects, against unreasonable searches and seizures, shall not be violated, and no Warrants shall issue, but upon probable cause, supported by Oath or affirmation, and particularly describing the place to be searched, and the persons or things to be seized.

Amendment [V.]

No person shall be held to answer for a capital, or otherwise infamous crime, unless on a presentment or indictment of a Grand Jury, except in cases arising in the land or naval forces, or in the Militia, when in actual service in time of War or public danger; nor shall any person be subject for the same offence to be twice put in jeopardy of life or limb; nor shall be compelled in any criminal case to be a witness against himself, nor be deprived of life, liberty, or property, without due process of law; nor shall private property be taken for public use, without just compensation.

Amendment [VI.]

In all criminal prosecutions, the accused shall enjoy the right to a speedy and public trial, by an impartial jury of the State and district wherein the crime shall have been committed, which district shall have been previously ascertained by law, and to be informed of the nature and cause of the accusation; to be confronted with the witnesses against him; to have compulsory process for obtaining witnesses in his favor, and to have the Assistance of Counsel for his defence.

Amendment [VII.]

In Suits at common law, where the value in controversy shall exceed twenty dollars, the right of trial by jury shall be preserved, and no fact tried by a jury, shall be otherwise re-examined in any Court of the United States, than according to the rules of the common law.

Amendment [VIII.]

Excessive bail shall not be required, nor excessive fines imposed, nor cruel and unusual punishments inflicted.

Amendment [IX.]

The enumeration in the Constitution, of certain rights, shall not be construed to deny or disparage others retained by the people.

Amendment [X.]

The powers not delegated to the United States by the Constitution, nor prohibited by it to the States, are reserved to the States respectively, or to the people.

Amendment [XI.]

The Judicial power of the United States shall not be construed to extend to any suit in law or equity, commenced or prosecuted against one of the United States by Citizens of another State, or by Citizens or Subjects of any Foreign State.

Amendment [XII.]

The Electors shall meet in their respective states, and vote by ballot for President and Vice-President, one of whom, at least, shall not be an inhabitant of the same state with themselves; they shall name in their ballots the person voted for as President, and in distinct ballots the person voted for as Vice-President, and they shall make distinct lists of all persons voted for as President, and of all persons voted for as Vice-President, and of the number of votes for each, which lists they shall sign and certify, and transmit sealed to the seat of the government of the United States, directed to the President of the Senate;—The President of the Senate shall, in the presence of the Senate and House of Representatives, open all the certificates and the votes shall then be counted;—The person having the greatest number of votes for President, shall be the President, if such number be a majority of the whole number of Electors appointed; and if no person have such majority, then from the persons having the highest numbers not exceeding three on the list of those voted for as President, the House of Representatives shall choose immediately, by ballot, the President. But in choosing the President, the votes shall be taken by states, the representation from each state having one vote; a quorum for this purpose shall consist of a member or members from two-thirds of the states, and a majority of all the states shall be necessary to a choice. And if the House of Representatives shall not choose a President whenever the right of choice shall devolve upon them, before the fourth day of March next following, then the Vice-President shall act as President, as in the case of the death or other constitutional disability of the President. *(See Note 14)*—

The person having the greatest number of votes as Vice-President, shall be the Vice-President, if such number be a majority of the whole number of Electors appointed, and if no person have a majority, then from the two highest numbers on the list, the Senate shall choose the Vice-President; a quorum for the purpose shall consist of two-thirds of the whole number of Senators, and a majority of the whole number shall be necessary to a choice. But no person constitutionally ineligible to the office of President shall be eligible to that of Vice-President of the United States.

Amendment [XIII.]

Section 1. Neither slavery nor involuntary servitude, except as a punishment for crime whereof the party shall have been duly convicted, shall exist within the United States, or any place subject to their jurisdiction.

Section 2. Congress shall have power to enforce this article by appropriate legislation.

Amendment [XIV.]

Section 1. All persons born or naturalized in the United States, and subject to the jurisdiction thereof, are citizens of the United States and of the State wherein they reside. No State shall make or enforce any law which shall abridge the privileges or immunities of citizens of the United States; nor shall any State deprive any person of life, liberty, or property, without due process of law; nor deny to any person within its jurisdiction the equal protection of the laws.

Section 2. Representatives shall be apportioned among the several States according to their respective numbers, counting the whole number of persons in each State, excluding Indians not taxed. But when the right to vote at any election for the choice of electors for President and Vice President of the United States, Representatives in Congress, the Executive and Judicial officers of a State, or the members of the Legislature thereof, is denied to any of the male inhabitants of such State, being twenty-one years of age,*(See Note 15)* and citizens of the United States, or in any way abridged, except for participation in rebellion, or other crime, the basis of representation therein shall be reduced in the proportion which the number of such male citizens shall bear to the whole number of male citizens twenty-one years of age in such State.

Section 3. No person shall be a Senator or Representative in Congress, or elector of President and Vice President, or hold any office, civil or military, under the United States, or under any State, who, having previously taken an oath, as a member of Congress, or as an officer of the United States, or as a member of any State legislature, or as an executive or judicial officer of any State, to support the Constitution of the United States, shall have engaged in insurrection or rebellion against the same, or given aid or comfort to the enemies thereof. But Congress may by a vote of two-thirds of each House, remove such disability.

Section 4. The validity of the public debt of the United States, authorized by law, including debts incurred for payment of pensions and bounties for services in suppressing insurrection or rebellion, shall not be questioned. But neither the United States nor any State shall assume or pay any debt or obligation incurred in aid of insurrection or rebellion against the United States, or any claim for the loss or emancipation of any slave; but all such debts, obligations and claims shall be held illegal and void.

Section 5. The Congress shall have power to enforce, by appropriate legislation, the provisions of this article.

Amendment [XV.]

Section 1. The right of citizens of the United States to vote shall not be denied or abridged by the United States or by any State on account of race, color, or previous condition of servitude.

Section 2. The Congress shall have power to enforce this article by appropriate legislation.

Amendment [XVI.]

The Congress shall have power to lay and collect taxes on incomes, from whatever source derived, without apportionment among the several States, and without regard to any census or enumeration.

Amendment [XVII.]

The Senate of the United States shall be composed of two Senators from each State, elected by the people thereof, for six years; and each Senator shall have one vote. The electors in each State shall have the qualifications requisite for electors of the most numerous branch of the State legislatures.

When vacancies happen in the representation of any State in the Senate, the executive authority of such State shall issue writs of election to fill such vacancies: Provided, That the legislature of any State may empower the executive thereof to make temporary appointments until the people fill the vacancies by election as the legislature may direct.

This amendment shall not be so construed as to affect the election or term of any Senator chosen before it becomes valid as part of the Constitution.

Amendment [XVIII]

Section 1. After one year from the ratification of this article the manufacture, sale, or transportation of intoxicating liquors within, the importation thereof into, or the exportation thereof from the United States and all territory subject to the jurisdiction thereof for beverage purposes is hereby prohibited.

Section. 2. The Congress and the several States shall have concurrent power to enforce this article by appropriate legislation.

Section. 3. This article shall be inoperative unless it shall have been ratified as an amendment to the Constitution by the legislatures of the several States, as provided in the Constitution, within seven years from the date of the submission hereof to the States by the Congress.

Amendment [XIX].

The right of citizens of the United States to vote shall not be denied or abridged by the United States or by any State on account of sex.

Congress shall have power to enforce this article by appropriate legislation.

Amendment [XX.]

Section 1. The terms of the President and Vice President shall end at noon on the 20th day of January, and the terms of Senators and Representatives at noon on the 3rd day of January, of the years in which such terms would have ended if this article had not been ratified; and the terms of their successors shall then begin.

Section. 2. The Congress shall assemble at least once in every year, and such meeting shall begin at noon on the 3rd day of January, unless they shall by law appoint a different day.

Section. 3. If, at the time fixed for the beginning of the term of the President, the President elect shall have died, the Vice President elect shall become President. If a President shall not have been chosen before the time fixed for the beginning of his term, or if the President elect shall have failed to qualify, then the Vice President elect shall act as President until a President shall have qualified; and the Congress may by law provide for the case wherein neither a President elect nor a Vice President elect shall have qualified, declaring who shall then act as President, or the manner in which one who is to act shall be selected, and such person shall act accordingly until a President or Vice President shall have qualified.

Section. 4. The Congress may by law provide for the case of the death of any of the persons from whom the House of Representatives may choose a President whenever the right of choice shall have devolved upon them, and for the case of the death of any of the persons from whom the Senate may choose a Vice President whenever the right of choice shall have devolved upon them.

Section. 5. Sections 1 and 2 shall take effect on the 15th day of October following the ratification of this article.

Section. 6. This article shall be inoperative unless it shall have been ratified as an amendment to the Constitution by the legislatures of three-fourths of the several States within seven years from the date of its submission.

Amendment [XXI.]

Section 1. The eighteenth article of amendment to the Constitution of the United States is hereby repealed.

Section 2. The transportation or importation into any State, Territory, or possession of the United States for delivery or use therein of intoxicating liquors, in violation of the laws thereof, is hereby prohibited.

Section 3. This article shall be inoperative unless it shall have been ratified as an amendment to the Constitution by conventions in the several States, as provided in the Constitution, within seven years from the date of the submission hereof to the States by the Congress.

Amendment [XXII.]

Section 1. No person shall be elected to the office of the President more than twice, and no person who has held the office of President, or acted as President, for more than two years of a term to which some other person was elected President shall be elected to the office of the President more than once. But this article shall not apply to any person holding the office of President when this article was proposed by the Congress, and shall not prevent any person who may be holding the office of President, or acting as President, during the term within which this article becomes operative from holding the office of President or acting as President during the remainder of such term.

Section 2. This article shall be inoperative unless it shall have been ratified as an amendment to the Constitution by the legislatures of three-fourths of the several states within seven years from the date of its submission to the states by the Congress.

Amendment [XXIII.]

Section 1. The District constituting the seat of government of the United States shall appoint in such manner as the Congress may direct:

A number of electors of President and Vice President equal to the whole number of

Senators and Representatives in Congress to which the District would be entitled if it were a state, but in no event more than the least populous state; they shall be in addition to those appointed by the states, but they shall be considered, for the purposes of the election of President and Vice President, to be electors appointed by a state; and they shall meet in the District and perform such duties as provided by the twelfth article of amendment.

Section 2. The Congress shall have power to enforce this article by appropriate legislation.

Amendment [XXIV.]

Section 1. The right of citizens of the United States to vote in any primary or other election for President or Vice President, for electors for President or Vice President, or for Senator or Representative in Congress, shall not be denied or abridged by the United States or any state by reason of failure to pay any poll tax or other tax.

Section 2. The Congress shall have power to enforce this article by appropriate legislation.

Amendment [XXV.]

Section 1. In case of the removal of the President from office or of his death or resignation, the Vice President shall become President.

Section 2. Whenever there is a vacancy in the office of the Vice President, the President shall nominate a Vice President who shall take office upon confirmation by a majority vote of both Houses of Congress.

Section 3. Whenever the President transmits to the President pro tempore of the Senate and the Speaker of the House of Representatives his written declaration that he is unable to discharge the powers and duties of his office, and until he transmits to them a written declaration to the contrary, such powers and duties shall be discharged by the Vice President as Acting President.

Section 4. Whenever the Vice President and a majority of either the principal officers of the executive departments or of such other body as Congress may by law provide, transmit to the President pro tempore of the Senate and the Speaker of the House of Representatives their written declaration that the President is unable to discharge the powers and duties of his office, the Vice President shall immediately assume the powers and duties of the office as Acting President.

Thereafter, when the President transmits to the President pro tempore of the Senate and the Speaker of the House of Representatives his written declaration that no inability exists, he shall resume the powers and duties of his office unless the Vice President and a majority of either the principal officers of the executive department or of such other body as Congress may by law provide, transmit within four days to the President pro tempore of the Senate and the Speaker of the House of Representatives their written declaration that the President is unable to discharge the powers and duties of his office. Thereupon Congress shall decide the issue, assembling within forty-eight hours for that purpose if not in session. If the Congress, within twenty-one days after receipt of the latter written declaration, or, if Congress is not in session, within twenty-one days after Congress is required to assemble, determines by two-thirds vote of both Houses that the President is unable to discharge the powers and duties of his office, the Vice President shall continue to discharge the same as Acting President; otherwise, the President shall resume the powers and duties of his office.

Amendment [XXVI.]

Section 1. The right of citizens of the United States, who are 18 years of age or older, to vote, shall not be denied or abridged by the United States or any state on account of age.

Section 2. The Congress shall have the power to enforce this article by appropriate legislation.

Amendment [XXVII.]

No law varying the compensation for the services of the Senators and Representatives shall take effect until an election of Representatives shall have intervened.

Section VII. Political Philosophy Section Review

Below is the review sheet for Part VII: Political Philosophy. Included in this review are the terms and concepts you should be familiar with to prepare for the exam. I have also included an example of the multiple choice questions that you will have to answer. It will give you an idea of what type of questions to expect.

We will be reviewing each of these terms and concepts and the multiple choice question in class prior to the exam.

You should be familiar with the following terms and concepts:

Political Philosophy
Democracy
Socialism
Communism
Capitalism
Social Contract
Hobbes' Political Theory
Anarchy
Commonwealth
Minimal of Morality
Right of Nature
State of Nature
Law of Nature
Leviathan
Locke's Political Theory

Will of the Majority

Representational Democracy

Natural rights

Life

Liberty

Property

Justified Revolution

3 things we get from government

Mill's Political Theory

Utilitarianism Justification

Tyranny of the Majority

Freedoms

Declaration of Independence

The Argument

Unalienable rights

Life

Liberty

Pursuit of Happiness

Consent of the Governed

U.S. Constitution

Domestic Tranquility

Double Jeopardy

Habeas Corpus

Impeachment

Suffrage

Welfare

Multiple Choice Example:

Which statements best describe John Stuart Mill's Political Theory?

A. Mill agrees with Locke in favoring a representational democracy. He also accepts Locke's concept of natural rights. The only reason to promote democracy and individual liberty is because it will maximize happiness. Mill also disagrees with Locke's idea of majority rule because this can lead to the Tyranny of the Majority whereby a minority is discriminated against. Every educated adult must be free to do what he/she desires. The only grounds for interfering with individual freedom is to protect others from harm.

B. Mill agrees with Locke in favoring a representational democracy. But he does not accept natural rights. The only reason to promote democracy and individual liberty is because it will maximize happiness. Mill also disagrees with Locke's idea of majority rule because this can lead to the Tyranny of the Majority whereby a minority is discriminated against. Every educated adult must be free to do what he/she desires. The only grounds for interfering with individual freedom is to protect others from harm.

C. Mill agrees with Locke in favoring a representational democracy. But he does not accept natural rights. The only reason to promote democracy and individual liberty is because it will maximize happiness. Mill agrees with Locke's idea of majority rule even though this can lead to the Tyranny of the Majority whereby a minority is discriminated against. Every educated adult must be free to do what he/she desires. The only grounds for interfering with individual freedom is to protect others from harm.

D. Mill agrees with Locke in favoring a representational democracy. But he does not accept natural rights. The only reason to promote democracy and individual liberty is because it will maximize happiness. Mill also disagrees with Locke's idea of majority rule because this can lead to the Tyranny of the Majority whereby a minority is discriminated against. Every educated adult must be free to do what he/she desires. The only grounds for interfering with individual freedom is to protect others from harm and us from hurting ourselves.

**For other books and audiotapes from
Windsor Group Publishing
go to
www.faithinquiry.com**

The Existence of God
by Joe Mixie

This book provides an analysis of the two major *a posteriori* proofs for the existence of God, which are:

Drawing Near To God
by Joe Mixie

This is a 31 day devotional guide on how to pray following the ACTS method of prayer.

Where Should I Serve in the Church?
by Joe Mixie

This pamphlet is designed to help Christians determine how they should serve in the church. It contains a spiritual gift survey.

The Path to Wisdom
Third Edition
By Joe Mixie

This introductory textbook contains the original reads that comprise the classical discussions for each of the main areas of the discipline of Philosophy: The Philosophy of Religion; The Problem of Evil; The Philosophy of Knowledge; Ethics and Political Philosophy.